the best of Cooking Light® everyday favorites

Spaghetti with Meat Sauce (page 140)

the best of Cooking Light®
everyday favorites

compiled and edited by

Heather Averett

©2008 by Oxmoor House, Inc.
Book Division of Southern Progress Corporation
P.O. Box 2262, Birmingham, Alabama 35201-2262

All rights reserved. No part of this book may be reproduced in any form or by any means without the prior written permission of the publisher, excepting brief quotes in connection with reviews written specifically for inclusion in a magazine or newspaper.

ISBN-13: 978-0-8487-3261-5
ISBN-10: 0-8487-3261-8

Printed in the United States of America
First printing 2008

Be sure to check with your health-care provider before making any changes in your diet.

Oxmoor House, Inc.

Editor in Chief: Nancy Fitzpatrick Wyatt
Executive Editor: Katherine M. Eakin
Art Director: Keith McPherson
Copy Chief: Allison Long Lowery

The Best of Cooking Light® Everyday Favorites

Editor: Heather Averett
Project Editor: Julie Boston
Nutrition Editor: Anne C. Cain, M.P.H., M.S., R.D.
Copy Editor: Donna Baldone
Editorial Assistant: Rachel Quinlivan, R.D.
Photography Director: Jim Bathie
Director of Production: Laura Lockhart
Senior Production Manager: Greg A. Amason
Production Manager: Theresa Beste-Farley
Production Assistant: Faye Porter Bonner

Contributors:
Compositor: Carol O. Loria
Designer: Carol Damsky
Copy Editor: Dolores Hydock
Indexer: Mary Ann Laurens
Editorial Interns: Amy Edgerton, Amelia Heying

For more books to enrich your life, visit
oxmoorhouse.com
To search, savor, and share thousands of recipes,
visit **myrecipes.com**

Cover: *Warm Chocolate Soufflé Cakes with Raspberry Sauce* (*page* 360)

Cooking Light®

Editor in Chief: Mary Kay Culpepper
Executive Editor: Billy R. Sims
Art Director: Susan Waldrip Dendy
Managing Editor: Maelynn Cheung
Senior Food Editor: Alison Mann Ashton
Features Editor: Phillip Rhodes
Projects Editor: Mary Simpson Creel, M.S., R.D.
Food Editor: Ann Taylor Pittman
Associate Food Editors: Julianna Grimes Bottcher, Timothy Q. Cebula, Kathy Kitchens Downie, R.D.
Assistant Editors: Cindy Hatcher, Brandy Rushing
Test Kitchens Director: Vanessa Taylor Johnson
Senior Food Stylist: Kellie Gerber Kelley
Food Stylist: M. Kathleen Kanen
Test Kitchens Professionals: SaBrina Bone, Kathryn Conrad, Mary H. Drennen, Jan Jacks Moon, Tiffany Vickers, Mike Wilson
Assistant Art Director: Maya Metz Logue
Senior Designers: Fernande Bondarenko, J. Shay McNamee
Designer: Brigette Mayer
Senior Photographer: Randy Mayor
Senior Photo Stylist: Cindy Barr
Photo Stylists: Jan Gautro, Leigh Ann Ross
Copy Chief: Maria Parker Hopkins
Senior Copy Editor: Susan Roberts
Copy Editor: Johannah Paiva
Production Manager: Liz Rhoades
Production Editors: Joanne McCrary Brasseal, Hazel R. Eddins
Production Assistant: Lauri Short
Administrative Coordinator: Carol D. Johnson
Office Manager: Rita K. Jackson
Editorial Assistant: Melissa Hoover
Correspondence Editor: Michelle Gibson Daniels
Interns: Caroline Glagola, Maggie Marlin

CookingLight.com
Editor: Jennifer Middleton Richards
Online Producer: Abigail Masters

contents

welcome

When do you like to cook? Is it daily? Once a week? Once a month? Ultimately, when you set foot in the kitchen isn't really important. What matters is that you do. And when you do, I hope that *Cooking Light* helps fuel the flame that gets you cooking—be it everyday or just on occasion.

Mary Kay Culpepper
Editor in Chief, *Cooking Light*

That's why at *Cooking Light* we're proud to introduce *The Best of Cooking Light Everyday Favorites.* With over 500 of our all-time greatest recipes at your fingertips, you'll be poised to tackle tonight's family dinner, tomorrow's brown-bag lunch, Saturday's supper club, or next November's Thanksgiving Day spread.

You'll find a variety of recipes ranging from American classics, such as Chicken and Dumplings from Scratch (page 223), to ethnic favorites from the other side of the world, such as Pot Stickers with Tangy Ginger Dipping Sauce (page 25).

We sincerely hope you'll want to keep *The Best of Cooking Light Everyday Favorites* at hand when you're planning your meals. It not only offers great ideas for any special occasion, but we also believe it will become one of your most indispensible tools in your kitchen everyday!

Here are just a few of our staff's favorites:

Shrimp in Green Sauce (page 106) is a quick-to-prepare entrée that's redolent of garlic and fresh herbs.

Easy Schnitzel (page 204) is ready to become a family favorite. Chicken makes this dish light and a snap to prepare.

Pork Posole (page 350) is as fun to prepare as it is to eat. Enjoy the pleasures of cooking this authentically Mexican dish.

Flaky Dinner Rolls (page 70) are a great way to connect with your family—especially over Sunday dinner.

Corn Fritter Casserole (page 303) is a homey side dish that tastes like a sweet corn fritter. Packaged corn muffin mix makes it a cinch to make.

Blueberry Cheesecake (page 364) is perfect for entertaining. Make-ahead steps free you from time in the kitchen so you can mingle with friends.

Plus, Camembert Mashed Potatoes (page 309), a choice side dish when company's coming. Key Lime Pie Parfaits (page 385)—a refreshing sweet-tart dessert that's a surefire summer treat. And Roasted Chicken with Onions, Potatoes, and Gravy (page 228) makes a complete meal when paired with a green vegetable and dinner rolls.

If you like to eat smart, be fit, and live well, this is the cookbook for you. My colleagues and I hope you enjoy finding, cooking, and sharing your best in *The Best of Cooking Light Everyday Favorites.*

Mary Kay Culpepper

Caramelized Black Bean "Butter," page 10, and Mango Mojitos, page 33

Appetizers and Beverages

Lemony Fruit Dip

Serve with fresh fruit, such as whole strawberries, pineapple chunks, and apple wedges.

- ¼ cup sugar, divided
- 1 large egg
- 2½ tablespoons fresh lemon juice
- ¼ cup water
- 1½ teaspoons cornstarch
- ½ teaspoon vanilla extract
- 1½ cups frozen reduced-calorie whipped topping, thawed

1. Combine 2 tablespoons sugar, egg, and juice in a small bowl; stir well with a whisk. Combine remaining 2 tablespoons sugar, water, and cornstarch in a small saucepan; bring to a boil. Cook 30 seconds or until thickened, stirring constantly. Remove from heat. Slowly pour beaten egg mixture into water mixture, stirring constantly. Cook over medium heat 2 minutes or until thick, stirring constantly. Remove from heat, and stir in vanilla. Cool completely. Fold in whipped topping. Place in a bowl; cover and chill. Yield: 1¾ cups (serving size: about 2 tablespoons).

CALORIES 39 (28% from fat); FAT 1.2g (sat 1g, mono 0.1g, poly 0.1g); PROTEIN 0.5g; CARB 6g; FIBER 0g; CHOL 15mg; IRON 0.1mg; SODIUM 7mg; CALC 2mg

Caramelized Black Bean "Butter"

(pictured on page 8)

- 1 tablespoon olive oil
- 4 cups chopped onion
- 2 (15-ounce) cans black beans, rinsed and drained
- 1 tablespoon balsamic vinegar
- 2 teaspoons unsweetened cocoa
- ½ teaspoon salt
- ½ teaspoon paprika
- 1 tablespoon chopped fresh parsley

1. Heat oil in a large nonstick skillet over medium-high heat. Add onion; sauté 10 minutes or until golden. Place onion, beans, vinegar, cocoa, salt, and paprika in a food processor; process until smooth. Place bean mixture in a medium bowl. Sprinkle with parsley. Yield: 3 cups (serving size: 1 tablespoon).

CALORIES 17 (2% from fat); FAT 0.4g (sat 0.1g, mono 0.2g, poly 0g); PROTEIN 0.7g; CARB 3.1g; FIBER 0.8g; CHOL 0mg; IRON 0.2mg; SODIUM 48mg; CALC 7mg

Lime-Spiked Black Bean Dip

This Tex-Mex dip is always a popular dish for casual gatherings.

- 2 (15-ounce) cans black beans, rinsed and drained
- 1 cup grated carrot
- ½ cup fresh lime juice (about 2 limes)
- ¼ cup finely chopped green onions
- ¼ cup chopped fresh cilantro
- 1 teaspoon minced garlic
- ¼ teaspoon salt
- ⅛ teaspoon ground red pepper

1. Place black beans in a food processor, and pulse until almost smooth. Combine beans, carrot, and remaining ingredients in a medium bowl, stirring until well blended. Let stand 30 minutes. Yield: 5 cups (serving size: 2 tablespoons).

CALORIES 19 (5% from fat); FAT 0.1g (sat 0g, mono 0.1g, poly 0g); PROTEIN 1.2g; CARB 3.9g; FIBER 1.3g; CHOL 0mg; IRON 0.3mg; SODIUM 61mg; CALC 8mg

Field Pea Dip

A take on Middle Eastern hummus, this dip uses field peas instead of chickpeas.

- 2 cups fresh pink-eyed peas
- 2 (14½-ounce) cans fat-free, less-sodium chicken broth
- 6 tablespoons low-fat mayonnaise
- 2 tablespoons tahini (sesame-seed paste)
- 2 tablespoons hot pepper vinegar (such as Crystal)
- 1 tablespoon fresh lemon juice
- 2 teaspoons paprika
- 2 garlic cloves, minced
- Chopped fresh chives

1. Combine peas and broth in a large saucepan; bring to a boil. Reduce heat; simmer, partially covered, 30 minutes or until tender. Drain peas. Place peas in a food processor; pulse 10 times or until coarsely chopped.

2. Combine peas, mayonnaise, and next 5 ingredients in a bowl, stirring until blended. Garnish with chives, if desired. Yield: 2 cups (serving size: 2 tablespoons).

CALORIES 109 (27% from fat); FAT 3.3g (sat 0.5g, mono 1.6g, poly 1g); PROTEIN 5.5g; CARB 15.2g; FIBER 2.5g; CHOL 2mg; IRON 1.9mg; SODIUM 53mg; CALC 28mg

Guacamole

Garlic and Sun-Dried Tomato Hummus

Sun-dried tomatoes replace tahini (sesame seed paste) to flavor this popular Middle Eastern dip. They also give the dish a warm, corallike color.

Cooking spray
2 (6-inch) pitas, each cut into 10 wedges
¼ cup water
2 tablespoons chopped oil-packed sun-dried tomato halves
½ teaspoon salt
¼ teaspoon freshly ground black pepper
2 garlic cloves
1 (15-ounce) can chickpeas (garbanzo beans), drained

1. Preheat oven to 425°.
2. Coat a baking sheet with cooking spray. Place pita wedges on pan; coat with cooking spray. Bake at 425° for 6 minutes or until golden.
3. Combine water, tomato, salt, pepper, garlic, and beans in a food processor; process until smooth. Serve with pita wedges. Yield: 5 servings (serving size: ¼ cup hummus and 4 pita wedges).

CALORIES 175 (9% from fat); FAT 1.7g (sat 0.2g, mono 0.5g, poly 0.6g); PROTEIN 6.6g; CARB 33.7g; FIBER 4.5g; CHOL 0mg; IRON 1.9mg; SODIUM 623mg; CALC 52mg

Guacamole

Lime juice, onion, cilantro, and cumin lend lots of flavor. When storing, press plastic wrap against the surface to help keep the guacamole from turning brown.

1 cup finely chopped onion
¼ cup minced fresh cilantro
2 tablespoons fresh lime juice
½ teaspoon salt
¼ teaspoon ground cumin
¼ teaspoon freshly ground black pepper
2 ripe peeled avocados, seeded and coarsely mashed
12 ounces unsalted baked tortilla chips
Cilantro sprigs (optional)

1. Combine first 7 ingredients in a medium bowl, stirring well. Cover and chill. Serve with baked tortilla chips. Garnish with cilantro sprigs, if desired. Yield: 16 servings (serving size: 2 tablespoons guacamole and about 10 chips).

CALORIES 122 (27% from fat); FAT 3.9g (sat 0.6g, mono 0g, poly 0g); PROTEIN 3g; CARB 21.1g; FIBER 3.6g; CHOL 0mg; IRON 0mg; SODIUM 74mg; CALC 3mg

Spinach and Artichoke Dip

Any potluck or open house will be complete with this lightened version of a popular restaurant appetizer.

- 2 cups (8 ounces) shredded part-skim mozzarella cheese, divided
- ½ cup fat-free sour cream
- ¼ cup (1 ounce) grated fresh Parmesan cheese, divided
- ¼ teaspoon black pepper
- 3 garlic cloves, crushed
- 1 (14-ounce) can artichoke hearts, drained and chopped
- 1 (8-ounce) block ⅓-less-fat cream cheese, softened
- 1 (8-ounce) block fat-free cream cheese, softened
- ½ (10-ounce) package frozen chopped spinach, thawed, drained, and squeezed dry
- 1 (13.5-ounce) package baked tortilla chips (about 16 cups)

1. Preheat oven to 350°.

2. Combine 1½ cups mozzarella, sour cream, 2 tablespoons Parmesan, and next 6 ingredients in a large bowl; stir until well blended. Spoon mixture into a 1½-quart baking dish. Sprinkle with remaining ½ cup mozzarella and remaining 2 tablespoons Parmesan. Bake at 350° for 30 minutes or until bubbly and golden brown. Serve with tortilla chips. Yield: 5½ cups (serving size: ¼ cup dip and about 6 tortilla chips).

CALORIES 148 (30% from fat); FAT 5g (sat 2.9g, mono 1.5g, poly 0.5g); PROTEIN 7.7g; CARB 18.3g; FIBER 1.5g; CHOL 17mg; IRON 0.6mg; SODIUM 318mg; CALC 164mg

Queso Dip

- ½ cup finely chopped onion
- 1½ teaspoons chili powder
- 1½ pounds light processed cheese, cubed (such as Velveeta Light)
- 2 (14.5-ounce) cans no-salt-added diced tomatoes, undrained
- 1 (4.5-ounce) can chopped green chiles, drained and finely chopped
- 2 garlic cloves, minced
- 12 ounces baked corn tortilla chips (such as Guiltless Gourmet)

1. Combine first 6 ingredients in an electric slow cooker. Cover and cook on LOW 2 hours or until cheese is melted, stirring after 1 hour. Serve with tortilla chips. Yield: 28 servings (serving size: ¼ cup dip and about 8 tortilla chips).

CALORIES 110 (29% from fat); FAT 3.5g (sat 1.7g, mono 0.1g, poly 0.1g); PROTEIN 6.4g; CARB 14.4g; FIBER 1.5g; CHOL 10mg; IRON 0.4mg; SODIUM 486mg; CALC 176mg

Chile con Queso Dip

Serve warm with baked tortilla chips.

- 1 (14.5-ounce) can diced tomatoes, undrained
- 1 (10-ounce) can diced tomatoes and green chiles, undrained
- 1 teaspoon olive oil
- ½ cup chopped onion
- 2 garlic cloves, minced
- 1 (8-ounce) block fat-free cream cheese, softened
- 1 teaspoon chili powder
- 6 ounces light processed cheese, cubed (such as Velveeta Light)
- Cilantro sprigs (optional)

1. Drain tomatoes and tomatoes with chiles in a colander over a bowl, reserving ⅓ cup liquid; set tomatoes and reserved liquid aside.

2. Heat oil in a medium saucepan over medium heat. Add onion and garlic; sauté 4 minutes. Add cream cheese; cook until cheese melts, stirring constantly. Add tomatoes, reserved liquid, and chili powder; bring to a boil. Add processed cheese; reduce heat, and simmer 3 minutes or until cheese melts, stirring constantly. Garnish with cilantro, if desired. Yield: 3½ cups (serving size: ¼ cup).

CALORIES 63 (24% from fat); FAT 1.7g (sat 0.9g, mono 0.2g, poly 0.1g); PROTEIN 5.5g; CARB 6.4g; FIBER 0.3g; CHOL 7mg; IRON 0.3mg; SODIUM 400mg; CALC 132mg

Antipasto Plate

DIP:

2 tablespoons golden raisins
2 tablespoons balsamic vinegar
3 tablespoons part-skim ricotta cheese
2 tablespoons chopped fresh parsley
2 tablespoons chopped fresh basil
2 tablespoons ⅓-less-fat cream cheese
¾ teaspoon honey
⅛ teaspoon salt
1 (5½-ounce) bottle roasted red bell peppers, rinsed and drained

SPREAD:

4 plum tomatoes, quartered and seeded
1 medium eggplant (about 1 pound), cubed
2 garlic cloves
½ medium onion, peeled and cut into 4 wedges
1 teaspoon olive oil
⅛ teaspoon salt
2 tablespoons chopped fresh basil
2 tablespoons balsamic vinegar
¼ teaspoon anchovy paste

REMAINING INGREDIENTS:

16 crackers
2 ounces very thin slices prosciutto

1. To prepare dip, combine golden raisins and 2 tablespoons balsamic vinegar in a microwave-safe bowl. Microwave at HIGH 45 seconds. Let stand 10 minutes; drain. Place raisins, ricotta, fresh parsley, 2 tablespoons chopped fresh basil, cream cheese, honey, salt, and roasted red peppers in a food processor; pulse until well combined.

2. Preheat oven to 450°.

3. To prepare spread, combine tomatoes, eggplant, garlic, and onion on a foil-lined jelly-roll pan; toss gently to combine. Drizzle with oil; sprinkle with ⅛ teaspoon salt. Toss to coat. Arrange vegetables in a single layer on pan. Bake at 450° for 20 minutes or until vegetables are lightly blistered and eggplant is tender, stirring after 10 minutes. Cool slightly. Place vegetable mixture, 2 tablespoons chopped fresh basil, 2 tablespoons balsamic vinegar, and anchovy paste in a food processor; pulse until combined. Serve dip and spread with crackers and prosciutto slices. Yield: 4 servings (serving size: 3 tablespoons dip, 3 tablespoons spread, 4 crackers, and ½ ounce prosciutto).

CALORIES 226 (30% from fat); FAT 7.5g (sat 2.5g, mono 2.9g, poly 0.6g); PROTEIN 10.2g; CARB 33.1g; FIBER 1.4g; CHOL 22mg; IRON 1.8mg; SODIUM 687mg; CALC 72mg

Adobo Chips with Warm Goat Cheese and Cilantro Salsa

The salsa derives smoky heat from chipotle chiles, and adobo sauce adds a vinegary touch to the chips.

SALSA:

- 1 (7-ounce) can chipotle chiles in adobo sauce
- 2 cups chopped fresh cilantro (about 1 bunch)
- 1 cup finely chopped tomatillos (about 4)
- ¼ cup minced red onion
- ¼ cup fresh lime juice

CHIPS:

- 2½ teaspoons fresh lime juice
- 1 teaspoon canola oil
- 1 teaspoon adobo sauce
- ½ teaspoon paprika
- ¼ teaspoon cumin
- 8 (6-inch) white corn tortillas

CHEESE:

- ½ cup (4 ounces) block-style fat-free cream cheese, softened
- ¼ cup (2 ounces) goat cheese

1. To prepare salsa, remove 2 chipotle chiles from can; finely chop to measure 2 teaspoons. Remove 1 teaspoon adobo sauce from can, and set aside (reserve remaining chipotle chiles and adobo sauce for another use). Combine 2 teaspoons chiles, cilantro, tomatillos, red onion, and ¼ cup lime juice in a medium bowl; cover and chill 1 hour.

2. Preheat oven to 375°.

3. To prepare chips, combine 2½ teaspoons lime juice, canola oil, adobo sauce, paprika, and cumin in a small bowl, stirring with a whisk. Brush 1 tortilla with about ¼ teaspoon juice mixture, spreading to edge. Top with another tortilla; repeat procedure with juice mixture. Repeat procedure 6 more times (you will have 1 stack of 8 tortillas). Using a sharp knife, cut tortilla stack into 6 wedges. Place wedges in a single layer on baking sheets. Bake at 375° for 15 minutes; turn wedges. Bake an additional 10 minutes.

4. Reduce oven temperature to 350°.

5. To prepare cheese, combine cream cheese and goat cheese in a small bowl; stir until blended. Spread cheese mixture into a shallow 6-ounce ramekin or baking dish; cover with foil. Bake at

350° for 10 minutes or just until warm. Yield: 8 servings (serving size: 6 chips, 1½ tablespoons cheese mixture, and about ¼ cup salsa).

CALORIES 95 (29% from fat); FAT 3.3g (sat 1.2g, mono 0.9g, poly 0.6g); PROTEIN 4.9g; CARB 13.4g; FIBER 1.8g; CHOL 4.4mg; IRON 0.5mg; SODIUM 131mg; CALC 60mg

Avocado-Mango Salsa with Roasted Corn Chips

For a light supper, add grilled shrimp on the side.

12 (6-inch) corn tortillas, each cut into 6 wedges
Cooking spray
¼ teaspoon kosher salt, divided
1¼ cups chopped peeled avocado
1 cup chopped peeled mango
1 tablespoon finely chopped fresh cilantro
4 teaspoons fresh lime juice
Cilantro sprigs (optional)

1. Preheat oven to 425°.
2. Arrange tortilla wedges in a single layer on baking sheets coated with cooking spray. Coat wedges with cooking spray, and sprinkle ⅛ teaspoon salt evenly over wedges. Bake at 425° for 8 minutes or until crisp.
3. Combine remaining ⅛ teaspoon salt, avocado, mango, chopped cilantro, and juice, tossing gently. Garnish with cilantro sprigs, if desired. Let stand 10 minutes. Serve with chips. Yield: 12 servings (serving size: about 3 tablespoons salsa and 6 chips).

CALORIES 92 (30% from fat); FAT 3.1g (sat 0.5g, mono 1.7g, poly 0.6g); PROTEIN 1.9g; CARB 15.8g; FIBER 2.4g; CHOL 0mg; IRON 0.6mg; SODIUM 83mg; CALC 49mg

Mixed Olive Tapenade

Serve at room temperature with baguette slices and lemon wedges or crackers.

1 cup kalamata olives, pitted (about 4 ounces)
1 cup green olives, pitted (about 4 ounces)
1 tablespoon chopped fresh flat-leaf parsley
1 tablespoon capers, rinsed and drained
2 teaspoons chopped fresh thyme
1 teaspoon grated lemon rind
¼ teaspoon freshly ground black pepper
10 oil-cured olives, pitted (about 1 ounce)
3 canned anchovy fillets (about ¼ ounce)
1 garlic clove, chopped
Flat-leaf parsley (optional)

1. Combine first 10 ingredients in a food processor; pulse 10 times or until olives are finely chopped. Spoon tapenade into a serving bowl; garnish with parsley, if desired. Yield: 16 servings (serving size: about 2 tablespoons).

CALORIES 39 (83% from fat); FAT 3.6g (sat 0.4g, mono 2.3g, poly 0.5g); PROTEIN 0.3g; CARB 2g; FIBER 0.4g; CHOL 0mg; IRON 0.1mg; SODIUM 310mg; CALC 5mg

Warm Olives with Fennel and Orange

It's amazing what changing the expected temperature of a dish can do. Gentle heat from the oven intensifies the richness of olives, fennel, and orange rind in this Mediterranean-accented appetizer. The multilayered flavors dazzle palates that expect lackluster olives straight from the jar. Buy pitted kalamata olives to speed up preparation.

1 tablespoon extravirgin olive oil
1½ teaspoons grated orange rind
1 teaspoon chopped fresh rosemary
½ teaspoon fennel seeds
1 small fennel bulb, cut into ¼-inch-thick wedges
12 kalamata olives, pitted
12 pimiento-stuffed olives
1 tablespoon balsamic vinegar

1. Heat oil in a large nonstick skillet over medium heat. Add rind, rosemary, fennel seeds, and fennel wedges; cook 5 minutes, stirring frequently. Add olives; cook 1 minute. Remove from heat; stir in vinegar. Place fennel mixture in an 8-inch square baking dish. Cover and let stand at least 2 hours.
2. Preheat oven to 250°.
3. Uncover olive mixture. Bake at 250° for 10 minutes or until heated, stirring once. Yield: 6 servings (serving size: about ⅓ cup).

CALORIES 72 (71% from fat); FAT 5.7g (sat 0.3g, mono 4.7g, poly 0.7g); PROTEIN 0.5g; CARB 5.2g; FIBER 1.3g; CHOL 0mg; IRON 0.4mg; SODIUM 331mg; CALC 24mg

Deviled Eggs

Prepare eggs up to a day in advance; store in an airtight container in the refrigerator.

12 large eggs
1/3 cup plain fat-free yogurt
3 tablespoons low-fat mayonnaise
1 tablespoon Dijon mustard
1 to 2 teaspoons hot pepper sauce
1/8 teaspoon salt
1/8 teaspoon paprika
1/8 teaspoon black pepper
2 tablespoons chopped green onions

1. Place eggs in a large saucepan. Cover with water to 1 inch above eggs; bring just to a boil. Remove from heat; cover and let stand 15 minutes. Drain and rinse with cold running water until cool. Slice eggs in half lengthwise; remove yolks. Discard 3 yolks.
2. Combine yogurt and next 4 ingredients in a medium bowl. Add remaining yolks; beat with a mixer at high speed until smooth. Spoon about 1 tablespoon yolk mixture into each egg white half. Cover and chill 1 hour. Sprinkle with paprika and black pepper. Garnish with green onions. Yield: 24 servings (serving size: 1 egg half).

CALORIES 38 (50% from fat); FAT 2.1g (sat 0.6g, mono 0.7g, poly 0.3g); PROTEIN 3.1g; CARB 1.3g; FIBER 0g; CHOL 80mg; IRON 0.3mg; SODIUM 82mg; CALC 21mg

French-Style Stuffed Eggs

Stuffed eggs are often served warm in France, and this recipe is similar to one from the Périgord region.

8 large eggs
1/3 cup minced reduced-fat ham
1 tablespoon minced green onions
1 tablespoon minced parsley
1 tablespoon low-fat mayonnaise
1 teaspoon mustard
1/4 teaspoon chopped fresh thyme
1/8 teaspoon salt
1/8 teaspoon freshly ground black pepper
2 (1-ounce) slices white bread, torn into large pieces
Cooking spray
Thyme leaves (optional)

1. Place eggs in a large saucepan. Cover with water to 1 inch above eggs; bring just to a boil. Remove from heat; cover and let stand 12 minutes. Drain and rinse with cold running water until cool.
2. Peel eggs, and slice in half lengthwise. Remove yolks; discard 4 yolks. Place remaining 4 yolks in a medium bowl. Add ham and next 7 ingredients; stir until combined.
3. Place bread in a food processor; pulse 10 times or until coarse crumbs measure 1 cup.
4. Spoon about 1 teaspoon egg yolk mixture into each egg white half. Top each half with 1 tablespoon breadcrumbs. Coat breadcrumbs with cooking spray.
5. Preheat broiler.
6. Place eggs on a baking sheet; broil 1 minute or until breadcrumbs are toasted. Garnish with thyme leaves, if desired. Yield: 16 servings (serving size: 1 egg half).

CALORIES 38 (38% from fat); FAT 1.6g (sat 0.5g, mono 0.6g, poly 0.2g); PROTEIN 3.3g; CARB 2.3g; FIBER 0.1g; CHOL 54mg; IRON 0.4mg; SODIUM 127mg; CALC 14mg

Tomato Crostini

The topping for this recipe can be made a few hours in advance and the crostini assembled at a moment's notice.

1/2 cup chopped plum tomato
1 tablespoon chopped fresh basil
1 tablespoon chopped pitted green olives
1 teaspoon capers
1/2 teaspoon balsamic vinegar
1/2 teaspoon olive oil
1/8 teaspoon sea salt
Dash of freshly ground black pepper
1 garlic clove, minced
4 (1-inch-thick) slices French bread baguette
Cooking spray
1 garlic clove, halved

1. Preheat oven to 375°.
2. Combine first 9 ingredients.
3. Lightly coat both sides of bread slices with cooking spray; arrange bread slices in a single layer on a baking sheet. Bake at 375° for about 4 minutes on each side or until lightly toasted.
4. Rub 1 side of bread slices with halved garlic, and top evenly with tomato mixture. Yield: 2 servings (serving size: 2 bread slices and about 1/3 cup tomato mixture).

CALORIES 109 (23% from fat); FAT 2.8g (sat 0.4g, mono 1.5g, poly 0.7g); PROTEIN 3.1g; CARB 18g; FIBER 1.4g; CHOL 0mg; IRON 1mg; SODIUM 373mg; CALC 30mg

Tomato Crostini

Vegetable and Tofu Lettuce Wraps with Miso Sambal

The creamy texture of the avocado pieces and tofu slices are a pleasant contrast to the crisp vegetables.

MISO SAMBAL:

- 2 tablespoons chile paste with garlic (such as sambal oelek)
- 2 tablespoons chopped peeled fresh ginger
- 2 tablespoons white miso (soybean paste)
- 2 tablespoons rice wine vinegar
- 1½ tablespoons sugar
- 1½ teaspoons dark sesame oil

WRAPS:

- 1 cup matchstick-cut English cucumber
- ½ cup cilantro sprigs
- 2 tablespoons chopped dry-roasted peanuts
- 1 (12.3-ounce) package reduced-fat firm tofu, drained and cut into ½-inch-thick strips
- ½ avocado, peeled and thinly sliced
- 12 large Boston lettuce leaves

1. To prepare miso sambal, combine first 6 ingredients in a blender; process until smooth.

2. To prepare wraps, divide cucumber, cilantro, peanuts, tofu, and avocado evenly among lettuce leaves. Drizzle each with about 1½ teaspoons sambal; roll up. Yield: 6 servings (serving size: 2 wraps).

CALORIES 106 (51% from fat); FAT 6g (sat 0.9g, mono 2.9g, poly 1.5g); PROTEIN 5.5g; CARB 8.5g; FIBER 1.5g; CHOL 0mg; IRON 1.1mg; SODIUM 261mg; CALC 27mg

Vegetable and Tofu Lettuce Wraps with Miso Sambal

Chunky Cherry Tomatoes with Basil

This vibrant-colored mixture shouldn't stand for much longer than an hour before serving or the salt will draw all the juices from the tomatoes. Serve with slices of toasted country bread, or use as a topping for grilled fish or roasted asparagus.

3 cups quartered cherry tomatoes
1 cup loosely packed, thinly sliced fresh basil
1 tablespoon extravirgin olive oil
1 tablespoon red wine vinegar
1 tablespoon balsamic vinegar
½ teaspoon salt
¼ teaspoon freshly ground black pepper
1 large garlic clove, minced

1. Combine all ingredients in a medium bowl; let stand 1 hour. Yield: 3 cups (serving size: ¼ cup).

CALORIES 20 (59% from fat); FAT 1.3g (sat 0.2g, mono 0.9g, poly 0.2g); PROTEIN 0.4g; CARB 2.3g; FIBER 0.6g; CHOL 0mg; IRON 0.3mg; SODIUM 101mg; CALC 9mg

Savory Yogurt Cheesecake with Caramelized Onions

FILLING:

1 (32-ounce) carton plain low-fat yogurt
½ cup (4 ounces) block-style fat-free cream cheese, softened
1 cup part-skim ricotta cheese
½ teaspoon salt
¼ teaspoon freshly ground black pepper
1 large egg yolk

CRUST:

½ cup all-purpose flour (about 2¼ ounces)
½ cup yellow cornmeal
1 teaspoon sugar
½ teaspoon salt
Dash of freshly ground black pepper
2½ tablespoons butter, chilled and cut into small pieces
¼ cup ice water
Cooking spray

ONIONS:

1 teaspoon butter
8 cups sliced onion (about 1½ pounds)
1 tablespoon sugar
½ teaspoon salt
¼ teaspoon freshly ground black pepper
1 teaspoon dried thyme

1. To prepare filling, place colander in a 2-quart glass measure or medium bowl. Line colander with 4 layers of cheesecloth, allowing cheesecloth to extend over outside edges. Spoon yogurt into colander. Cover loosely with plastic wrap, and refrigerate 12 hours. Spoon 1¾ cups yogurt cheese into a bowl; discard liquid. Place cream cheese in a bowl; beat with a mixer at medium speed until smooth. Add yogurt cheese, ricotta cheese, ½ teaspoon salt, ¼ teaspoon pepper, and egg yolk. Beat at low speed just until blended.

2. Preheat oven to 350°.

3. To prepare crust, lightly spoon flour into a dry measuring cup; level with a knife. Place flour, cornmeal, 1 teaspoon sugar, ½ teaspoon salt, and dash of pepper in a food processor; pulse 3 times or until combined. Add 2½ tablespoons butter; pulse 4 times or until mixture resembles coarse meal. With processor on, add ice water through food chute, processing just until moist (do not form a ball). Press cornmeal mixture into bottom of an 8-inch springform pan coated with cooking spray. Bake at 350° for 15 minutes or until lightly browned. Cool on a wire rack.

4. To prepare onions, while crust bakes, melt 1 teaspoon butter in a large nonstick skillet over medium heat. Add onion; cook 15 minutes, stirring occasionally. Stir in 1 tablespoon sugar, ½ teaspoon salt, and ¼ teaspoon pepper. Cover and cook 25 minutes or until browned and tender, stirring occasionally. Stir in thyme.

5. Spread yogurt mixture into prepared crust. Bake at 350° for 35 minutes or until almost set. Cool on a wire rack. (Cheesecake will continue to set as it cools.) Serve at room temperature. Cut cheesecake into wedges, and top each serving with onions. Yield: 10 servings (serving size: 1 cheesecake wedge and about 2 tablespoons onions).

CALORIES 198 (30% from fat); FAT 6.5g (sat 3.7g, mono 1.9g, poly 0.4g); PROTEIN 10.2g; CARB 25.6g; FIBER 2.5g; CHOL 37mg; IRON 1.1mg; SODIUM 454mg; CALC 240mg

Peaches with Mint-Almond Pesto and Brie

4 peaches
1 cup fresh mint leaves
¼ cup sugar
2 tablespoons balsamic vinegar
⅛ teaspoon black pepper
2 tablespoons chopped almonds, toasted
8 cups gourmet salad greens
1 (4½-ounce) round Brie cheese, cut into 8 wedges
8 (1-ounce) slices French bread

1. Cut an X on the bottom of each peach, carefully cutting just through the skin. Fill a large Dutch oven with water; bring to a boil. Immerse peaches for 20 seconds; remove with a slotted spoon, and plunge into ice water. Slip skins off peaches using a paring knife (skin will be very loose). Cut each peach in half, and remove pit.
2. Combine mint and sugar in a blender or food processor; process until chopped. Add vinegar and pepper; process until well blended. Pour mint mixture into a large bowl; add almonds and peach halves. Cover and chill 4 hours. Remove peaches with a slotted spoon, reserving marinade.
3. Arrange salad greens on each of 8 plates, and top with a peach half and a cheese wedge. Drizzle with marinade. Serve with French bread. Yield: 8 servings (serving size: 1 peach half, 1 cup salad greens, about ½ ounce Brie, and 1 slice bread).

CALORIES 202 (27% from fat); FAT 6g (sat 3.1g, mono 1.6g, poly 1.1g); PROTEIN 7.1g; CARB 30g; FIBER 3.3g; CHOL 11mg; IRON 1.6mg; SODIUM 279mg; CALC 108mg

Creamy Mushroom Phyllo Triangles

¾ cup dried porcini mushrooms
1 pound button mushrooms
1 large onion, cut into 1-inch pieces
2 tablespoons olive oil
1 teaspoon dried oregano
¾ teaspoon salt
½ teaspoon freshly ground black pepper
¼ teaspoon freshly grated nutmeg
6 ounces ⅓-less-fat cream cheese
½ cup finely chopped flat-leaf parsley
24 (18 x 14-inch) sheets frozen phyllo dough, thawed
Olive oil-flavored cooking spray

1. Cover porcini mushrooms with boiling water in a bowl. Let stand 1 hour. Drain well; chop.
2. Place half of button mushrooms in a food processor; pulse 8 times or until finely chopped. Remove from processor. Repeat procedure with remaining button mushrooms. Add onion to processor; pulse 8 times or until finely chopped.
3. Heat oil in a large nonstick skillet over medium heat. Add onion; sauté 5 minutes. Add button mushrooms; cook until tender and liquid evaporates. Stir in porcini mushrooms, oregano, salt, pepper, and nutmeg; cook 2 minutes. Remove from heat. Add cheese; stir until cheese melts. Stir in parsley.
4. Preheat oven to 375°.
5. Place 1 phyllo sheet on a large cutting board or work surface (cover remaining phyllo to prevent drying). Cut sheet in half lengthwise; lightly coat with cooking spray. Fold each phyllo piece in half lengthwise to form a (3½-inch-wide) strip. Spoon a level tablespoon of mushroom mixture onto 1 short end of each strip, leaving a 1-inch border. Fold 1 corner of edge with 1-inch border over mixture, forming a triangle; continue folding back and forth into a triangle to end of strip. Repeat procedure with remaining phyllo, cooking spray, and mushroom mixture. Place triangles, seam sides down, on baking sheets coated with cooking spray. Lightly coat tops with cooking spray.
6. Bake at 375° for 20 minutes or until golden. Serve warm. Yield: 24 servings (serving size: 2 triangles).

CALORIES 49 (37% from fat); FAT 2g (sat 0.8g, mono 1g, poly 0.2g); PROTEIN 1.5g; CARB 6.2g; FIBER 0.5g; CHOL 3mg; IRON 0.6mg; SODIUM 97mg; CALC 7mg

Antipasto Italian Roll-Ups

1 tablespoon fat-free sour cream
1 tablespoon sun-dried tomato spread (such as Alessi)
2 (6-inch) fat-free flour tortillas
½ cup fresh basil leaves
⅓ cup chopped bottled roasted red bell peppers
2 ounces part-skim mozzarella cheese, thinly sliced
1 ounce thinly sliced reduced-fat salami

1. Combine sour cream and sun-dried tomato spread. Spread 1 tablespoon tomato mixture down center of each tortilla. Top each tortilla with half of basil, bell peppers, mozzarella cheese, and salami; roll up. Yield: 2 servings (serving size: 1 roll-up).

CALORIES 274 (37% from fat); FAT 11.4g (sat 4.5g, mono 1.4g, poly 0.3g); PROTEIN 15.9g; CARB 27.7g; FIBER 1.7g; CHOL 29mg; IRON 1.8mg; SODIUM 824mg; CALC 315mg

Citrus-Herb Shrimp

Pinto Bean Nachos

12 (6-inch) corn tortillas, quartered
Cooking spray
1 tablespoon canola oil
2 teaspoons ground cumin
1 teaspoon chili powder
2 garlic cloves, minced
2 (15-ounce) cans pinto beans, undrained
1 cup (4 ounces) crumbled queso fresco
1 cup bottled salsa
1 cup diced peeled avocado
6 tablespoons chopped fresh cilantro

1. Preheat oven to 425°.
2. Arrange half of tortilla wedges in a single layer on a large baking sheet; lightly coat wedges with cooking spray. Bake at 425° for 8 minutes or until crisp. Repeat procedure with remaining tortilla wedges and cooking spray.
3. Heat oil in a medium saucepan over medium-high heat. Add cumin, chili powder, and garlic; cook 30 seconds, stirring constantly. Add pinto beans; bring to a boil, stirring frequently. Reduce heat to medium; simmer 10 minutes. Partially mash bean mixture with a potato masher until slightly thick. Place 8 chips on each of 6 plates. Spoon about ½ cup bean mixture evenly over tortilla chips on each plate; top each serving with about 2½ tablespoons queso fresco, 2½ tablespoons salsa, and 2½ tablespoons avocado. Sprinkle each serving with 1 tablespoon cilantro. Yield: 6 servings.

CALORIES 344 (27% from fat); FAT 10.5g (sat 2.2g, mono 4.8g, poly 2.3g); PROTEIN 13.5g; CARB 52.4g; FIBER 11.7g; CHOL 6mg; IRON 3.9mg; SODIUM 723mg; CALC 232mg

Citrus-Herb Shrimp

2 pounds unpeeled large shrimp
6 tablespoons chopped fresh mint
¼ cup chopped fresh cilantro
¼ cup fresh lime juice
2 tablespoons grated peeled fresh ginger
1 tablespoon canola oil
1 teaspoon salt
1 teaspoon crushed red pepper
½ teaspoon sugar
2 garlic cloves, minced

1. Peel and devein shrimp, leaving tails intact. Bring a large pot of water to a boil. Add shrimp; cook 5 minutes or just until shrimp are done. Drain; rinse under cold running water. Place shrimp in a large bowl; chill. Combine mint and next 8 ingredients. Add to shrimp; toss well to combine. Chill 1 hour. Yield: 10 servings (serving size: about 2½ ounces shrimp).

CALORIES 114 (24% from fat); FAT 3g (sat 0.5g, mono 0.6g, poly 1.4g); PROTEIN 18.7g; CARB 2.4g; FIBER 0.4g; CHOL 138mg; IRON 2.6mg; SODIUM 371mg; CALC 57mg

Chipotle Shrimp Cups

To make this ahead, assemble the filling the night before, and store it in the refrigerator.

- 36 wonton wrappers
- Cooking spray
- 1½ cups (6 ounces) reduced-fat shredded sharp Cheddar cheese
- 1 cup chopped cooked shrimp
- 1 cup chopped bottled roasted red bell peppers
- 1 cup bottled chipotle salsa
- ½ cup chopped green onions

1. Preheat oven to 350°.

2. Fit 1 wonton wrapper into each of 36 miniature muffin cups coated with cooking spray, pressing wrappers into sides of cups. Bake at 350° for 7 minutes or until lightly browned. Keep wontons in muffin cups.

3. Combine cheese and next 4 ingredients; spoon about 1 tablespoon cheese mixture into each wonton cup. Bake at 350° for 6 minutes or until cheese melts. Remove from muffin cups. Serve immediately. Yield: 3 dozen (serving size: 2 cups).

CALORIES 98 (24% from fat); FAT 2.6g (sat 1.6g, mono 0.6g, poly 0.4g); PROTEIN 7.6g; CARB 11.8g; FIBER 1.4g; CHOL 28mg; IRON 1mg; SODIUM 202mg; CALC 96mg

Crab-and-Scallop Sui Mei

These Cantonese open-faced dumplings (pronounced "shoe-MY") are made with round gyoza skins. If you can't find gyoza skins, buy wonton wrappers instead, and cut them into circles with a three-inch round biscuit cutter. You can make and refrigerate the seafood-and-vegetable filling up to a day in advance; fill and steam the dumplings shortly before serving. If you don't have a bamboo steamer, prepare these in two or three batches in a collapsible metal steamer basket. Line it with lettuce leaves so the dumplings don't stick.

DUMPLINGS:

- ⅓ cup chopped shiitake mushroom caps
- ⅓ cup chopped water chestnuts
- 3 tablespoons chopped green onions
- 2 garlic cloves, chopped
- 1 teaspoon grated peeled fresh ginger
- ½ teaspoon dark sesame oil
- ¼ teaspoon salt
- 5 ounces sea scallops, chopped
- 1 (6-ounce) can lump crabmeat, drained (such as Chicken of the Sea)
- 1 large egg, lightly beaten
- 18 gyoza skins
- 1 teaspoon cornstarch
- 8 lettuce leaves

DIPPING SAUCE:

- 1 tablespoon sugar
- 2 tablespoons rice vinegar
- 2 tablespoons low-sodium soy sauce
- 1 tablespoon water
- 1 teaspoon Thai chile paste

1. To prepare dumplings, place first 4 ingredients in a food processor; pulse 8 times or until finely chopped. Add ginger, oil, salt, and scallops; pulse 4 times or until scallops are finely chopped. Spoon mixture into a medium bowl; add crabmeat and egg, tossing to combine.

2. Working with 1 gyoza skin at a time (cover the remaining skins to prevent drying), spoon about 1 tablespoon filling into center of each skin. Gather up edges of skin around filling; lightly squeeze skin to adhere to filling, leaving top of dumpling open. Smooth surface of filling with back of a spoon dipped in water. Place dumplings on a baking sheet sprinkled with cornstarch; cover loosely with a damp towel to prevent drying.

3. Line each tier of a 2-tiered (10-inch) bamboo steamer with lettuce leaves. Arrange 9 dumplings, 1 inch apart, over lettuce in each steamer basket. Stack tiers; cover with steamer lid. Add water to a large skillet to a depth of 1 inch; bring to a boil. Place steamer in pan; steam dumplings 10 minutes. Remove dumplings from steamer.

4. To prepare dipping sauce, combine sugar and next 4 ingredients, stirring with a whisk until sugar dissolves. Serve dipping sauce with dumplings. Yield: 9 servings (serving size: 2 dumplings and about 1 teaspoon dipping sauce).

CALORIES 100 (13% from fat); FAT 1.4g (sat 0.3g, mono 0.4g, poly 0.4g); PROTEIN 8.1g; CARB 13.3g; FIBER 0.6g; CHOL 43mg; IRON 0.9mg; SODIUM 370mg; CALC 31mg

Spicy Fish Cakes

Make these as an appetizer, or serve atop lightly dressed greens for a simple dinner.

- ⅓ cup chopped green onions
- ¼ cup panko (Japanese breadcrumbs)
- 1 tablespoon chopped fresh basil
- 2 tablespoons chile paste with garlic
- 1 teaspoon grated peeled fresh ginger
- 2 garlic cloves, chopped
- 1 large egg white
- ¾ pound skinless halibut fillets, cut into ½-inch pieces
- ½ pound sea scallops
- 2 teaspoons vegetable oil
- Sliced green onions (optional)

1. Preheat oven to 350°.

2. Place first 9 ingredients in a food processor; pulse until coarsely ground. Divide fish mixture into 6 equal portions, shaping each portion into a ½-inch-thick patty.

3. Heat oil in a large nonstick skillet over medium-high heat. Add patties; cook 2 minutes on each side. Turn patties over; wrap handle of pan with foil. Bake at 350° for 5 minutes or until fish flakes easily when tested with a fork or until desired degree of doneness. Garnish with green onions, if desired. Yield: 6 servings (serving size: 1 patty).

CALORIES 134 (23% from fat); FAT 3.4g (sat 0.5g, mono 0.9g, poly 1.4g); PROTEIN 19.4g; CARB 6.1g; FIBER 0.4g; CHOL 31mg; IRON 0.9mg; SODIUM 211mg; CALC 49mg

Pot Stickers and Tangy Ginger Dipping Sauce

Pot Stickers

1 cup chopped napa (Chinese) cabbage
1 cup chopped spinach
¼ cup minced green onions
1 tablespoon low-sodium soy sauce
1 teaspoon minced peeled fresh ginger
½ teaspoon dark sesame oil
Dash of white pepper
3 garlic cloves, minced
⅓ pound lean ground pork
¼ pound peeled and deveined shrimp, chopped
24 round wonton wrappers or gyoza skins
1 tablespoon canola oil, divided
2 cups fat-free, less-sodium chicken broth, divided
Green onion strips (optional)

1. Combine first 10 ingredients in a bowl. Working with 1 wonton wrapper at a time (cover remaining wrappers with a damp towel to prevent drying), spoon about 1 heaping teaspoon filling into center of each wrapper. Moisten edges with water. Fold in half, pinching edges together to seal. Holding sealed edges between thumb and first two fingers of each hand, form 3 or 4 pleats along seal. Place dumpling, seam side up, on a platter. Repeat with remaining filling and wrappers to form 24 pot stickers.
2. Heat 1½ teaspoons canola oil in a large nonstick skillet over medium-high heat.
3. Arrange 12 pot stickers, seam sides up, in pan, and cook 30 seconds or until browned. Add 1 cup broth to pan; cover and cook 5 minutes. Uncover and cook about 1 minute or until liquid evaporates. Remove pot stickers from pan; cover and keep warm. Repeat procedure with remaining 1½ teaspoons canola oil, 12 pot stickers, and 1 cup broth. Garnish with green onion strips, if desired. Serve immediately. Yield: 8 servings (serving size: 3 pot stickers).

CALORIES 150 (27% from fat); FAT 4.5g (sat 1g, mono 1.3g, poly 0.9g); PROTEIN 11.1g; CARB 15.7g; FIBER 1g; CHOL 45mg; IRON 1.7mg; SODIUM 346mg; CALC 43mg

Tangy Ginger Dipping Sauce

½ cup chopped peeled tomato
⅓ cup chopped green onions
¼ cup fresh lime juice
¼ cup rice vinegar
1½ tablespoons sugar
2 teaspoons chopped peeled fresh ginger
2 garlic cloves, chopped
1 jalapeño pepper, seeded and chopped

1. Combine all ingredients in a small bowl; stir well with a whisk until sugar dissolves. Yield: 1 cup (serving size: 1 tablespoon).

CALORIES 11 (0% from fat); FAT 0g; PROTEIN 0.1g; CARB 2.7g; FIBER 0.2g; CHOL 0mg; IRON 0.1mg; SODIUM 1mg; CALC 2mg

Baked Hoisin Chicken Buns

Most often, you'll see this type of stuffed bun steamed, but many Chinese dim sum restaurants also serve baked versions. Frozen roll dough is convenient and saves the trouble of making homemade dough; just be sure to thaw it in the refrigerator overnight. Prepare the filling a day in advance, then fill the buns about an hour before you plan to serve them.

Cooking spray
12 ounces skinless, boneless chicken thighs
¼ cup finely chopped green onions
1½ tablespoons hoisin sauce
1 tablespoon oyster sauce
2 teaspoons rice vinegar
9 frozen white roll dough pieces, thawed (such as Rich's)
1 large egg, lightly beaten
1 teaspoon sesame seeds, toasted

1. Heat a nonstick skillet over medium-high heat. Coat pan with cooking spray. Add chicken; cook 4 minutes on each side or until done. Cool slightly; shred meat with 2 forks. Place chicken in a medium bowl. Add green onions, hoisin sauce, oyster sauce, and vinegar; toss well to combine.
2. Roll each dough piece into a 4-inch circle on a lightly floured surface. Spoon about 2 tablespoons chicken mixture into center of each dough circle. Gather edges of dough over filling; pinch to seal. Place filled dough, seam sides down, on a baking sheet coated with cooking spray. Lightly coat top of filled dough with cooking spray. Cover and let rise 20 minutes.
3. Preheat oven to 375°.
4. Uncover filled dough. Gently brush with egg; discard remaining egg. Sprinkle evenly with sesame seeds. Bake at 375° for 15 minutes or until golden brown. Serve warm. Yield: 9 servings (serving size: 1 filled bun).

CALORIES 143 (26% from fat); FAT 4.1g (sat 1g, mono 1.3g, poly 1g); PROTEIN 10.4g; CARB 16.6g; FIBER 1.2g; CHOL 43mg; IRON 1.4mg; SODIUM 220mg; CALC 29mg

Seared Beef Tenderloin Mini-Sandwiches with Mustard-Horseradish Sauce

Seared Beef Tenderloin Mini-Sandwiches with Mustard-Horseradish Sauce

These are a stylish choice for a special occasion such as an open house buffet. You can substitute arugula for watercress; it has a similar peppery bite.

- ⅔ cup fat-free sour cream
- ¼ cup Dijon mustard
- 2 tablespoons minced fresh tarragon
- 2 tablespoons prepared horseradish
- 1 (1½-pound) beef tenderloin, trimmed
- ½ teaspoon freshly ground black pepper
- Cooking spray
- 2 tablespoons fresh lemon juice
- 3 cups trimmed watercress (about 1 bunch)
- 1 (8-ounce) French bread baguette, cut diagonally into 16 slices
- 2 tablespoons capers
- ½ cup (2 ounces) shaved fresh Parmesan cheese

1. Combine first 4 ingredients, stirring well with a whisk. Cover and chill.

2. Heat a large nonstick skillet over medium-high heat. Sprinkle beef with pepper. Coat pan with cooking spray. Add beef to pan; cook 15 minutes or until desired degree of doneness, turning frequently. Let stand 15 minutes. Cut into 16 slices. Sprinkle with lemon juice.

3. Arrange watercress evenly on bread slices. Place 1 beef slice and about 1 tablespoon sauce over each bread slice. Arrange capers and cheese evenly over sauce. Yield: 16 servings (serving size: 1 sandwich).

CALORIES 136 (33% from fat); FAT 5g (sat 1.8g, mono 1.5g, poly 0.3g); PROTEIN 12.6g; CARB 10g; FIBER 0.6g; CHOL 25mg; IRON 1.7mg; SODIUM 314mg; CALC 94mg

Turkey Pot Stickers

You can assemble these bite-sized dumplings ahead and cook them just before serving. The food processor quickly chops the filling ingredients. Wonton wrappers can be substituted for gyoza skins.

DIPPING SAUCE:

2 tablespoons water
2 tablespoons rice vinegar
2 tablespoons low-sodium soy sauce
½ teaspoon dark sesame oil
2 garlic cloves, minced

DUMPLINGS:

1 cup sliced shiitake mushroom caps
½ cup sliced green onions
¼ cup sliced carrot
2 tablespoons minced peeled fresh ginger
2 tablespoons rice vinegar
3 large egg whites, lightly beaten
2 cups chopped cooked turkey
24 (4-inch) gyoza skins
2 teaspoons canola oil, divided
½ cup water, divided

1. To prepare dipping sauce, combine first 5 ingredients, stirring well with a whisk.
2. To prepare dumplings, place mushrooms, onions, carrot, ginger, and vinegar in a food processor; pulse until coarsely chopped, scraping sides. Combine mushroom mixture and egg whites in a large bowl; add turkey, stirring until combined.
3. Working with 1 gyoza skin at a time (cover remaining skins to keep from drying), spoon about 1 tablespoon turkey mixture into center of each skin. Moisten edges of skin with water. Fold in half, pinching edges together to seal. Place dumpling on a baking sheet (cover loosely with a towel to keep from drying). Repeat procedure with remaining gyoza skins and turkey mixture.
4. Heat 1 teaspoon canola oil in a large nonstick skillet over medium-high heat. Arrange half of dumplings in pan; cover and cook 5 minutes or until lightly browned. Turn dumplings; add ¼ cup water. Cover and simmer 5 minutes. Remove from pan.
5. Wipe pan dry with a paper towel. Repeat procedure with remaining canola oil, dumplings, and water. Serve warm with dipping sauce. Yield: 8 servings (serving size: 3 pot stickers and about 2 teaspoons dipping sauce).

CALORIES 144 (16% from fat); FAT 2.5g (sat 0.5g, mono 0.5g, poly 1g); PROTEIN 12.7g; CARB 16.5g; FIBER 0.9g; CHOL 30mg; IRON 1.6mg; SODIUM 332mg; CALC 25mg

Cinnamon-Spiced Hot Chocolate

½ cup water
⅓ cup honey
5 tablespoons unsweetened cocoa
½ teaspoon ground cinnamon
⅛ teaspoon ground nutmeg
¼ teaspoon salt
4 cups 2% reduced-fat milk
1 teaspoon vanilla extract

1. Combine water, honey, cocoa, cinnamon, nutmeg, and salt in a large, heavy saucepan. Bring to a boil over medium-high heat, stirring constantly. Gradually add milk and vanilla, stirring constantly with a whisk. Heat to 180° or until tiny bubbles form around edge, stirring with a whisk (do not boil). Yield: 8 servings (serving size: about ⅔ cup).

CALORIES 117 (23% from fat); FAT 3g (sat 1.8g, mono 0.2g, poly 0g); PROTEIN 4.8g; CARB 19.9g; FIBER 1.2g; CHOL 10mg; IRON 0.6mg; SODIUM 137mg; CALC 132mg

Apple Cider

A swivel-bladed vegetable peeler works well for removing the orange peel. Be sure to remove only the colored part of the peel, which contains the flavorful oils; the white pith is bitter.

4 cups cranberry juice cocktail
4 cups apple cider or apple juice
3 tablespoons brown sugar
5 (3 x 1-inch) strips orange rind
8 whole cloves
4 whole allspice
2 (3-inch) cinnamon sticks, halved
1 whole nutmeg
Whole cinnamon sticks (optional)

1. Combine first 8 ingredients in a large saucepan. Bring to a boil; cover, reduce heat, and simmer 30 minutes. Strain mixture through a fine sieve; discard solids. Serve warm with whole cinnamon sticks, if desired. Yield: 8 servings (serving size: 1 cup).

CALORIES 151 (0% from fat); FAT 0.1g (sat 0g, mono 0g, poly 0.1g); PROTEIN 0g; CARB 38.2g; FIBER 0.1g; CHOL 0mg; IRON 0.3mg; SODIUM 17mg; CALC 8mg

Hot Mulled Ginger-Spiced Cider

This party punch is prepared in a slow cooker, freeing up the stove top for other dishes on your menu.

- 3 whole cloves
- 2 (4 x 1-inch) strips orange rind
- 2 whole allspice
- 1 (3-inch) cinnamon stick
- 1 (½-inch) piece peeled fresh ginger
- 12 cups apple cider
- ½ cup apple jelly
- ¼ teaspoon ground nutmeg

1. Place first 5 ingredients on a 5-inch-square double layer of cheesecloth. Gather edges of cheesecloth together; tie securely.

2. Place cheesecloth bag, cider, jelly, and nutmeg in an electric slow cooker. Cover and cook on HIGH 4 hours. Remove and discard cheesecloth bag. Yield: 12 servings (serving size: 1 cup).

CALORIES 174 (0% from fat); FAT 0g; PROTEIN 1g; CARB 43.8g; FIBER 0g; CHOL 0mg; IRON 0mg; SODIUM 0mg; CALC 0mg

Fresh Ginger Beer

Iced Mint Tea

For a lighter minty flavor, remove the mint sprigs after they've steeped in the tea and before chilling. This tea is very sweet, but you can reduce the amount of sugar.

- 8 cups boiling water
- 1 tablespoon loose Chinese green tea
- 25 fresh mint sprigs (about 1½ ounces)
- ½ cup sugar

1. Combine 8 cups boiling water and tea in a medium bowl; cover with plastic wrap, and steep 2½ minutes. Remove plastic wrap, and strain tea mixture through a fine sieve into a large pitcher. Discard loose tea leaves. Add mint sprigs to tea, and steep 5 minutes. Add sugar; stir until sugar dissolves. Cool completely, and refrigerate. Serve over ice. Yield: 8 cups (serving size: 1 cup).

CALORIES 52 (2% from fat); FAT 0.1g (sat 0g, mono 0g, poly 0.1g); PROTEIN 0.2g; CARB 13.3g; FIBER 0.4g; CHOL 0mg; IRON 0.3mg; SODIUM 9mg; CALC 18mg

Fresh Ginger Beer

If you like ginger ale, you'll enjoy preparing this popular tangy carbonated beverage at home. Add your favorite rum to create a memorable cocktail. If you can't find superfine sugar, place granulated sugar in a blender, and process until fine. You can find bottled ground fresh ginger in the produce section of the supermarket.

- 2 cups cold water
- 1 cup fresh lime juice (about 4 limes)
- 4 teaspoons bottled ground fresh ginger (such as Spice World)
- ¾ cup superfine sugar
- 3 cups sparkling water
- Lime slices (optional)

1. Combine 2 cups water, juice, and ginger in a blender; process until blended.

2. Line a strainer with cheesecloth. Strain mixture over a pitcher; discard solids. Add sugar to pitcher; stir until dissolved.

3. Add sparkling water just before serving. Serve over ice. Garnish with lime slices, if desired. Yield: 8 servings (serving size: 1 cup).

CALORIES 81 (0% from fat); FAT 0g; PROTEIN 0.1g; CARB 21.5g; FIBER 0.1g; CHOL 0mg; IRON 0mg; SODIUM 3mg; CALC 21mg

Watermelon Agua Fresca

4 cups cubed seeded watermelon, divided
4 cups water
2 tablespoons sugar
2 tablespoons fresh lime juice

1. Finely chop 2 cups watermelon; set aside.
2. Place remaining 2 cups watermelon in a blender; process until smooth. Pour pureed watermelon through a sieve into a pitcher; discard solids. Add 4 cups water, sugar, and juice; stir until sugar dissolves. Stir in chopped watermelon. Cover and chill at least 1 hour. Yield: 6 servings (serving size: 1¼ cups).

CALORIES 72 (0% from fat); FAT 0g; PROTEIN 0.7g; CARB 22.9g; FIBER 1.4g; CHOL 0mg; IRON 0.5mg; SODIUM 6.8mg; CALC 14mg

Cantaloupe-Banana Slush

2 cups coarsely chopped cantaloupe
2 cups sliced ripe banana (about 2 medium)
2 cups pineapple-orange-banana juice
1 tablespoon sugar
1 tablespoon lime juice

1. Arrange cantaloupe and banana in a single layer on a baking sheet; freeze until firm. Place frozen fruit in a food processor; process until chunky. With processor on, slowly add pineapple-orange-banana juice and remaining ingredients; process until smooth. Serve immediately. Yield: 5 servings (serving size: 1 cup).

CALORIES 140 (3% from fat); FAT 0.5g (sat 0.2g, mono 0.1g, poly 0.1g); PROTEIN 2g; CARB 33.8g; FIBER 2.5g; CHOL 0mg; IRON 0.3mg; SODIUM 14mg; CALC 11mg

Wake-Up Shake

¾ cup prune juice, chilled
¾ cup 2% reduced-fat milk, chilled
½ cup vanilla low-fat yogurt
¾ teaspoon vanilla extract
8 bite-sized pitted dried plums
1 ripe banana, cut into chunks
Dash of ground allspice

1. Combine all ingredients in a blender; process until smooth. Yield: 3 servings (serving size: 1 cup).

CALORIES 215 (11% from fat); FAT 2.6g (sat 1.1g, mono 1.1g, poly 0.3g); PROTEIN 4.9g; CARB 45.2g; FIBER 1.9g; CHOL 7mg; IRON 1.5mg; SODIUM 71mg; CALC 161mg

Banana-Berry Smoothie

Banana-Berry Smoothie

Sip this power breakfast—which takes less time to whip up in a blender than toasting a bagel—while getting ready for work or on your way there. A scoop of powdered milk boosts the calcium contributed by the yogurt and the fortified orange juice. Additional nutritional benefits come from the potassium-rich banana and antioxidant-rich berries. Frozen berries ensure a thick, creamy consistency, but other fruits, such as frozen sliced peaches or bottled sliced mangoes, work well, too.

1¼ cups calcium-fortified orange juice
1¼ cups frozen mixed berries (such as Cascadian Farm Harvest Berries)
1 cup sliced ripe banana
½ cup vanilla fat-free yogurt
⅓ cup nonfat dry milk
1 tablespoon sugar

1. Combine all ingredients in a blender; process until smooth. Yield: 3 servings (serving size: 1 cup).

CALORIES 204 (3% from fat); FAT 0.6g (sat 0.2g, mono 0.1g, poly 0.2g); PROTEIN 6.6g; CARB 45.6g; FIBER 3.3g; CHOL 2mg; IRON 0.6mg; SODIUM 71mg; CALC 327mg

Blueberry Blender

3 cups fresh orange juice, chilled
¼ cup honey
1 pint fresh blueberries (2 cups)
1 medium cucumber, quartered

1. Combine all ingredients in a blender; process until smooth. Cover and chill 8 hours or overnight, if desired. Strain mixture through a cheesecloth-lined sieve into a medium bowl, pressing solids with a wooden spoon or a rubber spatula to squeeze out juice; discard solids. Yield: 4 servings (serving size: about 1 cup).

CALORIES 185 (3% from fat); FAT 0.7g (sat 0.1g, mono 0.1g, poly 0.2g); PROTEIN 2g; CARB 45.8g; FIBER 2.3g; CHOL 0mg; IRON 0.6mg; SODIUM 7mg; CALC 32mg

Chocolate–Peanut Butter Smoothie

Peel and slice bananas to freeze individually in zip-top bags for smoothies and shakes.

½ cup 1% low-fat milk
2 tablespoons chocolate syrup
2 tablespoons creamy peanut butter
1 frozen sliced ripe banana
1 (8-ounce) carton vanilla low-fat yogurt

1. Place all ingredients in a blender; process until smooth. Yield: 2 servings (serving size: about 1 cup).

CALORIES 332 (29% from fat); FAT 10.8g (sat 3.2g, mono 4.5g, poly 2.3g); PROTEIN 12.7g; CARB 49.8g; FIBER 3.1g; CHOL 8mg; IRON 1mg; SODIUM 194mg; CALC 282mg

Pimm's Cup

This drink derives most of its flavor from Pimm's No. 1, a gin-based aperitif with fruit juices and spices.

¾ cup Pimm's No. 1
2 cups ginger ale, chilled
1⅓ cups sparkling water, chilled
4 lemon slices
1 medium cucumber, halved lengthwise and cut into 4 spears

1. Fill 4 tall (12-ounce) glasses with ice cubes.
2. Pour 3 tablespoons Pimm's into each glass. Pour ½ cup ginger ale and ⅓ cup sparkling water into each glass; stir to combine. Garnish each serving with 1 lemon slice and 1 cucumber spear. Serve immediately. Yield: 4 servings.

CALORIES 150 (0% from fat); FAT 0g; PROTEIN 0.8g; CARB 13.3g; FIBER 0.8g; CHOL 0mg; IRON 0.3mg; SODIUM 13mg; CALC 15mg

Sparkling Peach Splash

Juicy, ripe peaches create a fruity cocktail based on the popular Bellini.

2 cups chopped peeled peaches (about 3 peaches)
½ cup peach schnapps
2 tablespoons fresh lime juice
1 (750-milliliter) bottle Champagne or sparkling wine, chilled
8 peach slices (optional)

1. Combine first 3 ingredients in a blender; process until smooth. Freeze 1 hour.
2. Pour Champagne into a pitcher. Spoon peach mixture into pitcher; stir to combine. Garnish with peach slices, if desired. Serve immediately. Yield: 8 servings (serving size: about ¾ cup).

CALORIES 133 (1% from fat); FAT 0.1g (sat 0g, mono 0g, poly 0.1g); PROTEIN 0.4g; CARB 12.1g; FIBER 0.9g; CHOL 0mg; IRON 0.4mg; SODIUM 6mg; CALC 11mg

Slushy Watermelon Mojito

Keep the limeade frozen so beverage will be slushy.

5 cups cubed seeded watermelon
1 cup sparkling water, chilled
¾ cup white rum
¼ cup chopped fresh mint
1 (6-ounce) can frozen limeade concentrate, undiluted
Mint sprigs (optional)
Lime slices (optional)

1. Arrange watermelon in a single layer on a baking sheet; freeze 2 hours or until completely frozen.
2. Combine frozen watermelon, sparkling water, rum, mint, and limeade in a blender; process until smooth. Pour into 8 (6-ounce) stemmed glasses. Garnish with mint sprigs and lime slices, if desired. Serve immediately. Yield: 8 servings (serving size: about ¾ cup).

CALORIES 119 (3% from fat); FAT 0.4g (sat 0.1g, mono 0.1g, poly 0.2g); PROTEIN 0.7g; CARB 17.5g; FIBER 0.6g; CHOL 0mg; IRON 0.3mg; SODIUM 2mg; CALC 11mg

Pimm's Cup, Sparkling Peach Splash, and Slushy Watermelon Mojito

Lemon Drop Liqueur

Lemon Drop Liqueur

Pour over ice with two parts sparkling water for a cool, delicious lemon spritzer. To serve straight up, coat the rim of a chilled martini glass in lemon juice, then dip the rim in sugar. Garnish with a slice of lemon.

- 2 cups sugar
- 1 cup water
- 5 lemon rinds, cut into strips
- 3 cups vodka
- ¼ cup lemon juice

1. Combine sugar and water in a saucepan; cook over medium heat 5 minutes or until sugar dissolves, stirring constantly. Remove from heat; stir in lemon rinds. Cool completely. Stir in vodka and juice.
2. Sterilize 2 wide-mouthed, 1-quart jars according to manufacturer's directions. Divide vodka mixture between jars. Cover each jar with metal lid; screw on band. Store in a cool, dark place for 3 weeks, shaking jar every other day.
3. Line a fine-mesh sieve with a double layer of cheesecloth; strain mixture through cheesecloth into a bowl. Discard solids. Return liqueur to jars or a clean decanter; store chilled in refrigerator or freezer. Yield: 4¾ cups (serving size: ¼ cup).

NOTE: Liqueur mixture will keep in the freezer for up to a year.

CALORIES 170 (0% from fat); FAT 0g; PROTEIN 0g; CARB 21.4g; FIBER 0.1g; CHOL 0mg; IRON 0mg; SODIUM 1mg; CALC 1mg

Grape Margarita Slush

- ¾ cup water
- ⅓ cup sugar
- 1 cup tequila
- ½ cup fresh lime juice (about 3 large limes)
- ⅓ cup Triple Sec (orange-flavored liqueur)
- 3 cups seedless green grapes
- 7 cups ice cubes

1. Combine ¾ cup water and sugar in a small saucepan over medium heat; cook 3 minutes or until sugar dissolves. Pour into a freezer-safe container; cool completely. Add tequila, juice, and Triple Sec to sugar mixture; stir to combine. Cover and freeze overnight. Place grapes in a large zip-top plastic bag; freeze overnight.
2. Place half of tequila mixture, 1½ cups grapes, and 3½ cups ice in a blender; process until desired consistency. Repeat with remaining tequila mixture, grapes, and ice. Serve immediately. Yield: 10 cups (serving size: 1 cup).

CALORIES 149 (2% from fat); FAT 0.3g (sat 0.1g, mono 0g, poly 0.1g); PROTEIN 0.4g; CARB 19.6g; FIBER 0.5g; CHOL 0mg; IRON 0.2mg; SODIUM 2mg; CALC 6mg

Winter-Spiced Red Wine Sangria

- 1 cup apple juice
- ⅓ cup Triple Sec (orange-flavored liqueur)
- ¼ cup sugar
- 4 whole cloves
- 3 navel oranges, cut into ¼-inch slices
- 2 lemons, cut into ¼-inch slices
- 2 (3-inch) cinnamon sticks
- 1 Bartlett pear, cut into ½-inch cubes
- 1 (750-milliliter) bottle fruity red wine

1. Combine all ingredients in a large pitcher; stir until sugar dissolves. Cover and refrigerate for at least 4 hours or overnight. Discard cloves and cinnamon sticks before serving. Yield: 10 servings (serving size: ¾ cup).

CALORIES 149 (0% from fat); FAT 0.1g (sat 0g, mono 0g, poly 0g); PROTEIN 0.5g; CARB 22g; FIBER 1.6g; CHOL 0mg; IRON 0.4mg; SODIUM 7mg; CALC 31mg

Easy Sangria

1 (1.5-liter) bottle dry red wine, divided
2 tablespoons brandy
2 tablespoons Triple Sec (orange-flavored liqueur)
⅓ cup sugar
⅔ cup fresh orange juice
2 tablespoons fresh lime juice
2 tablespoons fresh lemon juice
5 whole cloves
3 whole allspice
1 (3-inch) cinnamon stick
2 cups sparkling water, chilled
8 orange wedges
5 lemon slices
5 lime slices

1. Combine ½ cup wine, brandy, Triple Sec, and sugar in a 2-quart glass measure. Microwave at HIGH 1 minute or until mixture is warm; stir to dissolve sugar. Stir in remaining wine, juices, cloves, allspice, and cinnamon. Chill at least 2 hours.
2. Strain mixture into a pitcher, and discard spices. Just before serving, stir in sparkling water and remaining ingredients. Serve over ice. Yield: 8 servings (serving size: about ¾ cup).

CALORIES 199 (0% from fat); FAT 0.1g (sat 0g, mono 0g, poly 0.1g); PROTEIN 0.6g; CARB 15.8g; FIBER 0.1g; CHOL 0mg; IRON 0.9mg; SODIUM 10mg; CALC 18mg

Watermelon Margaritas

2 cups diced seeded watermelon, frozen
¾ cup tequila
⅓ cup Triple Sec (orange-flavored liqueur)
1 tablespoon sugar
2 tablespoons lime juice
2 cups crushed ice
Sugar (optional)
Lime slices (optional)
Orange slices (optional)

1. Place frozen watermelon, tequila, Triple Sec, sugar, and lime juice in a blender; process until smooth. Add ice, and process until smooth. Serve in glasses rimmed with sugar, and garnish with lime and orange slices, if desired. Yield: 5 servings (serving size: 1 cup).

CALORIES 157 (2% from fat); FAT 0.2g (sat 0.2g, mono 0g, poly 0g); PROTEIN 0.2g; CARB 6g; FIBER 0.4g; CHOL 0mg; IRON 0.1mg; SODIUM 2mg; CALC 6mg

Frozen Strawberry Daiquiris

3 cups sliced fresh strawberries
1 cup white rum
3 tablespoons fresh lime juice
1 (12-ounce) can thawed limeade concentrate, undiluted
1 cup crushed ice
6 lime slices (optional)

1. Place first 4 ingredients in a blender; process until smooth. Add ice; process until smooth. Serve immediately; garnish with lime slices, if desired. Yield: 6 servings (serving size: about 1 cup).

CALORIES 219 (2% from fat); FAT 0.4g (sat 0g, mono 0.1g, poly 0.2g); PROTEIN 0.7g; CARB 34.6g; FIBER 2.2g; CHOL 0mg; IRON 0.4mg; SODIUM 1mg; CALC 15mg

Mango Mojito

(pictured on page 8)

2 lime wedges
5 fresh mint leaves
¼ cup club soda
3 tablespoons rum
2 tablespoons Simple Syrup
1 tablespoon mango nectar
Crushed ice

1. Squeeze lime wedges into a small glass; add wedges and mint to glass. Crush with the back of a spoon for 30 seconds. Add soda, rum, Simple Syrup, and nectar; stir gently. Serve over ice. Yield: 1 serving (serving size: ½ cup).

(Totals include Simple Syrup) CALORIES 205 (0% from fat); FAT 0g; PROTEIN 0.1g; CARB 28.3g; FIBER 0.2g; CHOL 0mg; IRON 0.1mg; SODIUM 14mg; CALC 6mg

SIMPLE SYRUP:

2 cups sugar
1 cup water

1. Heat sugar and water in a small saucepan over medium-high heat until sugar dissolves (about 5 minutes), stirring constantly. Yield: 2 cups (serving size: 2 tablespoons).

CALORIES 97 (0% from fat); FAT 0g; PROTEIN 0g; CARB 25g; FIBER 0g; CHOL 0mg; IRON 0mg; SODIUM 0mg; CALC 1mg

Dinner Rolls, Five Ways, page 66

Breads

Cornmeal Buttermilk Biscuits

These tender biscuits are a new twist on a down-home Southern tradition.

- 1 cup all-purpose flour (about 4½ ounces)
- ½ cup cornmeal
- 1½ tablespoons sugar
- 2 teaspoons baking powder
- ½ teaspoon salt
- 3 tablespoons chilled butter, cut into small pieces
- ½ cup low-fat buttermilk

1. Preheat oven to 450°.
2. Lightly spoon flour into a dry measuring cup; level with a knife. Combine flour and next 4 ingredients in a medium bowl; cut in butter with a pastry blender or 2 knives until mixture resembles coarse meal. Add buttermilk; stir just until moist.
3. Turn dough out onto a lightly floured surface. Pat dough into an 8 x 4–inch rectangle. Cut dough by making 1 lengthwise cut and 3 crosswise cuts to form 8 biscuits. Place biscuits, 1 inch apart, on an ungreased baking sheet.
4. Bake at 450° for 12 minutes or until golden. Serve biscuits warm or at room temperature. Yield: 8 servings (serving size: 1 biscuit).

CALORIES 136 (30% from fat); FAT 4.5g (sat 2.3g, mono 1.8g, poly 0.2g); PROTEIN 2.8g; CARB 20.9g; FIBER 1g; CHOL 12mg; IRON 1.2mg; SODIUM 316mg; CALC 87mg

Sour Cream, Cheddar, and Green Onion Drop Biscuits

Roll out these biscuits, or drop into 12 muffin cups and bake the same amount of time. These are best the same day they're baked.

- 2 cups all-purpose flour (about 9 ounces)
- 1 tablespoon sugar
- 2 teaspoons baking powder
- 1 teaspoon salt
- ¼ teaspoon baking soda
- 3 tablespoons chilled butter, cut into small pieces
- ¾ cup (3 ounces) shredded reduced-fat sharp Cheddar cheese
- ¼ cup finely chopped green onions
- 1 cup fat-free buttermilk
- ½ cup fat-free sour cream
- Cooking spray

1. Preheat oven to 450°.
2. Lightly spoon flour into dry measuring cups; level with a knife. Combine flour, sugar, baking powder, salt, and baking soda in a large bowl, stirring with a whisk. Cut in butter with a pastry blender or 2 knives until mixture resembles coarse meal. Add cheese and onions; toss well. Add buttermilk and sour cream; stir just until moist.
3. Drop dough by ¼ cupfuls onto a baking sheet coated with cooking spray. Bake at 450° for 15 minutes or until edges are brown. Remove biscuits from pan; cool on wire racks. Yield: 1 dozen (serving size: 1 biscuit).

CALORIES 146 (29% from fat); FAT 4.7g (sat 2.9g, mono 0.8g, poly 0.2g); PROTEIN 5.2g; CARB 20.1g; FIBER 0.7g; CHOL 14mg; IRON 1mg; SODIUM 406mg; CALC 134mg

White Cheddar and Black Pepper Biscuits

The food processor's blades distribute the butter evenly throughout the biscuit dough. The richness of buttermilk and cheese mellows the spicy black pepper.

- 2 cups all-purpose flour (about 9 ounces)
- 1 tablespoon baking powder
- ½ teaspoon salt
- ½ teaspoon baking soda
- ½ teaspoon freshly ground black pepper
- ½ cup (2 ounces) shredded extrasharp white Cheddar cheese
- 3 tablespoons chilled butter, cut into small pieces
- 1 cup fat-free buttermilk
- Cooking spray

1. Preheat oven to 400°.
2. Lightly spoon flour into dry measuring cups; level with a knife. Place flour and next 4 ingredients in a food processor; pulse 5 times or until well combined. Add cheese and butter; pulse 5 times or until well combined.
3. Place mixture in a large bowl. Add buttermilk; stir just until moist.
4. Turn dough out onto a floured surface. Knead lightly 5 times. Roll dough to a ½-inch thickness; cut with a 2-inch biscuit cutter into 24 biscuits. Place on a baking sheet coated with cooking spray. Bake at 400° for 15 minutes or until golden. Yield: 12 servings (serving size: 2 biscuits).

CALORIES 129 (33% from fat); FAT 4.7g (sat 2.6g, mono 1.2g, poly 0.2g); PROTEIN 3.9g; CARB 17.4g; FIBER 0.6g; CHOL 13mg; IRON 1.1mg; SODIUM 342mg; CALC 130mg

Herb and Onion Wheat Biscuits

The sautéed onion is pureed so that its flavor carries throughout the biscuits. You can make and freeze the biscuits up to a week ahead. When ready to serve, thaw, wrap in foil, and heat in a 325° oven for 10 to 12 minutes or until thoroughly heated.

Cooking spray
- 1 cup chopped onion
- 3/4 cup fat-free milk
- 1 1/2 cups all-purpose flour (about 6 3/4 ounces)
- 1/2 cup whole wheat flour (about 2 1/3 ounces)
- 2 teaspoons baking powder
- 1/2 teaspoon salt
- 1/4 teaspoon sugar
- 1/4 teaspoon dried oregano
- 1/4 teaspoon dried basil
- 1/4 cup chilled butter, cut into small pieces

1. Preheat oven to 425°.

2. Heat a small skillet over medium heat. Coat pan with cooking spray. Add onion; cook 6 minutes or until tender, stirring frequently. Spoon onion into a blender. Add milk, and process until smooth. Cool.

3. Lightly spoon flours into dry measuring cups, and level with a knife. Combine flours and next 5 ingredients in a large bowl; cut in butter with a pastry blender or 2 knives until mixture resembles coarse meal. Add onion mixture; stir just until moist. Turn dough out onto a heavily floured surface (dough will be sticky); knead lightly 5 times with floured hands. Roll dough to a 1/2-inch thickness; cut into 10 biscuits with a 3-inch biscuit cutter. Place on a baking sheet coated with cooking spray. Bake at 425° for 12 minutes or until biscuits are golden. Yield: 10 servings (serving size: 1 biscuit).

CALORIES 119 (31% from fat); FAT 4.1g (sat 2.4g, mono 1.2g, poly 0.3g); PROTEIN 3.1g; CARB 17.9g; FIBER 1.3g; CHOL 11mg; IRON 1.1mg; SODIUM 227mg; CALC 73mg

Savory Two-Cheese Biscotti

Savory biscotti are a great alternative to breadsticks or rolls to serve with a meal. They're also good for dipping into chili or paired with a salad.

- 2¾ cups all-purpose flour (about 12⅓ ounces)
- ¾ cup (3 ounces) shredded extrasharp Cheddar cheese
- ½ cup (2 ounces) grated fresh Parmesan cheese
- 2 teaspoons baking powder
- ¾ teaspoon salt
- ¼ teaspoon ground red pepper
- ¼ cup fat-free milk
- 2 teaspoons olive oil
- 3 large eggs
- Cooking spray

1. Preheat oven to 350°.
2. Lightly spoon flour into dry measuring cups; level with a knife. Combine flour and next 5 ingredients in a large bowl. Combine milk, oil, and eggs; stir with a whisk. Add milk mixture to flour mixture, stirring until well blended (dough will be dry and crumbly). Turn out onto a lightly floured surface; knead 8 times. Divide dough in half. Shape each portion into an 8-inch-long roll. Place rolls, 6 inches apart, on a baking sheet coated with cooking spray; flatten to 1-inch thickness. Bake at 350° for 30 minutes. Remove from baking sheet; cool 10 minutes on a wire rack.
3. Reduce oven temperature to 325°.
4. Cut each roll diagonally into 12 (⅔-inch) slices. Place slices, cut sides down, on baking sheet. Bake at 325° for 10 minutes. Turn biscotti over; bake an additional 10 minutes (biscotti will be slightly soft in center but will harden as they cool). Remove from baking sheet; cool completely on wire rack. Yield: 2 dozen (serving size: 1 biscotto).

CALORIES 83 (30% from fat); FAT 2.8g (sat 1.5g, mono 0.5g, poly 0.1g); PROTEIN 3.9g; CARB 10.8g; FIBER 0.4g; CHOL 32mg; IRON 0.8mg; SODIUM 160mg; CALC 80mg

Sour Cream Scones

Whole wheat flour adds a nutty flavor. Split scones in half, and fill with a spoonful of commercial lemon curd, if desired.

- 1½ cups all-purpose flour (about 6¾ ounces)
- ⅔ cup whole wheat flour (about 3 ounces)
- ⅓ cup packed brown sugar
- 2 tablespoons granulated sugar
- 2 teaspoons baking powder
- ½ teaspoon baking soda
- ¼ teaspoon salt
- ⅔ cup reduced-fat sour cream
- 3 tablespoons butter, melted and cooled
- 1 large egg white
- ⅓ cup dried currants or raisins
- Cooking spray
- 1 tablespoon granulated sugar
- ¼ teaspoon ground cinnamon

1. Preheat oven to 400°.
2. Lightly spoon flours into dry measuring cups; level with a knife. Combine flours and next 5 ingredients in a large bowl; stir well with a whisk.
3. Combine sour cream, butter, and egg white in a small bowl. Add sour cream mixture to flour mixture, stirring just until moist. Stir in currants.
4. Turn dough out onto a lightly floured surface, and knead lightly 6 to 12 times with floured hands. (Dough will be crumbly.) Divide dough in half. Pat each half into a 6-inch circle on a baking sheet coated with cooking spray. Cut each circle into 6 wedges; do not separate.
5. Combine 1 tablespoon granulated sugar and cinnamon. Lightly coat top of dough with cooking spray. Sprinkle with cinnamon mixture. Bake at 400° for 15 minutes or until lightly browned. Yield: 12 servings (serving size: 1 scone).

CALORIES 175 (25% from fat); FAT 4.8g (sat 2.9g, mono 1.3g, poly 0.3g); PROTEIN 3.6g; CARB 30.2g; FIBER 1.4g; CHOL 14mg; IRON 1.3mg; SODIUM 219mg; CALC 81mg

Sour Cream Scones

Blueberry-Pecan Scones

These are easy to prepare for brunch or weekday breakfasts.

- ½ cup 2% reduced-fat milk
- ¼ cup sugar
- 2 teaspoons grated lemon rind
- 1 teaspoon vanilla extract
- 1 large egg
- 2 cups all-purpose flour (about 9 ounces)
- 1 tablespoon baking powder
- ½ teaspoon salt
- 3 tablespoons chilled butter, cut into small pieces
- 1 cup fresh or frozen blueberries
- ¼ cup finely chopped pecans, toasted
- Cooking spray
- 1 large egg white, lightly beaten
- 2 tablespoons sugar

1. Preheat oven to 375°.

2. Combine first 5 ingredients in a medium bowl, stirring with a whisk. Lightly spoon flour into dry measuring cups; level with a knife. Combine flour, baking powder, and salt in a large bowl, stirring with a whisk. Cut in butter with a pastry blender or 2 knives until mixture resembles coarse meal. Gently fold in blueberries and pecans. Add milk mixture, stirring just until moist (dough will be sticky).

3. Turn dough out onto a floured surface; pat dough into an 8-inch circle. Cut dough into 10 wedges, and place dough wedges on a baking sheet coated with cooking spray. Brush egg white over dough wedges; sprinkle with 2 tablespoons sugar. Bake scones at 375° for 18 minutes or until golden. Serve warm. Yield: 10 servings (serving size: 1 scone).

CALORIES 196 (30% from fat); FAT 6.6g (sat 2.2g, mono 2.9g, poly 1g); PROTEIN 4.4g; CARB 30.2g; FIBER 1.4g; CHOL 31mg; IRON 1.5mg; SODIUM 308mg; CALC 107mg

Fresh-Sage Drop Scones

- 1 cup all-purpose flour (about 4½ ounces)
- 1 cup yellow cornmeal
- 2 teaspoons baking powder
- ¼ teaspoon salt
- ¼ teaspoon black pepper
- 1 cup (4 ounces) shredded sharp Cheddar cheese
- ¼ cup minced green onions
- 2 tablespoons chopped fresh sage
- 1½ teaspoons chopped fresh thyme
- 1 cup 1% low-fat milk
- Cooking spray
- 12 sage leaves

1. Preheat oven to 400°.
2. Lightly spoon flour into a dry measuring cup; level with a knife. Combine flour and next 4 ingredients in a large bowl. Stir in cheese, onions, chopped sage, and thyme. Add milk, stirring just until moist. Drop dough by 2 level tablespoons 2 inches apart onto baking sheets coated with cooking spray. Gently press 1 sage leaf into top of each scone.
3. Bake at 400° for 20 minutes or until golden brown. Serve warm. Yield: 1 dozen (serving size: 1 scone).

CALORIES 129 (26% from fat); FAT 3.7g (sat 2.2g, mono 1g, poly 0.2g); PROTEIN 5.1g; CARB 18.4; FIBER 1g; CHOL 11mg; IRON 1.2mg; SODIUM 183mg; CALC 143mg

Paraguayan Corn Bread

Some of the ingredients are pureed in the food processor, which adds to the bread's moistness and superior texture.

- Cooking spray
- 2 tablespoons grated fresh Parmesan cheese
- 1 tablespoon butter
- 1 tablespoon canola oil
- 1 cup chopped onion
- ⅓ cup chopped green bell pepper
- 2 cups fresh corn kernels (about 4 ears), divided
- ½ cup 1% low-fat cottage cheese
- 1½ cups yellow cornmeal
- ¾ cup (3 ounces) shredded Muenster or sharp Cheddar cheese
- ½ cup fat-free milk
- 1 teaspoon salt
- ½ teaspoon black pepper
- 4 large egg whites
- ½ teaspoon cream of tartar

Paraguayan Corn Bread

1. Preheat oven to 400°.
2. Coat a 9-inch round cake pan with cooking spray. Sprinkle with Parmesan cheese; set aside.
3. Heat butter and oil in a medium skillet over medium heat. Add onion and bell pepper; cook 5 minutes or until soft. Place onion mixture in a food processor. Add 1½ cups corn and cottage cheese; process until almost smooth, scraping sides of bowl occasionally. Place pureed mixture in a large bowl. Stir in remaining ½ cup corn, cornmeal, Muenster cheese, milk, salt, and black pepper.
4. Place egg whites and cream of tartar in a large bowl; beat with a mixer at high speed until stiff peaks form. Gently stir one-fourth of egg white mixture into batter; gently fold in remaining egg white mixture. Spoon batter into prepared pan.
5. Bake at 400° for 30 minutes or until a wooden pick inserted in center comes out clean (cover loosely with foil if it becomes too brown). Cool in pan 10 minutes on a wire rack. Place a plate upside down on top of bread; invert onto plate. Cut into wedges. Yield: 8 servings (serving size: 1 wedge).

CALORIES 235 (30% from fat); FAT 7.9g (sat 3.7g, mono 2.2g, poly 1.5g); PROTEIN 10.9g; CARB 31g; FIBER 3.4g; CHOL 16mg; IRON 0.7mg; SODIUM 503mg; CALC 133mg

Banana Corn Muffins

½ cup mashed ripe banana (about 1 medium)
½ cup 2% reduced-fat milk
1 (8½-ounce) package corn muffin mix (such as Jiffy)
Cooking spray

1. Preheat oven to 350°.
2. Combine banana, milk, and mix in a medium bowl; stir just until moist. Spoon batter evenly into 6 muffin cups coated with cooking spray (batter will be slightly thin). Bake at 350° for 22 minutes or until a wooden pick inserted in center comes out clean. Cool in pan 10 minutes. Yield: 6 servings (serving size: 1 muffin).

CALORIES 199 (24% from fat); FAT 5.4g (sat 1.5g, mono 2.8g, poly 0.7g); PROTEIN 3.7g; CARB 34.2g; FIBER 3.2g; CHOL 2mg; IRON 1.1mg; SODIUM 457mg; CALC 49mg

Blueberry Oatmeal Muffins

1⅔ cups quick-cooking oats
⅔ cup all-purpose flour (about 3 ounces)
½ cup whole wheat flour (about 2⅓ ounces)
¾ cup packed light brown sugar
2 teaspoons ground cinnamon
1 teaspoon baking powder
1 teaspoon baking soda
¾ teaspoon salt
1½ cups fat-free buttermilk
¼ cup canola oil
2 teaspoons grated lemon rind
2 large eggs
2 cups frozen blueberries
2 tablespoons all-purpose flour
2 tablespoons granulated sugar

1. Preheat oven to 400°.
2. Place oats in a food processor; pulse 5 or 6 times until oats resemble coarse meal. Place in a bowl.
3. Lightly spoon flours into dry measuring cups; level with a knife. Add flours and next 5 ingredients to oats in bowl; stir well with a whisk. Make a well in center of mixture.
4. Combine buttermilk, oil, rind, and eggs in a small bowl; stir well with a whisk. Add to flour mixture, stirring just until moist.
5. Toss blueberries with 2 tablespoons flour; gently fold into batter.
6. Spoon batter into 16 muffin cups lined with paper liners; sprinkle batter with 2 tablespoons granulated sugar. Bake at 400° for 18 minutes or until muffins spring back when touched lightly in center. Remove from pans immediately. Place on a wire rack. Serve warm or at room temperature. Yield: 16 servings (serving size: 1 muffin).

CALORIES 170 (26% from fat); FAT 5g (sat 0.6g, mono 2.5g, poly 1.4g); PROTEIN 4g; CARB 28.6g; FIBER 2g; CHOL 27mg; IRON 1.2mg; SODIUM 256mg; CALC 65mg

Lemon-Blueberry Muffins

You can make these muffins up to two days ahead, and glaze them just before serving.

MUFFINS:
2 cups all-purpose flour (about 9 ounces)
½ cup sugar
1 teaspoon baking powder
½ teaspoon baking soda
½ teaspoon salt
⅛ teaspoon ground nutmeg
¼ cup butter
1¼ cups low-fat buttermilk
1 tablespoon grated lemon rind
1 large egg
1 cup fresh blueberries
Cooking spray

GLAZE:
1 tablespoon fresh lemon juice
½ cup powdered sugar

1. Preheat oven to 400°.
2. To prepare muffins, lightly spoon flour into dry measuring cups; level with a knife. Combine flour and next 5 ingredients in a medium bowl; cut in butter with a pastry blender or 2 knives until mixture resembles coarse meal.
3. Combine buttermilk, rind, and egg; stir well with a whisk. Add to flour mixture; stir just until moist. Gently fold in blueberries.
4. Spoon batter into 12 muffin cups coated with cooking spray. Bake at 400° for 20 minutes or until muffins spring back when lightly touched. Remove muffins from pans immediately; cool on a wire rack.
5. To prepare glaze, combine lemon juice and powdered sugar in a small bowl. Drizzle glaze evenly over cooled muffins. Yield: 1 dozen (serving size: 1 muffin).

NOTE: We recommend not using paper liners in the muffin cups because the muffins stick to the paper.

CALORIES 187 (23% from fat); FAT 4.8g (sat 2.7g, mono 1.4g, poly 0.3g); PROTEIN 3.7g; CARB 32.6g; FIBER 1g; CHOL 30mg; IRON 1.1mg; SODIUM 264mg; CALC 59mg

Lemon-Blueberry Muffins

Whole Wheat, Oatmeal, and Raisin Muffins

Whole Wheat, Oatmeal, and Raisin Muffins

With four whole grains and three dried fruits, these muffins are a great way to get a variety of antioxidants and fiber. Look for untoasted wheat germ in the organic food section of the supermarket. Or you can substitute toasted wheat germ, if you wish. Adding boiling water to the batter and allowing it to stand 15 minutes before baking allows the hearty oats, wheat germ, and bran to soak up the liquid for a more tender muffin.

- 1 cup whole wheat flour (about 4¾ ounces)
- ¼ cup granulated sugar
- ¼ cup packed brown sugar
- 2 tablespoons untoasted wheat germ
- 2 tablespoons wheat bran
- 1½ teaspoons baking soda
- 1 teaspoon ground cinnamon
- ½ teaspoon salt
- 1½ cups quick-cooking oats
- ⅓ cup chopped pitted dates
- ⅓ cup raisins
- ⅓ cup dried cranberries
- 1 cup low-fat buttermilk
- ¼ cup canola oil
- 1 teaspoon vanilla extract
- 1 large egg, lightly beaten
- ½ cup boiling water
- Cooking spray

1. Lightly spoon whole wheat flour into a dry measuring cup; level with a knife. Combine flour and next 7 ingredients in a large bowl, stirring with a whisk. Stir in quick-cooking oats, dates, raisins, and cranberries.

2. Make a well in center of mixture. Combine buttermilk, oil, vanilla, and egg; add to flour mixture, stirring just until moist. Stir in boiling water. Let batter stand 15 minutes.

3. Preheat oven to 375°.

4. Spoon batter evenly into 12 muffin cups coated with cooking spray. Bake at 375° for 20 minutes or until muffins spring back when touched lightly in center. Remove muffins from pans immediately, and place on a wire rack. Yield: 12 servings (serving size: 1 muffin).

CALORIES 204 (28% from fat); FAT 6.4g (sat 0.8g, mono 3.2g, poly 1.8g); PROTEIN 4.6g; CARB 34.7g; FIBER 3.4g; CHOL 19mg; IRON 1.4mg; SODIUM 288mg; CALC 43mg

Raspberry-Almond Muffins

Almond paste is coarser in texture and less sweet than marzipan, but either will work for this recipe. Both can be found on the baking aisle of the supermarket. They also make perfect bite-sized muffins for a brunch or when you need to serve a larger group. To make mini muffins, spoon one heaping teaspoon of batter into 48 mini muffin cups coated with cooking spray. Bake at 375° for 10 to 12 minutes.

- ½ cup granulated sugar
- ½ cup packed brown sugar
- 2½ tablespoons almond paste
- ¼ cup butter, softened
- 2 large eggs
- ½ cup fat-free buttermilk
- 1 teaspoon vanilla extract
- 1 teaspoon fresh lemon juice
- 2 cups all-purpose flour (about 9 ounces)
- ½ teaspoon baking powder
- ½ teaspoon baking soda
- ¼ teaspoon salt
- 1½ cups fresh raspberries
- Cooking spray
- 2 tablespoons turbinado sugar or granulated sugar

1. Preheat oven to 375°.

2. Place first 3 ingredients in a food processor; process until well blended. Add butter; pulse 4 or 5 times or just until combined. Add eggs, 1 at a time, pulsing after each addition. Add buttermilk, vanilla, and juice; pulse until blended.

3. Lightly spoon flour into dry measuring cups; level with a knife. Combine flour, baking powder, baking soda, and salt in a large bowl, stirring with a whisk. Make a well in center of mixture. Add buttermilk mixture; stir just until moist. Gently fold in raspberries. Let batter stand 5 minutes. Spoon batter into 12 muffin cups coated with cooking spray or lined with paper liners. Sprinkle with turbinado sugar. Bake at 375° for 22 minutes or until muffins spring back when touched lightly in center. Remove muffins from pans immediately; place on a wire rack. Yield: 12 servings (serving size: 1 muffin).

CALORIES 222 (23% from fat); FAT 5.7g (sat 2.7g, mono 2g, poly 0.6g); PROTEIN 4g; CARB 39.1g; FIBER 1.8g; CHOL 46mg; IRON 1.5mg; SODIUM 186mg; CALC 50mg

Oat Bran Muffins

The yield for this recipe is more than two dozen, but they freeze well for breakfasts during the week. Wrap cooled muffins in plastic wrap; freeze in zip-top plastic bags. Thaw at room temperature, or reheat in the microwave 15 seconds or until warm.

- 1 cup all-purpose flour (about 4½ ounces)
- 1 cup whole wheat flour (about 4¾ ounces)
- 1¾ cups oat bran
- ¾ cup packed brown sugar
- ⅓ cup nonfat dry milk
- ¼ cup flaxseed
- 4 teaspoons ground cinnamon
- 2 teaspoons baking soda
- 2 teaspoons baking powder
- ½ teaspoon salt
- 2 cups shredded carrot
- 2 cups chopped Granny Smith apple
- 1 cup raisins
- 1 cup fat-free milk
- ¼ cup canola oil
- 2 teaspoons vanilla extract
- 3 large egg whites
- 1 thin-skinned orange, unpeeled and quartered
- Cooking spray

1. Preheat oven to 375°.

2. Lightly spoon flours into dry measuring cups; level with a knife. Combine flours and next 8 ingredients in a large bowl, stirring well with a whisk. Stir in carrot, apple, and raisins.

3. Combine milk, oil, vanilla, egg whites, and orange in a blender or food processor; process until smooth. Make a well in center of flour mixture. Add milk mixture; stir until moist.

4. Spoon 3 tablespoons batter into each of 28 muffin cups coated with cooking spray or lined with paper liners. Bake in batches at 375° for 20 minutes or until muffins are browned and spring back when touched lightly in center. Remove muffins from pans immediately, and place on a wire rack. Yield: 28 muffins (serving size: 1 muffin).

CALORIES 114 (22% from fat); FAT 2.8g (sat 0.3g, mono 1.3g, poly 0.8g); PROTEIN 3.5g; CARB 22.6g; FIBER 3g; CHOL 0mg; IRON 1.1mg; SODIUM 188mg; CALC 61mg

Sour Cream Muffins with Poppy Seed Streusel

Keep these orange-scented muffins around for a quick breakfast or sweet snack.

STREUSEL:

3 tablespoons sugar
2 tablespoons all-purpose flour
1 tablespoon butter, melted
1 teaspoon poppy seeds

MUFFINS:

2 cups all-purpose flour (about 9 ounces)
¾ cup sugar
2 teaspoons baking powder
1 teaspoon baking soda
½ teaspoon salt
¾ cup fat-free buttermilk
¼ cup butter, melted
1 tablespoon grated orange rind
1 teaspoon vanilla extract
1 large egg, lightly beaten
1 (8-ounce) container reduced-fat sour cream
Cooking spray

1. Preheat oven to 375°.

2. To prepare streusel, combine first 4 ingredients in a small bowl; set aside.

3. To prepare muffins, lightly spoon 2 cups flour into dry measuring cups; level with a knife. Combine 2 cups flour, ¾ cup sugar, baking powder, baking soda, and salt in a medium bowl, stirring with a whisk. Make a well in center of mixture. Combine buttermilk and next 5 ingredients; add to flour mixture, stirring just until moist. Spoon batter into 15 muffin cups coated with cooking spray. Sprinkle streusel evenly over batter. Bake at 375° for 18 minutes or until golden brown. Remove from pans immediately; place on a wire rack. Yield: 15 servings (serving size: 1 muffin).

CALORIES 180 (32% from fat); FAT 6.3g (sat 3.2g, mono 2.3g, poly 0.4g); PROTEIN 3.3g; CARB 27.8g; FIBER 0.5g; CHOL 31mg; IRON 1mg; SODIUM 277mg; CALC 77mg

Low-Fat Strawberry-Cinnamon Muffins

- 1½ cups all-purpose flour (about 6¾ ounces)
- ½ cup sugar
- 2½ teaspoons baking powder
- 1 teaspoon ground cinnamon
- ¼ teaspoon salt
- ⅔ cup vanilla fat-free yogurt
- ¼ cup butter, melted
- 3 tablespoons 1% low-fat milk
- 1 large egg, lightly beaten
- Cooking spray
- ¼ cup strawberry jam
- 1 tablespoon sugar
- ½ teaspoon ground cinnamon

1. Preheat oven to 375°.

2. Lightly spoon flour into dry measuring cups; level with a knife. Combine flour and next 4 ingredients in a large bowl, stirring well with a whisk. Make a well in center of flour mixture. Combine yogurt, butter, milk, and egg in a bowl, stirring well with a whisk. Add yogurt mixture to flour mixture, stirring just until moist.

3. Place 12 foil cup liners in muffin cups; coat liners with cooking spray. Spoon 1 tablespoon batter into each liner. Top each with 1 teaspoon jam. Top evenly with remaining batter. Combine 1 tablespoon sugar and ½ teaspoon cinnamon; sprinkle evenly over batter. Bake at 375° for 15 minutes or until a wooden pick inserted in center comes out clean. Cool in pan on a wire rack 15 minutes. Remove from pan; place on a wire rack. Yield: 1 dozen (serving size: 1 muffin).

CALORIES 165 (24% from fat); FAT 4.4g (sat 2.6g, mono 1.3g, poly 0.3g); PROTEIN 3g; CARB 29g; FIBER 0.6g; CHOL 28mg; IRON 1mg; SODIUM 206mg; CALC 94mg

Cinnamon-Swirl Sour Cream Coffeecake Muffins

Fold the batter just four times to swirl in the brown sugar mixture, not fully blending it.

- ½ cup packed dark brown sugar
- ¼ cup chopped pecans
- 1½ teaspoons ground cinnamon
- 1 cup granulated sugar
- ¼ cup butter, softened
- ½ cup egg substitute
- 1 cup reduced-fat sour cream
- 2 tablespoons water
- 1 teaspoon vanilla extract
- 1¾ cups all-purpose flour (about 7¾ ounces)
- 1 teaspoon baking powder
- ½ teaspoon baking soda
- ½ teaspoon salt
- Cooking spray
- 6 tablespoons powdered sugar
- 1 tablespoon fresh orange juice
- Dash of salt

1. Preheat oven to 400°.

2. Combine first 3 ingredients; set aside.

3. Place granulated sugar and butter in a large bowl; beat with a mixer at medium speed until well blended (about 3 minutes). Add egg substitute; beat 3 minutes. Beat in sour cream, 2 tablespoons water, and vanilla.

4. Lightly spoon flour into dry measuring cups; level with a knife. Combine flour, baking powder, baking soda, and salt in a large bowl, stirring well with a whisk. Make a well in center of mixture; add sour cream mixture. Stir just until combined.

5. Place 3 tablespoons brown sugar mixture in a small bowl; set aside. Sprinkle surface of muffin batter with remaining brown sugar mixture. Gently fold batter 4 times.

6. Place 18 paper muffin cup liners in muffin cups; coat liners with cooking spray. Spoon batter into prepared cups. Sprinkle batter evenly with reserved brown sugar mixture. Bake at 400° for 25 minutes or until a wooden pick inserted in center comes out clean. Remove muffins from pans immediately; place on a wire rack. Cool 10 minutes.

7. Combine powdered sugar, juice, and dash of salt in a small bowl, stirring until smooth. Drizzle powdered sugar mixture evenly over muffins. Yield: 18 servings (serving size: 1 muffin).

CALORIES 182 (28% from fat); FAT 5.7g (sat 2.8g, mono 1.4g, poly 0.6g); PROTEIN 2.9g; CARB 30.4g; FIBER 0.6g; CHOL 14mg; IRON 1mg; SODIUM 176mg; CALC 53mg

Cinnamon-Swirl Sour Cream
Coffeecake Muffins

Cheddar–Green Onion Muffins

These can be made in advance; freeze in plastic bags. Thaw; wrap in foil, and reheat in the oven.

- 1¾ cups all-purpose flour (about 7¾ ounces)
- ¼ cup yellow cornmeal
- 1 teaspoon baking powder
- ½ teaspoon salt
- ¼ teaspoon baking soda
- ¼ teaspoon freshly ground black pepper
- ½ cup (2 ounces) reduced-fat shredded extrasharp Cheddar cheese, divided
- 3 tablespoons chilled butter, cut into pieces
- 1¼ cups fat-free buttermilk
- 2 tablespoons chopped green onions
- 1 teaspoon minced garlic
- 1 large egg, lightly beaten
- Cooking spray

1. Preheat oven to 375°.

2. Lightly spoon flour into dry measuring cups; level with a knife. Combine flour and next 5 ingredients in a food processor; pulse 3 times to combine. Add 5 tablespoons cheese and butter; pulse 5 times or until mixture resembles coarse crumbs. Spoon mixture into a medium bowl. Combine buttermilk, onions, garlic, and egg; stir with a whisk. Add to flour mixture, stirring just until moist. Spoon batter into 12 muffin cups coated with cooking spray. Sprinkle evenly with remaining 3 tablespoons cheese. Bake at 375° for 18 minutes or until a wooden pick inserted in center comes out clean. Cool 5 minutes in pan on a wire rack; remove from pan. Cool completely on a wire rack. Yield: 12 muffins (serving size: 1 muffin).

CALORIES 135 (30% from fat); FAT 4.5g (sat 2.7g, mono 0.9g, poly 0.2g); PROTEIN 4.9g; CARB 18.6g; FIBER 0.6g; CHOL 29mg; IRON 1.1mg; SODIUM 217mg; CALC 97mg

Butter Crust Sandwich Bread

1 tablespoon sugar
1 package dry yeast (about 2¼ teaspoons)
1 cup warm fat-free milk (100° to 110°)
2 tablespoons butter, melted and cooled, divided
3¼ cups all-purpose flour, divided (about 14½ ounces)
1 teaspoon salt
Cooking spray

1. Dissolve sugar and yeast in warm milk in a large bowl; let stand 5 minutes. Stir in 1 tablespoon butter. Lightly spoon flour into dry measuring cups, and level with a knife. Add 3 cups flour and salt to yeast mixture; stir until a soft dough forms. Turn dough out onto a floured surface. Knead until smooth and elastic (about 8 minutes); add enough of remaining ¼ cup flour, 1 tablespoon at a time, to prevent dough from sticking to hands (dough will feel tacky).

2. Place dough in a large bowl coated with cooking spray, turning to coat top. Cover and let rise in a warm place (85°), free from drafts, 1 hour or until doubled in size. (Gently press two fingers into dough. If indentation remains, dough has risen enough.) Punch dough down; cover and let rest 5 minutes.

3. Roll dough into a 14 x 7–inch rectangle on a lightly floured surface. Roll up rectangle tightly, starting with a short edge, pressing firmly to eliminate air pockets; pinch seam and ends to seal. Place roll, seam side down, in an 8 x 4½–inch loaf pan coated with cooking spray. Lightly coat surface of dough with cooking spray, and cover; let rise in a warm place (85°), free from drafts, 30 minutes or until doubled in size.

4. Preheat oven to 400°.

5. Uncover dough, and drizzle surface of dough with remaining 1 tablespoon butter, gently spreading with a pastry brush. Cut a (¼-inch-deep) slit lengthwise down center of loaf using a sharp knife.

6. Bake at 400° for 30 minutes or until bread is browned on bottom and sounds hollow when tapped. Cool on a wire rack. Yield: 1 loaf, 10 servings (serving size: 1 slice).

CALORIES 187 (16% from fat); FAT 3.3g (sat 1.5g, mono 0.9g, poly 0.5g); PROTEIN 5.3g; CARB 33.7g; FIBER 1.2g; CHOL 7mg; IRON 2mg; SODIUM 264mg; CALC 38mg

Breakfast Fig and Nut "Cookies"

¾ cup packed brown sugar
¼ cup butter, melted
2 large eggs
¼ cup finely chopped dried figs
¼ cup sweetened dried cranberries
1 teaspoon vanilla extract
1 cup all-purpose flour (about 4½ ounces)
½ cup whole wheat flour (about 2⅓ ounces)
½ cup unprocessed bran (about 1 ounce)
½ teaspoon baking soda
¼ teaspoon ground cinnamon
¼ teaspoon ground allspice
¼ cup sliced almonds
2 teaspoons granulated sugar

1. Preheat oven to 350°.

2. Combine first 3 ingredients in a large bowl. Stir in figs, cranberries, and vanilla.

3. Lightly spoon flours into dry measuring cups; level with a knife. Combine flours, bran, baking soda, cinnamon, and allspice, stirring with a whisk. Add flour mixture to egg mixture, stirring just until moist. Gently fold in almonds.

4. Drop by level ¼ cup measures 4 inches apart on 2 baking sheets lined with parchment paper. Sprinkle evenly with granulated sugar. Bake at 350° for 12 minutes or until almost set. Cool 2 minutes on pans. Remove from pans; cool completely on wire racks. Yield: 10 servings (serving size: 1 "cookie").

CALORIES 211 (31% from fat); FAT 7.1g (sat 3.3g, mono 2.4g, poly 0.8g); PROTEIN 4.5g; CARB 33.2g; FIBER 3.4g; CHOL 54mg; IRON 1.8mg; SODIUM 115mg; CALC 37mg

Breakfast Fig and Nut "Cookies"

Sour Cream, Cheddar, and Chive Potato Waffles

Cooking spray
1 teaspoon baking powder
1 (5.8-ounce) package shredded potato pancake mix (such as Panni)
1¾ cups fat-free milk
1 (8-ounce) carton reduced-fat sour cream
1 large egg
½ cup (2 ounces) reduced-fat shredded Cheddar cheese
¼ cup chopped fresh chives

1. Preheat waffle iron. Coat iron with cooking spray.
2. Combine baking powder and potato pancake mix in a large bowl. Place milk, sour cream, and egg in a medium bowl; stir well with a whisk. Add milk mixture to potato pancake mixture, stirring until smooth. Fold in cheese and chives.
3. Spoon about ½ cup batter onto hot waffle iron, spreading batter to edges. Cook 3 to 5 minutes or until steaming stops; repeat procedure with remaining batter. Yield: 7 servings (serving size: 1 waffle).

CALORIES 181 (26% from fat); FAT 5.3g (sat 3.1g, mono 0.5g, poly 0.1g); PROTEIN 8.9g; CARB 25g; FIBER 1.3g; CHOL 49mg; IRON 0.7mg; SODIUM 616mg; CALC 327mg

Banana-Cinnamon Waffles

Crown these lightly spiced waffles with cinnamon sugar, sliced bananas, and/or a drizzle of maple syrup. Buckwheat flour adds a somewhat tangy, robust nuttiness.

¼ cup flaxseed
1 cup all-purpose flour (about 4½ ounces)
½ cup whole wheat flour (about 2½ ounces)
¼ cup buckwheat flour (about 1 ounce)
2 tablespoons sugar
1½ teaspoons baking powder
½ teaspoon ground cinnamon
¼ teaspoon salt
1½ cups fat-free milk
3 tablespoons butter, melted
2 large eggs, lightly beaten
1 large ripe banana, mashed
Cooking spray

1. Place flaxseed in a blender or clean coffee grinder; process until ground. Lightly spoon flours into dry measuring cups; level with a knife. Combine flaxseed, flours, and next 4 ingredients in a medium bowl, stirring with a whisk.
2. Combine milk, butter, and eggs, stirring with a whisk; add milk mixture to flour mixture, stirring until blended. Fold in mashed banana.
3. Preheat a waffle iron. Coat iron with cooking spray. Spoon about ¼ cup batter per 4-inch waffle onto hot waffle iron, spreading batter to edges. Cook 3 to 4 minutes or until steaming stops; repeat procedure with remaining batter. Yield: 8 servings (serving size: 2 waffles).

CALORIES 215 (31% from fat); FAT 7.4g (sat 3.3g, mono 1.9g, poly 1.4g); PROTEIN 7.3g; CARB 31.1g; FIBER 3.4g; CHOL 65mg; IRON 1.9mg; SODIUM 205mg; CALC 133mg

Banana-Cinnamon Waffles

Strawberry Jam Crumb Cake

For convenience, you can freeze this breakfast treat for up to two weeks. Wrap in heavy-duty plastic wrap.

CRUMB TOPPING:

¼ cup all-purpose flour (about 1 ounce)
¼ cup packed brown sugar
¼ teaspoon ground cinnamon
2 tablespoons chilled butter, cut into small pieces

CAKE:

Cooking spray
1¼ cups all-purpose flour (about 5½ ounces)
½ teaspoon baking powder
¼ teaspoon baking soda
⅛ teaspoon salt
⅔ cup powdered sugar
¼ cup butter, softened
½ teaspoon vanilla extract
1 large egg
6 tablespoons fat-free milk
2 tablespoons fresh lemon juice
¼ cup reduced-sugar strawberry spread (such as Smucker's)

1. To prepare crumb topping, lightly spoon ¼ cup flour into a dry measuring cup; level with a knife. Combine ¼ cup flour, brown sugar, and cinnamon in a small bowl. Cut in 2 tablespoons butter with a pastry blender or 2 knives until mixture resembles coarse meal; set aside.
2. Preheat oven to 350°.
3. To prepare cake, lightly coat an 8-inch springform pan with cooking spray; set aside. Lightly spoon 1¼ cups flour into dry measuring cups; level with a knife. Combine flour, baking powder, baking soda, and salt in a small bowl; set aside.
4. Combine powdered sugar and ¼ cup butter in a large bowl; beat with a mixer at medium speed until well blended (about 2 minutes). Add vanilla and egg; beat 2 minutes. Combine milk and juice; add to sugar mixture. Beat 2 minutes.
5. Add half of flour mixture to sugar mixture; stir until smooth. Add remaining flour mixture, and stir just until combined.
6. Spoon half of batter into prepared pan, spreading evenly. Top with strawberry spread. Spoon remaining batter over strawberry layer, spreading evenly. Sprinkle reserved crumb topping evenly over batter. Bake at 350° for 45 minutes or until a wooden pick inserted in center comes out clean. Cool 10 minutes in pan on a wire rack; remove from pan. Cool completely on wire rack. Yield: 12 servings (serving size: 1 wedge).

CALORIES 191 (30% from fat); FAT 6.3g (sat 3.8g, mono 1.7g, poly 0.3g); PROTEIN 2.5g; CARB 31.7g; FIBER 0.5g; CHOL 33mg; IRON 0.9mg; SODIUM 123mg; CALC 32mg

Zucchini Bread

This quick bread recipe makes two loaves. Toasted slices are delicious for breakfast.

3 cups all-purpose flour (about 13½ ounces)
1 teaspoon baking powder
1 teaspoon ground cinnamon
½ teaspoon salt
¼ teaspoon baking soda
½ cup egg substitute
⅓ cup canola oil
1 teaspoon grated lemon rind
2 teaspoons vanilla extract
1 large egg, lightly beaten
1½ cups sugar
3 cups shredded zucchini (about 2 medium)
¼ cup coarsely chopped walnuts, toasted
Cooking spray

1. Preheat oven to 350°.
2. Lightly spoon flour into dry measuring cups; level with a knife. Combine flour and next 4 ingredients in a large bowl.
3. Combine egg substitute and next 4 ingredients in a large bowl; add sugar, stirring until combined. Add zucchini; stir until well combined. Add flour mixture; stir just until combined. Stir in walnuts.
4. Divide batter evenly between 2 (8 x 4–inch) loaf pans coated with cooking spray. Bake at 350° for 1 hour or until a wooden pick inserted in center comes out clean. Cool 10 minutes in pans on a wire rack; remove loaves from pans. Cool completely on wire rack. Yield: 2 loaves, 12 servings per loaf (serving size: 1 slice).

CALORIES 150 (26% from fat); FAT 4.3g (sat 0.4g, mono 2g, poly 1.6g); PROTEIN 2.7g; CARB 25.3g; FIBER 0.6g; CHOL 9mg; IRON 1mg; SODIUM 96mg; CALC 21mg

Chocolate Chip Zucchini Bread

Great for breakfast or an afternoon snack, this sweet bread is perfect with a glass of cold milk.

- ¾ cup sugar
- 3 tablespoons canola oil
- 2 large eggs
- 1 cup applesauce
- 2 cups all-purpose flour (about 9 ounces)
- 2 tablespoons unsweetened cocoa
- 1¼ teaspoons baking soda
- 1 teaspoon ground cinnamon
- ¼ teaspoon salt
- 1½ cups finely shredded zucchini (about 1 medium)
- ½ cup semisweet chocolate chips
- Cooking spray

1. Preheat oven to 350°.

2. Place first 3 ingredients in a large bowl, and beat with a mixer at low speed until well blended. Stir in 1 cup applesauce.

3. Lightly spoon flour into dry measuring cups; level with a knife. Combine flour and next 4 ingredients, stirring well with a whisk. Add flour mixture to sugar mixture in bowl, beating just until moist. Stir in zucchini and chips. Spoon batter into a 9 x 5–inch loaf pan coated with cooking spray. Bake at 350° for 1 hour or until a wooden pick inserted in center comes out almost clean. Cool in pan 10 minutes on a wire rack; remove from pan. Cool completely on wire rack. Yield: 1 loaf, 16 servings (serving size: 1 slice).

CALORIES 161 (29% from fat); FAT 5.1g (sat 1.6g, mono 1.4g, poly 1.7g); PROTEIN 2.9g; CARB 27.3g; FIBER 1.4g; CHOL 27mg; IRON 1.2mg; SODIUM 145mg; CALC 12mg

Banana-Oatmeal Loaf

Consider making this delicious loaf the night before you plan to serve it. We think it's better the next day. Allowing the loaf to stand overnight enhances the flavor and the moistness.

- 1½ cups all-purpose flour (about 6¾ ounces)
- ⅔ cup sugar
- 1½ teaspoons baking powder
- ¼ teaspoon baking soda
- ¼ teaspoon salt
- ¾ cup regular oats
- 1 cup mashed ripe banana (about 2 large)
- ⅓ cup low-fat buttermilk
- ¼ cup vegetable oil
- 1 teaspoon vanilla extract
- 2 large eggs, lightly beaten
- Cooking spray

1. Preheat oven to 350°.

2. Lightly spoon flour into dry measuring cups; level with a knife. Combine flour and next 4 ingredients in a large bowl, stirring well with a whisk. Stir in oats.

3. Combine banana, buttermilk, oil, vanilla, and eggs; add to flour mixture. Stir just until moist.

4. Spoon batter into an 8 x 4–inch loaf pan coated with cooking spray. Bake at 350° for 55 minutes or until a wooden pick inserted in center comes out clean. Cool 15 minutes in pan on a wire rack; remove from pan. Cool completely on wire rack. Yield: 12 servings (serving size: 1 slice).

CALORIES 192 (28% from fat); FAT 6g (sat 1.1g, mono 1.5g, poly 2.9g); PROTEIN 3.8g; CARB 31.4.g; FIBER 1.3g; CHOL 36mg; IRON 1.2mg; SODIUM 154mg; CALC 52mg

Sweet Potato Bread with Flaxseed and Honey

Flaxseeds need to be ground to release the healthful oils. A blender or clean coffee grinder is necessary; simply pounding them in a plastic bag on a countertop or with a mortar and pestle is not sufficient.

- ⅓ cup flaxseed
- 2 cups all-purpose flour (about 9 ounces)
- 1 teaspoon baking powder
- ½ teaspoon baking soda
- ¼ teaspoon salt
- ¼ cup (2 ounces) ⅓-less-fat cream cheese, softened
- 3 tablespoons butter, softened
- ½ cup packed brown sugar
- ¼ cup honey
- 1 large egg
- 1 large egg white
- 1 cup mashed cooked sweet potato
- Cooking spray

1. Preheat oven to 350°.

2. Place flaxseed in a blender or clean coffee grinder, and process until coarsely ground. Lightly spoon flour into dry measuring cups; level with a knife. Combine flaxseed, flour, baking powder, baking soda, and salt in a large bowl; make a well in center of mixture. Beat cream cheese and next 5 ingredients; stir in sweet potato. Add to flour mixture, stirring just until moist.

3. Spoon batter into an 8½ x 4½–inch loaf pan coated with cooking spray. Bake at 350° for 50 minutes or until a wooden pick inserted in center comes out clean. Cool 10 minutes in pan on a wire rack; remove from pan, and cool completely on wire rack. Yield: 16 servings (serving size: 1 [½-inch] slice).

NOTE: To freeze bread up to one month, place in an airtight container, or wrap in plastic wrap or heavy-duty foil. Thaw at room temperature.

CALORIES 171 (27% from fat); FAT 5.1g (sat 2.1g, mono 1.3g, poly 1.4g); PROTEIN 3.6g; CARB 29g; FIBER 1.8g; CHOL 22mg; IRON 1.4mg; SODIUM 157mg; CALC 44mg

Banana Bread

We give you two options for baking this classic. If you opt to make the smaller loaves, freeze some, and you'll have them on hand for last-minute invites.

- 1 cup sugar
- ¼ cup light butter, softened
- 1⅔ cups mashed ripe banana (about 3 bananas)
- ¼ cup fat-free milk
- ¼ cup reduced-fat sour cream
- 2 large egg whites
- 2 cups all-purpose flour (about 9 ounces)
- 1 teaspoon baking soda
- ½ teaspoon salt
- Cooking spray

1. Preheat oven to 350°.

2. Combine sugar and butter in a bowl; beat with a mixer at medium speed until well blended. Add banana, milk, sour cream, and egg whites; beat well.

3. Lightly spoon flour into dry measuring cups; level with a knife. Combine flour, baking soda, and salt; stir well. Add flour mixture to banana mixture, beating until blended.

4. Spoon batter into 4 (5 x 2½–inch) mini loaf pans coated with cooking spray. Bake at 350° for 45 minutes or until a wooden pick inserted in center comes out clean. Cool in pans 10 minutes on a wire rack; remove from pans. Cool completely. Yield: 4 loaves, 4 servings per loaf (serving size: 1 slice).

NOTE: To make a 9–inch loaf, spoon batter into a 9 x 5–inch loaf pan coated with cooking spray; bake at 350° for 1 hour and 10 minutes or until a wooden pick inserted in center comes out clean. Yield: 16 servings (serving size: 1 slice).

CALORIES 147 (14% from fat); FAT 2.2g (sat 1.4g, mono 0.2g, poly 0.1g); PROTEIN 2.5g; CARB 30.2g; FIBER 1.1g; CHOL 7mg; IRON 0.8mg; SODIUM 180mg; CALC 13mg

Fig, Date, and Walnut Quick Bread

Fig, Date, and Walnut Quick Bread

Dried fruits like figs and dates are good sources of fiber. Here they're paired with heart-healthy walnuts and a mixture of whole wheat and white flours.

- ¾ cup low-fat buttermilk
- ½ teaspoon finely grated lemon rind
- ¼ teaspoon ground nutmeg
- ⅛ teaspoon ground cloves
- ⅔ cup chopped dried figs
- ⅓ cup chopped pitted dates
- ½ cup packed brown sugar
- 2 tablespoons canola oil
- 2 large eggs
- ¾ cup all-purpose flour (about 3⅓ ounces)
- ¾ cup whole wheat flour (about 3½ ounces)
- 1½ teaspoons baking soda
- ⅛ teaspoon salt
- Cooking spray
- ⅓ cup chopped walnuts

1. Preheat oven to 350°.

2. Heat first 4 ingredients in a small, heavy saucepan over medium heat just until bubbles begin to form around edge (do not boil). Remove from heat; stir in figs and dates. Let stand 20 minutes or until fruit softens.

3. Combine brown sugar, oil, and eggs in a large bowl; stir with a whisk until well blended. Stir in cooled milk mixture.

4. Lightly spoon flours into dry measuring cups; level with a knife. Combine flours, baking soda, and salt in a large bowl; make a well in center of mixture. Add milk mixture to flour mixture, stirring just until moist. Spoon batter into an 8 x 4–inch loaf pan coated with cooking spray. Sprinkle walnuts evenly over batter. Bake at 350° for 40 minutes or until a wooden pick inserted in center comes out clean. Cool 10 minutes in pan on a wire rack; remove from pan. Cool completely on a wire rack. Yield: 12 servings (serving size: 1 slice).

CALORIES 192 (27% from fat); FAT 5.8g (sat 0.8g, mono 2g, poly 2.5g); PROTEIN 4.4g; CARB 32.5g; FIBER 2.9g; CHOL 36mg; IRON 1.4mg; SODIUM 216mg; CALC 55mg

Spicy Sriracha Bread

To make this Thai-inspired bread in a bread machine, follow the manufacturer's instructions for placing the first six ingredients in the bread pan. Brush melted butter over warm bread.

- ¾ cup warm water (100° to 110°)
- ¼ cup Sriracha (hot chile sauce, such as Huy Fong)
- 1 package dry yeast (about 2¼ teaspoons)
- 3 cups bread flour, divided (about 14¼ ounces)
- ¾ teaspoon salt
- 1 large egg
- Cooking spray
- 1 teaspoon butter, melted

1. Combine ¾ cup warm water, Sriracha, and yeast in a large bowl; let stand 5 minutes. Lightly spoon flour into dry measuring cups; level with a knife. Add 2¾ cups flour, salt, and egg to yeast mixture; stir until a soft dough forms. Turn dough out onto a floured surface. Knead until smooth and elastic (about 8 minutes); add enough of remaining flour, 1 tablespoon at a time, to prevent dough from sticking to hands (dough will feel sticky).

2. Place dough in a large bowl coated with cooking spray, turning to coat top. Cover and let rise in a warm place (85°), free from drafts, 1 hour or until doubled in size. (Gently press two fingers into dough. If indentation remains, dough has risen enough.) Punch dough down; cover and let rest 5 minutes. Roll dough into a 14 x 7–inch rectangle on a lightly floured surface. Roll up rectangle tightly, starting with a short edge, pressing firmly to eliminate air pockets; pinch seam and ends to seal. Place roll, seam side down, in an 8½ x 4½–inch loaf pan coated with cooking spray. Lightly coat surface of dough with cooking spray; cover and let rise in a warm place 30 minutes or until doubled in size.

3. Preheat oven to 375°.

4. Bake at 375° for 40 minutes or until lightly browned on bottom and loaf sounds hollow when tapped. Remove from pan, and brush with melted butter. Cool on a wire rack. Yield: 14 servings (serving size: 1 slice).

CALORIES 119 (8% from fat); FAT 1.1g (sat 0.4g, mono 0.3g, poly 0.3g); PROTEIN 4.2g; CARB 22.4g; FIBER 0.8g; CHOL 16mg; IRON 1.4mg; SODIUM 184mg; CALC 7mg

Greek Easter Bread

This sweet, spiced loaf is not only beautiful and delicious but also large enough to feed a crowd. Use leftovers to make French toast.

- 1 teaspoon whole allspice
- 1 (3-inch) cinnamon stick
- 1 cup warm water (100° to 110°)
- Dash of salt
- Dash of sugar
- 2 packages dry yeast (about 2¼ teaspoons each)
- 4¾ cups bread flour (about 22½ ounces), divided
- ½ cup sugar
- 3 tablespoons butter
- 3 large eggs
- 1 teaspoon salt
- Cooking spray
- 1 tablespoon water
- 1 large egg yolk

1. Place allspice and cinnamon in a spice or coffee grinder; process until finely ground. Set aside.

2. Combine water, dash of salt, dash of sugar, and yeast in a large bowl, stirring with a whisk. Let stand 5 minutes. Lightly spoon flour into dry measuring cups; level with a knife. Add 1 cup flour to yeast mixture, stirring until well combined. Let stand 20 minutes.

3. Place ½ cup sugar and butter in a large bowl; beat with a mixer at medium speed until light and fluffy. Add eggs, 1 at a time, beating well after each addition. Stir in allspice mixture. Add yeast mixture to butter mixture; stir with a whisk until well combined. Stir in 1 teaspoon salt. Add 3½ cups flour, about 1 cup at a time, stirring until a soft dough forms. Turn dough out onto a floured surface. Knead until smooth and elastic (about 8 minutes); add enough of remaining flour, 1 tablespoon at a time, to prevent dough from sticking to hands (dough will feel tacky).

4. Place dough in a large bowl coated with cooking spray, turning to coat top. Cover and let rise in a warm place (85°), free from drafts, 1 hour or until doubled in size. (Gently press two fingers into dough. If indentation remains, dough has risen enough.)

5. Divide dough into 3 equal portions, shaping each portion into a 14-inch-long rope. Place ropes lengthwise on a baking sheet coated with cooking spray (do not stretch); pinch ends together at one end to seal. Braid ropes; pinch loose ends to seal. Lightly coat dough with cooking spray. Cover and let rise 45 minutes or until doubled in size.

6. Preheat oven to 350°.

7. Combine 1 tablespoon water and egg yolk, stirring with a whisk. Brush half of yolk mixture over loaf. Let stand 5 minutes. Repeat procedure with remaining yolk mixture. Bake at 350° for 30 minutes or until loaf sounds hollow when tapped. Cool bread on a wire rack 20 minutes. Yield: 20 servings (serving size: 1 slice).

CALORIES 168 (18% from fat); FAT 3.3g (sat 1.5g, mono 0.9g, poly 0.4g); PROTEIN 5.3g; CARB 29.1g; FIBER 1.1g; CHOL 47mg; IRON 1.8mg; SODIUM 150mg; CALC 13mg

Ham-and-Swiss Stromboli

The fillings are baked into the bread, making it a hearty accompaniment with soup. To vary this recipe, use prosciutto and mozzarella cheese.

- 3 cups bread flour (about 14¼ ounces)
- 1 cup warm water (100° to 110°)
- 1 tablespoon nonfat dry milk
- 1 tablespoon olive oil
- 2½ teaspoons bread machine yeast
- 1 teaspoon salt
- ½ teaspoon dry mustard
- ½ cup (3 ounces) chopped ham
- ½ cup (2 ounces) cubed Swiss cheese
- 1½ teaspoons cornmeal
- 1 large egg, lightly beaten

1. Lightly spoon flour into dry measuring cups; level with a knife. Follow manufacturer's instructions for placing flour and next 6 ingredients into bread pan, and select dough cycle; start bread machine.
2. Remove dough from machine (do not bake). Turn dough out onto a floured surface; knead 30 seconds. Cover dough; let rest 10 minutes.
3. Roll dough into a 10 x 8–inch oval on a lightly floured surface. Sprinkle ham and cheese onto half of oval, lengthwise, leaving a 1-inch border. Fold dough over filling, and press edges and ends together to seal.
4. Cover a large baking sheet with parchment paper; dust with cornmeal. Place loaf, seam side down, on prepared pan. Make 3 diagonal cuts ¼ inch deep across top of loaf using a sharp knife. Cover and let rise in a warm place (85°), free from drafts, 1 hour or until doubled in size.
5. Preheat oven to 350°.
6. Uncover dough; brush with egg. Bake at 350° for 35 minutes or until browned. Cool slightly. Yield: 1 (1-pound) loaf, 8 servings (serving size: 1 slice).

CALORIES 262 (20% from fat); FAT 5.8g (sat 2g, mono 2.4g, poly 0.7g); PROTEIN 12.1g; CARB 39.1g; FIBER 0.4g; CHOL 40mg; IRON 2.8mg; SODIUM 453mg; CALC 93mg

Asiago-Pepper Bread

This flavorful loaf makes great bread for sandwiches and is also good toasted and served with an Italian meal.

- 3 cups bread flour (about 14¼ ounces)
- 1 cup warm water (100° to 110°)
- ½ cup nonfat dry milk
- ½ cup (2 ounces) grated Asiago cheese
- 1½ tablespoons minced green onions
- 1 tablespoon sugar
- 1 tablespoon butter, melted
- 2½ teaspoons bread machine yeast
- 1¼ teaspoons salt
- ½ teaspoon coarsely ground black pepper
- 1 large egg

1. Lightly spoon flour into dry measuring cups; level with a knife. Follow manufacturer's instructions for placing flour and remaining ingredients into bread pan. Select bake cycle, and start bread machine. Yield: 1 (1½-pound) loaf, 16 servings (serving size: 1 slice).

CALORIES 136 (17% from fat); FAT 2.5g (sat 1.2g, mono 0.7g, poly 0.3g); PROTEIN 6.2g; CARB 21.9g; FIBER 0.2g; CHOL 20mg; IRON 1.3mg; SODIUM 258mg; CALC 92mg

Multigrain Bread

Like an English muffin with its nooks and crannies, this bread is excellent for butter, jams, and other spreads.

- 3½ cups bread flour (about 16¾ ounces)
- 1 cup warm water (100° to 110°)
- ½ cup low-fat buttermilk
- ¼ cup yellow cornmeal
- ¼ cup regular oats
- ¼ cup wheat bran
- ¼ cup packed brown sugar
- 2 tablespoons honey
- 2½ teaspoons bread machine yeast
- 2 teaspoons salt

1. Lightly spoon flour into dry measuring cups; level with a knife. Follow manufacturer's instructions for placing flour and remaining ingredients into bread pan. Select bake cycle; start bread machine. Yield: 1 (2-pound) loaf, 16 servings (serving size: 1 slice).

CALORIES 150 (5% from fat); FAT 0.8g (sat 0.1g, mono 0.1g, poly 0.3g); PROTEIN 4.7g; CARB 31g; FIBER 0.8g; CHOL 0mg; IRON 1.8mg; SODIUM 299mg; CALC 19mg

Fig and Mascarpone Focaccia

This bread won our Test Kitchens highest rating.

- 1 teaspoon honey
- 1 package dry yeast (about 2¼ teaspoons)
- 1¼ cups warm water (100° to 110°), divided
- 2 tablespoons olive oil
- 3¼ cups all-purpose flour (about 14½ ounces), divided
- 1 teaspoon kosher salt, divided
- Cooking spray
- ¼ cup (2 ounces) mascarpone cheese
- 3 dried figs, quartered
- ½ teaspoon olive oil

1. Dissolve honey and yeast in ½ cup warm water in a large bowl; let stand 10 minutes. Add remaining ¾ cup water and 2 tablespoons oil; stir until blended. Lightly spoon flour into dry measuring cups; level with a knife. Add 2¾ cups flour and ½ teaspoon salt to yeast mixture; stir until blended. Turn dough out onto a floured surface. Knead until smooth and elastic (about 10 minutes); add enough of remaining ½ cup flour, 1 tablespoon at a time, to prevent dough from sticking to hands (dough will feel sticky).

2. Place dough in a large bowl coated with cooking spray, turning to coat top. Cover and let rise in a warm place (85°), free from drafts, 1 hour or until doubled in size. (Gently press two fingers into dough. If indentation remains, dough has risen enough.) Uncover dough.

3. Punch dough down. Place dough in a 13 x 9–inch baking pan coated with cooking spray. Pat dough to fit pan. Cover and let rise 30 minutes. Uncover dough. Make indentations in top of dough using handle of a wooden spoon or fingertips. Cover and let rise in a warm place (85°) for 45 minutes or until doubled in size.

4. Preheat oven to 400°.

5. Uncover dough. Spoon small dollops of cheese over dough. Gently spread cheese over dough. Sprinkle fig quarters evenly over cheese. Drizzle ½ teaspoon oil over dough. Sprinkle with ¼ teaspoon salt. Bake at 400° for 23 minutes or until browned on bottom and bread sounds hollow when tapped. Sprinkle with remaining ¼ teaspoon salt. Serve warm or at room temperature. Yield: 14 servings (serving size: 1 piece).

CALORIES 155 (25% from fat); FAT 4.3g (sat 1.4g, mono 2.2g, poly 0.3g); PROTEIN 3.6g; CARB 25.5g; FIBER 1.4g; CHOL 5mg; IRON 1.5mg; SODIUM 138mg; CALC 15mg

Fig and Mascarpone Focaccia

Garlic Flatbreads with Smoked Mozzarella and Tomato Vinaigrette

Garlic Flatbreads with Smoked Mozzarella and Tomato Vinaigrette

FLATBREADS:

- ¼ cup whole wheat flour (about 1 ounce)
- 1 cup warm water (100° to 110°), divided
- 1 package dry yeast (about 2¼ teaspoons)
- 2¼ cups all-purpose flour (about 10 ounces), divided
- ½ teaspoon salt
- Cooking spray
- 1 teaspoon cornmeal
- 4 garlic cloves, thinly sliced

TOPPING:

- 3 tablespoons balsamic vinegar
- 2 tablespoons extravirgin olive oil
- ¼ teaspoon salt
- ⅛ teaspoon freshly ground black pepper
- 1 garlic clove, minced
- ¾ cup halved red cherry tomatoes (about 4 ounces)
- ¾ cup halved yellow cherry tomatoes
- 1 cup (4 ounces) shredded smoked mozzarella cheese
- ½ cup thinly sliced fresh basil

1. To prepare flatbreads, lightly spoon whole wheat flour into a dry measuring cup; level with a knife. Combine whole wheat flour, ¼ cup water, and yeast in a bowl; let stand 10 minutes.

2. Lightly spoon all-purpose flour into dry measuring cups, and level with a knife. Combine 2 cups all-purpose flour, ½ teaspoon salt, and remaining ¾ cup water in a large bowl. Add yeast mixture, and stir until a dough forms. Turn dough out onto a lightly floured surface. Knead dough until smooth and elastic (about 10 minutes); add enough of remaining ¼ cup all-purpose flour, 1 tablespoon at a time, to prevent dough from sticking to hands (dough will feel sticky). Place dough in a large bowl coated with cooking spray, turning to coat top. Cover and let rise in a warm place (85°), free from drafts, 1 hour or until doubled in size. (Gently press two fingers into dough. If indentation remains, dough has risen enough.)

3. Preheat oven to 450°.

4. Punch dough down; cover and let rest 5 minutes. Divide dough in half. Roll each half into a 9-inch circle on a lightly floured surface; place on baking sheets sprinkled with cornmeal. Lightly coat dough with cooking spray. Sprinkle dough evenly with sliced garlic; press into dough using fingertips. Bake at 450° for 10 minutes or until crisp and garlic begins to brown. Remove flatbreads from oven; cool on wire racks.

5. To prepare topping, combine vinegar, oil, ¼ teaspoon salt, pepper, and minced garlic in a medium bowl. Add tomatoes; toss gently.

6. Preheat broiler.

7. Sprinkle each flatbread with ½ cup cheese; broil flatbreads 1 minute or until cheese melts. Remove from oven; top each flatbread with half of tomato mixture. Sprinkle each flatbread with ¼ cup thinly sliced basil. Cut each flatbread into 6 equal wedges. Yield: 12 servings (serving size: 1 wedge).

CALORIES 139 (27% from fat); FAT 4.1g (sat 1.3g, mono 2.1g, poly 0.4g); PROTEIN 5.3g; CARB 20.2g; FIBER 1.3g; CHOL 5mg; IRON 1.4mg; SODIUM 194mg; CALC 73mg

Basic Pizza Dough

- 2 teaspoons honey
- 1 package active dry yeast (about 2¼ teaspoons)
- ¾ cup warm water (100° to 110°)
- 2¼ cups all-purpose flour (about 10 ounces), divided
- ½ teaspoon salt
- Cooking spray
- 2 tablespoons stone-ground yellow cornmeal

1. Dissolve honey and yeast in ¾ cup warm water in a large bowl. Let stand 5 minutes or until bubbly. Lightly spoon flour into dry measuring cups; level with a knife. Add 2 cups flour and salt to yeast mixture; stir until a soft dough forms. Turn dough out onto a lightly floured surface. Knead until smooth and elastic (about 6 minutes); add enough of remaining flour, 1 tablespoon at a time, to prevent dough from sticking to hands (dough will feel slightly sticky).

2. Place dough in a large bowl coated with cooking spray, turning to coat top. Cover and let rise in a warm place (85°), free from drafts, 30 minutes or until doubled in size. (Gently press two fingers into dough. If indentation remains, dough has risen enough.)

3. Roll dough into a 12-inch circle (about ¼ inch thick) on a lightly floured surface. Place dough on a rimless baking sheet sprinkled with cornmeal. Crimp edges of dough with fingers to form a rim. Lightly spray surface of dough with cooking spray; cover with plastic wrap. Place dough in refrigerator up to 30 minutes. Use dough in your favorite homemade pizza recipe. Yield: 1 (12-inch) crust.

(Totals are for 1 [12-inch] pizza crust) CALORIES 1,155 (3% from fat); FAT 3.4g (sat 0.6g, mono 0.5g, poly 1.3g); PROTEIN 33.8g; CARB 242.5g; FIBER 10.8g; CHOL 0mg; IRON 14.3mg; SODIUM 1,195mg; CALC 49mg

Dinner Rolls, Five Ways

(pictured on page 34)

One simple dough yields five rich dinner roll variations.

- 2 teaspoons sugar
- 1 package dry yeast (about 2¼ teaspoons)
- 1 (12-ounce) can evaporated fat-free milk, warmed (100° to 110°)
- 4 cups all-purpose flour (about 18 ounces), divided
- 1 large egg, lightly beaten
- 1 teaspoon salt
- Cooking spray
- ½ teaspoon cornmeal
- 2 tablespoons butter, melted and cooled

1. Dissolve sugar and yeast in warm milk in a large bowl; let stand 5 minutes.
2. Lightly spoon flour into dry measuring cups; level with a knife. Add 3 cups flour and egg to milk mixture, stirring until smooth; cover and let stand 15 minutes.
3. Add ¾ cup flour and salt; stir until a soft dough forms. Turn dough out onto a floured surface. Knead until smooth and elastic (about 8 minutes); add enough of remaining flour, 1 tablespoon at a time, to prevent dough from sticking to hands (dough will feel tacky).
4. Place dough in a large bowl coated with cooking spray, turning to coat top. Cover and let rise in a warm place (85°), free from drafts, 30 minutes or until doubled in size. (Press two fingers into dough. If indentation remains, dough has risen enough.) Punch dough down; cover and let rest 5 minutes.
5. Divide dough into 16 equal portions. Working with one portion at a time (cover remaining dough to prevent drying), shape each portion into desired form. Place shaped dough portions on a baking sheet lightly sprinkled with cornmeal. Lightly coat shaped dough portions with cooking spray; cover with plastic wrap. Let rise in a warm place (85°), free from drafts, 20 minutes or until doubled in size.
6. Preheat oven to 400°.
7. Gently brush shaped dough portions with butter. Bake at 400° for 20 minutes or until lightly browned on top and rolls sound hollow when tapped on bottom. Place on wire racks. Serve warm, or cool completely on wire racks. Yield: 16 servings (serving size: 1 roll).

CALORIES 151 (13% from fat); FAT 2.1g (sat 1.1g, mono 0.5g, poly 0.2g); PROTEIN 5.4g; CARB 27g; FIBER 0.9g; CHOL 18mg; IRON 1.7mg; SODIUM 187mg; CALC 69mg

How to Shape Dinner Rolls

Roll: Divide dough into 16 equal portions; shape each portion into a ball.

Knot: Divide dough into 16 equal portions; shape each portion into an 8-inch rope. Tie each rope into a single knot; tuck top end of rope under bottom edge of roll.

Cloverleaf: Divide dough into 16 equal portions; divide each portion into three balls. Working with three balls at a time, press balls together to form a cloverleaf roll on a baking sheet (be sure balls are touching each other).

Twist: Divide dough into 16 equal portions; shape each portion into an 18-inch rope. Fold each rope in half so that both ends meet. Working with one folded rope at a time, hold ends of rope in one hand and folded end in the other hand; gently twist.

Snail: Divide dough into 16 equal portions; shape each portion into a 20-inch rope. On a flat surface, coil each rope around itself in a spiral; pinch tail of coil to seal.

Glazed Cinnamon-Raisin Rolls

If you're a weekend baker, the unbaked rolls can be prepared up to two months in advance and stored in the freezer. When you're ready to eat them, let the rolls stand 30 minutes, then bake 20 minutes. Prepare glaze while rolls bake.

DOUGH:

1 package dry yeast (about 2¼ teaspoons)
¼ cup warm water (100° to 110°)
½ cup fat-free milk
⅓ cup granulated sugar
¼ cup butter, melted and cooled
1 teaspoon vanilla extract
½ teaspoon salt
1 large egg, lightly beaten
3¾ cups all-purpose flour (about 17 ounces), divided
Cooking spray

FILLING:

⅔ cup packed brown sugar
½ cup golden raisins
½ cup chopped dried apricots
½ cup chopped pecans
1 tablespoon ground cinnamon
2 tablespoons butter, melted and cooled

GLAZE:

1 cup powdered sugar
2 tablespoons fat-free milk

1. Dissolve yeast in warm water in a large bowl; let stand 5 minutes. Stir in ½ cup milk and next 5 ingredients. Lightly spoon flour into dry measuring cups; level with a knife. Add 3½ cups flour to yeast mixture; stir until blended. Turn dough out onto a floured surface. Knead until smooth and elastic (about 10 minutes); add enough of remaining flour, 1 tablespoon at a time, to prevent dough from sticking to hands (dough will feel sticky).

2. Place dough in a large bowl coated with cooking spray, turning to coat top. Cover and let rise in a warm place (85°), free from drafts, 1 hour or until doubled in size. (Gently press two fingers into dough. If indentation remains, dough has risen enough.) Punch dough down; cover and let rest 5 minutes.

3. To prepare filling, combine brown sugar, golden raisins, dried apricots, chopped pecans, and cinnamon.

4. Roll dough into an 18 x 10–inch rectangle on a floured surface. Brush 2 tablespoons melted butter over dough; sprinkle with 1½ cups filling, leaving a ½-inch border. Beginning with a long side, roll up jelly-roll fashion, and pinch seam to seal (do not seal ends of roll).

5. Place a long piece of dental floss under dough ¾ inch from end of roll. Cross ends of floss over top of roll; slowly pull ends to cut through dough. Repeat procedure to make 24 rolls. Coat 2 (8-inch) square foil baking pans with cooking spray. Sprinkle ½ cup filling into each pan. Place 12 rolls, cut sides up, in each pan. Cover and let rise 1½ hours or until doubled in size.

6. Preheat oven to 350°.

7. Uncover rolls. Bake at 350° for 20 minutes or until browned.

8. To prepare glaze, combine powdered sugar and 2 tablespoons milk, stirring until smooth. Drizzle over warm rolls. Yield: 24 servings (serving size: 1 roll).

TO FREEZE UNBAKED ROLLS: Prepare through Step 5. Cover with plastic wrap. Wrap tightly with heavy-duty foil. Freeze up to 2 months.

TO PREPARE FROZEN UNBAKED ROLLS: Remove rolls from freezer, and let stand at room temperature 30 minutes. Uncover and bake at 350° for 20 minutes or until browned.

CALORIES 193 (24% from fat); FAT 5.1g (sat 2g, mono 1.9g, poly 0.8g); PROTEIN 3.1g; CARB 34.4g; FIBER 1.4g; CHOL 17mg; IRON 1.5mg; SODIUM 87mg; CALC 28mg

Flaky Dinner Rolls

- 3 tablespoons sugar
- 1 package dry yeast (about 2¼ teaspoons)
- 1 cup warm fat-free milk (100° to 110°)
- 3 cups all-purpose flour (about 13½ ounces), divided
- ¾ teaspoon salt
- 3 tablespoons butter, softened
- Cooking spray

1. Dissolve sugar and yeast in warm milk in a large bowl; let stand 5 minutes. Lightly spoon flour into dry measuring cups; level with a knife. Add 2¾ cups flour and salt to yeast mixture; stir until a dough forms. Turn dough out onto a lightly floured surface. Knead until smooth (about 5 minutes); add enough of remaining flour, 1 tablespoon at a time, to prevent dough from sticking to hands (dough will feel slightly sticky). Cover dough with plastic wrap, and let rest 10 minutes.

2. Roll dough into a 12 x 10–inch rectangle on a lightly floured baking sheet. Gently spread butter over dough. Working with a long side, fold up bottom third of dough. Fold top third of dough over first fold to form a 12 x 3–inch rectangle. Cover dough with plastic wrap, and place in freezer 10 minutes.

3. Remove dough from freezer; remove plastic wrap. Roll dough, still on baking sheet (sprinkle on a little more flour, if needed), into a 12 x 10–inch rectangle. Working with a long side, fold up bottom third of dough. Fold top third of dough over first fold to form a 12 x 3–inch rectangle. Cover with plastic wrap; place in freezer 10 minutes.

4. Remove dough from freezer; remove plastic wrap. Roll dough, still on baking sheet, into a 12 x 8–inch rectangle. Beginning with a long side, roll up dough jelly-roll fashion; pinch seam to seal (do not seal ends). Cut into 12 equal slices. Place slices, cut sides up, in muffin cups coated with cooking spray. Lightly coat tops of slices with cooking spray. Cover and let rise in a warm place (85°), free from drafts, 45 minutes or until doubled in size.

5. Preheat oven to 375°.

6. Bake at 375° for 20 minutes or until golden brown. Remove from pan; cool 5 minutes on a wire rack. Serve warm. Yield: 1 dozen (serving size: 1 roll).

CALORIES 160 (18% from fat); FAT 3.2g (sat 1.5g, mono 1.2g, poly 0.2g); PROTEIN 4.2g; CARB 28.3g; FIBER 1g; CHOL 8mg; IRON 1.7mg; SODIUM 178mg; CALC 25mg

Orange Rolls

Keep any remaining rolls in the baking pan. Cover pan with foil, and store in the refrigerator. To reheat, place foil-covered pan in a 300° oven for 15 minutes or until rolls are warm.

DOUGH:

- 1 package dry yeast (about 2¼ teaspoons)
- ½ cup warm water (100° to 110°)
- 1 cup sugar, divided
- ½ cup reduced-fat sour cream
- 2 tablespoons butter, softened
- 1 teaspoon salt
- 1 large egg, lightly beaten
- 3½ cups all-purpose flour (about 15¾ ounces), divided
- Cooking spray
- 2 tablespoons butter, melted
- 2 tablespoons grated orange rind

GLAZE:

- ¾ cup sugar
- ¼ cup butter
- 2 tablespoons fresh orange juice
- ½ cup reduced-fat sour cream

1. To prepare dough, dissolve yeast in warm water in a large bowl; let stand 5 minutes. Add ¼ cup sugar, ½ cup sour cream, 2 tablespoons softened butter, salt, and egg; beat with a mixer at medium speed until smooth. Lightly spoon flour into dry measuring cups; level with a knife. Add 2 cups flour to yeast mixture, beating until smooth. Add 1 cup flour to yeast mixture, stirring until a soft dough forms. Turn dough out onto a floured surface. Knead until smooth and elastic (about 10 minutes); add enough remaining flour, 1 tablespoon at a time, to prevent dough from sticking to hands (dough will feel sticky).

2. Place dough in a large bowl coated with cooking spray, turning to coat top. Cover and let rise in a warm place (85°), free from drafts, 1 hour and 15 minutes or until doubled in size. (Gently press two fingers into dough. If indentation remains, dough has risen enough.)

3. Punch dough down; cover and let rest 5 minutes. Divide dough in half. Working with one portion at a time (cover remaining dough to prevent drying), roll each dough portion into a 12-inch circle on a floured surface. Brush surface of each circle with 1 tablespoon melted butter. Combine ¾ cup sugar and rind. Sprinkle half of sugar mixture over each circle. Cut each circle into 12 wedges. Roll up each wedge tightly, beginning at wide end. Place rolls, point sides down, in a 13 x 9–inch baking pan coated with cooking spray. Cover and let rise 25 minutes or until doubled in size.

4. Preheat oven to 350°.

5. Uncover dough. Bake at 350° for 25 minutes or until golden brown.

6. While rolls bake, prepare glaze. Combine ¾ cup sugar, ¼ cup butter, and orange juice in a small saucepan; bring to a boil over medium-high heat. Cook 3 minutes or until sugar dissolves, stirring occasionally. Remove from heat; cool slightly. Stir in ½ cup sour cream. Drizzle glaze over warm rolls; let stand 20 minutes before serving. Yield: 2 dozen (serving size: 1 roll).

CALORIES 178 (28% from fat); FAT 5.6g (sat 3.2g, mono 1.3g, poly 0.3g); PROTEIN 2.8g; CARB 30g; FIBER 0.6g; CHOL 24mg; IRON 1mg; SODIUM 146mg; CALC 23mg

Soft Pretzels

Be sure to cover the pretzels while they rise to prevent them from deflating. For a lower sodium option, top the pretzels with two teaspoons of sesame seeds instead of kosher salt.

- 1 package dry yeast (about 2¼ teaspoons)
- 1½ teaspoons sugar
- 1 cup warm water (100° to 110°)
- 3¼ cups all-purpose flour (about 14½ ounces), divided
- 1 teaspoon salt
- Cooking spray
- 6 cups water
- 2 tablespoons baking soda
- 1 teaspoon cornmeal
- 1 teaspoon water
- 1 large egg
- 2 teaspoons kosher salt

1. Dissolve yeast and sugar in warm water in a large bowl, and let stand 5 minutes.

2. Lightly spoon flour into dry measuring cups; level with a knife. Add 3 cups flour and 1 teaspoon salt to yeast mixture; stir until a soft dough forms. Turn dough out onto a lightly floured surface; knead until smooth and elastic (about 8 minutes). Add enough of remaining flour, 1 tablespoon at a time, to prevent dough from sticking to hands (dough will feel slightly sticky).

3. Place dough in a large bowl coated with cooking spray, turning to coat top. Cover and let rise in a warm place (85°), free from drafts, 40 minutes or until doubled in size. (Gently press two fingers into dough. If indentation remains, dough has risen enough.) Punch dough down; cover and let rest 5 minutes.

4. Preheat oven to 425°.

5. Divide dough into 12 equal portions. Working with one portion at a time (cover remaining dough to prevent drying), roll each portion into an 18-inch-long rope with tapered ends. Cross one end of rope over other to form a circle, leaving about 4 inches at end of each rope. Twist rope at base of circle. Fold ends over circle and into a traditional pretzel shape, pinching gently to seal. Place pretzels on a baking sheet lightly coated with cooking spray. Cover and let rise 10 minutes (pretzels will rise only slightly).

6. Combine 6 cups water and baking soda in a nonaluminum Dutch oven. Bring to a boil; reduce heat, and simmer. Gently lower 1 pretzel into simmering water mixture; cook 15 seconds. Turn pretzel over with a slotted spatula; cook an additional 15 seconds. Transfer pretzel to a wire rack coated with cooking spray. Repeat procedure with remaining pretzels.

7. Place pretzels on a baking sheet sprinkled with cornmeal. Combine 1 teaspoon water and egg in a small bowl, stirring with a fork until smooth. Brush a thin layer of egg mixture over pretzels; sprinkle evenly with kosher salt. Bake at 425° for 12 minutes or until pretzels are deep golden brown. Transfer to a wire rack to cool. Yield: 12 servings (serving size: 1 pretzel).

CALORIES 141 (12% from fat); FAT 1.9g (sat 0.2g, mono 0.6g, poly 0.6g); PROTEIN 4.3g; CARB 26.8g; FIBER 1.1g; CHOL 18mg; IRON 1.8mg; SODIUM 541mg; CALC 8mg

How to Shape Soft Pretzels

Cross one end of rope over the other to form a circle, leaving about 4 inches at end of each rope. Twist the rope at the base of the circle.

Fold the ends over the circle and into a traditional pretzel shape, pinching gently to seal.

Prussian Leaf–Wrapped Breadsticks

Mennonites who emigrated from west Prussia brought with them the tradition of baking dough on leaves of cabbage, kale, horseradish, or sweet calamus. The practice survives in the custom of wrapping buttermilk bread dough in beet greens brushed with butter and salt. Serve this novelty bread on a large platter with a bowl of sour cream.

- 12 young beet leaves (6 to 8 inches long), stems trimmed
- 1 package dry yeast (about 2¼ teaspoons)
- ⅓ cup warm water (100° to 110°)
- ½ cup low-fat buttermilk
- ½ teaspoon salt
- 1¼ cups bread flour (about 6 ounces), divided
- 1 cup all-purpose flour (about 4½ ounces)
- Cooking spray
- 2 tablespoons butter, melted
- ½ teaspoon kosher salt
- Reduced-fat sour cream (optional)

1. Wash beet leaves. Pat leaves dry; set aside.

2. Dissolve yeast in warm water in a large bowl; let stand 5 minutes. Stir in buttermilk and ½ teaspoon salt. Lightly spoon flours into dry measuring cups; level with a knife. Add 1 cup bread flour and all-purpose flour to buttermilk mixture; stir to form a soft dough. Turn dough out onto a lightly floured surface. Knead until smooth and elastic (about 8 minutes); add enough of remaining bread flour, 1 tablespoon at a time, to prevent dough from sticking to hands (dough will feel tacky).

3. Place dough in a large bowl coated with cooking spray, turning to coat top. Cover and let rise in a warm place (85°), free from drafts, 1 hour or until doubled in size. (Gently press two fingers into dough. If indentation remains, dough has risen enough.) Uncover dough. Punch dough down; cover and let rest 5 minutes.

4. Roll dough into a 12 x 4–inch rectangle on a lightly floured surface. Cut rectangle crosswise into 12 (1-inch) strips. Working with one portion at a time (cover remaining dough to prevent drying), wrap a leaf around middle of each dough strip, starting with stem end. (Ends of breadsticks should not be covered by leaf.) Place breadsticks, leaf tips down, on a baking sheet covered with parchment paper. Brush breadsticks with melted butter; sprinkle with kosher salt. Cover and let rise 45 minutes or until doubled in size.

5. Preheat oven to 375°.

6. Bake breadsticks at 375° for 35 minutes or until browned on bottom and lightly browned on top. Remove from pan; cool on a wire rack. Serve with low-fat sour cream, if desired. Yield: 12 servings (serving size: 1 breadstick).

CALORIES 105 (17% from fat); FAT 2g (sat 1.4g, mono 0g, poly 0g); PROTEIN 3.9g; CARB 18.9g; FIBER 1.9g; CHOL 6mg; IRON 2.3mg; SODIUM 265mg; CALC 50mg

How to Wrap Breadsticks

Working with one portion at a time (cover remaining dough to prevent drying), wrap a leaf around middle of each dough strip, starting with the stem end. (Ends of breadsticks should not be covered by the leaf.) Place breadsticks, leaf-tips down, on a baking sheet covered with parchment paper.

Fish and Shellfish

Grilled Salmon with Corn and Pepper Relish,
page 91

Striped Bass with Heirloom Tomatoes and Herbs

Try using tomatoes of different colors for the prettiest presentation. Spinach can be substituted for sorrel.

FISH:

- 4 (6-ounce) striped bass fillets
- ¼ teaspoon kosher salt
- ½ teaspoon freshly ground black pepper
- ¼ teaspoon ground red pepper
- 1 teaspoon olive oil

SALAD:

- 3 tomatoes, cut into (½-inch-thick) slices (about 1¼ pounds)
- ¾ teaspoon kosher salt, divided
- ⅓ cup fresh mint leaves
- ⅓ cup fresh basil leaves
- ⅓ cup fresh flat-leaf parsley leaves
- ⅓ cup fresh chervil leaves
- ⅓ cup (1-inch) slices fresh chives
- 1 tablespoon extravirgin olive oil
- 1 tablespoon balsamic vinegar
- ¼ teaspoon freshly ground black pepper
- 8 sorrel leaves, coarsely chopped

1. To prepare fish, sprinkle fillets evenly with ¼ teaspoon salt, black pepper, and red pepper. Heat olive oil in a large nonstick skillet over medium-high heat. Add fillets, skin side down. Cook 2 minutes or until skin is browned; turn fish over. Reduce heat to medium, and cook 10 minutes or until fish flakes easily when tested with a fork or until desired degree of doneness.

2. To prepare salad, place tomato slices in a medium bowl, and sprinkle evenly with ½ teaspoon salt. Let stand 10 minutes. Combine remaining ¼ teaspoon salt, mint, and next 8 ingredients in a small bowl, tossing gently.

3. Divide tomato slices evenly among 4 plates. Top each serving with 1 fillet and ½ cup herb mixture. Yield: 4 servings (serving size: 1 fillet).

CALORIES 248 (33% from fat); FAT 9.2g (sat 1.6g, mono 4.5g, poly 1.9g); PROTEIN 32.3g; CARB 9.1g; FIBER 2.8g; CHOL 136mg; IRON 3.4mg; SODIUM 609mg; CALC 69mg

Asian Marinated Striped Bass

Only four ingredients give this quick marinade a lot of flavor.

2 tablespoons minced fresh cilantro
1 tablespoon sugar
3 tablespoons fish sauce
2 garlic cloves, minced
4 (6-ounce) striped bass fillets
Cooking spray

1. Combine first 4 ingredients in a large zip-top plastic bag; add fish to bag. Seal and marinate in refrigerator 20 minutes, turning once. Remove fish from bag, reserving marinade.
2. Heat a large nonstick skillet over medium-high heat. Coat pan with cooking spray. Add fish to pan; cook 4 minutes on each side or until fish flakes easily when tested with a fork or until desired degree of doneness. Remove from pan. Add marinade to pan; bring to a boil. Cook 30 seconds; serve with fish. Yield: 4 servings (serving size: 1 fillet and 2 teaspoons sauce).

CALORIES 185 (19% from fat); FAT 4g (sat 0.9g, mono 1.1g, poly 1.3g); PROTEIN 31g; CARB 4.2g; FIBER 0.1g; CHOL 136mg; IRON 1.6mg; SODIUM 1,146mg; CALC 10mg

Bayou Catfish Fillets

Bake the fish on a ventilated broiler pan to keep the spicy cornmeal breading crisp. You can also use yellow cornmeal. Try this breading on other white fish fillets, such as cod, haddock, or snapper.

2 tablespoons white cornmeal
1½ teaspoons seasoned salt
1½ teaspoons dried oregano
1 teaspoon garlic powder
1 teaspoon onion powder
¾ teaspoon ground red pepper
½ teaspoon chili powder
¼ teaspoon ground cumin
¼ teaspoon black pepper
6 (6-ounce) catfish fillets
Cooking spray
6 lemon wedges (optional)

1. Preheat broiler.
2. Combine first 9 ingredients in a zip-top plastic bag. Add 1 catfish fillet. Seal bag; shake well. Remove fillet from bag; place on a broiler pan coated with cooking spray. Repeat procedure with remaining fillets and cornmeal mixture. Broil 6 inches from heat 6 minutes. Carefully turn fillets over; broil 6 minutes or until fish flakes easily when tested with a fork. Serve with lemon wedges, if desired. Yield: 6 servings (serving size: 1 fillet and 1 lemon wedge).

CALORIES 247 (48% from fat); FAT 13.2g (sat 3.1g, mono 6.1g, poly 2.8g); PROTEIN 27g; CARB 3.8g; FIBER 0.8g; CHOL 80mg; IRON 1.3mg; SODIUM 474mg; CALC 27mg

Catfish with Dill Sauce

Unlike a traditional chunky tartar sauce, this sauce is pureed in the food processor for a creamy texture.

¾ cup fat-free sour cream
½ cup fresh parsley leaves
½ cup fresh dill
½ cup chopped green onions
3 tablespoons rice vinegar
1 tablespoon honey
1 garlic clove, chopped
¾ teaspoon salt, divided
1 tablespoon canola oil
6 (6-ounce) catfish fillets
¼ teaspoon freshly ground black pepper

1. Combine first 7 ingredients in a food processor; add ½ teaspoon salt. Process until smooth.
2. Heat 1½ teaspoons oil in a large nonstick skillet over medium-high heat. Sprinkle fish with remaining ¼ teaspoon salt and pepper. Add 3 fillets to pan; cook 3 minutes on each side or until fish flakes easily when tested with a fork. Remove from pan; keep warm. Repeat procedure with remaining oil and fillets; serve with sauce. Yield: 6 servings (serving size: 1 fillet and about 2 tablespoons sauce).

CALORIES 231 (29% from fat); FAT 7.5g (sat 1.8g, mono 3.1g, poly 1.7g); PROTEIN 29.7g; CARB 9.2g; FIBER 0.4g; CHOL 102mg; IRON 1.1mg; SODIUM 395mg; CALC 85mg

Pan-Seared Cod with Basil Sauce

If you have a minichopper, use it to make the basil sauce. Otherwise, take the time to chop the herb finely before stirring in the remaining ingredients.

- ¼ cup fresh basil, minced
- ¼ cup fat-free, less-sodium chicken broth
- 2 tablespoons grated fresh Parmesan cheese
- 4 teaspoons extravirgin olive oil
- 1 teaspoon salt, divided
- 2 garlic cloves, minced
- 4 (6-ounce) cod fillets
- ¼ teaspoon freshly ground black pepper
- Cooking spray

1. Combine basil, chicken broth, cheese, olive oil, ½ teaspoon salt, and minced garlic in a bowl.
2. Sprinkle fish with remaining ½ teaspoon salt and black pepper. Heat a large nonstick skillet over medium-high heat. Coat pan with cooking spray. Add fish; cook 5 minutes on each side or until fish flakes easily when tested with a fork or until desired degree of doneness. Serve fish with basil sauce. Yield: 4 servings (serving size: 1 fillet and about 1½ tablespoons sauce).

CALORIES 199 (30% from fat); FAT 6.6g (sat 1.3g, mono 3.5g, poly 0.8g); PROTEIN 32g; CARB 1.3g; FIBER 0.6g; CHOL 76mg; IRON 0.7mg; SODIUM 765mg; CALC 85mg

Pan-Seared Grouper with Roasted Tomato Sauce

- 12 plum tomatoes, halved lengthwise and cut into ½-inch slices
- 1 red bell pepper, cut into 1-inch strips
- Cooking spray
- 2 tablespoons olive oil, divided
- ¾ teaspoon salt, divided
- ½ teaspoon dried Italian seasoning
- 1 tablespoon red wine vinegar
- ¼ teaspoon freshly ground black pepper
- 5 basil leaves
- 2 tablespoons all-purpose flour
- 1 tablespoon cornmeal
- 4 (6-ounce) grouper fillets (about 1 inch thick)

1. Preheat oven to 350°.
2. Arrange tomato slices and bell pepper strips in a single layer on a jelly-roll pan coated with cooking spray; drizzle with 1 tablespoon oil. Sprinkle with ¼ teaspoon salt and Italian seasoning; stir to coat. Bake at 350° for 40 minutes or until edges are lightly browned. Remove from oven.
3. Increase oven temperature to 400°.
4. Transfer tomato mixture to a food processor. Add ¼ teaspoon salt, vinegar, black pepper, and basil leaves; process until smooth. Spoon tomato mixture into a bowl. Cover and keep warm.
5. Heat remaining 1 tablespoon oil in a large oven-proof skillet over medium-high heat. Combine flour and cornmeal in a shallow dish. Sprinkle fish with remaining ¼ teaspoon salt; dredge in flour mixture. Add fish to pan; cook 3 minutes. Turn fish over; bake at 400° for 8 minutes or until fish flakes easily when tested with a fork or until desired degree of doneness. Serve with sauce. Yield: 4 servings (serving size: 1 fillet and about ¼ cup sauce).

CALORIES 278 (29% from fat); FAT 9g (sat 1.4g, mono 5.4g, poly 1.5g); PROTEIN 35.4g; CARB 13.4g; FIBER 3g; CHOL 63mg; IRON 2.5mg; SODIUM 543mg; CALC 70mg

Grilled Grouper with Apricot-Ginger Relish

Peaches, mangoes, or nectarines would also work in place of apricots.

- 2 cups diced fresh apricots (about 6 medium)
- ½ cup diced red bell pepper
- ⅓ cup rice wine vinegar
- ¼ cup minced green onions
- 2 tablespoons sugar
- 2 tablespoons minced peeled fresh ginger
- ½ teaspoon freshly ground black pepper
- ¼ teaspoon salt
- ¼ teaspoon hot sauce
- 1 tablespoon chile paste with garlic (such as sambal oelek)
- 4 (6-ounce) grouper fillets (½ inch thick)
- Cooking spray

1. Combine first 9 ingredients in a small bowl. Let stand 1 hour.
2. Prepare grill.
3. Rub chile paste over both sides of fillets.
4. Place fillets on a grill rack coated with cooking spray; grill 6 minutes on each side or until fish flakes easily when tested with a fork or until desired degree of doneness. Serve fillets with apricot-ginger relish. Yield: 4 servings (serving size: 1 fillet and about ½ cup relish).

CALORIES 234 (9% from fat); FAT 2.4g (sat 0.5g, mono 0.5g, poly 0.7g); PROTEIN 34.5g; CARB 17.3g; FIBER 2.2g; CHOL 63mg; IRON 2.4mg; SODIUM 342mg; CALC 64mg

Pan-Roasted Grouper with Provençal Vegetables

Use a broiler pan for both components of this recipe. The fennel-tomato mixture cooks in the bottom of the pan, helping to steam the fish on the rack above.

- 2 cups thinly sliced fennel bulb (about 1 medium bulb)
- 2 tablespoons fresh orange juice
- 1 (28-ounce) can whole tomatoes, drained and coarsely chopped
- 16 picholine olives, pitted and chopped
- ½ teaspoon salt, divided
- ½ teaspoon black pepper, divided
- Cooking spray
- 2 teaspoons olive oil
- 1 garlic clove, minced
- 4 (6-ounce) grouper fillets

1. Preheat oven to 450°.

2. Combine first 4 ingredients. Add ¼ teaspoon salt and ¼ teaspoon pepper; toss well. Spoon mixture into a broiler pan coated with cooking spray. Bake at 450° for 10 minutes; stir once.

3. Combine ¼ teaspoon salt, ¼ teaspoon pepper, oil, and garlic; brush evenly over fish. Remove pan from oven. Place fish on rack of pan coated with cooking spray; place rack over fennel mixture.

4. Bake at 450° for 10 minutes or until fish flakes easily when tested with a fork or until desired degree of doneness. Yield: 4 servings (serving size: 1 fillet and ¾ cup fennel mixture).

CALORIES 247 (25% from fat); FAT 6.9g (sat 0.7g, mono 3.4g, poly 2.1g); PROTEIN 33.6g; CARB 11.5g; FIBER 2.8g; CHOL 60mg; IRON 2.6mg; SODIUM 898mg; CALC 91m

Grilled Grouper with Browned Butter–Orange Couscous

A stainless steel pan makes it easy to watch the browning process and prevent the butter from burning. Pomegranate seeds are a colorful addition to the couscous, but you can omit them if they're out of season.

COUSCOUS:

- 2 tablespoons butter
- ¼ cup slivered almonds
- 1 cup uncooked couscous
- 1 (14-ounce) can fat-free, less-sodium chicken broth
- ½ cup coarsely chopped orange sections
- ¼ cup pomegranate seeds (optional)
- 3 tablespoons chopped fresh parsley
- ¼ teaspoon salt

GROUPER:

- ¼ teaspoon salt
- ½ teaspoon coriander seeds
- ½ teaspoon black peppercorns
- Dash of ground red pepper
- 4 (6-ounce) grouper fillets
- Cooking spray

1. To prepare couscous, melt butter in a large stainless steel skillet over medium-high heat. Add almonds; sauté 2 minutes or until almonds are toasted and butter is lightly browned. Add couscous; cook 1 minute, stirring constantly. Remove from heat.
2. Bring broth to a boil in a medium saucepan over high heat. Gradually add broth to couscous mixture in pan; cover and let stand 5 minutes. Fluff with a fork. Stir in oranges, pomegranate seeds, parsley, and ¼ teaspoon salt.
3. To prepare grouper, place ¼ teaspoon salt, coriander, peppercorns, and red pepper in a spice or clean coffee grinder, and process until finely ground. Rub spice mixture evenly over fish.
4. Heat a grill pan over medium-high heat. Coat pan with cooking spray. Arrange fillets in pan; cook 4 minutes. Turn fillets over; cook 4 minutes or until fish flakes easily when tested with a fork or until desired degree of doneness. Serve fillets with couscous. Yield: 4 servings (serving size: 1 fillet and 1 cup couscous).

CALORIES 453 (24% from fat); FAT 12.1g (sat 3.6g, mono 5.5g, poly 1.8g); PROTEIN 42.2g; CARB 42g; FIBER 3.9g; CHOL 78mg; IRON 2.6mg; SODIUM 704mg; CALC 95mg

Sesame Halibut en Papillote

En papillote refers to the method of steaming in the oven where the food is baked in parchment paper. Steam is trapped inside, keeping the food moist and flavorful. The impressive presentation belies this dish's simple preparation.

- 1 tablespoon dark sesame oil, divided
- 2 garlic cloves, minced
- 4 cups shredded bok choy
- ½ teaspoon salt, divided
- ½ teaspoon chile paste with garlic (such as sambal oelek)
- 4 (6-ounce) halibut fillets (about 1 inch thick)
- ¼ teaspoon freshly ground black pepper
- 1 teaspoon sesame seeds, toasted

1. Preheat oven to 400°.
2. Heat 1 teaspoon sesame oil in a large nonstick skillet over medium-high heat. Add garlic; sauté 30 seconds. Add bok choy and ¼ teaspoon salt; sauté 5 minutes or until crisp-tender. Remove from heat; stir in chile paste. Sprinkle fish evenly with remaining ¼ teaspoon salt and pepper.
3. Cut 4 (15-inch) squares of parchment paper. Fold each square in half, and open each. Place ½ cup bok choy near fold; top with 1 fillet. Drizzle each serving with ½ teaspoon oil; sprinkle with ¼ teaspoon sesame seeds. Fold papers; seal edges with narrow folds. Place packets on a baking sheet. Bake at 400° for 18 minutes or until paper is puffy and lightly browned. Place 1 packet on each of 4 plates; cut open. Serve immediately. Yield: 4 servings (serving size: 1 fillet and 1 cup bok choy).

CALORIES 233 (30% from fat); FAT 7.8g (sat 1.1g, mono 2.8g, poly 2.9g); PROTEIN 36.7g; CARB 2.3g; FIBER 0.9g; CHOL 54mg; IRON 2.1mg; SODIUM 459mg; CALC 158mg

Cornflake-Crusted Halibut with Chile-Cilantro Aïoli

Make the mayonnaise-based aïoli ahead, if you like. To crush the cornflakes, place them in a zip-top plastic bag, seal, and press with a rolling pin.

AÏOLI:

- 2 tablespoons minced fresh cilantro
- 3 tablespoons fat-free mayonnaise
- 1 serrano chile, seeded and minced
- 1 garlic clove, minced

FISH:

- 1 cup fat-free milk
- 1 large egg white, lightly beaten
- 2 cups cornflakes, finely crushed
- ¼ cup all-purpose flour
- ½ teaspoon salt
- ¼ teaspoon black pepper
- 2 tablespoons olive oil
- 4 (6-ounce) halibut fillets
- Lemon wedges

1. To prepare aïoli, combine first 4 ingredients, stirring well.

2. To prepare fish, combine milk and egg white in a shallow dish, stirring well with a whisk. Combine cornflakes, flour, salt, and pepper in a shallow dish.

3. Heat oil in a large nonstick skillet over medium-high heat. Dip fish in milk mixture; dredge in cornflake mixture. Add fish to pan; cook 4 minutes on each side or until fish flakes easily when tested with a fork or until desired degree of doneness. Serve with aïoli and lemon wedges. Yield: 4 servings (serving size: 1 fillet, about 1 tablespoon aïoli, and 1 lemon wedge).

CALORIES 367 (27% from fat); FAT 11.2g (sat 1.6g, mono 6.3g, poly 1.9g); PROTEIN 40.8g; CARB 25.1g; FIBER 2.2g; CHOL 56mg; IRON 2.4mg; SODIUM 645mg; CALC 166mg

Steamed Fish with Spicy Ginger Sauce

Steamed Fish with Spicy Ginger Sauce

Steaming is a common cooking method used in Asian cuisine to prepare fish quickly to perfect doneness without added fat. Mild-flavored fish works best in this easy recipe. Mirin is a sweet, low-alcohol rice wine that's found in the Asian food sections of most large supermarkets; sweet sherry, however, is an acceptable substitute.

SAUCE:

- ¼ cup fresh orange juice
- 1 tablespoon grated peeled fresh ginger
- 2 tablespoons mirin (sweet rice wine)
- 2 tablespoons low-sodium soy sauce
- 1 tablespoon dark sesame oil
- ½ to 1 teaspoon crushed red pepper

FISH:

- 4 (6-ounce) halibut or trout fillets
- ½ cup chopped green onions
- 1 tablespoon grated peeled fresh ginger
- ¼ teaspoon salt
- ¼ teaspoon freshly ground black pepper
- 1 cup thinly sliced leek (about 1 large)
- ½ cup (1-inch) julienne-cut carrot
- ½ cup (1-inch) julienne-cut red bell pepper
- 4 cups water
- 4 cilantro sprigs (optional)

1. To prepare sauce, combine first 6 ingredients, stirring with a whisk.

2. To prepare fish, lightly score each fillet by making 3 (¼-inch-deep) crosswise cuts with a sharp knife. Combine onions and 1 tablespoon ginger, tossing well. Rub about 2 tablespoons onion mixture evenly into slits of each fillet. Sprinkle fillets with salt and black pepper. Combine leek, carrot, and bell pepper; arrange half of leek mixture in a 10-inch pie plate. Pour half of sauce over leek mixture, and arrange fillets in a single layer over leek mixture. Top fillets with remaining leek mixture; drizzle with remaining sauce.

3. Open a small metal vegetable steamer; place steamer upside down in a large, deep wok. Add 4 cups water; bring to a simmer. Wearing oven mitts, carefully place pie plate on top of inverted steamer. Cover and cook 12 minutes or until fish flakes easily when tested with a fork or until desired degree of doneness. Wearing oven mitts, carefully remove pie plate from wok. Garnish with cilantro sprigs, if desired. Yield: 4 servings (serving size: 1 fillet, about 3 tablespoons leek mixture, and about 3 tablespoons sauce).

CALORIES 279 (25% from fat); FAT 7.6g (sat 1.1g, mono 2.7g, poly 2.7g); PROTEIN 36.7g; CARB 12.2g; FIBER 2g; CHOL 54mg; IRON 2.3mg; SODIUM 537mg; CALC 104mg

Sweet Black Pepper Fish

For most of its flavor, this Vietnamese classic relies on sugar and pepper, which most have on hand. The sugar makes a slightly bitter caramel sauce with fabulous results.

- ½ cup water, divided
- 3 tablespoons sugar
- 2½ tablespoons Thai fish sauce
- 3 tablespoons minced peeled fresh lemongrass
- 1 tablespoon minced garlic
- 1 teaspoon freshly ground black pepper
- 1 cup chopped green onions
- 4 (6-ounce) halibut fillets
- 1 tablespoon chopped fresh cilantro

1. Combine ¼ cup water, sugar, and fish sauce in a large nonstick skillet; bring to a boil, stirring to dissolve sugar. Add lemongrass, garlic, and pepper. Cook 1½ minutes or until slightly reduced.

2. Add ¼ cup water, green onions, and fish; cook over medium-high heat 7 minutes or until fish flakes easily when tested with a fork or until desired degree of doneness, turning once. Sprinkle with cilantro. Yield: 4 servings (serving size: 1 fillet and 2 tablespoons sauce).

CALORIES 247 (14% from fat); FAT 3.9g (sat 0.6g, mono 1.3g, poly 1.3g); PROTEIN 36.3g; CARB 13.9g; FIBER 1.2g; CHOL 54mg; IRON 1.9mg; SODIUM 911mg; CALC 89mg

Fish Tacos with Two Salsas

You can prepare one or the other salsa, or make both of them and serve the extra with baked tortilla chips.

TOMATO SALSA:
- 1 cup chopped seeded tomato (about 2 medium)
- ½ cup chopped seeded yellow or orange tomato (about 1 medium)
- ¼ cup finely chopped red onion
- 1 tablespoon chopped fresh parsley
- 1 tablespoon fresh lime juice
- ½ teaspoon minced habanero pepper
- ½ teaspoon extravirgin olive oil
- ¼ teaspoon salt

MANGO SALSA:
- 1 cup chopped peeled mango
- ½ cup chopped seeded peeled cucumber
- ¼ cup chopped green onions
- ¼ cup chopped fresh cilantro
- 2 tablespoons minced jalapeño pepper
- 1 tablespoon fresh lime juice
- 1 teaspoon extravirgin olive oil
- ⅛ teaspoon salt

FISH:
- 2 tablespoons lime juice
- 2 teaspoons olive oil
- ¼ teaspoon ground cumin
- 2 garlic cloves, minced
- 4 (6-ounce) halibut fillets
- ¼ teaspoon salt
- Cooking spray

REMAINING INGREDIENTS:
- 4 (10-inch) flour tortillas
- 1 cup shredded red cabbage
- ¼ cup reduced-fat sour cream
- Lime wedges (optional)

1. To prepare tomato salsa, combine first 8 ingredients in a small bowl; cover and chill at least 1 hour.
2. To prepare mango salsa, combine mango and next 7 ingredients in a small bowl. Cover and chill at least 1 hour.
3. Prepare grill.
4. To prepare fish, combine 2 tablespoons lime juice, 2 teaspoons olive oil, cumin, and garlic in a large zip-top plastic bag. Add fish to bag; seal and marinate in refrigerator 15 minutes, turning once. Remove fish from bag; discard marinade. Sprinkle both sides of fish evenly with ¼ teaspoon salt. Place fish on grill rack coated with cooking spray; grill 4 minutes on each side or until fish flakes easily when tested with a fork or until desired degree of doneness. Flake fish into large chunks.
5. To prepare tacos, place tortillas on grill rack coated with cooking spray; grill 10 seconds on each side. Divide fish and cabbage evenly over one half of each tortilla; top each tortilla with salsa and 1 tablespoon sour cream. Fold tortillas in half. Serve with lime wedges, if desired. Yield: 4 servings (serving size: 1 taco and about ¼ cup salsa).

CALORIES 541 (25% from fat); FAT 15.3g (sat 3.6g, mono 7.1g, poly 2.5g); PROTEIN 43.9g; CARB 55.9g; FIBER 4.6g; CHOL 62mg; IRON 4.5mg; SODIUM 835mg; CALC 162mg

Apple and Horseradish–Glazed Salmon

Mild apple jelly and hot horseradish are naturals with rich salmon. Serve couscous and fresh asparagus on the side.

- ⅓ cup apple jelly
- 1 tablespoon finely chopped fresh chives
- 2 tablespoons prepared horseradish
- 1 tablespoon champagne or white wine vinegar
- ½ teaspoon kosher salt, divided
- 4 (6-ounce) salmon fillets (about 1 inch thick), skinned
- ¼ teaspoon freshly ground black pepper
- 2 teaspoons olive oil

1. Preheat oven to 350°.
2. Combine apple jelly, chives, horseradish, vinegar, and ¼ teaspoon salt, stirring well with a whisk.
3. Sprinkle salmon with ¼ teaspoon salt and pepper. Heat oil in a large nonstick skillet over medium heat. Add salmon; cook 3 minutes. Turn salmon over; brush with half of apple mixture. Wrap handle of skillet with foil; bake at 350° for 5 minutes or until fish flakes easily when tested with a fork or until desired degree of doneness. Brush with remaining apple mixture. Yield: 4 servings (serving size: 1 fillet).

CALORIES 375 (40% from fat); FAT 16.8g (sat 4.3g, mono 7.7g, poly 3.4g); PROTEIN 36.4g; CARB 18.1g; FIBER 0.1g; CHOL 90mg; IRON 0.7mg; SODIUM 376mg; CALC 30mg

Apple and Horseradish-Glazed Salmon

Roasted Salmon with Citrus and Herbs

Here's a nice alternative for preparing salmon. Watch the fish carefully so it doesn't overcook.

- 1 tablespoon finely chopped fresh parsley
- 1 tablespoon finely chopped fresh thyme
- 1 tablespoon minced garlic
- 2 teaspoons grated lemon rind
- 2 teaspoons grated lime rind
- 1 teaspoon sea salt
- ½ teaspoon freshly ground black pepper
- 1 (2¼-pound) salmon fillet
- Cooking spray

1. Preheat oven to 400°.
2. Combine first 7 ingredients in a small bowl. Place salmon on a broiler pan coated with cooking spray. Rub parsley mixture over salmon. Bake at 400° for 15 minutes or until fish flakes easily when tested with a fork or until desired degree of doneness. Yield: 6 servings (serving size: 4½ ounces).

CALORIES 282 (42% from fat); FAT 13.3g (sat 3.1g, mono 5.7g, poly 3.2g); PROTEIN 36.3g; CARB 1g; FIBER 0.3g; CHOL 87mg; IRON 0.7mg; SODIUM 464mg; CALC 26mg

Sweet-Spicy Glazed Salmon

Chinese-style hot mustard has a sharp bite similar to wasabi. If you can't find it, use Dijon mustard or one teaspoon of a dry mustard such as Colman's.

- 3 tablespoons dark brown sugar
- 1 tablespoon low-sodium soy sauce
- 4 teaspoons Chinese-style hot mustard
- 1 teaspoon rice vinegar
- 4 (6-ounce) salmon fillets (about 1 inch thick)
- Cooking spray
- ¼ teaspoon salt
- ¼ teaspoon freshly ground black pepper

1. Preheat oven to 425°.
2. Combine first 4 ingredients in a saucepan; bring to a boil. Remove from heat.
3. Place fish on a foil-lined jelly-roll pan coated with cooking spray; sprinkle with salt and pepper. Bake at 425° for 10 minutes. Remove from oven.
4. Preheat broiler.
5. Brush sugar mixture over fish; broil 3 inches from heat 3 minutes or until fish flakes easily when tested with a fork or until desired degree of doneness. Yield: 4 servings (serving size: 1 fillet).

CALORIES 252 (37% from fat); FAT 10.3g (sat 2.3g, mono 4.4g, poly 2.5g); PROTEIN 27.7g; CARB 11g; FIBER 0.1g; CHOL 65mg; IRON 0.9mg; SODIUM 470mg; CALC 33mg

Curried Salmon with Tomato Jam

SALMON:

- 1 tablespoon all-purpose flour
- 2 teaspoons curry powder
- ½ teaspoon dried basil
- ¼ teaspoon salt
- 2 (6-ounce) skinned salmon fillets (about 1 inch thick)
- Cooking spray
- 1 teaspoon canola oil

TOMATO JAM:

- 2½ cups diced tomato
- ½ cup chopped onion
- 2 teaspoons minced peeled fresh ginger
- ¼ cup dried currants
- 1 tablespoon cider vinegar
- 1½ cups hot cooked basmati rice

1. To prepare salmon, combine first 4 ingredients in a shallow dish. Dredge salmon in flour mixture. Reserve remaining flour mixture for tomato jam.
2. Heat a large nonstick skillet over medium-high heat. Coat pan with cooking spray; add oil to pan. Add salmon; cook 4 minutes on each side or until golden and fish flakes easily when tested with a fork or until desired degree of doneness. Remove salmon from pan; keep warm.
3. To prepare tomato jam, place pan over medium-high heat. Add tomato, onion, and ginger; sauté 1 minute. Stir in reserved flour mixture, currants, and vinegar; bring to a boil. Cook until reduced to 1 cup (about 10 minutes). Spoon ¾ cup rice onto each of 2 plates; top each serving with 1 salmon fillet and ¼ cup tomato jam. Yield: 2 servings.

NOTE: Store remaining tomato jam in an airtight container in refrigerator for up to three days.

CALORIES 545 (29% from fat); FAT 17.7g (sat 2.9g, mono 7.6g, poly 4.4g); PROTEIN 40.1g; CARB 54.9g; FIBER 3.3g; CHOL 111mg; IRON 3.8mg; SODIUM 393mg; CALC 60mg

Thyme-Scented Salmon with Tuscan White Bean Salad

Garnish each serving with a mixture of whatever fresh herbs you happen to have on hand. The recipe comes together quickly and makes a nice presentation. It's ideal for a dinner party when you want to impress.

BEAN SALAD:

- 1 tablespoon extravirgin olive oil
- ⅓ cup finely chopped celery
- ½ cup finely chopped carrot
- ½ cup finely chopped shallots
- 2 garlic cloves, minced
- 3 tablespoons lemon juice
- 2 tablespoons water
- 2 teaspoons chopped fresh parsley
- 2 teaspoons chopped fresh mint
- 2 teaspoons chopped fresh basil
- 1 (15-ounce) can cannellini beans or other white beans, drained

SALMON:

- 2 teaspoons chopped fresh thyme
- 1 teaspoon chopped fresh parsley
- ½ teaspoon salt
- ⅛ teaspoon black pepper
- 4 (6-ounce) salmon fillets (about 1 inch thick)
- 3 tablespoons lemon juice

1. Preheat oven to 375°.

2. To prepare bean salad, heat oil in a medium nonstick skillet; add celery, carrot, shallots, and garlic. Cook 4 minutes or until tender; add 3 tablespoons juice and next 5 ingredients. Cook 2 minutes or until thoroughly heated, stirring constantly. Remove from heat; cover.

3. To prepare salmon, combine thyme, 1 teaspoon parsley, salt, and pepper in a small bowl; sprinkle evenly over fish. Place fish on a baking sheet or broiler pan lined with aluminum foil. Bake at 375° for 14 minutes or until fish flakes easily when tested with a fork or until desired degree of doneness. Remove from oven, and sprinkle evenly with 3 tablespoons lemon juice. Serve with bean salad. Yield: 4 servings (serving size: 1 fillet and ½ cup salad).

CALORIES 414 (37% from fat); FAT 17g (sat 3.6g, mono 8.2g, poly 3.9g); PROTEIN 41g; CARB 22g; FIBER 5g; CHOL 87mg; IRON 2.6mg; SODIUM 616mg; CALC 78mg

Spice-Rubbed Salmon with Cucumber Relish

Spice-Rubbed Salmon with Cucumber Relish

The bold spice rub works well with rich-flavored salmon and would also be good on pork. Serve with mashed potatoes or couscous.

1 tablespoon brown sugar
1 teaspoon garlic powder
1 teaspoon dried oregano
1 teaspoon ground cumin
1 teaspoon chili powder
1 teaspoon paprika
½ teaspoon salt, divided
¼ teaspoon dried thyme
4 (6-ounce) salmon fillets, skinned
Cooking spray
2 cups chopped cucumber
½ cup chopped red bell pepper
¼ cup chopped onion
2 tablespoons chopped fresh mint
1 tablespoon capers
1 tablespoon cider vinegar

1. Preheat broiler.
2. Combine first 6 ingredients, ¼ teaspoon salt, and dried thyme; rub evenly over fish. Place fish on a jelly-roll pan coated with cooking spray. Broil 8 minutes or until fish flakes easily when tested with a fork or until desired degree of doneness.
3. Combine remaining ¼ teaspoon salt, cucumber, and next 5 ingredients; serve with fish. Yield: 4 servings (serving size: 1 fillet and about ½ cup relish).

CALORIES 312 (39% from fat); FAT 13.6g (sat 3.2g, mono 5.7g, poly 3.3g); PROTEIN 37.3g; CARB 8.9g; FIBER 2.3g; CHOL 87mg; IRON 1.7mg; SODIUM 450mg; CALC 53mg

Lime-Marinated Broiled Salmon

⅓ cup low-sodium soy sauce
¼ cup fresh lime juice
1 teaspoon minced peeled fresh ginger
½ teaspoon chopped fresh thyme
2 garlic cloves, chopped
4 (6-ounce) skinless salmon fillets (about 1 inch thick)
Cooking spray
4 lime wedges

1. Place first 5 ingredients in a blender; process until smooth. Pour into a large zip-top plastic bag. Add salmon; seal and marinate in refrigerator 1 hour, turning bag occasionally.
2. Preheat broiler.
3. Remove salmon from bag; discard marinade. Place salmon on a broiler pan coated with cooking spray; broil 8 minutes. Turn salmon, and broil an additional 4 minutes or until fish flakes easily when tested with a fork or until desired degree of doneness. Serve with lime wedges. Yield: 4 servings (serving size: 1 fillet and 1 lime wedge).

CALORIES 281 (42% from fat); FAT 13.1g (sat 3.1g, mono 5.7g, poly 3.2g); PROTEIN 36.8g; CARB 7.9g; FIBER 0.1g; CHOL 87mg; IRON 0.8mg; SODIUM 414mg; CALC 25mg

Grilled Salmon with Corn and Pepper Relish

(pictured on page 76)

4 teaspoons olive oil, divided
1 (6-inch) lemon rind strip
6 (6-ounce) skinless salmon fillets
1 cup fresh corn kernels (about 2 ears)
1 cup coarsely chopped yellow bell pepper
1 cup coarsely chopped red bell pepper
1 cup coarsely chopped green bell pepper
1 cup finely chopped red onion
2 tablespoons chopped fresh parsley
3 tablespoons red wine vinegar
½ teaspoon salt, divided
½ teaspoon freshly ground black pepper
2 garlic cloves, minced
Cooking spray
Lemon wedges

1. Place 2 teaspoons oil, lemon rind, and salmon in a large zip-top plastic bag. Seal bag, and marinate in refrigerator at least 1 hour or overnight.
2. Prepare grill.
3. Combine corn and next 6 ingredients in a bowl. Stir in remaining 2 teaspoons oil, ¼ teaspoon salt, ¼ teaspoon black pepper, and garlic.
4. Sprinkle salmon with remaining ¼ teaspoon salt and remaining ¼ teaspoon black pepper. Place salmon on grill rack coated with cooking spray; grill 4 minutes on each side or until fish flakes easily when tested with a fork or until desired degree of doneness. Serve fish with relish and lemon wedges. Yield: 6 servings (serving size: 1 fillet and about ¾ cup relish).

CALORIES 274 (28% from fat); FAT 8.5g (sat 1.3g, mono 3.3g, poly 2.7g); PROTEIN 35.8g; CARB 13.3g; FIBER 2.6g; CHOL 88mg; IRON 2mg; SODIUM 314mg; CALC 40mg

Grilled Salmon with Nectarine-Red Onion Relish

Refreshing on a hot day, this grilled salmon makes a perfect summer meal. If you can't find nectarines try substituting peaches or mangoes.

- 2½ cups coarsely chopped nectarines (about 2 pounds)
- 1 cup coarsely chopped red bell pepper
- 1 cup coarsely chopped red onion
- ¼ cup thinly sliced fresh basil
- ¼ cup white wine vinegar
- ½ teaspoon grated orange rind
- ¼ cup fresh orange juice
- 2 tablespoons minced seeded jalapeño pepper
- 2 tablespoons fresh lime juice
- 2 teaspoons sugar
- 2 garlic cloves, minced
- ¼ teaspoon salt, divided
- ½ teaspoon freshly ground black pepper
- 4 (6-ounce) salmon fillets
- Cooking spray

1. Combine first 11 ingredients and ⅛ teaspoon salt in a medium bowl. Let stand 2 hours.
2. Prepare grill.
3. Sprinkle pepper and remaining ⅛ teaspoon salt over salmon. Place salmon on grill rack coated with cooking spray; grill 5 minutes on each side or until fish flakes easily when tested with a fork or until desired degree of doneness. Serve immediately with relish. Yield: 4 servings (serving size: 1 fillet and 1 cup relish).

CALORIES 380 (36% from fat); FAT 15.4g (sat 2.6g, mono 7.2g, poly 3.5g); PROTEIN 38.1g; CARB 21.6g; FIBER 3.5g; CHOL 115mg; IRON 1.6mg; SODIUM 236mg; CALC 36mg

Ponzu Grilled Salmon with Golden Beet Couscous

COUSCOUS:

- 1 teaspoon olive oil
- 2 tablespoons thinly sliced peeled shallots
- 8 ounces small golden beets, thinly sliced, peeled, and quartered (about 1½ cups)
- 1 cup uncooked Israeli couscous
- 2 cups water
- ¼ teaspoon salt
- 1 cup fresh spinach leaves, trimmed

SAUCE:

- ½ cup orange juice
- 2 tablespoons brown sugar
- 3 tablespoons low-sodium soy sauce
- 2 tablespoons sake (rice wine)
- 1 tablespoon fresh lime juice
- ½ teaspoon cornstarch
- ⅛ teaspoon crushed red pepper

REMAINING INGREDIENTS:

- 4 (6-ounce) salmon fillets with skin (about 1 inch thick)
- Cooking spray
- Lime wedges

1. Preheat grill.
2. To prepare couscous, heat oil in a large nonstick skillet over medium-high heat. Add shallots and beets; sauté 5 minutes or until shallots are tender and just beginning to brown. Stir in couscous; cook 1 minute, stirring frequently. Add water and salt; cover and simmer 8 minutes or until couscous is tender. Remove from heat; stir in spinach. Toss gently until combined and spinach wilts. Keep warm.
3. To prepare sauce, combine orange juice and next 6 ingredients in a small saucepan, stirring well with a whisk; bring to a boil over medium-high heat. Cook 1 minute.
4. To prepare fish, brush cut sides of fillets with ¼ cup sauce; place, skin sides up, on grill rack coated with cooking spray. Grill salmon, skin sides up, 2 minutes. Turn fillets; brush with remaining ¼ cup sauce. Grill 3 minutes or until fish flakes easily when tested with a fork or until desired degree of doneness. Serve with couscous and lime wedges. Yield: 4 servings (serving size: 1 fillet and ¾ cup couscous).

CALORIES 500 (22% from fat); FAT 12.4g (sat 1.9g, mono 4.5g, poly 4.6g); PROTEIN 41.4g; CARB 51.6g; FIBER 4.1g; CHOL 94mg; IRON 3mg; SODIUM 828mg; CALC 60mg

Ponzu Grilled Salmon with Golden Beet Couscous

Baked Snapper with Tomato-Orange Sauce

Serve this dish with a side of couscous to capture the sauce. Add a salad topped with crumbled blue cheese.

- 3 cups chopped red tomato (about 2 pounds)
- 2 cups chopped yellow tomato (about 1½ pounds)
- ½ cup chopped onion
- ¼ cup dry white wine
- 1 teaspoon grated orange rind
- ¼ cup fresh orange juice
- ⅛ teaspoon ground turmeric
- 2 garlic cloves, minced
- 4 (6-ounce) red snapper, grouper, or other firm white fish fillets
- 1 teaspoon olive oil
- ¼ teaspoon salt
- ⅛ teaspoon black pepper

1. Preheat oven to 400°.
2. Combine first 8 ingredients in an 11 x 7–inch baking dish. Bake at 400° for 20 minutes. Arrange fish on tomato mixture. Drizzle with oil; sprinkle with salt and pepper. Cover with foil; bake 20 minutes or until fish flakes easily when tested with a fork or until desired degree of doneness. Yield: 4 servings (serving size: 1 fillet and 1 cup sauce).

CALORIES 246 (15% from fat); FAT 4.2g (sat 0.7g, mono 1.4g, poly 1.2g); PROTEIN 37.3g; CARB 14.9g; FIBER 2.9g; CHOL 63mg; IRON 1.5mg; SODIUM 278mg; CALC 77mg

Sautéed Tilapia with Lemon-Peppercorn Pan Sauce

- ¾ cup fat-free, less-sodium chicken broth
- ¼ cup fresh lemon juice
- 1½ teaspoons drained brine-packed green peppercorns, lightly crushed
- 1 teaspoon butter
- 1 teaspoon vegetable oil
- 2 (6-ounce) tilapia or sole fillets
- ¼ teaspoon salt
- ¼ teaspoon freshly ground black pepper
- ¼ cup all-purpose flour
- 2 teaspoons butter
- Lemon wedges (optional)

1. Combine chicken broth, fresh lemon juice, and green peppercorns.
2. Melt 1 teaspoon butter with oil in a large nonstick skillet over low heat.
3. While butter melts, sprinkle fillets with salt and black pepper. Place flour in a shallow dish. Dredge fillets in flour; shake off excess flour.
4. Increase heat to medium-high; heat 2 minutes or until butter turns golden brown. Add fillets to pan; sauté 3 minutes on each side or until fish flakes easily when tested with a fork. Remove fillets from pan. Add broth mixture to pan, scraping to loosen browned bits. Bring to a boil; cook until reduced to ½ cup (about 3 minutes). Remove from heat. Stir in 2 teaspoons butter with a whisk. Serve sauce over fillets. Garnish with lemon wedges, if desired. Yield: 2 servings (serving size: 1 fillet and 2 tablespoons sauce).

CALORIES 282 (26% from fat); FAT 8.3g (sat 3.2g, mono 2g, poly 2.1g); PROTEIN 35g; CARB 15.3g; FIBER 0.8g; CHOL 92mg; IRON 1.5mg; SODIUM 739mg; CALC 43mg

Tilapia in Mustard Cream Sauce

Orange roughy, flounder, or sole are good substitutes for tilapia. Serve with sautéed spinach, instant polenta, or steamed rice on the side.

- 4 (6-ounce) tilapia fillets
- ½ teaspoon chopped fresh thyme
- ½ teaspoon freshly ground black pepper
- ¼ teaspoon salt
- Cooking spray
- ¾ cup fat-free, less-sodium chicken broth
- 1 ounce portobello mushrooms, thinly sliced (about 1 cup)
- 2 tablespoons whipping cream
- 2 tablespoons Dijon mustard

1. Sprinkle fish with thyme, pepper, and salt. Heat a large nonstick skillet over medium-high heat. Coat pan with cooking spray. Add fish; cook 1 minute on each side. Add chicken broth; bring to a boil. Cover, reduce heat, and simmer 5 minutes. Add mushrooms; cook, uncovered, 1 minute or until mushrooms are tender. Remove fish from pan; keep warm.
2. Add cream and mustard to mushrooms in pan; stir with a whisk until well combined. Cook 1 minute or until thoroughly heated. Serve sauce over fish. Yield: 4 servings (serving size: 1 fillet and ¼ cup sauce).

CALORIES 184 (22% from fat); FAT 4.6g (sat 2.1g, mono 1g, poly 0.4g); PROTEIN 32.7g; CARB 1.2g; FIBER 0.6g; CHOL 134mg; IRON 2.2mg; SODIUM 536mg; CALC 40mg

Pecan-Crusted Tilapia

- ½ cup dry breadcrumbs
- 2 tablespoons finely chopped pecans
- ½ teaspoon salt
- ¼ teaspoon garlic powder
- ¼ teaspoon black pepper
- ½ cup low-fat buttermilk
- ½ teaspoon hot sauce
- 3 tablespoons all-purpose flour
- 4 (6-ounce) tilapia or red snapper fillets
- 1 tablespoon vegetable oil, divided
- 4 lemon wedges

1. Combine first 5 ingredients in a shallow dish. Combine buttermilk and hot sauce in a medium bowl; place flour in a shallow dish. Dredge 1 fillet in flour. Dip in buttermilk mixture; dredge in breadcrumb mixture. Repeat procedure with remaining fillets, flour, buttermilk, and breadcrumb mixtures.

2. Heat 1½ teaspoons oil in a large nonstick skillet over medium-high heat. Add 2 fillets; cook 3 minutes on each side or until fish flakes easily when tested with a fork. Repeat procedure with remaining oil and fillets. Serve with lemon wedges. Yield: 4 servings (serving size: 1 tilapia fillet).

CALORIES 302 (27% from fat); FAT 9.1g (sat 1.1g, mono 3.9g, poly 2.6g); PROTEIN 38.4g; CARB 14.2g; FIBER 0.9g; CHOL 64mg; IRON 1.3mg; SODIUM 530mg; CALC 98mg

Caribbean Mango Tilapia

4 serrano chiles, seeded
3 garlic cloves, peeled
2 large shallots, peeled
2 cups chopped peeled mango
⅓ cup cider vinegar
¼ cup fresh orange juice
1 tablespoon chopped fresh thyme
2 teaspoons olive oil
¼ teaspoon salt
4 (6-ounce) tilapia fillets
Cooking spray

1. Combine first 3 ingredients in a food processor; process until minced. Add mango and next 5 ingredients; process until smooth. Place mango mixture and fish in a zip-top plastic bag; seal and marinate in refrigerator 20 minutes. Remove fish from bag, reserving marinade. Pour reserved marinade into a small saucepan; bring to a boil. Reduce heat, and simmer 5 minutes. Remove from heat.
2. Prepare grill or broiler.
3. Place fish on a grill rack or broiler pan coated with cooking spray. Cook 4 minutes on each side or until fish flakes easily when tested with a fork. Serve with sauce. Yield: 4 servings (serving size: 1 fillet and ¼ cup sauce).

CALORIES 263 (23% from fat); FAT 6.8g (sat 0.8g, mono 3.3g, poly 2g); PROTEIN 32.7g; CARB 19.3g; FIBER 1.6g; CHOL 75mg; IRON 0.5mg; SODIUM 239mg; CALC 21mg

Trout with Lentils

Serve this dish warm or as a chilled salad over a bed of greens.

1 teaspoon olive oil
¼ cup chopped leek
¼ cup finely chopped carrot
2 garlic cloves, minced
1 cup dried lentils
½ cup water
1 (14-ounce) can fat-free, less-sodium chicken broth
¼ cup chopped celery
1 tablespoon chopped fresh parsley
1 tablespoon sherry vinegar
¾ teaspoon salt, divided
¼ teaspoon black pepper, divided
2 (6-ounce) trout fillets
Cooking spray

1. Heat oil in a medium saucepan over medium-high heat. Add chopped leek, carrot, and garlic; sauté 2 minutes. Stir in lentils, water, and broth; bring to a boil. Cover, reduce heat, and simmer 25 minutes or until lentils are tender. Remove from heat. Add celery, parsley, vinegar, ½ teaspoon salt, and ⅛ teaspoon pepper, stirring to combine.
2. Preheat broiler.
3. Sprinkle trout with remaining ¼ teaspoon salt and ⅛ teaspoon pepper. Place fish on a baking sheet coated with cooking spray; broil 5 minutes or until fish flakes easily when tested with a fork. Break fish into chunks; add to lentil mixture, tossing gently. Yield: 4 servings (serving size: 1 cup).

CALORIES 311 (18% from fat); FAT 6.2g (sat 1.6g, mono 2.2g, poly 1.9g); PROTEIN 32.8g; CARB 31.3g; FIBER 15.2g; CHOL 50mg; IRON 5mg; SODIUM 668mg; CALC 96mg

Greek Tuna Steaks

The combination of Mediterranean flavors works equally well not only with the tuna steaks in this recipe, but also with striped bass or red snapper fillets.

1½ teaspoons chopped fresh or ½ teaspoon dried oregano
1 teaspoon olive oil
¾ teaspoon chopped fresh or ¼ teaspoon dried thyme
½ teaspoon salt
¼ teaspoon black pepper
4 (6-ounce) tuna steaks (about ¾ inch thick)
Cooking spray
4 lemon wedges

1. Combine first 5 ingredients in a small bowl, and rub evenly over steaks. Cover steaks; marinate in refrigerator 15 minutes.
2. Heat a large grill pan over medium-high heat. Coat pan with cooking spray. Add steaks; cook 5 minutes on each side or until desired degree of doneness. Serve steaks with lemon wedges. Yield: 4 servings (serving size: 1 steak).

CALORIES 250 (35% from fat); FAT 9.7g (sat 2.3g, mono 3.6g, poly 2.7g); PROTEIN 38.2g; CARB 0.2g; FIBER 0.1g; CHOL 63mg; IRON 1.8mg; SODIUM 357mg; CALC 4mg

Mediterranean Tuna Cakes with Citrus Mayonnaise

CITRUS MAYONNAISE:

2 tablespoons fat-free mayonnaise
1 tablespoon fat-free milk
1 tablespoon fresh lime juice
½ teaspoon grated lime rind
⅛ teaspoon ground cumin

TUNA CAKES:

¾ pound tuna steaks, finely chopped
¾ cup finely chopped red bell pepper
1 tablespoon chopped fresh or 1 teaspoon dried mint
1 tablespoon chopped fresh cilantro
1 tablespoon dry breadcrumbs
1 tablespoon finely chopped onion
1 tablespoon fat-free mayonnaise
1 teaspoon lemon juice
⅛ teaspoon salt
2 tablespoons dry breadcrumbs
Cooking spray
1 teaspoon olive oil
Lime wedges (optional)

1. To prepare citrus mayonnaise, combine first 5 ingredients in a small bowl. Cover and chill.

2. To prepare tuna cakes, combine tuna and next 8 ingredients in a bowl; stir until well blended. Divide tuna mixture into 4 equal portions, and shape each into a ½-inch-thick patty. Dredge patties in 2 tablespoons breadcrumbs.

3. Heat a nonstick skillet over medium-high heat. Coat pan with cooking spray; add oil to pan. Add patties; cook 3 minutes on each side or until browned. Serve with citrus mayonnaise. Garnish with lime wedges, if desired. Yield: 2 servings (serving size: 2 tuna cakes and 2 tablespoons mayonnaise).

CALORIES 345 (31% from fat); FAT 11.7g (sat 2.6g, mono 4.2g, poly 3.3g); PROTEIN 41.8g; CARB 16.2g; FIBER 1.3g; CHOL 65mg; IRON 3.3mg; SODIUM 582mg; CALC 41mg

Tuna-Noodle Casserole

Perfect for a weeknight dinner, here's a tasty update of a traditional favorite. Mushrooms make a nice addition to this comfort food classic.

- 1 (1-ounce) slice white bread
- 1 tablespoon butter
- ¾ cup diced onion
- 1 cup 2% reduced-fat milk
- 1 (10.75-ounce) can condensed 30% reduced-sodium 98% fat-free cream of mushroom soup, undiluted (such as Campbell's)
- 3 cups hot cooked egg noodles (about 6 ounces uncooked pasta)
- 1¼ cups frozen green peas, thawed
- 1 tablespoon lemon juice
- ¼ teaspoon salt
- ¼ teaspoon pepper
- 2 (6-ounce) cans low-sodium tuna in water, drained and flaked
- 1 (2-ounce) jar diced pimiento, drained
- 2 tablespoons grated Parmesan cheese

1. Preheat oven to 450°.
2. Place bread in a food processor; pulse 10 times or until coarse crumbs measure ⅓ cup. Set aside.
3. Melt butter in a saucepan over medium-high heat. Add onion; sauté 3 minutes. Add milk and soup. Cook 3 minutes, stirring constantly with a whisk. Combine soup mixture, egg noodles, and next 6 ingredients in a 2-quart casserole. Combine breadcrumbs and cheese; sprinkle on top. Bake at 450° for 15 minutes or until bubbly. Yield: 4 servings (serving size: 1¼ cups).

CALORIES 402 (17% from fat); FAT 7.7g (sat 2.2g, mono 2.4g, poly 1.5g); PROTEIN 28.8g; CARB 52.5g; FIBER 5.2g; CHOL 84mg; IRON 3.4mg; SODIUM 795mg; CALC 144mg

Vegetable Panzanella with Tuna

Make sure your bread is dry so the croutons won't get soggy when tossed with the dressing. If you're using fresh bread, bake the bread cubes at 350° for five minutes. Serve this salad immediately, while the bread is still crunchy.

VINAIGRETTE:

- 2 tablespoons chopped fresh parsley
- 2 tablespoons chopped fresh basil
- 2 tablespoons olive oil
- 2 tablespoons red wine vinegar
- ¼ teaspoon freshly ground black pepper
- 1 garlic clove, minced

SALAD:

- 2½ pounds cucumber, peeled, halved lengthwise, seeded, and sliced (about 4 cups)
- 1¼ cups diced zucchini
- 1 cup diced red bell pepper
- ¾ cup halved pitted kalamata olives
- ½ cup thinly sliced red onion
- ¼ teaspoon salt
- 3 tomatoes, each cut into 8 wedges (about 1½ pounds)
- 1 (6-ounce) can albacore tuna in water, drained and flaked
- 4 cups (½-inch) cubed day-old whole wheat bread (about 13 [1-ounce] slices)

1. To prepare vinaigrette, combine first 6 ingredients; stir with a whisk.
2. To prepare salad, combine cucumber, zucchini, red bell pepper, olives, red onion, ¼ teaspoon salt, tomatoes, and tuna in a large bowl. Add bread. Drizzle with vinaigrette; toss gently to combine. Yield: 6 servings (serving size: 2 cups).

CALORIES 298 (30% from fat); FAT 10g (sat 1.7g, mono 6g, poly 1.8g); PROTEIN 13.6g; CARB 41.1g; FIBER 5.9g; CHOL 9mg; IRON 4mg; SODIUM 668mg; CALC 109mg

Louisiana Crab Cakes with Creole Tartar Sauce

Lump crabmeat makes great crab cakes, but they're prone to falling apart. Handle them patiently and gently when shaping into patties for the best results.

TARTAR SAUCE:

- ½ cup low-fat mayonnaise
- 3 tablespoons sweet pickle relish
- 2 tablespoons capers, rinsed and drained
- 1 teaspoon Creole mustard
- ¼ teaspoon salt-free Cajun-Creole seasoning (such as The Spice Hunter)
- ¼ teaspoon hot pepper sauce (such as Tabasco)

CRAB CAKES:

- 4 (1-ounce) slices white bread
- ¼ cup finely chopped onion
- ¼ cup finely chopped red bell pepper
- 1 tablespoon chopped fresh parsley
- 1 tablespoon fresh lemon juice
- 1 tablespoon hot pepper sauce (such as Tabasco)
- ¼ teaspoon freshly ground black pepper
- 1 pound lump crabmeat, shell pieces removed
- 1 large egg, lightly beaten
- 1 large egg white, lightly beaten
- 4 teaspoons vegetable oil, divided
- Flat-leaf parsley sprigs (optional)
- Lemon wedges (optional)

1. To prepare tartar sauce, combine first 6 ingredients, stirring with a whisk. Let stand 10 minutes.

2. To prepare crab cakes, place bread in a food processor; pulse 10 times or until coarse crumbs measure 2 cups. Combine 1 cup breadcrumbs, onion, and next 8 ingredients; mix well. Divide crab mixture into 8 equal portions. Form each portion into a ½-inch-thick patty. Place 1 cup breadcrumbs in a shallow dish. Dredge patties, one at a time, in breadcrumbs.

3. Heat 2 teaspoons oil in a large nonstick skillet over medium-high heat. Add 4 patties; cook 3 minutes on each side or until golden brown. Repeat procedure with remaining oil and patties. Serve with tartar sauce. Garnish with parsley sprigs and lemon wedges, if desired. Yield: 4 servings (serving size: 2 crab cakes and 2 tablespoons tartar sauce).

CALORIES 331 (30% from fat); FAT 11g (sat 1.8g, mono 2.6g, poly 5.3g); PROTEIN 28.2g; CARB 29.1g; FIBER 1.4g; CHOL 167mg; IRON 2.5mg; SODIUM 992mg; CALC 163mg

Scallops with Cucumber-Horseradish Sauce

Serve with a salad and bread or over cooked angel hair pasta tossed with a little olive oil and salt. Add extra horseradish if you want more heat in the sauce. Substitute shrimp for scallops, if you wish.

1 tablespoon olive oil
Cooking spray
1 cup chopped seeded peeled cucumber
1 cup plain fat-free yogurt
2 tablespoons finely chopped fresh parsley
1½ tablespoons prepared horseradish
⅛ teaspoon kosher salt
⅛ teaspoon coarsely ground black pepper
2 tablespoons Italian-seasoned breadcrumbs
12 large sea scallops (about 1½ pounds)

1. Heat oil in a large nonstick skillet coated with cooking spray over medium-high heat.
2. Combine cucumber, yogurt, parsley, horseradish, salt, and pepper; set aside. Place breadcrumbs in a shallow dish; dredge scallops in breadcrumbs.
3. Add scallops to pan; cook 4 minutes on each side or until done. Serve immediately. Yield: 4 servings (serving size: 3 scallops and about ⅓ cup sauce).

CALORIES 220 (25% from fat); FAT 6g (sat 1.4g, mono 3.1g, poly 0.8g); PROTEIN 28.2g; CARB 11.7g; FIBER 0.4g; CHOL 50mg; IRON 0.8mg; SODIUM 393mg; CALC 174mg

Scallops with Chipotle-Orange Sauce

2 tablespoons butter, divided
Cooking spray
12 large sea scallops (about 1½ pounds)
½ teaspoon paprika
¼ teaspoon salt, divided
½ cup fresh orange juice
1 tablespoon finely chopped canned chipotle chile in adobo sauce
¼ cup finely chopped green onions

1. Melt 1 tablespoon butter in a large skillet coated with cooking spray over medium-high heat. Sprinkle scallops with paprika and ⅛ teaspoon salt. Add scallops to pan, and cook 3 minutes on each side or until browned. Remove from pan; set aside, and keep warm.
2. Add orange juice and chile to pan, scraping to loosen browned bits. Bring to a boil; cook until reduced to ¼ cup (about 1 minute). Add remaining 1 tablespoon butter and remaining ⅛ teaspoon salt, stirring with a whisk until smooth. Serve with scallops; sprinkle with onions. Yield: 4 servings (serving size: 3 scallops, about 1 tablespoon sauce, and 1 tablespoon onions).

CALORIES 218 (29% from fat); FAT 7.1g (sat 3.7g, mono 1.7g, poly 0.7g); PROTEIN 28.9g; CARB 8.1g; FIBER 0.4g; CHOL 72mg; IRON 0.6mg; SODIUM 488mg; CALC 47mg

Cornmeal-Crusted Scallops with Mint Chimichurri

Chimichurri is a thick herb sauce commonly made with parsley and oregano, and served with grilled meat in South American cuisine. Mint gives this version a more delicate taste, making it perfect for seafood. Serve over a bed of rice to soak up the flavorful sauce.

CHIMICHURRI:
1½ cups loosely packed fresh mint leaves
¾ cup sliced green onions
2 tablespoons water
1½ tablespoons fresh lime juice
1 tablespoon honey
1 teaspoon minced seeded serrano chile
½ teaspoon salt
½ teaspoon freshly ground black pepper
1 garlic clove

SCALLOPS:
3 tablespoons yellow cornmeal
1½ pounds sea scallops
1 tablespoon olive oil
Green onion strips (optional)

1. To prepare chimichurri, place first 9 ingredients in a food processor, and process until finely chopped. Set aside.
2. To prepare scallops, place cornmeal in a shallow dish. Dredge scallops in cornmeal. Heat oil in a large nonstick skillet over medium-high heat. Add scallops; cook 3 minutes or until browned. Turn scallops over using tongs; cook 3 minutes or until done. Serve with chimichurri, and garnish with green onion strips, if desired. Yield: 4 servings (serving size: about 4 ounces scallops and 2 tablespoons chimichurri).

CALORIES 237 (19% from fat); FAT 4.9g (sat 0.6g, mono 2.6g, poly 0.9g); PROTEIN 29.6g; CARB 17.3g; FIBER 2.1g; CHOL 56mg; IRON 1.4mg; SODIUM 576mg; CALC 68mg

Cornmeal-Crusted Scallops with Mint Chimichurri

Seared Scallops on Braised Wild Mushrooms

Although this dish is quick and easy to prepare, its luxury comes from truffle oil–enhanced mushrooms. The crisp crust on the scallops renders a textural contrast to the tender mushrooms. To get the best crust, be sure your skillet is very hot, and turn the scallops only once during cooking.

- 4 teaspoons olive oil, divided
- 2 cups sliced cremini mushrooms (about 4 ounces)
- 1 cup sliced shiitake mushroom caps (about 2 ounces)
- 1 cup sliced oyster mushroom caps (about 2 ounces)
- ½ teaspoon salt, divided
- ½ teaspoon freshly ground black pepper, divided
- ¼ cup dry white wine
- 1 teaspoon chopped fresh thyme
- 1 teaspoon fresh lemon juice
- 1 teaspoon truffle oil or extravirgin olive oil
- 12 large sea scallops (about 1½ pounds)
- ¼ cup yellow cornmeal
- 2 cups trimmed watercress

1. Heat 2 teaspoons olive oil in a large cast-iron skillet over medium-high heat. Add mushrooms, ¼ teaspoon salt, and ¼ teaspoon black pepper; sauté 2 minutes or until mushrooms begin to soften. Add wine, thyme, and juice; reduce heat to low. Cook 5 minutes or until mushrooms are tender. Pour mushroom mixture into a bowl. Stir in truffle oil; cover and keep warm.

2. Wipe pan dry with paper towels. Pat scallops dry with paper towels; sprinkle with ¼ teaspoon salt and ¼ teaspoon black pepper. Place cornmeal in a shallow dish; dredge scallops in cornmeal. Heat 2 teaspoons olive oil in pan over high heat. Add scallops; cook 3 minutes on each side or until golden brown. Serve over trimmed watercress and mushroom mixture. Yield: 4 servings (serving size: about 5 ounces scallops, ½ cup watercress, and ½ cup mushroom mixture).

CALORIES 252 (26% from fat); FAT 7.3g (sat 1g, mono 4.3g, poly 1.1g); PROTEIN 31.8g; CARB 14.3g; FIBER 1.7g; CHOL 56mg; IRON 1.8mg; SODIUM 578mg; CALC 69mg

Spiced Shrimp with Peach Salsa

Mangoes and nectarines can be used in place of peaches, if desired. If you use nectarines, don't bother with peeling.

PEACH SALSA:

- 3½ cups coarsely chopped peeled peaches (about 2¼ pounds)
- 1 cup coarsely chopped red bell pepper
- 1 cup coarsely chopped green bell pepper
- ⅓ cup coarsely chopped red onion
- ¼ cup fresh cilantro leaves
- 1 tablespoon lime juice
- ¼ teaspoon salt
- 1 jalapeño pepper, seeded and chopped

SHRIMP:

- 2 teaspoons brown sugar
- 1 teaspoon ground cumin
- ¼ teaspoon salt
- ¼ teaspoon freshly ground black pepper
- 1½ pounds large shrimp, peeled and deveined
- 1 tablespoon canola oil

1. To prepare salsa, place first 8 ingredients in a food processor; pulse 8 times. Set aside.

2. To prepare shrimp, combine sugar, cumin, ¼ teaspoon salt, pepper, and shrimp in a large bowl; toss gently to coat. Heat oil in a large nonstick skillet over medium-high heat. Add shrimp mixture; sauté 4 minutes or until shrimp are done. Serve with peach salsa. Yield: 4 servings (serving size: 5 ounces shrimp and 1 cup salsa).

CALORIES 272 (23% from fat); FAT 6.9g (sat 0.8g, mono 2.5g, poly 2.2g); PROTEIN 35.7g; CARB 16.1g; FIBER 2.5g; CHOL 259mg; IRON 4.8mg; SODIUM 612mg; CALC 110mg

Shrimp and Pasta with Peanut Sauce

You can also try this recipe with cooked, cut-up chicken or pork tenderloin. Sticky rice or Asian noodles can be substituted for rigatoni, if desired.

- 1 tablespoon minced fresh cilantro
- 1 tablespoon grated peeled fresh ginger
- 3 tablespoons low-sodium soy sauce
- 2 tablespoons crunchy peanut butter
- 1 teaspoon sugar
- 1 teaspoon rice vinegar
- ¼ teaspoon hot sauce
- 1 garlic clove, minced
- 1 teaspoon dark sesame oil
- 8 ounces medium shrimp, peeled and deveined
- 1 cup vertically sliced onion
- ½ red bell pepper, cut into ¼-inch strips
- 1 cup bagged prewashed spinach
- 2 cups hot cooked rigatoni (about 1¼ cups uncooked pasta)

1. Combine first 8 ingredients in a medium bowl, stirring well with a whisk.

2. Heat a large nonstick skillet over medium-high heat; add oil. Add shrimp; sauté 3 minutes or until done. Remove shrimp from pan. Add onion and bell pepper to pan; sauté 3 minutes. Add soy sauce mixture, shrimp, and spinach. Reduce heat to medium; cook 2 minutes or until spinach wilts. Serve over pasta. Yield: 2 servings (serving size: 1 cup shrimp mixture and 1 cup pasta).

CALORIES 483 (25% from fat); FAT 13.4g (sat 2.4g, mono 5.1g, poly 4.4g); PROTEIN 36.1g; CARB 55.1g; FIBER 4.8g; CHOL 172mg; IRON 6.2mg; SODIUM 1,003mg; CALC 108mg

Shrimp Tacos

Shredded rotisserie chicken or flaked, cooked fish also works well in these tacos. Serve with a side of corn and avocado salsa to round out the meal.

- 3 tablespoons black peppercorns
- 3 quarts water
- 1 tablespoon salt
- 1 teaspoon ground red pepper
- 2 limes, quartered
- 1 pound medium shrimp, peeled and deveined
- ½ cup coarsely chopped fresh cilantro
- ¼ cup fresh lime juice
- 1 tablespoon minced seeded jalapeño pepper
- 12 (6-inch) corn tortillas
- ¾ cup chopped peeled tomato
- ½ cup reduced-fat sour cream
- ½ cup chopped green onions

1. Place black peppercorns on a double layer of cheesecloth. Gather edges of cheesecloth together, and tie securely. Combine cheesecloth bag, water, salt, red pepper, and lime quarters in a Dutch oven. Bring to a boil; cook 2 minutes. Add shrimp; cook 2 minutes or until done. Drain. Discard cheesecloth bag and lime quarters.

2. Combine shrimp, fresh cilantro, lime juice, and jalapeño pepper, tossing well to coat. Heat tortillas according to package directions. Spoon ⅓ cup shrimp mixture into each tortilla; top each taco with 1 tablespoon tomato, 2 teaspoons sour cream, and 2 teaspoons onions. Yield: 4 servings (serving size: 3 tacos).

CALORIES 358 (20% from fat); FAT 7.8g (sat 3g, mono 0.8g, poly 1.7g); PROTEIN 29.3g; CARB 43.6g; FIBER 5.1g; CHOL 188mg; IRON 4.1mg; SODIUM 612mg; CALC 250mg

Shrimp Pad Thai

Pad thai is the most popular noodle dish in Thailand. Pungent fish sauce (also called *nam pla*) is an important flavoring for this dish; you can find it in the Asian foods section of most large supermarkets or in Asian markets. Substitute four cups hot cooked linguine for the rice stick noodles if you can't find them.

- 8 ounces wide rice stick noodles (*banh pho*)
- 1/4 cup ketchup
- 2 tablespoons sugar
- 3 tablespoons fish sauce
- 1/2 teaspoon crushed red pepper
- 2 tablespoons canola oil, divided
- 1 pound medium shrimp, peeled and deveined
- 2 large eggs, lightly beaten
- 1 cup fresh bean sprouts
- 3/4 cup (1-inch) sliced green onions
- 1 garlic clove, minced
- 2 tablespoons chopped unsalted, dry-roasted peanuts

1. Place noodles in a large bowl. Add hot water to cover; let stand 12 minutes or until tender. Drain.
2. Combine ketchup, sugar, fish sauce, and pepper in a small bowl.
3. Heat 2 teaspoons oil in a large nonstick skillet over medium-high heat. Add shrimp; sauté 2 minutes or until shrimp are done. Remove shrimp from pan; keep warm.
4. Heat 4 teaspoons oil in pan over medium-high heat. Add eggs; cook 30 seconds or until soft-scrambled, stirring constantly. Add sprouts, green onions, and garlic; cook 1 minute. Add noodles, ketchup mixture, and shrimp; cook 3 minutes or until heated. Sprinkle with peanuts. Yield: 6 servings (serving size: 1 1/2 cups).

CALORIES 346 (25% from fat); FAT 9.3g (sat 1.3g, mono 4.3g, poly 2.6g); PROTEIN 22.2g; CARB 41.9g; FIBER 2.3g; CHOL 185mg; IRON 4mg; SODIUM 945mg; CALC 78mg

Fettuccine with Shrimp and Portobellos

Serve this entrée in a bowl with toasted bread to soak up the flavorful broth.

- 8 ounces uncooked fettuccine
- 1 (4-inch) portobello mushroom cap (about 5 ounces)
- 1 tablespoon olive oil
- 1 cup finely chopped onion
- 1/4 cup chopped fresh flat-leaf parsley
- 1/4 teaspoon salt
- 1 garlic clove, minced
- 1 cup fat-free, less-sodium chicken broth
- 1/4 cup dry white wine
- 3/4 pound large shrimp, peeled and deveined
- 1/2 cup (2 ounces) shredded Asiago cheese
- 1 tablespoon chopped fresh chives

1. Cook pasta according to package directions, omitting salt and fat. Drain and rinse under cold water. Drain.
2. Remove brown gills from underside of mushroom cap using a spoon; discard gills. Cut cap into thin slices. Cut slices in half crosswise.
3. Heat olive oil in a large saucepan over medium-high heat. Add mushroom, onion, parsley, salt, and garlic; sauté 4 minutes or until mushroom releases moisture, stirring frequently. Stir in broth, wine, and shrimp; bring to a boil. Add pasta; cook 3 minutes or until shrimp are done, tossing to combine. Sprinkle with cheese and chives. Yield: 4 servings (serving size: 1 3/4 cups shrimp mixture, 2 tablespoons cheese, and about 1 teaspoon chives).

CALORIES 384 (21% from fat); FAT 9.1g (sat 3.3g, mono 2.7g, poly 0.9g); PROTEIN 23.8g; CARB 48.9g; FIBER 2.8g; CHOL 114mg; IRON 4.5mg; SODIUM 540mg; CALC 156mg

Shrimp in Green Sauce

Reminiscent of shrimp scampi, this dish gets a flavor boost from fresh parsley and green onions. Preparation is a breeze, thanks to a food processor. Good bread to soak up the rich sauce is a must.

3½ tablespoons extravirgin olive oil
6 garlic cloves, peeled
1 cup coarsely chopped green onions
1 cup coarsely chopped fresh flat-leaf parsley
½ teaspoon salt
½ teaspoon freshly ground black pepper
¼ teaspoon crushed red pepper
2¼ pounds large shrimp, peeled and deveined
⅓ cup dry white wine
6 ounces sourdough or French bread, torn into 6 (1-ounce) pieces

1. Preheat oven to 500°.
2. Place oil and garlic in a food processor; process until garlic is finely chopped, scraping sides of bowl occasionally. Add green onions and parsley to food processor; pulse until minced. Spoon garlic mixture into a large bowl. Add salt, black pepper, red pepper, and shrimp to garlic mixture; toss well to coat.
3. Spoon shrimp mixture into a shallow roasting pan; add wine. Bake at 500° for 7 minutes or until shrimp are done, stirring once. Serve with bread. Yield: 6 servings (serving size: about 5 ounces shrimp mixture and 1 ounce bread).

CALORIES 352 (30% from fat); FAT 11.8g (sat 1.8g, mono 6.6g, poly 2g); PROTEIN 37.6g; CARB 19.5g; FIBER 2g; CHOL 259mg; IRON 5.6mg; SODIUM 630mg; CALC 131mg

Spiced Shrimp with Avocado Oil

These vividly seasoned shrimp are great on their own, served atop pasta, or as part of a tapas tray. A light drizzle of the oil over the shrimp at the end results in an essence of avocado flavor in every bite.

1½ pounds medium shrimp, peeled and deveined
1 teaspoon sugar
¼ teaspoon kosher salt
1 tablespoon chili powder
½ teaspoon ground cumin
½ teaspoon ground coriander
½ teaspoon dried oregano
1½ tablespoons avocado oil
Lime wedges

1. Sprinkle shrimp with sugar and salt. Combine chili powder, cumin, coriander, and oregano. Lightly coat shrimp with spice mixture.
2. Heat a large nonstick skillet over medium-high heat. Add 1 teaspoon oil and half of shrimp; sauté 4 minutes or until done. Remove from pan. Repeat procedure with 1 teaspoon oil and remaining shrimp. Place shrimp on a platter, and drizzle remaining 2½ teaspoons oil over shrimp. Serve with lime wedges. Yield: 4 servings (serving size: about 5 ounces shrimp).

CALORIES 234 (32% from fat); FAT 8.3g (sat 1.2g, mono 4.1g, poly 1.9g); PROTEIN 34.6g; CARB 3.2g; FIBER 0.2g; CHOL 259mg; IRON 4.3mg; SODIUM 430mg; CALC 94mg

Coconut-Curry Shrimp over Rice

Shrimp need just a short marinating time to absorb the flavors of the aromatic sauce, making this tasty entrée quick enough for a busy weeknight.

¼ cup coconut milk
3 tablespoons finely chopped red bell pepper
1 tablespoon minced fresh cilantro
1½ tablespoons fish sauce
1 tablespoon fresh lemon juice
1 teaspoon sugar
1 teaspoon curry powder
1½ pounds large shrimp, peeled and deveined
4 cups water
3 cups hot cooked basmati rice
4 lemon wedges
Fresh cilantro sprigs (optional)

1. Combine first 7 ingredients in a large zip-top plastic bag. Add shrimp; seal and marinate in refrigerator 30 minutes, turning bag occasionally. Place shrimp mixture in a 10-inch pie plate.
2. Open a small metal vegetable steamer; place steamer upside down in a large, deep wok. Add 4 cups water; bring to a simmer. Wearing oven mitts, carefully place pie plate on top of inverted steamer. Cover and cook 4 minutes or until shrimp are done. Wearing oven mitts, carefully remove pie plate from wok. Serve shrimp mixture over rice; serve with lemon wedges. Garnish with cilantro, if desired. Yield: 4 servings (serving size: 1 cup shrimp mixture, ¾ cup rice, and 1 lemon wedge).

CALORIES 375 (15% from fat); FAT 6.4g (sat 3.3g, mono 0.7g, poly 1.3g); PROTEIN 38.6g; CARB 38.3g; FIBER 1g; CHOL 259mg; IRON 6.3mg; SODIUM 777mg; CALC 111mg

Coconut-Curry Shrimp over Rice

Coconut Curry Shrimp Cakes with Papaya-Lime Sauce

Take a little extra time picking out a ripe papaya for this sauce. It should have a vivid golden-yellow color and give slightly when pressed with the palm. It will blend better and yield a more flavorful and smooth sauce than unripe fruit. If you're unable to find fresh papaya, substitute another soft-texture tropical fruit, such as mango. The presentation on gourmet salad greens adds texture as well as visual appeal.

SHRIMP CAKES:

- ¾ teaspoon curry powder
- 1 cup panko (Japanese breadcrumbs)
- 2 tablespoons flaked sweetened coconut
- 2 tablespoons finely chopped fresh cilantro
- 2 tablespoons minced red bell pepper
- 2 tablespoons minced green onions
- 1 tablespoon minced peeled fresh ginger
- 3 tablespoons light coconut milk
- 2 teaspoons minced seeded serrano chile
- 1 teaspoon low-sodium soy sauce
- ¼ teaspoon salt
- 12 ounces medium shrimp, peeled, deveined, and chopped
- 1 large egg
- 1 garlic clove, minced
- Cooking spray

SAUCE:

- 1 cup diced peeled ripe papaya
- ¼ cup water
- ¼ cup fresh lime juice
- 2 teaspoons sugar

REMAINING INGREDIENTS:

- 4 cups gourmet salad greens
- 2 teaspoons sesame seeds, toasted

1. To prepare shrimp cakes, heat a large nonstick skillet over medium heat. Add curry powder; cook 30 seconds or until lightly toasted and fragrant, stirring constantly. Combine curry powder and next 13 ingredients, stirring well. Cover and chill 1 hour. Divide shrimp mixture into 8 equal portions; shape each portion into a ½-inch-thick patty. Heat pan over medium-high heat. Coat pan with cooking spray. Add shrimp cakes to pan; cook 4 minutes on each side or until browned. Remove pan from heat; cover and let stand 5 minutes.

2. To prepare sauce, combine papaya and next 3 ingredients in a food processor; process until smooth.

3. Place 1 cup salad greens on each of 4 plates. Top each serving with 2 shrimp cakes; spoon about ¼ cup sauce over each serving, and sprinkle with ½ teaspoon toasted sesame seeds. Serve immediately. Yield: 4 servings.

CALORIES 256 (20% from fat); FAT 5.7g (sat 1.9g, mono 1.1g, poly 1.2g); PROTEIN 22.9g; CARB 28.5g; FIBER 3g; CHOL 182mg; IRON 3.4mg; SODIUM 402mg; CALC 101mg

Cajun Shrimp and Catfish

Look for light Alfredo sauce in plastic tubs in the refrigerated dairy section of your supermarket.

- 2 tablespoons low-fat buttermilk
- 1 tablespoon low-salt blackening seasoning
- 1½ pounds catfish fillets, cut into ½-inch strips
- Cooking spray
- 1 tablespoon butter
- 1 cup chopped green onions
- 1 cup presliced mushrooms
- ½ cup chopped fresh parsley
- 1 pound small shrimp, peeled and deveined
- ½ cup light Alfredo sauce (such as Contadina)
- 1 tablespoon fat-free, less-sodium chicken broth or fat-free milk
- 2 tablespoons grated fresh Parmesan cheese
- 5½ cups hot cooked long-grain rice
- Parsley sprigs (optional)

1. Preheat oven to 350°.

2. Place buttermilk and seasoning in a large bowl, stirring to blend. Add catfish; toss gently to coat.

3. Heat a large nonstick skillet over medium-high heat. Coat pan with cooking spray. Add catfish mixture; cook 3 minutes, stirring frequently. Place catfish mixture in a 2½-quart shallow casserole coated with cooking spray.

4. Melt butter in pan over medium-high heat. Add onions, mushrooms, and chopped parsley; sauté 3 minutes. Add shrimp; sauté 3 minutes. Spoon shrimp mixture over catfish. Combine Alfredo sauce and broth, stirring with a whisk. Drizzle over shrimp mixture; sprinkle with cheese. Bake at 350° for 20 minutes or until bubbly. Serve shrimp mixture over rice. Garnish with parsley sprigs, if desired. Yield: 8 servings (serving size: about ¾ cup shrimp mixture and about ⅔ cup rice).

CALORIES 382 (28% from fat); FAT 12g (sat 4.4g, mono 3.8g, poly 1.9g); PROTEIN 30.4g; CARB 35.7g; FIBER 1.1g; CHOL 139mg; IRON 3.7mg; SODIUM 511mg; CALC 110mg

Jambalaya with Shrimp and Andouille Sausage

- 1 tablespoon olive oil
- 1 cup chopped onion
- 1 cup chopped red bell pepper
- 1 tablespoon minced garlic
- 6 ounces andouille sausage, sliced
- 1 cup uncooked long-grain white rice
- 1 teaspoon paprika
- 1 teaspoon freshly ground black pepper
- 1 teaspoon dried oregano
- ½ teaspoon onion powder
- ½ teaspoon dried thyme
- ¼ teaspoon garlic salt
- 1 bay leaf
- 2 cups fat-free, less-sodium chicken broth
- ¾ cup water
- 1 tablespoon tomato paste
- ½ teaspoon hot pepper sauce
- 1 (14.5-ounce) can no-salt-added diced tomatoes, undrained
- ½ pound peeled and deveined medium shrimp
- 2 tablespoons chopped fresh parsley

1. Heat oil in a large Dutch oven over medium-high heat. Add chopped onion, bell pepper, garlic, and sausage; sauté 5 minutes or until vegetables are tender.

2. Add rice and next 7 ingredients; cook 2 minutes. Add broth, water, tomato paste, pepper sauce, and tomatoes, and bring to a boil. Cover, reduce heat, and simmer 20 minutes. Add shrimp; cook 5 minutes. Let stand 5 minutes. Discard bay leaf. Stir in parsley. Yield: 4 servings (serving size: 1½ cups).

CALORIES 426 (27% from fat); FAT 12.7g (sat 3.9g, mono 2.8g, poly 1g); PROTEIN 25g; CARB 52.7g; FIBER 4.9g; CHOL 117mg; IRON 5.1mg; SODIUM 763mg; CALC 99mg

Lasagna Rolls with Roasted Red Pepper Sauce, page 122

Meatless Main Dishes

Pain Perdu

Pain Perdu

Pain Perdu—literally "lost bread"—is a simple breakfast of day-old French bread dredged in beaten eggs and pan-fried in butter.

1½ cups fat-free milk
¾ cup egg substitute
¼ cup granulated sugar
½ teaspoon ground cinnamon
½ teaspoon ground nutmeg
1½ teaspoons vanilla extract
¼ teaspoon salt
16 (1-inch-thick) slices diagonally cut French bread baguette
¼ cup butter
2 cups water
½ cup dry white wine
¼ cup granulated sugar
1 tablespoon cornstarch
2 cups fresh raspberries
1 cup fresh blackberries
1 cup fresh blueberries
½ cup halved fresh strawberries
1 tablespoon powdered sugar

1. Combine first 7 ingredients, stirring well with a whisk. Arrange bread slices in a single layer in a large shallow dish. Pour milk mixture over bread slices, and let stand until milk is absorbed (about 2 minutes).

2. Melt 2 tablespoons butter in a large cast-iron skillet over medium heat. Arrange 8 bread slices in pan; cook 3 minutes on each side or until bread is golden brown. Remove from pan; keep warm. Repeat procedure with remaining 2 tablespoons butter and 8 bread slices.

3. Combine 2 cups water, wine, ¼ cup granulated sugar, and cornstarch in a large saucepan, stirring with a whisk. Bring to a boil; cook until reduced to 1 cup (about 5 minutes). Remove pan from heat. Add fruit to pan, stirring gently to coat. Serve sauce with bread slices. Sprinkle each serving with powdered sugar. Yield: 8 servings (serving size: 2 bread slices and about ½ cup sauce).

CALORIES 270 (26% from fat); FAT 7.8g (sat 4g, mono 2.3g, poly 1g); PROTEIN 7.6g; CARB 40.9g; FIBER 4.7g; CHOL 16mg; IRON 1.7mg; SODIUM 373mg; CALC 112mg

Coconut French Toast with Grilled Pineapple and Tropical Salsa

Easy to make, this rich dish is best prepared with day-old bread. You can serve the pineapple slices raw, but the deep, caramelized flavors you get from cooking them in a grill pan are worth the extra effort.

SALSA:
2 tablespoons flaked sweetened coconut
2 teaspoons fresh lime juice
2 cups chopped peeled ripe mangoes
1 pint strawberries, chopped

FRENCH TOAST:
1 cup egg substitute
1 cup light coconut milk
1 cup 1% low-fat milk
½ cup granulated sugar
½ teaspoon vanilla extract
¼ teaspoon salt
2 large eggs
1 (16-ounce) loaf French bread, cut into 16 slices
Cooking spray

REMAINING INGREDIENTS:
1 medium pineapple, peeled, cored, and cut crosswise into 8 slices
Powdered sugar (optional)

1. To prepare salsa, combine first 4 ingredients; cover and chill.

2. Preheat oven to 400°.

3. To prepare French toast, combine egg substitute and next 6 ingredients in a large bowl, stirring well with a whisk. Place bread in egg mixture; press down with spatula to completely submerge bread in egg mixture. Let bread mixture stand 15 minutes.

4. Arrange soaked bread in a single layer on a jelly-roll pan coated with cooking spray. Bake at 400° for 12 minutes or until set. Remove from oven, and keep warm.

5. While bread bakes, heat a grill pan over medium-high heat. Coat pan with cooking spray. Arrange 4 pineapple slices in pan; cook 4 minutes on each side or until pineapple begins to brown. Remove from pan; keep warm. Repeat procedure with remaining pineapple and cooking spray. Arrange 2 French toast pieces on each of 8 plates; top each serving with 1 pineapple slice and ½ cup salsa. Sprinkle with powdered sugar, if desired. Yield: 8 servings.

CALORIES 350 (15% from fat); FAT 5.7g (sat 2.3g, mono 1.4g, poly 0.8g); PROTEIN 11.4g; CARB 64.8g; FIBER 4.4g; CHOL 54mg; IRON 2.8mg; SODIUM 523mg; CALC 112mg

Frittata with Mushrooms, Linguine, and Basil

Break pasta in half before cooking so it's easier to stir into the egg mixture. Add a small salad of gourmet greens for color on the plate.

Cooking spray
3 cups sliced cremini or button mushrooms
1¼ cups thinly sliced leek (about 2 large)
½ cup 1% low-fat milk
2 teaspoons butter, melted
¾ teaspoon salt
⅛ teaspoon freshly ground black pepper
4 large egg whites
3 large eggs
2 cups hot cooked linguine (about 4 ounces uncooked pasta)
⅓ cup chopped fresh basil
½ cup (2 ounces) shredded part-skim mozzarella cheese

1. Preheat oven to 450°.
2. Heat a large nonstick skillet over medium heat. Coat pan with cooking spray. Add mushrooms and sliced leek; cook 6 minutes or until leek is tender, stirring frequently.
3. Combine milk and next 5 ingredients in a large bowl, stirring with a whisk. Add leek mixture, pasta, and basil; toss gently to combine.
4. Heat pan over medium-low heat. Coat pan with cooking spray. Add egg mixture; cook until edges begin to set (about 4 minutes). Gently lift edge of egg mixture, tilting pan to allow some uncooked mixture to come in contact with pan. Cook 5 minutes or until almost set. Sprinkle with cheese; wrap handle of pan with foil. Bake at 450° for 7 minutes or until golden brown. Cut into 8 wedges. Yield: 4 servings (serving size: 2 wedges).

CALORIES 269 (29% from fat); FAT 8.8g (sat 4.1g, mono 2.8g, poly 0.9g); PROTEIN 18.4g; CARB 28g; FIBER 2.8g; CHOL 174mg; IRON 2.6mg; SODIUM 661mg; CALC 177mg

Cheese Enchilada Casserole

Unlike most enchilada casseroles, in which the tortillas are rolled up, this dish layers them like lasagna noodles. It can be prepped and baked in less than 45 minutes.

1 cup (4 ounces) reduced-fat shredded extrasharp Cheddar cheese
1 cup chopped tomato
1 cup fat-free cottage cheese
⅓ cup sliced green onions
2 teaspoons chili powder
2 garlic cloves, minced
9 (6-inch) corn tortillas
Cooking spray
1 cup taco sauce
¼ cup (1 ounce) shredded Monterey Jack cheese
2 tablespoons chopped green onions

1. Preheat oven to 375°.
2. Combine first 6 ingredients. Arrange 3 tortillas in a 1½-quart baking dish coated with cooking spray. Spread half of cheese mixture over tortillas. Repeat procedure with 3 tortillas and remaining cheese mixture; top with remaining tortillas.
3. Pour taco sauce over tortillas; sprinkle with Monterey Jack cheese. Bake at 375° for 20 minutes or until cheese melts. Sprinkle with 2 tablespoons green onions. Yield: 4 servings (serving size: 1¼ cups).

CALORIES 299 (18% from fat); FAT 6g (sat 2.8g, mono 1.7g, poly 0.9g); PROTEIN 19.1g; CARB 42.3g; FIBER 4.3g; CHOL 15mg; IRON 1.4mg; SODIUM 1,029mg; CALC 332mg

Frittata with Mushrooms, Linguine, and Basil

Cheese Enchilada
Casserole

Huevos Rancheros with Queso Fresco

Queso fresco is a soft, crumbly, salty Mexican cheese. Look for it in cottage cheese-style tubs in the dairy section of large grocery stores and Hispanic markets. Substitute crumbled feta or goat cheese, if you prefer.

- 1 (10-ounce) can diced tomatoes and green chiles, undrained
- 1 (10-ounce) can red enchilada sauce
- ⅓ cup chopped fresh cilantro
- 1 tablespoon fresh lime juice
- 2 tablespoons water
- 1 (16-ounce) can pinto beans, rinsed and drained
- Cooking spray
- 4 large eggs
- 4 (8-inch) fat-free flour tortillas
- 1 cup (4 ounces) crumbled queso fresco

1. Combine tomatoes and enchilada sauce in a medium saucepan; bring to a boil. Reduce heat; simmer, uncovered, 5 minutes or until slightly thick. Remove from heat; stir in cilantro and juice, and set aside.

2. Place water and pinto beans in a microwave-safe bowl, and partially mash with a fork. Cover and microwave at HIGH 2 minutes or until hot.

3. Heat a large nonstick skillet over medium-high heat. Coat pan with cooking spray. Add eggs, and cook 1 minute on each side or until desired degree of doneness.

4. Warm tortillas according to package directions. Spread about ⅓ cup beans over each tortilla; top each tortilla with 1 egg. Spoon ½ cup sauce around each egg; sprinkle each serving with ¼ cup cheese. Yield: 4 servings (serving size: 1 topped tortilla).

CALORIES 340 (26% from fat); FAT 9.8g (sat 3.2g, mono 2.7g, poly 1g); PROTEIN 15.7g; CARB 37.8g; FIBER 6.1g; CHOL 222mg; IRON 2.1mg; SODIUM 970mg; CALC 153mg

Southwestern Bean Casserole

This Tex-Mex dish is perfect for a weeknight dinner with the family. Use medium-hot salsa to enhance the flavor.

1 teaspoon canola oil
Cooking spray
1 cup chopped onion
2 garlic cloves, minced
1 cup canned no-salt-added cream-style corn, divided
½ cup drained canned chopped green chiles, divided
½ cup bottled salsa
½ teaspoon salt
¼ teaspoon ground cumin
¼ teaspoon black pepper
2 (16-ounce) cans pinto beans, drained
1 (14.5-ounce) can no-salt-added stewed tomatoes, undrained
1 cup (4 ounces) reduced-fat shredded Cheddar cheese, divided
¾ cup yellow cornmeal
¼ cup all-purpose flour (about 1 ounce)
1 teaspoon sugar
¼ teaspoon salt
½ cup low-fat buttermilk
¼ cup canola oil
2 egg whites, lightly beaten

1. Preheat oven to 375°.
2. Heat 1 teaspoon oil in a large saucepan coated with cooking spray over medium-high heat. Add onion and garlic; sauté 3 minutes. Add ½ cup corn, ¼ cup chiles, salsa, and next 5 ingredients; bring to a boil. Reduce heat, and simmer 15 minutes. Pour mixture into a 13 x 9–inch baking dish coated with cooking spray. Sprinkle with ½ cup cheese; set aside.
3. Combine cornmeal, flour, sugar, and ¼ teaspoon salt in a medium bowl. Combine remaining ½ cup corn, remaining ¼ cup chiles, remaining ½ cup cheese, buttermilk, ¼ cup oil, and egg whites; add to cornmeal mixture, stirring just until moist. Spread corn bread batter evenly over bean mixture. Bake casserole at 375° for 25 minutes or until corn bread is lightly browned. Let stand 5 minutes. Yield: 7 servings (serving size: 1 cup).

CALORIES 376 (30% from fat); FAT 12.5g (sat 3.5g, mono 2.7g, poly 4.5g); PROTEIN 16.5g; CARB 51.3g; FIBER 5.2g; CHOL 11mg; IRON 3.6mg; SODIUM 680mg; CALC 225mg

Cuban Beans and Rice

Dry beans lend themselves well to slow cooking because unlike on the stove top, there is no risk of burning over the long simmering period. This meatless entrée reheats well the next day for lunch.

1 pound dried black beans
2 cups water
2 cups organic vegetable broth (such as Swanson Certified Organic)
2 cups chopped onion
1½ cups chopped red bell pepper
1 cup chopped green bell pepper
2 tablespoons olive oil
3 teaspoons salt
2 teaspoons fennel seeds, crushed
2 teaspoons ground coriander
2 teaspoons ground cumin
2 teaspoons dried oregano
2 tablespoons sherry or red wine vinegar
2 (10-ounce) cans diced tomatoes and green chiles, drained
5 cups hot cooked rice
Hot sauce (optional)

1. Sort and wash beans; place in a large bowl. Cover with water to 2 inches above beans; cover and let stand 8 hours. Drain beans.
2. Combine beans, 2 cups water, and next 10 ingredients in an electric slow cooker. Cover and cook on HIGH 5 hours or until beans are tender. Stir in vinegar and tomatoes. Serve over rice. Sprinkle with hot sauce, if desired. Yield: 10 servings (servings size: 1 cup bean mixture and ½ cup rice).

CALORIES 314 (9% from fat); FAT 3.3g (sat 0.4g, mono 2g, poly 0.5g); PROTEIN 12.1g; CARB 58.3g; FIBER 6g; CHOL 0mg; IRON 3.7mg; SODIUM 816mg; CALC 24mg

Bell Pepper-and-Potato Tagine over Couscous

Harissa is a fiery-hot condiment available in Middle Eastern markets.

2 teaspoons olive oil
1¾ cups diced onion
2 tablespoons tomato paste
1 tablespoon chopped fresh mint
½ teaspoon crushed red pepper
6 garlic cloves, crushed
2 baking potatoes, peeled and each cut into 6 wedges (about 1 pound)
2 cups (1-inch) red bell pepper strips
2 cups (1-inch) green bell pepper strips
1 teaspoon salt
1 (15½-ounce) can chickpeas, drained
3 cups chopped seeded tomato
3 cups water
1 teaspoon harissa (optional)
¾ cup uncooked couscous
3 tablespoons chopped fresh parsley

1. Heat oil in a Dutch oven over medium-high heat. Add onion and next 5 ingredients; cook 10 minutes, stirring occasionally. Add peppers, salt, and chickpeas; sauté 5 minutes. Stir in tomato and water. Bring to a boil; partially cover, reduce heat, and simmer 25 minutes or until potatoes are tender. Remove vegetables with a slotted spoon; set aside. Reserve 1 cup cooking liquid.

2. Bring reserved cooking liquid to a boil in a medium saucepan; stir in harissa, if desired. Gradually stir in couscous. Remove from heat; cover and let stand 5 minutes. Fluff with a fork. Serve with vegetables; sprinkle with chopped parsley. Yield: 5 servings (serving size: about 1⅓ cups tagine and ½ cup couscous).

CALORIES 382 (11% from fat); FAT 4.6g (sat 0.7g, mono 1.9g, poly 1.5g); PROTEIN 13.6g; CARB 74.3g; FIBER 9g; CHOL 0mg; IRON 4.5mg; SODIUM 596mg; CALC 77mg

Spicy Yellow Soybean, Lentil, and Carrot Curry

A dollop of cool yogurt balances the heat and spiciness from the curry paste, red pepper, and cilantro.

1 tablespoon olive oil
2⅓ cups finely chopped onion
1 tablespoon red curry paste
4 cups vegetable broth, divided
2 cups finely chopped carrot
2 tablespoons minced peeled fresh ginger
⅛ teaspoon ground red pepper
3 garlic cloves, minced
1 cup dried small red lentils
1 (15-ounce) can yellow soybeans, rinsed and drained
⅓ cup minced fresh cilantro
¼ teaspoon salt
¼ teaspoon freshly ground black pepper
6 tablespoons plain fat-free yogurt
Fresh cilantro sprigs (optional)

1. Heat oil in a large saucepan over medium-high heat. Add onion; sauté 3 minutes or until tender. Stir in curry paste; cook 1 minute. Add ½ cup broth, carrot, ginger, red pepper, and garlic; cook 6 minutes or until carrot is tender, stirring occasionally. Add 3½ cups broth, lentils, and soybeans; bring to a boil. Reduce heat; simmer 10 minutes or until lentils are tender. Stir in cilantro, salt, and black pepper. Divide evenly among 6 shallow bowls; dollop with yogurt. Garnish with cilantro sprigs, if desired. Yield: 6 servings (serving size: 1 cup curry and 1 tablespoon yogurt).

CALORIES 314 (28% from fat); FAT 9.7g (sat 1.3g, mono 3.2g, poly 3.9g); PROTEIN 22.8g; CARB 39.5g; FIBER 11.8g; CHOL 0mg; IRON 6.2mg; SODIUM 937mg; CALC 163mg

Spicy Yellow Soybean, Lentil, and Carrot Curry

Spaghetti Squash with Edamame-Cilantro Pesto

Spaghetti Squash with Edamame-Cilantro Pesto

- 2 (2½-pound) spaghetti squashes
- Cooking spray
- ½ teaspoon salt, divided
- 1¼ cups chopped fresh cilantro
- 1 cup vegetable broth
- 1 tablespoon extravirgin olive oil
- ¼ teaspoon freshly ground black pepper
- 2 garlic cloves, minced
- 1 pound frozen shelled edamame (green soybeans), thawed
- ¼ cup (1 ounce) grated fresh Parmesan cheese

1. Preheat oven to 350°.
2. Cut each squash in half lengthwise; discard seeds. Place squash halves, cut sides down, on a baking sheet coated with cooking spray. Bake at 350° for 1 hour or until tender. Cool slightly. Scrape inside of squash with a fork to remove spaghetti-like strands to measure about 8 cups. Place in a large bowl. Sprinkle with ¼ teaspoon salt; toss gently to combine. Cover and keep warm.
3. Place cilantro, broth, oil, pepper, remaining ¼ teaspoon salt, garlic, and edamame in a food processor; pulse until coarsely chopped. Serve edamame pesto over squash; sprinkle with cheese. Yield: 6 servings (serving size: 1½ cups squash, ½ cup edamame pesto, and 2 teaspoons cheese).

CALORIES 233 (29% from fat); FAT 7.6g (sat 1.3g, mono 2.8g, poly 2.4g); PROTEIN 12.5g; CARB 31.3g; FIBER 8.8g; CHOL 3mg; IRON 3mg; SODIUM 533mg; CALC 182mg

Vegetarian Stuffed Peppers

- 6 medium red bell peppers
- 1 teaspoon olive oil
- ¾ cup finely chopped shallots
- 4 cups chopped mushrooms
- 1 cup chopped fresh parsley
- ¼ cup slivered almonds, toasted
- 3 tablespoons dry sherry
- 1½ teaspoons ancho chile powder
- 2½ cups cooked brown rice
- 1 cup tomato juice
- ½ teaspoon freshly ground black pepper
- ½ teaspoon garlic powder
- ¼ teaspoon salt
- 6 tablespoons (1½ ounces) grated fresh Parmesan cheese

1. Preheat oven to 350°.
2. Cut tops off bell peppers; discard seeds and membranes. Cook peppers in boiling water 5 minutes; drain.
3. Heat oil in a large nonstick skillet over medium-high heat. Add shallots; sauté 3 minutes or until tender. Add mushrooms, and sauté 4 minutes or until tender. Add parsley, almonds, sherry, and chile powder; sauté 3 minutes. Add rice, juice, black pepper, garlic powder, and salt; sauté 3 minutes. Spoon ¾ cup rice mixture into each bell pepper; top each with 1 tablespoon cheese. Place peppers in a 13 x 9–inch baking dish; bake at 350° for 15 minutes. Yield: 6 servings (serving size: 1 stuffed pepper).

CALORIES 223 (25% from fat); FAT 6.3g (sat 1.5g, mono 2.3g, poly 1.2g); PROTEIN 9.5g; CARB 35.1g; FIBER 5.5g; CHOL 5mg; IRON 2.4mg; SODIUM 336mg; CALC 155mg

Portobello Mushroom Fajitas

Portobello mushrooms and red onions make a meaty fajita filling with satisfying, pungent flavors.

- 1 tablespoon olive oil
- 4 cups (½-inch-thick) slices portobello mushrooms (about 8 ounces)
- 1 cup vertically sliced red onion
- 1 cup (¼-inch-thick) green bell pepper strips
- 2 garlic cloves, minced
- 3 tablespoons chopped fresh cilantro
- 1 tablespoon fresh lime juice
- ¼ teaspoon salt
- ¼ teaspoon freshly ground black pepper
- 1 serrano chile, minced
- 12 (6-inch) flour tortillas
- 1 cup (4 ounces) crumbled queso fresco
- ¾ cup salsa verde

1. Heat oil in a large nonstick skillet over medium-high heat. Add mushrooms; sauté 5 minutes. Add onion, bell pepper, and garlic. Reduce heat to medium, and cook 4 minutes or until bell pepper is crisp-tender, stirring frequently. Remove from heat; stir in cilantro and next 4 ingredients.
2. Warm tortillas according to package directions. Spoon about ¼ cup of mushroom mixture down center of each tortilla; top each tortilla with 4 teaspoons cheese and 1 tablespoon salsa. Roll up. Yield: 4 servings (serving size: 3 fajitas).

CALORIES 437 (26% from fat); FAT 12.7g (sat 3.6g, mono 6.8g, poly 1.5g); PROTEIN 13.8g; CARB 65.9g; FIBER 4.9g; CHOL 9mg; IRON 3.9mg; SODIUM 792mg; CALC 219mg

Zucchini, Olive, and Cheese Quesadillas

If you want a change of pace from the usual bean, cheese, and salsa quesadillas, this recipe is for you. Just add a mixed greens salad to round out your meal.

- 1 teaspoon olive oil
- Cooking spray
- 1/3 cup finely chopped onion
- 1/2 teaspoon bottled minced garlic
- 1 1/4 cups shredded zucchini
- 1/4 teaspoon dried oregano
- 1/8 teaspoon salt
- 1/8 teaspoon black pepper
- 4 (8-inch) fat-free flour tortillas
- 1/2 cup (2 ounces) preshredded part-skim mozzarella cheese
- 1/2 cup diced tomato
- 1/4 cup chopped pitted kalamata olives, divided
- 1/4 cup (1 ounce) crumbled feta cheese, divided

1. Heat oil in a large nonstick skillet coated with cooking spray over medium-high heat. Add onion and garlic; sauté 1 minute. Add zucchini; sauté 2 minutes or until lightly browned. Remove from heat; stir in oregano, salt, and pepper.

2. Wipe pan clean with paper towels, and coat with cooking spray. Heat pan over medium heat. Add 1 tortilla to pan, and sprinkle with 1/4 cup mozzarella. Top with half of zucchini mixture, 1/4 cup tomato, 2 tablespoons olives, 2 tablespoons feta, and 1 tortilla. Cook 3 minutes or until lightly browned on bottom. Carefully turn quesadilla; cook 2 minutes or until lightly browned. Place quesadilla on a cutting board; cut in half using a serrated knife. Repeat procedure with remaining tortillas, mozzarella, zucchini mixture, tomato, olives, and feta. Serve warm. Yield: 2 servings.

CALORIES 447 (32% from fat); FAT 15.8g (sat 6.6g, mono 7.4g, poly 1.1g); PROTEIN 17.4g; CARB 58.7g; FIBER 4g; CHOL 33mg; IRON 3.1mg; SODIUM 1,466mg; CALC 307mg

Lasagna Rolls with Roasted Red Pepper Sauce

(pictured on page 110)

These rolls require some assembly time but are a nice change of pace from layered pasta. They also make a pretty presentation on a plate.

LASAGNA:

- 8 uncooked lasagna noodles
- 4 teaspoons olive oil
- 1/2 cup finely chopped onion
- 1 (8-ounce) package presliced mushrooms
- 1 (6-ounce) package baby spinach
- 3 garlic cloves, minced
- 1/2 cup (2 ounces) shredded mozzarella cheese
- 1/2 cup part-skim ricotta cheese
- 1/4 cup minced fresh basil, divided
- 1/2 teaspoon salt
- 1/4 teaspoon crushed red pepper

SAUCE:

- 1 tablespoon red wine vinegar
- 1/4 teaspoon salt
- 1/8 teaspoon black pepper
- 2 garlic cloves, minced
- 1 (14.5-ounce) can diced tomatoes
- 1 (7-ounce) bottle roasted red bell peppers, undrained
- 1/8 teaspoon crushed red pepper

1. To prepare lasagna, cook noodles according to package directions, omitting salt and fat. Drain and rinse noodles under cold water. Drain.

2. Heat oil in a large nonstick skillet over medium-high heat. Add onion, mushrooms, spinach, and 3 garlic cloves; sauté 5 minutes or until onion and mushrooms are tender. Remove from heat; stir in cheeses, 2 tablespoons basil, 1/2 teaspoon salt, and 1/4 teaspoon crushed red pepper.

3. To prepare sauce, place vinegar and next 6 ingredients in a blender; process until smooth.

4. Place cooked noodles on a flat surface; spread 1/4 cup cheese mixture over each noodle. Roll up noodles, jelly-roll fashion, starting with short side. Place rolls, seam sides down, in a shallow 2-quart microwave-safe dish. Pour 1/4 cup sauce over each roll, and cover with heavy-duty plastic wrap. Microwave at HIGH 5 minutes or until thoroughly heated. Sprinkle with remaining 2 tablespoons basil. Yield: 4 servings (serving size: 2 rolls).

CALORIES 393 (27% from fat); FAT 11.7g (sat 4.3g, mono 3.6g, poly 1.5g); PROTEIN 19.3g; CARB 58.3g; FIBER 5.9g; CHOL 20mg; IRON 3.8mg; SODIUM 924mg; CALC 253mg

Penne with Tomatoes, Olives, and Capers

Penne with Tomatoes, Olives, and Capers

This simple dish depends on fresh basil, garlic, and tomatoes to deliver big flavor. You can use almost any small pasta, such as macaroni, farfalle, rotelle, or tubetti.

- 1 tablespoon olive oil
- ¼ teaspoon crushed red pepper
- 3 garlic cloves, finely chopped
- 3 cups chopped plum tomato (about 1¾ pounds)
- ½ cup chopped pitted kalamata olives
- 1½ tablespoons capers
- ¼ teaspoon salt
- 6 cups hot cooked penne (about 4 cups uncooked tube-shaped pasta)
- ¾ cup (3 ounces) grated fresh Parmesan cheese
- 3 tablespoons chopped fresh basil

1. Heat olive oil in a large nonstick skillet over medium-high heat. Add red pepper and chopped garlic, and sauté 30 seconds. Add tomato, olives, capers, and salt. Reduce heat, and simmer 8 minutes, stirring occasionally. Add pasta to pan, tossing gently to coat; cook 1 minute or until thoroughly heated. Remove from heat.

2. Spoon pasta mixture in a large bowl; top with cheese and basil, tossing gently. Yield: 4 servings (serving size: about 1¾ cups).

CALORIES 484 (28% from fat); FAT 15.1g (sat 4.7g, mono 7.7g, poly 1.7g); PROTEIN 19.1g; CARB 67.8g; FIBER 4.3g; CHOL 14mg; IRON 3.9mg; SODIUM 870mg; CALC 287mg

Triple Mushroom Pizza with Truffle Oil

Triple Mushroom Pizza with Truffle Oil

Truffle oil takes this pizza from fine to sublime. In a pinch, you can substitute extravirgin olive oil for the truffle oil.

- 1 teaspoon sugar
- 1 package quick-rise yeast (about 2¼ teaspoons)
- ½ cup warm water (100° to 110°)
- 1½ cups all-purpose flour (about 6¾ ounces), divided
- ½ teaspoon salt, divided
- Cooking spray
- 2 teaspoons cornmeal
- 2 teaspoons olive oil
- 2 cups thinly sliced shiitake mushroom caps (about 4 ounces)
- 2 cups sliced cremini mushrooms (about 4 ounces)
- 1½ cups (¼-inch-thick) slices portobello mushrooms (about 4 ounces)
- ⅔ cup (about 2½ ounces) shredded sharp fontina cheese, divided
- 2 teaspoons chopped fresh thyme
- ½ teaspoon truffle oil
- ¼ cup (1 ounce) grated fresh Parmesan cheese
- ¼ teaspoon sea salt

1. Dissolve sugar and yeast in warm water in a large bowl; let stand 5 minutes. Lightly spoon flour into dry measuring cups; level with a knife. Add 1¼ cups flour and ¼ teaspoon salt to yeast mixture; stir until a soft dough forms. Turn dough out onto a lightly floured surface. Knead until smooth and elastic (about 10 minutes); add enough of remaining flour, 1 tablespoon at a time, to prevent dough from sticking to hands (dough will feel tacky).

2. Place dough in a large bowl coated with cooking spray, turning to coat top. Cover and let rise in a warm place (85°), free from drafts, 30 minutes or until doubled in size. (Gently press two fingers into dough. If indentation remains, dough has risen enough.) Punch dough down; cover and let stand 5 minutes. Line a baking sheet with parchment paper; sprinkle with cornmeal. Roll dough into a 12-inch circle on a floured surface. Place dough on prepared baking sheet. Crimp edges of dough with fingers to form a rim; let rise 10 minutes.

3. Preheat oven to 475°.

4. While dough rises, heat 2 teaspoons olive oil in a large nonstick skillet over medium heat. Add ¼ teaspoon salt and mushrooms; cook 7 minutes or until mushrooms soften and moisture almost evaporates, stirring frequently.

5. Sprinkle ¼ cup fontina cheese evenly over dough, and arrange mushroom mixture evenly over fontina. Sprinkle with 2 teaspoons thyme, and drizzle dough evenly with ½ teaspoon truffle oil. Sprinkle remaining fontina and Parmesan cheese evenly over top. Bake at 475° for 15 minutes or until crust is lightly browned. Remove to cutting board, and sprinkle with ¼ teaspoon sea salt. Cut into 8 slices. Serve immediately. Yield: 4 servings (serving size: 2 slices).

CALORIES 331 (29% from fat); FAT 10.6g (sat 4.9g, mono 4.2g, poly 0.8g); PROTEIN 14.8g; CARB 42.8g; FIBER 3.1g; CHOL 25mg; IRON 3.5mg; SODIUM 693mg; CALC 180mg

Potato Gnocchi with Spinach and Yellow Squash

Look for gnocchi (Italian dumplings) in the dry pasta section of your supermarket.

- 1 (1-pound) package vacuum-packed potato gnocchi (such as Ferrara)
- 1 tablespoon olive oil
- 1 yellow squash, quartered lengthwise and thinly sliced
- 1½ teaspoons bottled minced garlic
- 1 (10-ounce) package fresh spinach, torn
- ¼ cup fat-free milk
- ¼ teaspoon freshly ground black pepper
- ⅛ teaspoon salt
- ½ cup (2 ounces) shredded smoked Gouda cheese or grated sharp provolone cheese

1. Cook gnocchi in boiling water according to package directions.

2. While gnocchi cooks, heat oil in a large skillet over medium heat. Add squash; sauté 4 minutes or until crisp-tender. Add garlic; sauté 1 minute. Add spinach, and cover and cook 2 minutes or just until spinach wilts. Reduce heat to low; stir in milk, pepper, and salt. Add gnocchi and cheese; stir gently. Serve immediately. Yield: 4 servings (serving size: 1 cup).

CALORIES 234 (29% from fat); FAT 7.7g (sat 3g, mono 3.6g, poly 0.5g); PROTEIN 10.8g; CARB 44.5g; FIBER 5.7g; CHOL 16mg; IRON 3.7mg; SODIUM 655mg; CALC 203mg

Roasted Fresh Corn, Poblano, and Cheddar Pizza

Refrigerated dough tends to shrink when removed from the can. Be sure to let the dough rest a few minutes before you start to work with it so it will be more pliable.

- 2 poblano chiles
- Cooking spray
- 2 cups fresh corn kernels (about 4 ears)
- ½ cup chopped green onions
- 1 garlic clove, minced
- ½ cup 1% low-fat milk
- 2 large egg whites
- 1 large egg
- ½ teaspoon salt
- ¼ teaspoon freshly ground black pepper
- 1 cup (4 ounces) shredded sharp Cheddar cheese
- 1 (13.8-ounce) can refrigerated pizza crust dough
- 2 tablespoons fat-free sour cream
- 2 tablespoons chopped fresh cilantro

1. Preheat broiler.
2. Place poblano chiles on a foil-lined baking sheet; broil 10 minutes or until blackened and charred, turning occasionally. Place in a zip-top plastic bag; seal. Let chiles stand 10 minutes. Peel and discard skins, seeds, and stems. Chop chiles.
3. Lower oven temperature to 425°.
4. Heat a large nonstick skillet over medium-high heat. Coat pan with cooking spray. Add corn, green onions, and garlic; sauté 2 minutes or until lightly browned. Stir in milk; cook over medium heat 2 minutes or until liquid almost evaporates. Cool slightly. Place egg whites, egg, salt, and black pepper in a bowl; stir with a whisk. Stir in poblano chiles, corn mixture, and cheese.
5. Line a baking sheet with parchment paper. Unroll dough onto parchment paper; pat dough to form a 13 x 8–inch rectangle. Spread corn mixture over dough, leaving a 1-inch border. Fold 1 inch of dough over corn mixture. Bake at 425° for 12 minutes or until set. Serve with sour cream; sprinkle with cilantro. Yield: 6 servings (serving size: 1 piece, 1 teaspoon sour cream, and 1 teaspoon cilantro).

CALORIES 331 (28% from fat); FAT 10.3g (sat 4.4g, mono 2.2g, poly 0.3g); PROTEIN 15.8g; CARB 44.5g; FIBER 1.6g; CHOL 57mg; IRON 2.5mg; SODIUM 808mg; CALC 186mg

Grilled Salad Pizza

- 1 package dry yeast (about 2¼ teaspoons)
- ⅔ cup warm water (100° to 110°)
- 3½ teaspoons olive oil, divided
- 1⅔ cups all-purpose flour (about 7½ ounces)
- 1 teaspoon sugar
- ½ teaspoon salt
- ½ teaspoon dried oregano
- ¼ teaspoon dried thyme
- Cooking spray
- ½ cup (2 ounces) shredded part-skim mozzarella cheese
- ¼ cup (1 ounce) grated fresh Parmesan cheese
- 2½ cups coarsely chopped trimmed arugula (about 4 ounces)
- 1½ cups chopped seeded tomato
- ¼ cup chopped fresh basil
- 2 teaspoons balsamic vinegar
- 1½ teaspoons Dijon mustard
- 1 (14-ounce) can artichoke hearts, drained and chopped

1. Dissolve yeast in ⅔ cup warm water in a large bowl, and let stand 5 minutes. Stir in 1½ teaspoons oil. Lightly spoon flour into dry measuring cups; level with a knife. Combine flour, sugar, salt, oregano, and thyme. Add to yeast mixture; stir well. Turn dough out onto a lightly floured surface. Knead until smooth and elastic (about 10 minutes).
2. Place dough in a large bowl coated with cooking spray, turning to coat top. Cover and let rise in a warm place (85°), free from drafts, 45 minutes or until doubled in size. (Press two fingers into dough. If indentation remains, dough has risen enough.) Punch dough down; cover and let rest 5 minutes. Divide in half. Roll each half into a 9-inch circle on a floured surface.
3. Heat a grill pan over medium heat. Coat pan with cooking spray. Place one dough portion on pan; cook 10 minutes. Turn dough over; sprinkle with ¼ cup mozzarella and 2 tablespoons Parmesan. Cook 10 minutes; remove from pan. Repeat procedure with remaining dough and cheeses.
4. Combine 2 teaspoons oil, arugula, and next 5 ingredients in a medium bowl. Spoon 2 cups salad onto each pizza crust using a slotted spoon. Cut each pizza into 4 wedges. Serve immediately. Yield: 4 servings (serving size: ½ pizza).

CALORIES 357 (25% from fat); FAT 9.8g (sat 3.3g, mono 4.4g, poly 1.1g); PROTEIN 15.5g; CARB 53.5g; FIBER 3.8g; CHOL 13mg; IRON 4.2mg; SODIUM 572mg; CALC 269mg

Grilled Salad Pizza

Tofu Fried Rice

Using frozen peas and carrots, plus bottled minced garlic and ginger, is an easy way to speed up the preparation of this simple Chinese standby. You can keep any leftover sake tightly capped in the refrigerator for up to three weeks, or substitute one tablespoon of rice wine vinegar for the sake.

- 2 cups uncooked instant rice
- 2 tablespoons vegetable oil, divided
- 1 (14-ounce) package reduced-fat firm tofu, drained and cut into (½-inch) cubes
- 2 large eggs, lightly beaten
- 1 cup (½-inch-thick) slices green onions
- 1 cup frozen peas and carrots, thawed
- 2 teaspoons bottled minced garlic
- 1 teaspoon bottled minced fresh ginger
- 2 tablespoons sake (rice wine)
- 3 tablespoons low-sodium soy sauce
- 1 tablespoon hoisin sauce
- ½ teaspoon dark sesame oil
- Thinly sliced green onions (optional)

1. Cook rice according to package directions, omitting salt and fat.

2. While rice cooks, heat 1 tablespoon vegetable oil in a large nonstick skillet over medium-high heat. Add tofu; cook 4 minutes or until lightly browned, stirring occasionally. Remove from pan. Add eggs to pan; cook 1 minute or until done, breaking egg into small pieces. Remove from pan. Add 1 tablespoon vegetable oil to pan. Add 1 cup onions, peas and carrots, garlic, and ginger; sauté 2 minutes.

3. While vegetable mixture cooks, combine sake, soy sauce, hoisin sauce, and sesame oil. Add cooked rice to pan; cook 2 minutes, stirring constantly. Add tofu, egg, and soy sauce mixture; cook 30 seconds, stirring constantly. Garnish with sliced green onions, if desired. Yield: 4 servings (serving size: 1½ cups).

CALORIES 376 (26% from fat); FAT 11g (sat 2g, mono 3g, poly 5.1g); PROTEIN 15.8g; CARB 50.6g; FIBER 3.2g; CHOL 106mg; IRON 3.8mg; SODIUM 629mg; CALC 79mg

Kung Pao Tofu Rice

To save on cleanup, microwave the rice first and use the same container for combining the remaining ingredients. Packaged grilled tofu can be found in most supermarkets in the refrigerated case along with the other soy and organic products.

- 1 cup water
- ½ cup instant brown rice
- ½ cup shredded carrot
- ½ cup thinly sliced bok choy
- ¼ cup chopped green onions
- 2 tablespoons chopped fresh cilantro
- 3 ounces packaged grilled tofu, cut into ½-inch cubes (such as Marjon, about ½ cup)
- 1 tablespoon rice vinegar
- 1½ tablespoons creamy peanut butter
- 2 teaspoons water
- 2 teaspoons low-sodium soy sauce
- ½ teaspoon chili garlic sauce (such as Lee Kum Kee)
- ⅛ teaspoon salt

1. Combine 1 cup water and brown rice in a medium microwave-safe bowl; cover. Microwave at HIGH 4 minutes. Microwave at MEDIUM 5 minutes. Fluff with a fork. Let cool to room temperature. Add carrot and next 4 ingredients; toss gently to combine.

2. Combine vinegar and next 5 ingredients, stirring with a whisk. Add to rice mixture; toss gently to combine. Yield: 2 servings (serving size: about 1 cup).

CALORIES 217 (37% from fat); FAT 9g (sat 1.5g, mono 2.3g, poly 2.8g); PROTEIN 10g; CARB 25.7g; FIBER 3.4g; CHOL 0mg; IRON 1.2mg; SODIUM 471mg; CALC 48mg

Thai Summer Squash and Tofu with Fresh Corn

This dish is rich and soupy; the basmati rice makes a flavorful base. Fresh corn adds a natural sweetness.

- 1 teaspoon canola oil
- 1 cup diced yellow squash
- 1 cup diced zucchini
- 1 (12.3-ounce) package reduced-fat extra-firm tofu, drained and cut into ½-inch cubes
- ½ teaspoon salt, divided
- 3 cups fresh corn kernels (about 6 ears)
- 1 cup light coconut milk
- ¾ cup (½-inch) sliced green onions
- ⅓ cup water
- 1 tablespoon chopped fresh basil
- 1 tablespoon chopped fresh cilantro
- 1 teaspoon low-sodium soy sauce
- ¼ teaspoon freshly ground black pepper
- 1 jalapeño pepper, seeded and chopped
- 2 cups hot cooked basmati rice
- 2 tablespoons chopped unsalted cashews, toasted

1. Heat oil in a large nonstick skillet over medium-high heat. Add squash, zucchini, and tofu; sprinkle with ¼ teaspoon salt. Stir-fry 8 minutes or until lightly browned. Stir in remaining ¼ teaspoon salt, corn, and next 8 ingredients. Reduce heat, and simmer 8 minutes or until corn is tender. Serve with rice. Sprinkle with cashews. Yield: 4 servings (serving size: 1¼ cups vegetables, ½ cup rice, and 1½ teaspoons nuts).

CALORIES 283 (28% from fat); FAT 8.7g (sat 3g, mono 2.4g, poly 2.1g); PROTEIN 12.9g; CARB 43.4g; FIBER 5.5g; CHOL 0mg; IRON 3.1mg; SODIUM 462mg; CALC 78mg

Curried Noodles with Tofu

Coconut milk gives this meatless dish a velvety richness. Look for green curry paste in the Asian foods section of your supermarket. Use it conservatively, though—a little goes a long way.

- 6 ounces uncooked rice sticks (rice-flour noodles), angel hair pasta, or vermicelli
- 1 cup light coconut milk
- 1 tablespoon sugar
- 2 tablespoons low-sodium soy sauce
- 1½ tablespoons grated peeled fresh ginger
- 1 teaspoon green curry paste
- ½ teaspoon salt
- 4 garlic cloves, minced
- Cooking spray
- 1 (12.3-ounce) package extra-firm tofu, drained and cut into 1-inch cubes
- 1 cup red bell pepper strips
- 4 cups shredded napa (Chinese) cabbage
- 1 cup chopped green onions
- 3 tablespoons chopped fresh cilantro

1. Place noodles in a large bowl. Add hot water to cover; let stand 5 minutes. Drain.
2. Combine light coconut milk, sugar, soy sauce, fresh ginger, green curry paste, salt, and minced garlic in a small bowl.
3. Heat a large nonstick skillet over medium-high heat. Coat pan with cooking spray. Add tofu; sauté 10 minutes or until golden brown. Remove tofu from pan; keep warm.
4. Add bell pepper to pan; sauté 1 minute or until crisp-tender. Add cabbage; sauté 30 seconds. Stir in noodles, coconut milk mixture, and tofu; cook 2 minutes or until noodles are tender. Stir in onions and fresh cilantro. Yield: 4 servings (serving size: 1¼ cups).

CALORIES 300 (15% from fat); FAT 4.9g (sat 2.3g, mono 0.4g, poly 1.1g); PROTEIN 11.5g; CARB 51.4g; FIBER 4.5g; CHOL 0mg; IRON 3.6mg; SODIUM 678mg; CALC 89mg

Rice Noodles with Tofu and Bok Choy

Look for water-packed tofu, which will hold its shape when cooked and tossed with the rice noodles. If rice noodles are unavailable, substitute angel hair pasta.

- 1 (6-ounce) package rice noodles
- ¼ cup low-sodium soy sauce
- 2 tablespoons rice vinegar
- 1 teaspoon sugar
- 1 teaspoon dark sesame oil
- ½ teaspoon crushed red pepper
- Cooking spray
- 2 cups (¼-inch-thick) red bell pepper strips
- 5 cups sliced bok choy
- ½ pound firm water-packed tofu, drained and cut into ½-inch cubes
- 3 garlic cloves, minced
- ½ cup thinly sliced green onions
- 3 tablespoons chopped fresh cilantro

1. Cook noodles in boiling water 6 minutes; drain. Combine soy sauce, vinegar, sugar, oil, and crushed red pepper, stirring well with a whisk.
2. Heat a large nonstick skillet over medium-high heat. Coat pan with cooking spray. Add bell pepper strips; sauté 2 minutes. Add bok choy; sauté 1 minute. Add tofu and garlic; sauté 2 minutes. Add noodles and soy sauce mixture; cook 2 minutes or until thoroughly heated, tossing well to coat. Sprinkle with onions and cilantro. Yield: 4 servings (serving size: 2 cups).

CALORIES 281 (17% from fat); FAT 5.2g (sat 0.8g, mono 0.9g, poly 2.3g); PROTEIN 12.9g; CARB 46.7g; FIBER 4.2g; CHOL 0mg; IRON 3.8mg; SODIUM 575mg; CALC 190mg

Rice Noodles with Tofu and Bok Choy

Vegetarian Meat Loaf

Using heart-healthy meatless ground beef and fat-free crumbles instead of ground round saves about 10 grams of fat per serving and adds almost five grams of fiber. Serve with mashed potatoes and sautéed green beans for a hearty dinner.

- 1 cup chopped celery
- 1 cup sliced carrots
- 1 medium onion, peeled and quartered
- 3 garlic cloves, minced
- 1 tablespoon canola oil
- ¾ cup ketchup, divided
- ⅓ cup dry breadcrumbs
- 2 large eggs
- 1 (12-ounce) package meatless ground burger (such as Boca)
- 1 (12-ounce) package meatless fat-free crumbles (such as Lightlife Smart Ground)

Cooking spray

1. Preheat oven to 350°.
2. Combine first 4 ingredients in a food processor; process until finely chopped.
3. Heat oil in a large nonstick skillet over medium-high heat. Add onion mixture; sauté 5 minutes or until tender. Place onion mixture, ½ cup ketchup, breadcrumbs, eggs, ground burger, and crumbles in a large bowl; mix well.
4. Place mixture in a 9 x 5–inch loaf pan coated with cooking spray. Spread remaining ¼ cup ketchup over loaf. Bake at 350° for 35 minutes. Let stand 10 minutes. Cut loaf into 8 slices. Yield: 8 servings.

CALORIES 197 (16% from fat); FAT 3.7g (sat 0.7g, mono 1g, poly 1.3g); PROTEIN 20.5g; CARB 22.3g; FIBER 5.9g; CHOL 53mg; IRON 3mg; SODIUM 667mg; CALC 41mg

Vegetarian Chicken-Green Chile Enchilada Casserole

This meatless version of a family favorite uses soy-based chicken strips and has the heartiness and flavor of its classic counterpart. Meatless alternatives are low in saturated fat and cholesterol and are often high in fiber. Incorporating them in recipes is a great way to get the heart-health benefits of soy.

1 teaspoon vegetable oil
1 cup chopped onion
3 garlic cloves, minced
1 (4.5-ounce) can chopped green chiles, undrained
2 (6-ounce) packages meatless fat-free chicken strips (such as Lightlife Smart Menu), chopped
½ teaspoon ground cumin
½ teaspoon chili powder
2 (10-ounce) cans green chile enchilada sauce
Cooking spray
14 (6-inch) corn tortillas, cut into quarters
1½ cups (6 ounces) preshredded reduced-fat Mexican blend cheese, divided
Chopped fresh cilantro (optional)

1. Preheat oven to 375°.
2. Heat oil in a large nonstick skillet over medium-high heat. Add onion and garlic; sauté 5 minutes or until onion is tender. Add chiles; cook 3 minutes, stirring constantly. Remove from heat; stir in chopped chicken strips.
3. Combine ½ teaspoon cumin, ½ teaspoon chili powder, and enchilada sauce. Pour one-third of sauce mixture into an 11 x 7–inch baking dish coated with cooking spray. Arrange half of tortilla quarters over sauce mixture; top with onion mixture. Sprinkle with ¾ cup Mexican blend cheese; top with one-third of sauce mixture. Top with remaining tortillas and sauce mixture. Bake at 375° for 15 minutes. Sprinkle with remaining ¾ cup cheese; bake an additional 10 minutes. Sprinkle with cilantro, if desired. Yield: 8 servings.

CALORIES 218 (29% from fat); FAT 7.3g (sat 2.3g, mono 1.4g, poly 1g); PROTEIN 17.8g; CARB 22.9g; FIBER 5.5g; CHOL 15 mg; IRON 0.1mg; SODIUM 889mg; CALC 145mg

Biscuits and Vegetarian Sausage Gravy

Vegetarian sausage has a firmer texture than pork sausage. Crumbling the sausage helps distribute it evenly throughout the gravy.

1 (16.3-ounce) can reduced-fat refrigerated biscuit dough
1 tablespoon vegetable oil
½ (14-ounce) package meatless fat-free sausage (such as Lightlife Gimme Lean)
¼ cup all-purpose flour (about 1 ounce)
3 cups 1% low-fat milk
½ teaspoon salt
¼ teaspoon freshly ground black pepper

1. Prepare biscuits according to package directions.
2. Heat oil in a large nonstick skillet over medium-high heat. Add sausage; cook 3 minutes or until browned, stirring to crumble. Remove from heat; cool slightly. Crumble sausage into ½-inch pieces; return to pan.
3. Lightly spoon flour into a dry measuring cup; level with a knife. Combine flour and milk, stirring with a whisk until smooth. Add milk mixture, salt, and pepper to pan; bring to a boil over medium-high heat. Cover, reduce heat, and simmer 3 minutes or until thick. Split biscuits in half. Place 2 biscuit halves on each of 8 plates; top each serving with about ⅓ cup gravy. Serve immediately. Yield: 8 servings.

CALORIES 268 (29% from fat); FAT 8.7g (sat 2.4g, mono 4g, poly 1g); PROTEIN 11.4g; CARB 36.9g; FIBER 0.6g; CHOL 4mg; IRON 1mg; SODIUM 910mg; CALC 131mg

Meats

Fresh Herb-Coated Beef Tenderloin Steaks with Mushroom Gravy, page 155

Meat Loaf

The meat loaf is easy to lift out of the slow cooker with the foil "hammock" that holds it.

1½ pounds extralean ground beef
¾ cup finely chopped onion
½ cup seasoned breadcrumbs
¼ cup finely chopped green bell pepper
¼ cup ketchup
2 tablespoons prepared mustard
1 teaspoon garlic powder
1 teaspoon dried oregano
¼ teaspoon salt
¼ teaspoon freshly ground black pepper
1 large egg white
Cooking spray
2 tablespoons ketchup

1. Combine first 11 ingredients in a large bowl; mix well. Form mixture into an 8½ x 4½–inch loaf.
2. Fold a 12-inch-long piece of foil in half lengthwise. Spray foil with cooking spray. Place meat loaf on foil, leaving a 2- to 3-inch border at each end of foil. Lift foil, and place in an electric slow cooker. Spread 2 tablespoons ketchup over top of meat loaf. Cook on HIGH 4 hours or until a thermometer registers 170°. Using foil, carefully lift meat loaf out of cooker. Let stand 10 minutes; cut into 6 slices. Yield: 6 servings (serving size: 1 slice).

CALORIES 263 (38% from fat); FAT 11g (sat 4.3g, mono 4.7g, poly 0.7g); PROTEIN 26.1g; CARB 13.9g; FIBER 1.3g; CHOL 41mg; IRON 3.3mg; SODIUM 590mg; CALC 44mg

Moroccan Meatballs in Spicy Tomato Sauce

Sweet and savory seasoned meatballs simmer in an aromatic tomato sauce for a Mediterranean-style dinner. Use kitchen shears to coarsely chop the tomatoes while they are still in the can. You can shape the meatballs in advance and store them in the freezer to save time. The rest of the recipe is best prepared and cooked the same day.

MEATBALLS:
½ cup dry breadcrumbs
¼ cup dried currants
¼ cup finely chopped onion
½ teaspoon salt
½ teaspoon ground cumin
½ teaspoon dried oregano
¼ teaspoon ground cinnamon
1½ pounds lean ground beef
1 large egg white
Cooking spray

SAUCE:
¼ cup tomato paste
1 teaspoon fennel seeds
1 teaspoon grated orange rind
½ teaspoon ground cumin
¼ teaspoon ground cinnamon
¼ teaspoon salt
¼ teaspoon ground red pepper
1 (28-ounce) can whole tomatoes, coarsely chopped

REMAINING INGREDIENTS:
3 cups hot cooked couscous
Chopped fresh parsley (optional)

1. To prepare meatballs, combine first 9 ingredients in a bowl; shape meat mixture into 30 meatballs. Heat a large nonstick skillet over medium-high heat. Coat pan with cooking spray. Add half of meatballs to pan; cook 3 minutes or until browned, stirring frequently. Place browned meatballs in an electric slow cooker. Coat pan with cooking spray; repeat procedure with remaining 15 meatballs.
2. To prepare sauce, combine tomato paste and next 7 ingredients. Add to slow cooker; stir gently to coat. Cover and cook on LOW 6 hours. Serve over couscous. Garnish with parsley, if desired. Yield: 6 servings (serving size: 5 meatballs, 1 cup sauce, and ½ cup couscous).

CALORIES 312 (17% from fat); FAT 6g (sat 2.2g, mono 2.2g, poly 0.9g); PROTEIN 28.7g; CARB 37.8g; FIBER 4.2g; CHOL 60mg; IRON 4.6mg; SODIUM 696mg; CALC 85mg

Moroccan Meatballs in Spicy Tomato Sauce

Stuffed Peppers

Precooking the peppers and bringing the sauce to a boil before adding it to the dish cuts down on the baking time.

- 1 (3½-ounce) bag boil-in-bag long-grain rice
- 4 medium red bell peppers
- ¾ pound ground sirloin
- 1 cup chopped onion
- ½ cup chopped fresh parsley
- 1 teaspoon paprika
- ½ teaspoon salt
- ⅛ teaspoon ground allspice
- 2 cups bottled tomato-and-basil pasta sauce (such as Classico), divided
- ½ cup (2 ounces) grated fresh Parmesan cheese
- ½ cup dry red wine
- Cooking spray

1. Preheat oven to 450°.

2. Cook rice according to package directions, omitting salt and fat.

3. While rice cooks, cut tops off bell peppers; reserve tops. Discard seeds and membranes. Place peppers, cut sides down, in an 8-inch square baking dish; cover with plastic wrap. Microwave at HIGH 2 minutes or until peppers are crisp-tender. Cool.

4. Heat a large nonstick skillet over medium-high heat. Add beef and next 5 ingredients; cook 4 minutes or until beef is lightly browned, stirring to crumble. Remove from heat. Add cooked rice, ½ cup pasta sauce, and cheese to beef mixture, stirring to combine.

5. While beef cooks, combine 1½ cups pasta sauce and wine in a small saucepan; bring to a boil.

6. Spoon about ¾ cup beef mixture into each pepper. Place peppers in a 2-quart baking dish coated with cooking spray, and add wine mixture to pan. Cover with foil.

7. Bake at 450° for 20 minutes. Uncover; bake an additional 5 minutes or until lightly browned. Serve peppers with sauce. Garnish with pepper tops. Yield: 4 servings (serving size: 1 stuffed pepper and ⅓ cup sauce).

CALORIES 347 (20% from fat); FAT 7.9g (sat 3.9g, mono 2.6g, poly 0.7g); PROTEIN 26.6g; CARB 39.9g; FIBER 4.6g; CHOL 55mg; IRON 4.1mg; SODIUM 747mg; CALC 284mg

Skillet Stuffed Peppers

Use any color bell pepper in this 20-minute recipe. Save time with packaged refrigerated mashed potatoes.

- 2 large green bell peppers, halved lengthwise and seeded
- Cooking spray
- ¾ pound ground round
- ½ cup water
- 1 (1.25-ounce) package taco seasoning
- 1 (20-ounce) package refrigerated mashed potatoes (such as Simply Potatoes)
- ¼ cup (1 ounce) reduced-fat shredded Cheddar cheese
- Cracked black pepper (optional)

1. Place bell pepper halves, cut sides down, on a microwave-safe dish; cover with plastic wrap. Microwave at HIGH 3 minutes and 30 seconds or until pepper halves are crisp-tender. Let stand, covered, 3 minutes (peppers will soften).
2. Heat a large nonstick skillet over medium-high heat. Coat pan with cooking spray. Add beef to pan; cook 3 minutes, stirring to crumble. Add ½ cup water and seasoning; stir to combine. Cover, reduce heat, and cook 5 minutes or until done.
3. While beef cooks and peppers stand, cook potatoes in microwave according to package directions, omitting salt and fat.
4. Spoon ½ cup beef mixture into each pepper half; top each with ⅔ cup potatoes. Sprinkle each pepper half with 1 tablespoon cheese. Garnish with black pepper, if desired. Yield: 4 servings (serving size: 1 stuffed pepper half).

CALORIES 338 (36% from fat); FAT 13.4g (sat 5.3g, mono 5.7g, poly 0.4g); PROTEIN 20.1g; CARB 29.3g; FIBER 5.1g; CHOL 59mg; IRON 2.4mg; SODIUM 663mg; CALC 48mg

Beef-Taco Rice with Refried Beans

This is an easy dish to serve a crowd. It's quick to assemble by using instant rice, taco seasoning, canned refried beans, and preshredded cheese. You can even find chopped onion and bell peppers in many produce sections.

- 4 cups water
- 1 cup chopped onion
- 1 cup chopped green bell pepper
- ¼ teaspoon salt
- ¼ teaspoon black pepper
- 1 (1.25-ounce) package taco seasoning, divided
- 4 cups uncooked instant rice
- 2 (8-ounce) cans no-salt-added tomato sauce
- 1 pound ground round
- Cooking spray
- 1 (16-ounce) can fat-free refried beans
- 1 (8-ounce) package preshredded reduced-fat Mexican blend or Cheddar cheese

1. Preheat oven to 350°.
2. Combine first 5 ingredients in a large saucepan; add half of taco seasoning. Bring to a boil. Remove from heat. Stir in rice; cover and let stand 5 minutes. Stir in tomato sauce.
3. Cook meat in a large nonstick skillet over medium-high heat until browned, stirring to crumble. Drain; return meat to pan. Stir in remaining taco seasoning.
4. Spread half of rice mixture in a 13 x 9–inch baking dish coated with cooking spray. Spread beans evenly over rice mixture; top with beef mixture and half of cheese. Spread remaining rice mixture over cheese; top with remaining cheese. Bake at 350° for 10 minutes or until cheese melts. Yield: 10 servings (serving size: about 1¼ cups).

CALORIES 371 (18% from fat); FAT 7.5g (sat 3.6g, mono 2.5g, poly 0.4g); PROTEIN 23.7g; CARB 51.2g; FIBER 3.8g; CHOL 42mg; IRON 4.4mg; SODIUM 696mg; CALC 221mg

Spaghetti with Meat Sauce

A few additions to this bottled spaghetti sauce render customized flavor from a convenience product.

- 12 ounces uncooked spaghetti
- ¾ pound ground sirloin
- 1 cup chopped onion
- 1½ teaspoons bottled minced garlic
- ¾ cup dry red wine
- 1 (26-ounce) jar low-fat spaghetti sauce (such as Healthy Choice)
- ⅔ cup 2% reduced-fat milk
- ½ teaspoon salt
- ¼ teaspoon black pepper

1. Cook pasta according to package directions, omitting salt and fat.
2. While pasta cooks, heat a large nonstick skillet over medium-high heat. Add beef; cook until browned, stirring to crumble. Drain beef; set aside.
3. Add onion and garlic to pan; sauté 3 minutes. Add wine; cook 3 minutes or until liquid almost evaporates.
4. Stir in beef and spaghetti sauce; bring to a boil. Reduce heat, and simmer 5 minutes, stirring occasionally. Stir in milk, salt, and pepper; cook 3 minutes, stirring occasionally. Serve sauce over pasta. Yield: 6 servings (serving size: about 1 cup pasta and ⅔ cup sauce).

CALORIES 401 (15% from fat); FAT 6.9g (sat 1.8g, mono 2.9g, poly 1.1g); PROTEIN 22.8g; CARB 60.1g; FIBER 4.9g; CHOL 37mg; IRON 4.7mg; SODIUM 544mg; CALC 77mg

Make-Ahead Cheese-and-Hamburger Casserole

The penne doesn't have to be cooked beforehand because it absorbs the liquid when the dish is refrigerated overnight. If you want to make it the same day, cook the pasta before adding it to the other ingredients.

- 1 pound ground round
- 1 cup chopped onion
- 3 garlic cloves, crushed
- 1 (8-ounce) package presliced mushrooms
- 6 tablespoons tomato paste
- 1 teaspoon sugar
- 1 teaspoon dried thyme
- 1 teaspoon dried oregano
- ¼ teaspoon pepper
- 1 (28-ounce) can whole tomatoes, undrained and chopped
- ⅓ cup all-purpose flour (about 1½ ounces)
- 2½ cups 2% reduced-fat milk
- 1 cup (4 ounces) crumbled feta cheese
- ¾ cup (3 ounces) shredded part-skim mozzarella cheese
- 4 cups uncooked penne (tube-shaped pasta)
- 1 tablespoon chopped fresh parsley (optional)

1. Combine first 3 ingredients in a large nonstick skillet, and cook over medium-high heat until browned, stirring to crumble. Add mushrooms; cook 5 minutes or until tender. Add tomato paste and next 5 ingredients; stir well. Bring to a boil; reduce heat, and simmer, uncovered, 20 minutes. Remove from heat.
2. Lightly spoon flour into a dry measuring cup; level with a knife. Place flour in a medium saucepan. Gradually add milk, stirring with a whisk until blended. Place over medium heat; cook 10 minutes or until thick, stirring constantly. Stir in cheeses; cook 3 minutes or until cheeses melt, stirring constantly. Reserve ½ cup cheese sauce; set aside. Pour remaining cheese sauce, beef mixture, and pasta in a 13 x 9–inch baking dish; stir gently. Drizzle reserved cheese sauce over pasta mixture. Cover and refrigerate 24 hours.
3. Preheat oven to 350°.
4. Bake at 350°, covered, for 1 hour and 10 minutes or until thoroughly heated. Sprinkle with fresh parsley, if desired. Yield: 8 servings (serving size: about 1½ cups).

CALORIES 412 (23% from fat); FAT 10.8g (sat 5.5g, mono 3.2g, poly 0.9g); PROTEIN 27.5g; CARB 51.1g; FIBER 3.2g; CHOL 60mg; IRON 4.9mg; SODIUM 448mg; CALC 286mg

Mini Meat Loaves

A tangy mixture of ketchup and Dijon mustard not only flavors the meat loaves but also acts as a glaze that helps them brown nicely as they cook. Serve with mashed potatoes.

½ cup ketchup
1½ tablespoons Dijon mustard
1 pound ground sirloin
¾ cup finely chopped onion
¼ cup seasoned breadcrumbs
½ teaspoon salt
½ teaspoon dried oregano
⅛ teaspoon black pepper
1 large egg, lightly beaten
Cooking spray

1. Preheat oven to 400°.

2. Combine ketchup and mustard, stirring well with a whisk. Reserve 2½ tablespoons ketchup mixture. Combine remaining ketchup mixture, beef, and next 6 ingredients in a large bowl, stirring to combine.

3. Divide beef mixture into 4 equal portions. Shape each portion into a 4 x 2½–inch loaf; place loaves on a jelly-roll pan coated with cooking spray.

4. Spread about 2 teaspoons reserved ketchup mixture evenly over each meat loaf. Bake at 400° for 25 minutes or until done. Yield: 4 servings (serving size: 1 meat loaf).

CALORIES 255 (28% from fat); FAT 7.9g (sat 2.8g, mono 3.2g, poly 0.4g); PROTEIN 27.4g; CARB 15.7g; FIBER 0.9g; CHOL 120mg; IRON 2.7mg; SODIUM 944mg; CALC 31mg

Cape Malay Curry

Curries from South Africa's Cape Malay are known for combining sweet and savory flavors with sweet spices like cinnamon and ginger, dried fruit (especially apricots), and savory seasonings. This beef stew is great over rice, mashed potatoes, or egg noodles.

- 1½ teaspoons ground turmeric
- 1½ teaspoons ground cumin
- 1½ teaspoons ground coriander
- 1½ teaspoons chili powder
- ¾ teaspoon ground cinnamon
- ½ teaspoon salt
- 2 teaspoons canola oil
- 2 cups chopped onion
- 1½ tablespoons minced peeled fresh ginger
- 2 bay leaves
- 1 garlic clove, minced
- 1 pound beef stew meat, cut into bite-sized pieces
- 1¼ cups less-sodium beef broth
- 1 cup water
- 1 cup chopped green bell pepper (about 1 medium)
- ⅓ cup chopped dried apricots
- ⅓ cup apricot spread (such as Polaner All Fruit)
- 2 teaspoons red wine vinegar
- ¼ cup low-fat buttermilk

1. Combine first 6 ingredients in a small bowl.

2. Heat oil in a Dutch oven over medium-high heat. Add spice mixture; cook 15 seconds, stirring constantly. Add onion; sauté 2 minutes. Add ginger, bay leaves, and garlic; sauté 15 seconds. Add beef; sauté 3 minutes. Add broth and next 5 ingredients; bring to a boil. Cover, reduce heat, and simmer 1½ hours. Uncover; discard bay leaves. Simmer 30 minutes or until beef is very tender. Remove from heat; stir in buttermilk. Yield: 4 servings (serving size: 1¼ cups).

CALORIES 349 (30% from fat); FAT 11.5g (sat 3.4g, mono 5.1g, poly 1.2g); PROTEIN 25.7g; CARB 35.3g; FIBER 3.9g; CHOL 71mg; IRON 4.3mg; SODIUM 396mg; CALC 77mg

Beef Burgundy with Egg Noodles

This entrée actually tastes better when made a day in advance, which makes it a great choice for entertaining. Cook the egg noodles while you reheat the stew.

- ⅓ cup all-purpose flour (about 1½ ounces)
- 2 teaspoons salt, divided
- ¾ teaspoon freshly ground black pepper, divided
- 2¼ pounds beef stew meat
- 3 bacon slices, chopped and divided
- 1 cup chopped onion
- 1 cup sliced carrot
- 4 garlic cloves, minced
- 1½ cups dry red wine
- 1 (14-ounce) can less-sodium beef broth
- 8 cups halved mushrooms (about 1½ pounds)
- 2 tablespoons tomato paste
- 2 teaspoons chopped fresh thyme
- 2 bay leaves
- 1 (16-ounce) package frozen pearl onions
- 7 cups hot cooked medium egg noodles (about 6 cups uncooked noodles)
- 3 tablespoons chopped fresh flat-leaf parsley

1. Lightly spoon flour into a dry measuring cup; level with a knife. Combine flour, 1 teaspoon salt, and ¼ teaspoon pepper in a large zip-top plastic bag. Add beef; seal and shake to coat.

2. Cook half of bacon in a large Dutch oven over medium-high heat until crisp. Remove bacon from pan with a slotted spoon; set aside. Add half of beef mixture to drippings in pan; cook 5 minutes, browning on all sides. Remove beef from pan; cover and keep warm. Repeat procedure with remaining bacon and beef mixture. Remove beef from pan; cover and keep warm.

3. Add chopped onion, carrot, and garlic to pan; sauté 5 minutes. Stir in wine and beef broth, scraping pan to loosen browned bits. Add bacon, beef, remaining 1 teaspoon salt, remaining ½ teaspoon black pepper, mushrooms, tomato paste, thyme, bay leaves, and pearl onions; bring to a boil. Cover, reduce heat, and simmer 45 minutes. Uncover and cook 1 hour or until beef is tender. Discard bay leaves. Serve beef mixture over noodles, and sprinkle with parsley. Yield: 9 servings (serving size: about 1 cup beef mixture, ¾ cup noodles, and 1 teaspoon parsley).

CALORIES 447 (29% from fat); FAT 14.6g (sat 5.1g, mono 6.1g, poly 1.5g); PROTEIN 32.7g; CARB 45.7g; FIBER 3.9g; CHOL 117mg; IRON 6mg; SODIUM 677mg; CALC 47mg

Beef Burgundy with Egg Noodles

Guinness-Braised Chuck Steaks with Horseradish Mashed Potatoes

Guinness-Braised Chuck Steaks with Horseradish Mashed Potatoes

STEAK:

- 1 (1½-pound) boneless chuck steak, trimmed
- ½ teaspoon freshly ground black pepper
- ¼ teaspoon salt
- 2 teaspoons olive oil
- 1½ cups finely chopped onion
- ½ cup chopped carrot
- ½ cup fat-free, less-sodium chicken broth, divided
- 1 teaspoon dark brown sugar
- 1 teaspoon chopped fresh rosemary
- 1 (8-ounce) package presliced mushrooms
- 1 garlic clove, minced
- 2 bay leaves
- 1 (12-ounce) bottle Guinness Stout

POTATOES:

- 2 pounds peeled baking potatoes, quartered
- 2 tablespoons butter
- ½ cup fat-free milk
- ¼ cup finely chopped green onions
- ¼ cup reduced-fat sour cream
- 2 tablespoons prepared horseradish
- ½ teaspoon salt
- ½ teaspoon freshly ground black pepper

1. To prepare steak, sprinkle steak with ½ teaspoon pepper and ¼ teaspoon salt. Heat oil in a Dutch oven over medium-high heat. Add steak; cook 5 minutes on each side or until browned. Remove steak from pan; set aside. Add 1½ cups onion, chopped carrot, 2 tablespoons broth, and sugar. Cover, reduce heat to medium, and cook 10 minutes. Stir in rosemary, mushrooms, and garlic. Cover and cook 2 minutes. Add bay leaves, Guinness Stout, remaining broth, and steak; bring to a boil. Cover, reduce heat, and simmer 1 hour and 30 minutes or until steak is tender.

2. To prepare potatoes, place potatoes in a large saucepan; cover with water. Bring to a boil. Simmer 20 minutes or until potatoes are tender; drain. Return potatoes to pan. Add butter; beat with a mixer at medium speed just until smooth. Stir in butter and next 6 ingredients. Keep warm.

3. Remove steak from pan; keep warm. Discard bay leaves. Increase heat to medium-high; cook 5 minutes or until slightly thick. Spoon stout mixture over steak. Serve with mashed potatoes. Yield: 6 servings (serving size: 3 ounces beef, ¾ cup potatoes, and ⅓ cup sauce).

CALORIES 428 (27% from fat); FAT 13.1g (sat 5g, mono 6g, poly 0.9g); PROTEIN 35.2g; CARB 42.3g; FIBER 4.6g; CHOL 86mg; IRON 4.3mg; SODIUM 872mg; CALC 82mg

Marinated Flank Steak with Horseradish Raita

This tender, marinated beef is crusted with a dry spice rub and served with spicy-sweet yogurt sauce. The cooling raita also has a little bite of its own.

RAITA:

- 1½ teaspoons finely grated fresh horseradish root
- ½ teaspoon finely grated peeled fresh ginger
- ¼ teaspoon salt
- ¼ teaspoon sugar
- 1 (8-ounce) carton fat-free yogurt

STEAK:

- 1 tablespoon mustard seeds
- 2 teaspoons Szechuan peppercorns
- 1½ teaspoons whole allspice
- 1½ teaspoons coriander seeds
- 1 teaspoon cumin seeds
- ½ teaspoon kosher salt
- 1 (1-pound) flank steak, trimmed
- Cooking spray
- Parsley sprigs (optional)

1. To prepare raita, combine first 5 ingredients in a small bowl. Cover and chill.

2. To prepare steak, combine mustard seeds and next 4 ingredients in a spice or coffee grinder; pulse until coarsely ground. Stir kosher salt into spice mixture. Rub spice mixture over both sides of steak; cover and chill 4 hours.

3. Heat a large nonstick skillet over medium-high heat. Coat pan with cooking spray. Add steak; cook 3 minutes on each side or until desired degree of doneness. Place steak on a platter or cutting board; let stand 5 minutes. Cut steak diagonally across grain into thin slices. Serve with raita. Garnish with parsley, if desired. Yield: 4 servings (serving size: 3 ounces steak and ¼ cup raita).

CALORIES 216 (33% from fat); FAT 7.8g (sat 2.9g, mono 3.2g, poly 0.4g); PROTEIN 27.1g; CARB 7.7g; FIBER 1.6g; CHOL 46mg; IRON 3.2mg; SODIUM 475mg; CALC 165mg

Grilled Steak Soft Tacos

The sweet, caramelized flavor of grilled corn makes an excellent addition to these steak tacos. Place the shucked ears on the grill rack immediately after you remove the meat. The arugula is an unexpected topping. This aromatic salad green adds a peppery mustard bite. Use shredded lettuce, if you prefer. Omit the jalapeño pepper slices for those with delicate palates.

1 cup fresh lime juice (about 8 limes)
1 (2-pound) flank steak, trimmed
2 tablespoons ground cumin
2 tablespoons ground coriander
½ teaspoon kosher salt
½ teaspoon cracked black pepper
6 garlic cloves, minced
Cooking spray
4 ears shucked corn
8 (8-inch) fat-free flour tortillas
2 cups trimmed arugula
2 cups thinly sliced red onion
1 cup cilantro sprigs
1 cup chopped tomato
1 cup diced peeled avocado
½ cup sliced seeded jalapeño pepper (about 4 peppers)
8 lime wedges

1. Combine lime juice and steak in a large zip-top plastic bag. Seal and marinate in refrigerator 1 hour, turning bag occasionally.
2. Prepare grill.
3. Remove steak from bag, and discard marinade. Combine cumin and next 4 ingredients; rub over both sides of steak.
4. Place steak on a grill rack coated with cooking spray; grill 8 minutes on each side or until desired degree of doneness. Place on a cutting board; cover loosely with foil. Let stand 5 minutes. Cut steak diagonally across grain into thin slices.
5. Place corn on grill rack coated with cooking spray; grill 8 minutes or until tender, turning occasionally. Cut kernels from ears of corn; discard cobs.
6. Heat flour tortillas according to package directions. Divide steak evenly among tortillas; top each serving with about ¼ cup corn, ¼ cup arugula, ¼ cup red onion, 2 tablespoons cilantro, 2 tablespoons tomato, 2 tablespoons avocado, and 1 tablespoon jalapeño pepper. Fold each tortilla in half. Serve with lime wedges. Yield: 8 servings (serving size: 1 taco).

CALORIES 397 (29% from fat); FAT 12.8g (sat 4.3g, mono 5.4g, poly 1g); PROTEIN 28.1g; CARB 34.3g; FIBER 6.7g; CHOL 57mg; IRON 3.6mg; SODIUM 425mg; CALC 56mg

Beef-Broccoli Lo Mein

Asian condiments and sauces have such concentrated flavors, a little goes a long way.

8 ounces uncooked spaghetti
1 teaspoon dark sesame oil
1 tablespoon peanut oil
1 tablespoon minced peeled fresh ginger
4 garlic cloves, minced
3 cups chopped broccoli
1½ cups vertically sliced onion
1 (1-pound) flank steak, trimmed and cut across grain into long, thin strips
3 tablespoons low-sodium soy sauce
2 tablespoons brown sugar
1 tablespoon oyster sauce
1 tablespoon chile paste with garlic (such as sambal oelek)

1. Cook pasta according to package directions, omitting salt and fat; drain. Combine pasta and sesame oil, tossing well to coat.
2. While pasta cooks, heat peanut oil in a large nonstick skillet over medium-high heat. Add ginger and garlic; sauté 30 seconds. Add broccoli and onion; sauté 3 minutes. Add steak; sauté 5 minutes or until done. Add pasta mixture, soy sauce, and remaining ingredients; cook 1 minute or until lo mein is thoroughly heated, stirring constantly. Yield: 6 servings (serving size: 1⅓ cups).

CALORIES 327 (26% from fat); FAT 9.3g (sat 3g, mono 3.6g, poly 1.6g); PROTEIN 21.7g; CARB 39.1g; FIBER 2.9g; CHOL 36mg; IRON 3.6mg; SODIUM 382mg; CALC 47mg

Beef-Broccoli Lo Mein

Tequila-Marinated Beef-and-Pepper Fajitas

The convenience of using a stove-top grill pan is that it gives meat and vegetables the appearance and taste of food cooked outside without having to wait for the grill to preheat. These fajitas are a great weeknight supper, but you can also serve them with salsa and a dollop of light sour cream for an appetizer. Add a pitcher of sangría and you have all you need for a festive Tex-Mex menu.

- ¼ cup tequila
- 2 tablespoons chopped fresh cilantro
- 2 tablespoons fresh lime juice
- 1 tablespoon Worcestershire sauce
- 1 teaspoon ground cumin
- ½ teaspoon canola oil
- ¼ teaspoon ground red pepper
- 2 garlic cloves, minced
- 1 (1-pound) flank steak, trimmed
- 1 green bell pepper, cut into 4 wedges
- 1 red bell pepper, cut into 4 wedges
- 4 (¼-inch-thick) slices red onion
- ¼ teaspoon salt
- ¼ teaspoon black pepper
- Cooking spray
- 4 (8-inch) fat-free flour tortillas

1. Combine first 8 ingredients in a large zip-top plastic bag; stir with a whisk. Add steak; seal bag, and marinate in refrigerator 1 hour. Remove steak from bag; discard marinade.
2. Sprinkle bell pepper wedges and onion slices with salt and pepper.
3. Heat a large grill pan over medium-high heat. Coat pan with cooking spray. Add bell pepper wedges to pan; cook 5 minutes. Turn bell pepper wedges over; add onion slices to pan. Cook 5 minutes, turning onion slices once. Remove bell pepper wedges and onion slices from pan; set aside, and keep warm. Add steak to pan; cook about 5 minutes on each side or until desired degree of doneness. Cut steak diagonally across grain into thin slices.
4. Warm tortillas according to package directions. Arrange about 3 ounces steak, 2 bell pepper wedges, and 1 onion slice down center of each tortilla; fold tortillas in half. Yield: 4 servings.

CALORIES 346 (30% from fat); FAT 11.7g (sat 4.6g, mono 4.5g, poly 0.7g); PROTEIN 26.1g; CARB 28.4g; FIBER 2g; CHOL 58mg; IRON 4mg; SODIUM 577mg; CALC 19mg

Cajun Flank Steak

- 1 tablespoon garlic powder
- 1 tablespoon onion powder
- 2 teaspoons sugar
- 2 teaspoons paprika
- 1 teaspoon chili powder
- ¾ teaspoon salt
- ½ teaspoon black pepper
- ¼ teaspoon ground red pepper
- 1 (1-pound) flank steak, trimmed
- Cooking spray

1. Combine first 8 ingredients in a small bowl. Rub spice mixture over both sides of flank steak.
2. Heat a nonstick grill pan over medium-high heat. Coat pan with cooking spray. Add steak; cook 5 minutes on each side. Cut steak diagonally across grain into thin slices. Yield: 4 servings (serving size: 3 ounces).

CALORIES 195 (42% from fat); FAT 9g (sat 3.6g, mono 3.3g, poly 0.5g); PROTEIN 22.7g; CARB 6.1g; FIBER 0.9g; CHOL 54mg; IRON 2.6mg; SODIUM 512mg; CALC 19mg

Pepper Steak

You can toss in other vegetables, such as sliced onion or water chestnuts, when you add the red bell pepper.

- Cooking spray
- 2 tablespoons all-purpose flour
- 2 tablespoons bottled minced garlic (about 6 cloves)
- 1 tablespoon minced peeled fresh ginger
- ¼ teaspoon salt
- ⅛ teaspoon black pepper
- 1 (1-pound) sirloin steak, trimmed and cut across grain into ¼-inch-thick strips
- 1 cup red bell pepper strips
- ½ cup beef consommé
- 1 teaspoon low-sodium soy sauce
- 1 teaspoon dark sesame oil

1. Heat a large nonstick skillet over medium-high heat. Coat pan with cooking spray. Combine flour and next 5 ingredients, tossing to coat. Add beef mixture to pan; sauté 3 minutes. Add bell pepper and remaining ingredients to pan; cover and cook 7 minutes or until peppers are crisp-tender, stirring occasionally. Yield: 4 servings (serving size: 1 cup).

CALORIES 197 (28% from fat); FAT 6.2g (sat 1.9g, mono 2.5g, poly 0.8g); PROTEIN 26.5g; CARB 7.7g; FIBER 0.9g; CHOL 69mg; IRON 3.7mg; SODIUM 419mg; CALC 22mg

Pepper Steak

Cumin-Coriander Sirloin Steak

The combination of cumin, coriander, and ground red pepper creates a tasty rub for the beef. Brown sugar aids in a crusty caramelization. Serve with baked sweet potato spears and collard greens.

Cooking spray
1 tablespoon brown sugar
½ teaspoon salt
½ teaspoon ground cumin
½ teaspoon ground coriander seeds
¼ teaspoon ground red pepper
1 (1-pound) boneless sirloin steak (about 1¼ inches thick), trimmed

1. Preheat oven to 450°.

2. Coat an 8-inch cast-iron skillet with cooking spray. Place pan in a 450° oven for 5 minutes.

3. Combine brown sugar and next 4 ingredients, and rub evenly over both sides of steak. Place steak in preheated pan.

4. Bake at 450° for 7 minutes on each side or until desired degree of doneness. Let steak stand 5 minutes. Cut steak diagonally across grain into thin slices. Yield: 4 servings (serving size: 3 ounces).

CALORIES 198 (39% from fat); FAT 8.6g (sat 3.4g, mono 3.6g, poly 0.3g); PROTEIN 25.1g; CARB 3.7g; FIBER 0.3g; CHOL 76mg; IRON 2.9mg; SODIUM 350mg; CALC 17mg

Shepherd's Pie Peppers

Shepherd's Pie assumes a new identity when stuffed into pepper shells. Cooking the peppers for a short time in boiling water softens them before stuffing.

2 large green bell peppers (about 1 pound)
Cooking spray
6 ounces lean boneless sirloin steak, cut into ¾-inch cubes
¾ cup fat-free beef broth
⅔ cup frozen peas and carrots
⅓ cup chopped onion
2 tablespoons tomato paste
1 teaspoon Worcestershire sauce
¼ teaspoon black pepper
⅛ teaspoon salt
1 tablespoon cornstarch
1 tablespoon water
1 cup frozen mashed potatoes
½ cup fat-free milk
2 teaspoons grated Parmesan cheese
Dash of paprika

1. Preheat oven to 400°.
2. Cut tops off bell peppers; discard tops, seeds, and membranes. Cook peppers in boiling water 5 minutes; drain and set aside.
3. Heat a large nonstick skillet over medium-high heat. Coat pan with cooking spray. Add beef; cook 6 minutes or until browned, stirring frequently. Drain and pat dry with paper towels. Wipe drippings from pan with a paper towel.
4. Return meat to pan; add beef broth and next 6 ingredients. Bring to a boil; cover, reduce heat, and simmer 10 minutes. Combine cornstarch and 1 tablespoon water, stirring well with a whisk. Add to meat mixture; bring to a boil. Cook 1 minute, stirring constantly. Divide meat mixture evenly between peppers. Place stuffed peppers in an 8-inch square baking dish.
5. Combine potatoes and milk in a microwave-safe bowl, stirring well. Microwave at HIGH 2 minutes, stirring after 1 minute. Let stand 2 minutes. Spoon warm potato mixture evenly over tops of stuffed peppers; lightly coat potato mixture with cooking spray. Combine Parmesan cheese and dash of paprika; sprinkle over potato mixture.
6. Bake at 400° for 20 minutes or until potatoes are golden. Yield: 2 servings (serving size: 1 pepper).

CALORIES 386 (21% from fat); FAT 9g (sat 3.3g, mono 3.4g, poly 1.1g); PROTEIN 30.1g; CARB 43.3g; FIBER 6.2g; CHOL 66mg; IRON 3.7mg; SODIUM 991mg; CALC 173mg

Beef, Okra, and Potato Kebabs

This recipe features an unusual, delicious grilled okra. Grilling infuses the okra pods with smoky flavor, and it allows them to maintain their firm texture.

8 fingerling potatoes, each cut in half lengthwise
2 tablespoons chopped fresh parsley
1½ tablespoons prepared horseradish
1½ tablespoons whole-grain Dijon mustard
1 tablespoon Worcestershire sauce
1½ teaspoons sugar
2 teaspoons olive oil
¼ teaspoon freshly ground black pepper
½ teaspoon salt, divided
1 cup (1-inch-square) cut red bell pepper
16 small okra pods
8 shallots, peeled and halved
1 (1-pound) boneless sirloin steak, trimmed and cut into 1-inch cubes
1 medium yellow squash, halved lengthwise and cut into ½-inch slices (about 2 cups)
Cooking spray

1. Place potatoes in a saucepan; cover with water. Bring to a boil. Reduce heat, and simmer 15 minutes or until tender; drain. Cool.
2. Combine parsley, horseradish, Dijon mustard, Worcestershire sauce, sugar, olive oil, and ¼ teaspoon black pepper in a large bowl, stirring well. Stir in ¼ teaspoon salt. Add potatoes, bell pepper, okra, shallots, beef, and squash; toss well to coat. Cover and chill 1 hour.
3. Prepare grill.
4. Thread vegetables and beef alternately onto each of 8 (10-inch) skewers. Sprinkle kebabs evenly with remaining ¼ teaspoon salt. Place kebabs on grill rack coated with cooking spray, and grill 10 minutes or until desired degree of doneness, turning occasionally. Yield: 4 servings (serving size: 2 kebabs).

CALORIES 338 (30% from fat); FAT 11.3g (sat 3.7g, mono 5.3g, poly 0.7g); PROTEIN 30.6g; CARB 30.4g; FIBER 3.9g; CHOL 76mg; IRON 4.8mg; SODIUM 564mg; CALC 76mg

Grilled Steak and Summer Vegetables with Pesto

Grilled Steak and Summer Vegetables with Pesto

Grilling the meat and vegetables at the same time gets dinner on the table quickly. Asparagus, portobello mushroom caps, and corn on the cob are also great grilled instead of squash and bell peppers.

- 1 (1-pound) lean boneless sirloin steak, trimmed
- ¾ teaspoon salt, divided
- ½ teaspoon black pepper, divided
- ¼ cup red wine vinegar
- 4 small zucchini, halved lengthwise
- 4 small yellow squash, halved lengthwise
- 2 red bell peppers, quartered
- 4 green onions
- 4 garlic cloves, minced
- Cooking spray
- 2 tablespoons commercial pesto
- Oregano sprigs (optional)

1. Prepare grill or broiler.
2. Sprinkle steak with ¼ teaspoon salt and ¼ teaspoon black pepper.
3. Combine ½ teaspoon salt, ¼ teaspoon black pepper, vinegar, and next 5 ingredients in a large zip-top plastic bag. Seal and shake to coat.
4. Place steak on grill rack or broiler pan coated with cooking spray; cook 4 minutes on each side or until desired degree of doneness. Let stand 5 minutes; cut steak into ¼-inch slices. Place zucchini and squash on grill rack or broiler pan coated with cooking spray; cook 4 minutes on each side or until tender. Place bell peppers and onions on grill rack or broiler pan; cook 2 minutes or just until tender.
5. Coarsely chop vegetables; place in a bowl. Add pesto; stir gently. Garnish with oregano, if desired. Yield: 4 servings (serving size: 3 ounces steak and 1 cup vegetable mixture).

CALORIES 380 (30% from fat); FAT 12.8g (sat 4.5g, mono 6.1g, poly 0.7g); PROTEIN 40.7g; CARB 24.1g; FIBER 9.4g; CHOL 103mg; IRON 6mg; SODIUM 583mg; CALC 159mg

Steak Diane

This recipe will impress your family and guests with very little effort. For an easy side of roasted potatoes, start with precut potato wedges from the refrigerated section of the grocery store.

- ½ teaspoon salt, divided
- ¼ teaspoon black pepper
- 6 (4-ounce) beef tenderloin steaks, trimmed (about 1 inch thick)
- 1 teaspoon butter
- ½ cup finely chopped shallots
- ⅓ cup water
- 2 tablespoons Worcestershire sauce
- 1½ tablespoons fresh lemon juice
- 1½ tablespoons dry sherry
- 2 tablespoons chopped fresh parsley

1. Heat a large, heavy skillet over medium-high heat. Sprinkle ¼ teaspoon salt and black pepper evenly over steaks. Add steaks to pan; cook 4 minutes on each side or until desired degree of doneness. Remove from pan; cover and keep warm.
2. Melt butter in pan over medium heat. Add shallots; cook 2 minutes or until tender, stirring occasionally. Add water, Worcestershire sauce, lemon juice, and sherry, stirring with a whisk. Reduce heat; simmer 1 minute. Stir in remaining ¼ teaspoon salt. Spoon sauce over steaks; sprinkle with parsley. Yield: 6 servings (serving size: 1 steak and 1½ tablespoons sauce).

CALORIES 197 (40% from fat); FAT 8.7g (sat 3.3g, mono 3.3g, poly 0.3g); PROTEIN 24.2g; CARB 3.8g; FIBER 0.1g; CHOL 73mg; IRON 3.5mg; SODIUM 312mg; CALC 18mg

Vietnamese Grilled Steak with Portobellos and Mint-Cilantro Mojo

Vietnamese Grilled Steak with Portobellos and Mint-Cilantro Mojo

A hint of nutmeg in the sauce reflects the French influence in Vietnamese cooking. Combining mint with cilantro adds a refreshing element to the mojo, a Caribbean condiment consisting of garlic, citrus juice, and oil. Mojo is also good with grilled or roasted lamb. Steamed green beans make a colorful side on the plate.

SAUCE:

¼ cup chopped green onions
¼ cup low-sodium soy sauce
1½ tablespoons chopped peeled fresh ginger
1 tablespoon brown sugar
1 tablespoon dark sesame oil
1 tablespoon honey
⅛ teaspoon ground nutmeg
1 garlic clove

MOJO:

½ cup cilantro leaves
½ cup mint leaves
3 tablespoons water
1 tablespoon olive oil
1 tablespoon fresh lemon juice
1 garlic clove

REMAINING INGREDIENTS:

2 portobello mushroom caps (about 4 ounces)
1 pound green beans, trimmed
Cooking spray
1 (1-pound) boneless beef shoulder steak

1. To prepare sauce, combine first 8 ingredients in a food processor; process until smooth. Place in a small bowl.
2. To prepare mojo, combine cilantro and next 5 ingredients in a food processor; process until smooth. Place mojo in a small bowl.
3. Remove brown gills from undersides of portobello mushrooms using a spoon; discard gills. Cut each mushroom into 6 slices; set aside.
4. Steam green beans 3 minutes or until tender; keep warm.
5. Heat a nonstick grill pan over medium-high heat. Coat pan with cooking spray. Add steak, and cook 2 minutes on each side or until browned. Remove from pan; cut steak diagonally across grain into thin slices. Toss mushrooms with half of sauce; add to pan. Stir-fry 1 minute; remove from pan. Return steak to pan; cook 2 minutes or until desired degree of doneness. Drizzle steak with remaining sauce. Arrange steak, mushrooms, and green beans on serving plates. Serve with mojo. Yield: 4 servings (serving size: 3 ounces steak, 3 mushroom slices, 1 cup green beans, and about 1 tablespoon mojo).

CALORIES 364 (41% from fat); FAT 16.6g (sat 4.9g, mono 7.6g, poly 2.2g); PROTEIN 35.6g; CARB 18.9g; FIBER 4.5g; CHOL 62mg; IRON 4.2mg; SODIUM 608mg; CALC 84mg

Fresh Herb–Coated Beef Tenderloin Steaks with Mushroom Gravy

(pictured on page 134)

BEEF:

1 teaspoon salt
1 teaspoon chopped fresh thyme
1 teaspoon chopped fresh rosemary
½ teaspoon freshly ground black pepper
4 garlic cloves, minced
4 (4-ounce) beef tenderloin steaks, trimmed (1 inch thick)
Cooking spray

GRAVY:

1 teaspoon olive oil
½ teaspoon chopped fresh thyme
1 (8-ounce) package presliced cremini mushrooms
4 garlic cloves, minced
½ cup fat-free, less-sodium chicken broth
½ cup white wine
1 tablespoon water
1 teaspoon cornstarch

1. Preheat oven to 450°.
2. Combine first 5 ingredients. Coat both sides of steaks with cooking spray; rub steaks evenly with thyme mixture. Place steaks on rack of a broiler or roasting pan coated with cooking spray; bake at 450° for 8 minutes on each side or until desired degree of doneness. Remove from oven; keep warm.
3. To prepare gravy, heat oil in a large nonstick skillet over medium-high heat. Add ½ teaspoon thyme, mushrooms, and 4 garlic cloves; cook 5 minutes or until mushrooms are tender. Add broth and wine; bring to a boil. Cook until reduced by half (about 4 minutes).
4. Combine water and cornstarch in a small bowl, stirring with a whisk. Add cornstarch mixture to mushroom mixture in pan; bring to a boil. Cook 1 minute or until slightly thick, stirring constantly. Serve with steaks. Yield: 4 servings (serving size: 1 steak and ¼ cup gravy).

CALORIES 202 (29% from fat); FAT 6.5g (sat 2.2g, mono 2.9g, poly 0.4g); PROTEIN 24.5g; CARB 6.3g; FIBER 0.7g; CHOL 52mg; IRON 2mg; SODIUM 692mg; CALC 44mg

Beef Tenderloin Steaks with Creole Spice Rub

The steaks need to stand for a few minutes after cooking to allow their juices to reabsorb. Try this sassy side dish: Sauté chopped bell peppers, onion, garlic, and ground red pepper, and then add frozen corn. Make a quick dessert—slice strawberries, and toss them with sour cream and brown sugar.

- 1 teaspoon dry mustard
- 1 teaspoon garlic powder
- 1 teaspoon ground sage
- 1 teaspoon dried thyme
- ¾ teaspoon salt
- ½ teaspoon ground cumin
- ½ teaspoon ground red pepper
- ½ teaspoon freshly ground black pepper
- 4 (4-ounce) beef tenderloin steaks, trimmed (1 inch thick)
- Cooking spray

1. Combine first 8 ingredients; rub mixture evenly over steaks.

2. Heat a large nonstick skillet over medium-high heat. Coat pan with cooking spray. Add steaks to pan; cook 4 minutes on each side or until desired degree of doneness. Remove from heat; let stand 5 minutes. Yield: 4 servings (serving size: 1 steak).

CALORIES 155 (35% from fat); FAT 6g (sat 2g, mono 2.2g, poly 0.4g); PROTEIN 22.8g; CARB 1.4g; FIBER 0.5g; CHOL 52mg; IRON 2.1mg; SODIUM 490mg; CALC 31mg

Pepper-Crusted Filet Mignon with Horseradish Cream

Horseradish and sour cream make a cooling yet spicy sauce for the peppery steaks.

- 2 (4-ounce) beef tenderloin steaks, trimmed (about ¾ inch thick)
- ½ teaspoon sea salt
- ¼ teaspoon freshly ground black pepper
- 1 teaspoon butter
- Cooking spray
- 1 garlic clove, minced
- ¼ cup fat-free sour cream
- ½ teaspoon prepared horseradish

1. Sprinkle steaks with salt and pepper.
2. Melt butter in a nonstick skillet coated with cooking spray over medium heat. Add steaks; cook 3 minutes on each side or until desired degree of doneness. Sprinkle steaks evenly with garlic; cook 1 minute on each side over medium-low heat.
3. Combine sour cream and horseradish; serve with steaks. Yield: 2 servings (serving size: 1 steak and 2 tablespoons horseradish cream).

CALORIES 231 (44% from fat); FAT 11.3g (sat 4.8g, mono 4g, poly 0.5g); PROTEIN 25.2g; CARB 5.6g; FIBER 0.1g; CHOL 78mg; IRON 3.3mg; SODIUM 684mg; CALC 58mg

Filet Mignon with Red Currant–Green Peppercorn Sauce

Green peppercorns are soft and a bit milder than black peppercorns. We prefer red currant jelly for this recipe because it makes a clear, shiny sauce.

- 1½ cups merlot or other dry red wine
- ¼ cup finely chopped shallots
- ¼ cup red currant jelly
- 1 tablespoon drained brine-packed green peppercorns, finely chopped
- 2 teaspoons butter
- 4 (4-ounce) beef tenderloin steaks, trimmed (1 inch thick)
- ¼ teaspoon kosher salt
- ¼ teaspoon freshly ground black pepper

1. Prepare grill.
2. Combine wine and shallots in a small saucepan; bring to a boil. Cook until reduced to ¼ cup (about 10 minutes). Strain through a fine sieve over a bowl; discard solids. Return wine to pan; add jelly and green peppercorns. Cook over medium heat until jelly melts (about 2 minutes), stirring occasionally. Remove from heat. Stir in butter; keep warm.
3. Sprinkle steaks with kosher salt and freshly ground black pepper. Place steaks on grill rack; grill 4 minutes on each side or until desired degree of doneness. Serve sauce with beef. Yield: 4 servings (serving size: 1 filet and 1 tablespoon sauce).

CALORIES 302 (39% from fat); FAT 13g (sat 5.5g, mono 4.9g, poly 0.5g); PROTEIN 23.3g; CARB 14.9g; FIBER 0.2g; CHOL 77mg; IRON 3.2mg; SODIUM 294mg; CALC 23mg

Guinness-Braised Beef Brisket

Tender from gentle cooking, this entrée is a classic preparation made without the usual pot watching. Serve it with grainy, coarse-ground mustard. Use the leftovers in classic Reuben sandwiches: sliced corned beef with Thousand Island dressing, Swiss cheese, and sauerkraut on sourdough, rye, or pumpernickel bread.

- 2 cups water
- 1 cup chopped onion
- 1 cup chopped carrot
- 1 cup chopped celery
- 1 cup Guinness Stout
- ⅔ cup packed brown sugar
- ¼ cup tomato paste
- ¼ cup chopped fresh or 1 tablespoon dried dill
- 1 (14-ounce) can less-sodium beef broth
- 6 black peppercorns
- 2 whole cloves
- 1 (3-pound) cured corned beef brisket, trimmed

1. Combine first 11 ingredients in a large electric slow cooker, stirring until well blended; top with beef. Cover and cook on HIGH 8 hours or until beef is tender. Remove beef; cut diagonally across grain into ¼-inch slices. Discard broth mixture. Yield: 6 servings (serving size: 3 ounces).

CALORIES 226 (39% from fat); FAT 9.7g (sat 3.2g, mono 4.7g, poly 0.4g); PROTEIN 17.9g; CARB 15.2g; FIBER 0.9g; CHOL 87mg; IRON 2.2mg; SODIUM 1,105mg; CALC 28mg

New England–Style Pickled Beef

Soaking meat in a salt solution is the traditional way to make corned beef. The three-day brining period is a great technique for keeping the brisket moist.

- 7 cups water, divided
- 2 tablespoons black peppercorns
- 2 tablespoons pickling spice
- 1 tablespoon juniper berries, crushed
- 1 tablespoon coriander seeds
- 8 bay leaves
- 6 thyme sprigs
- 4 garlic cloves, crushed
- ¾ cup kosher salt
- ½ cup sugar
- 2 cups ice cubes
- 1 (4½-pound) beef brisket, trimmed
- 1½ cups (2-inch-thick) slices carrot
- 1 (2-pound) head green cabbage, cored and quartered
- 9 small red potatoes, quartered
- 6 small onions, peeled and halved

1. Combine 1 cup water, peppercorns, and next 6 ingredients in a small saucepan; bring to a boil. Reduce heat, and simmer 5 minutes. Remove from heat. Pour into a large bowl; cool to room temperature. Add remaining 6 cups water, salt, and sugar, stirring until salt and sugar dissolve. Pour salt mixture into a 2-gallon zip-top plastic bag. Add ice and brisket; seal. Refrigerate 3 days, turning bag occasionally. Remove brisket from bag; discard brine. Pat brisket dry with paper towels.
2. Place brisket in a large stockpot; cover with water. Bring to a boil; skim foam from surface. Cover, reduce heat, and simmer 2½ to 3 hours or until brisket is tender. Remove brisket from pan; keep warm. Reserve cooking liquid in pan. Add carrot, cabbage, potatoes, and onions to reserved cooking liquid; bring to a boil. Reduce heat, and simmer 30 minutes or until tender. Discard bay leaves. Yield: 12 servings (serving size: about 3 ounces beef, 3 potato wedges, 1 onion half, and about ½ cup carrot and cabbage).

CALORIES 256 (34% from fat); FAT 9.8g (sat 3.5g, mono 4.4g, poly 0.4g); PROTEIN 29.9g; CARB 11.2g; FIBER 2.6g; CHOL 88mg; IRON 3.2mg; SODIUM 508mg; CALC 42mg

Garlic and Herb Standing Rib Roast

A standing rib roast makes a grand statement at the table. You do not need to ask your butcher for a frenched roast (one that has had the meat stripped from the bones); a regular standing rib roast will work just as well.

- 1 (5-pound) standing rib roast, trimmed
- Cooking spray
- 1½ tablespoons chopped fresh thyme
- ½ teaspoon salt
- ¼ teaspoon freshly ground black pepper
- 4 garlic cloves, minced
- Parsley sprigs (optional)
- Roasted garlic heads (optional)

1. Preheat oven to 450°.
2. Place roast on a broiler pan coated with cooking spray. Combine thyme, salt, pepper, and 4 garlic cloves; rub over roast. Bake at 450° for 45 minutes.
3. Reduce heat to 350° (do not remove roast from oven). Bake roast at 350° for 1 hour and 20 minutes or until a thermometer registers 145° (medium-rare) or desired degree of doneness. Let stand 10 minutes before slicing. Garnish with parsley and roasted garlic, if desired. Yield: 12 servings (serving size: about 3 ounces meat).

CALORIES 226 (53% from fat); FAT 13.3g (sat 5.3g, mono 5.6g, poly 0.4g); PROTEIN 24.4g; CARB 0.4g; FIBER 0.1g; CHOL 72mg; IRON 2.6mg; SODIUM 162mg; CALC 10mg

How to Roast Garlic Heads

Remove white papery skin from garlic head (do not peel or separate cloves). Cut top third off head, and discard.
Drizzle 1 teaspoon oil over cut side of garlic; wrap in foil. Bake at 375° for 50 minutes, cut side up, or until tender and cut side is lightly golden; cool 10 minutes.

Garlic and Herb Standing Rib Roast

Veal Piccata

Enjoy this lemony Italian favorite with simple steamed green beans and mashed sweet potatoes.

2 tablespoons all-purpose flour
1/4 teaspoon black pepper
Dash of salt
1 tablespoon water
1 large egg white
1/3 cup Italian-seasoned breadcrumbs
4 (2-ounce) veal cutlets
2 teaspoons olive oil
1 cup fat-free, less-sodium chicken broth
1 teaspoon grated lemon rind
2 to 3 tablespoons fresh lemon juice
1 tablespoon capers, drained and rinsed
Lemon wedges (optional)

1. Combine flour, pepper, and salt in a shallow dish. Combine water and egg white in another shallow dish, stirring with a whisk. Place breadcrumbs in a third shallow dish. Working with 1 cutlet at a time, dredge in flour mixture. Dip floured cutlet in egg white mixture; dredge in breadcrumbs.
2. Heat oil in a large nonstick skillet over medium-high heat. Add cutlets to pan; cook 2 minutes on each side or until lightly browned. Remove from pan; keep warm.
3. Add broth, rind, juice, and capers to pan; simmer 2 minutes, stirring constantly. Pour over cutlets; serve immediately. Garnish with lemon wedges, if desired. Yield: 2 servings (serving size: 2 cutlets and 3 tablespoons sauce).

CALORIES 281 (24% from fat); FAT 7.6g (sat 1.2g, mono 4g, poly 0.6g); PROTEIN 30.4g; CARB 21.2g; FIBER 1.3g; CHOL 89mg; IRON 2.2mg; SODIUM 964mg; CALCIUM 89mg

Breaded Veal Topped with Tomatoes, Spinach, and Lemon

Small boneless, skinless chicken breasts pounded 1/4 inch thick can be substituted for the veal.

1/2 cup all-purpose flour (about 2 1/4 ounces)
2 large eggs, lightly beaten
1 cup dry breadcrumbs
4 (4-ounce) veal cutlets (about 1/4 inch thick)
1/2 teaspoon salt
1/4 teaspoon black pepper
4 teaspoons olive oil, divided
Cooking spray
2 teaspoons balsamic vinegar
1/8 teaspoon salt
3 cups fresh spinach
1 cup grape tomatoes, halved (about 1/4 pound)
1 lemon, quartered

1. Place flour in shallow dish. Place eggs in another dish. Place breadcrumbs in another dish. Sprinkle veal with 1/2 teaspoon salt and pepper. Working with 1 cutlet at a time, dredge veal in flour, turning to coat other side; shake off excess flour. Dip veal in egg, and then dredge in breadcrumbs.
2. Heat 2 teaspoons oil in a large nonstick skillet coated with cooking spray over medium-high heat. Add veal; cook 4 minutes. Turn veal over; cook 3 minutes or until done. Keep warm.
3. Combine remaining 2 teaspoons oil, vinegar, and 1/8 teaspoon salt in a large bowl. Add spinach and tomatoes; toss gently to coat. Top veal with spinach mixture; serve with lemon wedges. Yield: 4 servings (serving size: 1 cutlet, 3/4 cup spinach mixture, and 1 lemon wedge).

CALORIES 384 (29% from fat); FAT 12.5g (sat 2.9g, mono 6.2g, poly 2.8g); PROTEIN 32.5g; CARB 33.8g; FIBER 2.4g; CHOL 197mg; IRON 4.2mg; SODIUM 730mg; CALC 97mg

Grilled Bread with Tuscan-Style Lamb

Ask the butcher to cut the leg of lamb into thin slices, or scaloppine (the Italian word for very thin slices of veal). Also, try the lamb over couscous or inside a warm pita.

- 1 tablespoon chopped fresh flat-leaf parsley
- 1 tablespoon chopped fresh rosemary
- 1 tablespoon chopped fresh thyme
- 1 tablespoon chopped fresh sage
- 1 tablespoon white wine vinegar
- 1 teaspoon extravirgin olive oil
- ¼ teaspoon freshly ground black pepper
- 2 garlic cloves, minced
- 1 (1-pound) boneless leg of lamb, trimmed
- ½ teaspoon salt
- Cooking spray
- 1 (8-ounce) French bread baguette
- ½ cup thinly sliced bottled roasted red bell peppers
- Flat-leaf parsley sprigs (optional)

1. Combine first 8 ingredients, stirring well; place mixture in a large zip-top plastic bag. Cut lamb crosswise into 8 (¼-inch-thick) slices. Place each slice between 2 sheets of heavy-duty plastic wrap; pound each piece to ⅛-inch thickness using a meat mallet or rolling pin. Add lamb to bag; seal and marinate in refrigerator 8 hours or overnight, turning bag occasionally. Remove lamb; discard marinade.

2. Prepare grill or broiler.

3. Sprinkle lamb evenly with salt. Place lamb on grill rack or broiler pan coated with cooking spray, and grill 1 minute on each side or until desired degree of doneness.

4. Cut baguette in half horizontally. Coat cut sides of bread with cooking spray. Place bread, cut sides down, on grill rack or broiler pan; grill 2 minutes or until golden. Cut bread into 16 slices. Serve lamb with grilled bread and bell peppers. Garnish with parsley sprigs, if desired. Yield: 4 servings (serving size: about 2 slices lamb, 4 slices bread, and 2 tablespoons peppers).

CALORIES 207 (29% from fat); FAT 6.6g (sat 1.7g, mono 2.5g, poly 1.7g); PROTEIN 14.2g; CARB 22.3g; FIBER 1.9g; CHOL 37mg; IRON 1.7mg; SODIUM 353mg; CALC 18mg

Curried Lamb Chops with Minted Chutney

Look for mango chutney with other condiments; it's a terrific flavor booster to a simple grilled chop.

- 2 teaspoons curry powder
- ½ teaspoon salt
- ¼ teaspoon crushed red pepper
- 4 (6-ounce) lamb rib chops, trimmed
- ½ cup mango chutney
- 2 tablespoons chopped fresh mint

1. Combine curry powder, salt, and pepper; rub evenly over lamb.
2. Heat a grill pan over medium-high heat. Add lamb; cook 5 minutes on each side or until desired degree of doneness. Combine chutney and mint; serve with lamb. Yield: 4 servings (serving size: 1 chop and 2 tablespoons chutney).

CALORIES 300 (31% from fat); FAT 10.4g (sat 3.7g, mono 4.1g, poly 1g); PROTEIN 36.1g; CARB 14.2g; FIBER 1.2g; CHOL 112mg; IRON 4mg; SODIUM 414mg; CALC 38mg

All About Mint

Mint isn't just a little sprig that garnishes your dessert plate. It's extremely versatile and can be used in both sweet and savory dishes. In the Mediterranean, it's treasured as a companion to lamb and is used in fruit and vegetable salads.

Spicy Lamb Kebabs

The yogurt-based marinade would also work well with cubed beef sirloin steak.

- 1 cup plain fat-free yogurt
- 1 tablespoon grated lemon rind
- 2 tablespoons fresh lemon juice
- 1½ tablespoons grated peeled fresh ginger
- 2 teaspoons paprika
- 1½ teaspoons salt
- 1 teaspoon ground coriander
- 1 teaspoon ground cumin
- ½ teaspoon freshly ground black pepper
- ¼ teaspoon ground red pepper
- 2 garlic cloves, minced
- 2½ pounds boneless leg of lamb, trimmed and cubed
- Cooking spray
- 2 tablespoons chopped fresh mint
- 8 lemon wedges

1. Combine first 11 ingredients in a large zip-top plastic bag. Add lamb to bag; seal and marinate in refrigerator 3 hours, turning bag occasionally.
2. Prepare grill.
3. Remove lamb from bag; discard marinade. Thread lamb onto 8 (10-inch) skewers. Place kebabs on grill rack coated with cooking spray; grill 8 minutes or until desired degree of doneness, turning occasionally. Place kebabs on a platter; sprinkle with mint. Serve with lemon wedges. Yield: 8 servings (serving size: 1 kebab and 1 lemon wedge).

CALORIES 163 (29% from fat); FAT 5.2g (sat 1.8g, mono 2.1g, poly 0.5g); PROTEIN 24.8g; CARB 3.5g; FIBER 0.4g; CHOL 73mg; IRON 2.2mg; SODIUM 528mg; CALC 52mg

Meatballs and Rice Noodles

An Asian spin on an Italian classic, pork and beef balls are nestled atop spicy noodles. Serve with thinly sliced cucumbers tossed with rice wine vinegar.

- 3 tablespoons chopped shallots
- 2 teaspoons fish sauce
- 1 teaspoon fresh lime juice
- 2 garlic cloves, minced
- 1 bacon slice
- 6 ounces lean ground pork
- 6 ounces ground sirloin
- Cooking spray
- 10 ounces rice vermicelli or thin rice stick noodles
- ½ cup warm water
- 6 tablespoons sugar
- ¼ cup fresh lime juice
- 1½ tablespoons fish sauce
- 2 teaspoons chili garlic sauce (such as Lee Kum Kee)
- 4 garlic cloves, minced
- 1 tablespoon chopped fresh basil
- 1 tablespoon chopped fresh cilantro
- 1 tablespoon chopped fresh mint

1. Combine first 5 ingredients in a food processor; process until smooth. Add pork and beef; pulse to combine.

2. Divide meat mixture into 12 equal portions, shaping each into a (1-inch) ball. Heat a large nonstick skillet over medium-high heat. Coat pan with cooking spray. Add meatballs; cook 10 minutes or until meatballs are done, browning on all sides.

3. Cook noodles in boiling water 6 minutes; drain. Combine warm water and next 5 ingredients, stirring with a whisk until sugar dissolves. Combine fresh basil, cilantro, and mint. Divide noodles evenly among 4 plates; top each serving with 3 meatballs. Drizzle each serving with about ⅓ cup sauce; sprinkle with about 2 teaspoons herb mixture. Yield: 4 servings.

CALORIES 487 (28% from fat); FAT 15.1g (sat 5.6g, mono 6.6g, poly 1.2g); PROTEIN 19.1g; CARB 66.7g; FIBER 2.1g; CHOL 59mg; IRON 1.9mg; SODIUM 905mg; CALC 36mg

Pan-Seared Pork Cutlets with Nectarine Salsa

The rub gives a boost to a potentially bland cut of meat. The contrast of hot and sweet is sure to make this a family favorite. You can substitute peaches for the nectarines if you prefer.

- 2 teaspoons chili powder
- 1 teaspoon ground coriander
- ½ teaspoon ground cumin
- ½ teaspoon paprika
- ¼ teaspoon salt
- ¼ teaspoon freshly ground black pepper
- 8 (2-ounce) pork loin cutlets
- 1 teaspoon olive oil
- Cooking spray
- ½ cup bottled salsa
- ¼ cup apricot preserves
- 4 cups sliced peeled nectarines (about 3 pounds)
- ¼ cup chopped fresh cilantro
- 2 tablespoons chopped fresh oregano

1. Combine first 6 ingredients; rub mixture over both sides of pork. Heat oil in a large nonstick skillet coated with cooking spray over medium-high heat. Add pork; sauté 2 minutes on each side or until done. Remove from pan; keep warm.

2. Add salsa and preserves to pan; bring to a boil. Cook 1 minute. Stir in nectarines, cilantro, and oregano; cook mixture 1 minute or until thoroughly heated. Serve salsa with pork. Yield: 4 servings (serving size: 2 cutlets and 1 cup salsa).

CALORIES 322 (31% from fat); FAT 11g (sat 1.6g, mono 4.1g, poly 1.1g); PROTEIN 25.5g; CARB 32.6g; FIBER 4.7g; CHOL 68mg; IRON 2.7mg; SODIUM 327mg; CALC 60mg

Bourbon-Glazed Pork Chops and Peaches

The bourbon-and-honey marinade also yields a sauce for the dish. Be sure the marinade comes to a full boil, which is for food safety and a recommended practice whenever a meat marinade is later used as a sauce.

- ⅓ cup bourbon
- ¼ cup honey
- 3 tablespoons low-sodium soy sauce
- 1 tablespoon canola oil
- ½ teaspoon ground ginger
- ¼ teaspoon crushed red pepper
- ¼ teaspoon freshly ground black pepper
- 4 (4-ounce) boneless center-cut loin pork chops (about ¾ inch thick)
- 2 peaches, halved and pitted
- Cooking spray

1. Combine bourbon, honey, soy sauce, canola oil, ginger, red pepper, and ¼ teaspoon black pepper in a large bowl. Add pork and peaches; toss well to coat.

2. Heat a nonstick grill pan over medium-high heat. Coat pan with cooking spray. Remove pork and peaches from bowl, reserving marinade. Place pork and peaches on grill pan; cook 4 minutes on each side or until pork is done.

3. While pork cooks, place marinade in a microwave-safe bowl; microwave at HIGH 2 minutes. Spoon over pork and peaches. Yield: 4 servings (serving size: 1 chop, 1 peach half, and 2 tablespoons sauce).

CALORIES 285 (29% from fat); FAT 9.3g (sat 3.1g, mono 4.3g, poly 1.1g); PROTEIN 26.4g; CARB 24.3g; FIBER 1.2g; CHOL 73mg; IRON 1.4mg; SODIUM 489mg; CALC 27mg

Bourbon-Glazed Pork Chops and Peaches

Pork Loin Chops with Cinnamon Apples

Tart Granny Smiths balance the caramel sweetness of brown sugar. Braeburn apples work well, too.

- 1 teaspoon dried rubbed sage
- ½ teaspoon salt
- ¼ teaspoon freshly ground black pepper
- 4 (4-ounce) boneless center-cut loin pork chops (about ½ inch thick)
- ½ teaspoon vegetable oil
- Cooking spray
- 1 teaspoon butter
- 4 cups (½-inch) slices peeled Granny Smith apples (about 4 medium)
- 1 tablespoon brown sugar
- 1 teaspoon fresh lemon juice
- ½ teaspoon ground cinnamon
- Dash of salt

1. Combine dried sage, ½ teaspoon salt, and black pepper; sprinkle over pork. Heat oil in a large nonstick skillet coated with cooking spray over medium heat. Add pork; cook 3 minutes on each side or until done. Remove pork from pan; cover and keep warm.

2. Melt butter in pan over medium heat. Add apples and next 4 ingredients; cook 5 minutes or until tender, stirring frequently. Serve apple mixture with pork chops. Yield: 4 servings (serving size: 1 pork chop and ¾ cup apple mixture).

CALORIES 251 (30% from fat); FAT 8.3g (sat 3.1g, mono 3.3g, poly 0.9g); PROTEIN 24.1g; CARB 20.2g; FIBER 2.3g; CHOL 67mg; IRON 0.9mg; SODIUM 388mg; CALC 38mg

Buttermilk-Brined Pork Chops

Though these pork chops require overnight brining, they make dinner the next night a breeze. Brine chops up to two days beforehand. Just remove from brine after an overnight soak, discarding brine; cover chops in plastic wrap, and refrigerate until ready to cook. Add roasted butternut squash and steamed green beans.

- 2 cups fat-free buttermilk
- 2 tablespoons kosher salt
- 2 tablespoons sugar
- 1 tablespoon grated lemon rind
- 1 teaspoon chopped fresh rosemary
- 1 teaspoon chopped fresh sage
- 4 (6-ounce) bone-in center-cut pork chops (about ½ inch thick)
- 2 teaspoons freshly ground black pepper
- Cooking spray

1. Combine first 6 ingredients in a large zip-top plastic bag; shake well to dissolve salt and sugar. Add pork to bag; seal and refrigerate at least 8 hours or overnight, turning bag occasionally.

2. Remove pork from bag; discard buttermilk mixture. Pat pork dry with a paper towel. Sprinkle pork with pepper.

3. Heat a large nonstick grill pan over medium-high heat. Coat pan with cooking spray. Add pork chops; cook about 3½ minutes on each side or until desired degree of doneness. Yield: 4 servings (serving size: 1 chop).

CALORIES 183 (35% from fat); FAT 7.2g (sat 2.5g, mono 3.2g, poly 0.6g); PROTEIN 26g; CARB 2g; FIBER 0.3g; CHOL 69mg; IRON 0.8mg; SODIUM 345mg; CALC 43mg

Buttermilk-Brined Pork Chops

Ginger-Curry Pork and Rice

If you don't have dried apricots on hand, you can substitute golden raisins instead. Coat your knife with cooking spray for chopping the dried fruit. Fresh ginger livens up this dish and gives it a mild, peppery heat. The sauce is also good with skinless, boneless chicken thighs.

- 2 (4-ounce) boneless center-cut loin pork chops
- 1/8 teaspoon black pepper
- Dash of salt
- 1 tablespoon canola oil, divided
- 1/2 teaspoon grated lime rind
- 1 tablespoon fresh lime juice
- 1 1/2 teaspoons grated peeled fresh ginger
- 1/2 cup chopped onion
- 1/2 teaspoon red curry paste
- 1 cup fat-free, less-sodium chicken broth
- 2 tablespoons chopped dried apricots
- 1 teaspoon honey
- 1 garlic clove, minced
- 1 1/2 cups cooked basmati rice
- 2 tablespoons thinly sliced green onions

1. Sprinkle pork with pepper and salt. Heat 2 teaspoons oil in a medium nonstick skillet over medium-high heat. Add pork; cook 2 1/2 minutes on each side or until browned. Remove from heat. Combine rind, juice, and ginger in a shallow dish; add pork, turning to coat.

2. Add remaining 1 teaspoon oil to pan, and place over medium heat. Add 1/2 cup onion and curry paste; cook 2 minutes or until onion is tender, stirring frequently. Add pork mixture, broth, apricots, honey, and garlic; bring to a boil. Cover, reduce heat, and simmer 10 minutes or until pork is done. Remove pork from pan. Increase heat to medium-high. Add rice; cook 2 minutes or until thoroughly heated, stirring frequently. Serve rice with pork; top each serving with 1 tablespoon green onions. Yield: 2 servings (serving size: 1 pork chop and 1 cup rice mixture).

CALORIES 486 (26% from fat); FAT 14.3g (sat 3.3g, mono 4.8g, poly 5.1g); PROTEIN 33.5g; CARB 53.7g; FIBER 4.8g; CHOL 62mg; IRON 2mg; SODIUM 965mg; CALC 56mg

Pan-Seared Pork Chops with Molasses-Plum Sauce

Aside from seasoning the meat, salt also brings the sweet-savory flavors of the sauce into balance. If you prefer, you can easily substitute dried cherries or cranberries for the blueberries and still get a great-tasting dish. Serve these saucy pork chops alongside rice or couscous.

- 2 teaspoons olive oil
- ½ cup chopped onion
- ¾ cup fat-free, less-sodium chicken broth
- ¼ cup dried blueberries
- 3 tablespoons cider vinegar
- 2 tablespoons molasses
- ½ teaspoon salt, divided
- ½ teaspoon freshly ground black pepper, divided
- ⅛ teaspoon ground coriander
- 3 plums, pitted, peeled, and coarsely chopped (about 1¾ cups)
- Cooking spray
- 4 (6-ounce) bone-in center-cut pork chops (about 1 inch thick)
- Fresh parsley sprigs (optional)

1. Heat oil in a medium saucepan over medium heat. Add onion; cook 3 minutes or until tender, stirring frequently. Stir in chicken broth, blueberries, vinegar, molasses, ¼ teaspoon salt, ¼ teaspoon black pepper, coriander, and plums; bring to a boil. Reduce heat, and simmer 20 minutes or until plums are tender and mixture is thick.

2. Heat a large nonstick skillet over medium-high heat. Coat pan with cooking spray. Sprinkle remaining ¼ teaspoon salt and ¼ teaspoon pepper over chops. Add chops to pan; cook 2 minutes on each side or until browned. Reduce heat to medium; cook 4 minutes or until done. Remove chops from pan; cover and keep warm. Add plum mixture to pan, and bring to a simmer. Cook 2 minutes, scraping pan to loosen browned bits. Spoon plum mixture over pork. Garnish with parsley, if desired. Yield: 4 servings (serving size: 1 pork chop and ¼ cup sauce).

CALORIES 299 (29% from fat); FAT 9.6g (sat 2.9g, mono 5g, poly 0.8g); PROTEIN 27.1g; CARB 26.6g; FIBER 1.9g; CHOL 69mg; IRON 1.7mg; SODIUM 434mg; CALC 61mg

Shredded Pork Tacos

Shredded Pork Tacos

Since pork tenderloin is already a lean cut of meat, it literally falls apart after eight hours. Use two forks to shred the meat while the mixture is still in the slow cooker. You can also serve the pork mixture on sandwich buns. Serve with a fruit salad of kiwi, oranges, honeydew melon, and grapes.

- ½ cup chopped onion
- ½ cup beer or water
- 2 tablespoons tomato paste
- 1 (1-pound) pork tenderloin, trimmed and cut into 1-inch pieces
- 1 (1.25-ounce) package 40%-less-sodium taco seasoning
- 1 jalapeño pepper, seeded and chopped
- 2 tablespoons chopped fresh cilantro
- 8 (6-inch) corn tortillas
- 2 cups shredded iceberg lettuce
- ½ cup (2 ounces) reduced-fat shredded sharp Cheddar cheese
- ¼ cup finely chopped onion
- ¼ cup reduced-fat sour cream

1. Combine first 6 ingredients in an electric slow cooker. Cover and cook on LOW 6 hours. Stir in cilantro.

2. Warm tortillas according to package directions. Spoon ¼ cup pork mixture onto each tortilla, and top each tortilla with ¼ cup lettuce, 1 tablespoon cheese, 1½ teaspoons finely chopped onion, and 1½ teaspoons sour cream. Fold tacos in half. Yield: 4 servings (serving size: 2 tacos).

CALORIES 379 (28% from fat); FAT 11.6g (sat 4.8g, mono 2.9g, poly 1.2g); PROTEIN 42g; CARB 28.1g; FIBER 3.2g; CHOL 119mg; IRON 2.1mg; SODIUM 343mg; CALC 142mg

Rosemary and Pepper–Crusted Pork Tenderloin

Use a mortar and pestle to crush the fennel and celery seeds. Or place them in a zip-top plastic bag, and crush with a rolling pin.

- 2 teaspoons cracked black pepper
- 1 teaspoon dried rosemary, crushed
- ½ teaspoon kosher salt
- ½ teaspoon fennel seeds, crushed
- ½ teaspoon celery seeds, crushed
- ½ teaspoon dry mustard
- 1 (1-pound) pork tenderloin, trimmed
- Cooking spray
- 2 tablespoons chopped fresh flat-leaf parsley

1. Preheat oven to 425°.

2. Combine first 6 ingredients; rub over pork. Place pork in a shallow roasting pan coated with cooking spray. Bake at 425° for 30 minutes or until a thermometer registers 160° (slightly pink). Let stand 5 minutes; cut into thin slices. Sprinkle with parsley. Yield: 4 servings (serving size: 3 ounces).

CALORIES 158 (31% from fat); FAT 5.4g (sat 1.8g, mono 2.2g, poly 0.5g); PROTEIN 24.7g; CARB 1.3g; FIBER 0.6g; CHOL 75mg; IRON 1.8mg; SODIUM 289mg; CALC 23mg

Pork Tenderloin with Olive-Mustard Tapenade

This quick entrée is great served with orzo and a tossed Greek salad with feta cheese. To quickly flatten pork, press with the heel of your hand. A little of this tapenade adds a lot of flavor.

1 (1-pound) pork tenderloin, trimmed and cut crosswise into 8 pieces
½ teaspoon salt
¼ teaspoon black pepper
¼ teaspoon ground fennel
Cooking spray
¼ cup chopped pitted kalamata olives
¼ cup chopped pitted green olives or onion-stuffed green olives
1 tablespoon chopped fresh parsley
1 tablespoon Dijon mustard
2 teaspoons balsamic vinegar
1 garlic clove, minced, or ½ teaspoon bottled minced garlic

1. Heat a large nonstick skillet over medium-high heat. Press pork pieces into ½-inch-thick medallions. Combine salt, pepper, and fennel; rub evenly over pork. Lightly coat pork with cooking spray. Add pork to pan; cook 4 minutes on each side or until done.
2. While pork cooks, combine olives and next 4 ingredients. Serve olive mixture over pork. Yield: 4 servings (serving size: 2 pork medallions and 2 tablespoons olive mixture).

CALORIES 163 (33% from fat); FAT 6g (sat 1.6g, mono 3.2g, poly 0.7g); PROTEIN 24.3g; CARB 2.2g; FIBER 0.7g; CHOL 74mg; IRON 2.2mg; SODIUM 590mg; CALC 31mg

Caribbean Pork and Plantain Hash

Use semiripe yellow plantains—not green or soft, ripe black ones. The plantains brown better if not stirred too much as they cook. Serve with a side of tomato and hearts of palm salad and mango slices drizzled with lime juice for an authentic island meal.

1 tablespoon low-sodium soy sauce
¾ teaspoon salt, divided
¾ teaspoon dried thyme
¼ teaspoon ground ginger
¼ teaspoon ground red pepper
⅛ teaspoon ground allspice
1 (1-pound) pork tenderloin, trimmed and cut into ½-inch pieces
1½ tablespoons vegetable oil, divided
1 tablespoon butter
1½ cups coarsely chopped onion
1 cup chopped green bell pepper
2 large yellow plantains, chopped (about 3 cups)
½ teaspoon black pepper
4 garlic cloves, minced
1 teaspoon habanero hot pepper sauce
2 tablespoons chopped fresh cilantro

1. Combine soy sauce, ¼ teaspoon salt, thyme, and next 4 ingredients; toss well to coat. Heat 1½ teaspoons oil in a large nonstick skillet over medium-high heat. Add pork mixture; sauté 4 minutes or until done. Remove from pan. Add 1 tablespoon oil and butter to pan. Add onion, bell pepper, plantains, ½ teaspoon salt, and black pepper; cook 6 minutes, stirring occasionally. Stir in garlic; sauté 2 minutes or until plantains are tender. Drizzle with hot sauce, and stir well. Sprinkle with cilantro. Yield: 4 servings (serving size: about 1½ cups).

CALORIES 384 (29% from fat); FAT 12.5g (sat 4g, mono 3.8g, poly 3.7g); PROTEIN 26.8g; CARB 44.9g; FIBER 4.7g; CHOL 81mg; IRON 2.8mg; SODIUM 674mg; CALC 38mg

Caribbean Pork and Plantain Hash

Roasted Pork Tenderloin Medallions with Dried Cranberry Sauce

Roasted Pork Tenderloin Medallions with Dried Cranberry Sauce

A tablespoon of grape jelly helps thicken the tangy-sweet sauce. Tenderloin is lean and juicy when it's properly prepared. Use a meat thermometer to avoid overcooking. Add broccoli and whole wheat couscous to round out the meal.

PORK:

1 teaspoon dried sage
1 teaspoon dried thyme
¾ teaspoon salt
½ teaspoon freshly ground black pepper
1 (1-pound) pork tenderloin, trimmed
Cooking spray

SAUCE:

1 cup fat-free, less-sodium chicken broth
1 cup dried cranberries
½ cup cranberry juice cocktail (such as Ocean Spray)
1 tablespoon grape jelly

1. Preheat oven to 400°.
2. To prepare pork, combine first 4 ingredients; rub evenly over pork.
3. Heat a large ovenproof nonstick skillet over medium-high heat. Coat pan with cooking spray. Add pork; cook 4 minutes on each side or until browned. Place pan in oven; cook pork at 400° for 12 minutes or until a meat thermometer registers 160° (slightly pink). Place pork on a cutting board; keep warm.
4. To prepare sauce, add broth, dried cranberries, and juice to pan; bring to a boil, scraping pan to loosen browned bits. Stir in jelly; cook 8 minutes or until mixture is slightly thick, stirring occasionally. Cut pork into (½-inch) slices. Serve with sauce. Yield: 4 servings (serving size: about 3 ounces pork and ¼ cup sauce).

CALORIES 282 (20% from fat); FAT 6.3g (sat 2.2g, mono 2.8g, poly 0.7g); PROTEIN 24g; CARB 33.6g; FIBER 2.1g; CHOL 75mg; IRON 2.1mg; SODIUM 596mg; CALC 21mg

Pork with Apricots, Dried Plums, and Sauerkraut

Sauerkraut balances the sweetness of the apricot preserves and orange juice. Slow cooking nicely tenderizes the pork and dried fruit.

1 (2-pound) pork tenderloin, trimmed
1 cup chopped onion
¾ cup apricot preserves
½ cup dried apricots
½ cup pitted dried plums
¼ cup fat-free, less-sodium chicken broth
¼ cup orange juice
2 tablespoons cornstarch
1 teaspoon salt
½ teaspoon dried thyme
¼ teaspoon freshly ground black pepper
1 (10-ounce) package refrigerated sauerkraut

1. Place pork in an electric slow cooker. Combine onion and next 10 ingredients in a large bowl; pour sauerkraut mixture over pork. Cover and cook on LOW 7 hours. Remove pork from slow cooker, and let pork stand 10 minutes. Cut pork into ¼-inch-thick slices; serve with sauerkraut mixture. Yield: 8 servings (serving size: 3 ounces pork and about ½ cup sauerkraut mixture).

CALORIES 313 (19% from fat); FAT 6.6g (sat 2.2g, mono 3g, poly 0.7g); PROTEIN 25.4g; CARB 38.3g; FIBER 2.5g; CHOL 67mg; IRON 1.7mg; SODIUM 41mg; CALC 594mg

Thyme-Coated Pork Tenderloin

Pork tenderloin is an ideal choice for weeknight meals. It's as versatile as chicken and as quick and easy to prepare. In this version, the pork is rolled in a mixture of fresh breadcrumbs, dried thyme, and dried onion flakes. Day-old bread makes superior crumbs.

1 teaspoon dried thyme
1 teaspoon instant onion flakes
1 slice day-old hearty white bread (such as Pepperidge Farm), torn
2 large egg whites, lightly beaten
1 (1-pound) pork tenderloin, trimmed
¼ teaspoon salt
¼ teaspoon freshly ground black pepper
Cooking spray

1. Preheat oven to 400°.
2. Place thyme, onion, and bread in a food processor; pulse until fine breadcrumbs measure ⅓ cup. Place breadcrumb mixture in a shallow dish. Place egg whites in a shallow dish. Sprinkle pork with salt and pepper. Dip pork in egg whites; dredge in breadcrumb mixture. Place pork on a broiler pan coated with cooking spray. Bake at 400° for 30 minutes or until a thermometer registers 160° (slightly pink). Let stand 5 minutes. Cut pork into ¼-inch-thick slices. Yield: 4 servings (serving size: 3 ounces).

CALORIES 165 (22% from fat); FAT 4.1g (sat 1.3g, mono 1.5g, poly 0.3g); PROTEIN 25.1g; CARB 5.5g; FIBER 0.8g; CHOL 63mg; IRON 1.7mg; SODIUM 267mg; CALC 17mg

Honey-Hoisin Pork Tenderloin

Look for hoisin sauce in the Asian section of your market. Serve this pork dish with a salad and mashed potatoes.

2 tablespoons sliced green onions
2 tablespoons hoisin sauce
2 tablespoons low-sodium soy sauce
2 tablespoons sage or clover honey
1 tablespoon hot water
2 garlic cloves, minced
1 (1-pound) pork tenderloin, trimmed
¼ teaspoon salt
Cooking spray
½ teaspoon sesame seeds

1. Preheat oven to 400°.
2. Combine first 6 ingredients in a small bowl. Pour ¼ cup honey mixture into a large zip-top plastic bag; reserve remaining honey mixture. Add pork to bag; seal and marinate in refrigerator 30 minutes, turning bag occasionally.
3. Remove pork from bag; discard marinade. Sprinkle pork with salt. Heat a large ovenproof skillet over medium-high heat. Coat pan with cooking spray. Add pork; cook 2 minutes, browning on all sides. Brush 1 tablespoon reserved honey mixture over pork; sprinkle with sesame seeds. Place pan in oven. Bake at 400° for 20 minutes or until a thermometer registers 160° (slightly pink) or until desired degree of doneness.
4. Place pork on a platter; let stand 5 minutes. Cut pork diagonally across grain into thin slices. Drizzle with remaining honey mixture. Yield: 4 servings (serving size: 3 ounces pork).

CALORIES 195 (20% from fat); FAT 4.3g (sat 1.4g, mono 1.9g, poly 0.6g); PROTEIN 24.7g; CARB 13.6g; FIBER 0.5g; CHOL 74mg; IRON 1.7mg; SODIUM 633mg; CALC 12mg

Honey-Hoisin Pork Tenderloin

Pork Tenderloin with Plum Sauce

Pork Tenderloin with Plum Sauce

Serve with polenta and sugar snap peas; add a sprig of parsley, if desired.

- 1 teaspoon grated peeled fresh ginger
- ½ teaspoon kosher salt, divided
- ¼ teaspoon freshly ground black pepper, divided
- 1 (1-pound) pork tenderloin, trimmed
- 1 teaspoon olive oil
- 2½ tablespoons minced shallots (about 1 medium)
- 2 cups chopped peeled ripe plums (about 4 medium)
- 1 tablespoon brown sugar
- ¼ teaspoon ground ginger
- ¼ cup dry white wine
- 1 teaspoon balsamic vinegar
- 1 teaspoon butter
- Cooking spray
- 1 tablespoon chopped walnuts, toasted

1. Combine fresh ginger, ¼ teaspoon salt, and ⅛ teaspoon pepper. Cut pork crosswise into 8 pieces; rub pork with ginger mixture. Let stand 15 minutes.
2. Heat oil in a large nonstick skillet over medium heat. Add shallots; cook 5 minutes or until tender, stirring frequently. Stir in remaining ¼ teaspoon salt, ⅛ teaspoon pepper, plums, sugar, and ground ginger. Cook 8 minutes or until plums are tender; stir in wine and vinegar. Reduce heat; simmer 10 minutes. Add butter; stir until butter melts.
3. Heat a large nonstick skillet over medium-high heat. Coat pan with cooking spray. Add pork to pan; cook 3 minutes on each side or until desired degree of doneness. Serve sauce over pork. Sprinkle with walnuts. Yield: 4 servings (serving size: 2 pork pieces, ¼ cup sauce, and ¾ teaspoon walnuts).

CALORIES 232 (30% from fat); FAT 7.7g (sat 2.2g, mono 3.4g, poly 1.6g); PROTEIN 25g; CARB 16g; FIBER 1.5g; CHOL 76mg; IRON 1.8mg; SODIUM 305mg; CALC 19mg

Simply Roasted Pork

Apple jelly can be used in place of the apricot preserves; it will give the glaze a slightly sweeter flavor.

- ½ cup apricot preserves
- 1 teaspoon salt
- 1 teaspoon dried oregano
- ¾ teaspoon garlic powder
- ½ teaspoon freshly ground black pepper
- 1 (3-pound) boneless pork loin roast, trimmed
- Cooking spray
- Flat-leaf parsley sprigs (optional)

1. Preheat oven to 425°.
2. Place preserves in a small saucepan over medium-low heat; cook 10 minutes or until melted, stirring occasionally. Keep warm over low heat.
3. Combine salt, oregano, garlic powder, and pepper; rub evenly over pork. Place pork on a rack coated with cooking spray; place rack in a shallow roasting pan. Bake at 425° for 30 minutes. Brush ¼ cup preserves evenly over pork. Bake an additional 10 minutes. Brush remaining preserves evenly over pork. Bake an additional 10 minutes or until a thermometer registers 160° (slightly pink). Let pork stand 10 minutes before slicing. Garnish with flat-leaf parsley sprigs, if desired. Yield: 14 servings (serving size: about 3 ounces).

CALORIES 159 (27% from fat); FAT 4.7g (sat 1.6g, mono 2.1g, poly 0.5g); PROTEIN 20.6g; CARB 7.6g; FIBER 0.2g; CHOL 59mg; IRON 0.9mg; SODIUM 232mg; CALC 24mg

Fig and Chile-Glazed Pork Tenderloin

Fig and Chile–Glazed Pork Tenderloin

- ½ cup fig preserves
- ¼ cup rice vinegar
- 1 tablespoon chile paste with garlic
- 1 tablespoon low-sodium soy sauce
- ½ teaspoon kosher salt, divided
- 2 (1-pound) pork tenderloins, trimmed
- ½ teaspoon freshly ground black pepper
- Cooking spray
- Fresh chives, cut into 1-inch pieces (optional)

1. Prepare grill.
2. Combine preserves, vinegar, chile paste, soy sauce, and ¼ teaspoon salt, stirring with a whisk.
3. Sprinkle pork with ¼ teaspoon salt and pepper. Place pork on a grill rack coated with cooking spray; grill 18 minutes or until a thermometer registers 160° (slightly pink), turning occasionally and basting with fig mixture. Garnish with chives, if desired. Yield: 8 servings (serving size: about 3 ounces).

CALORIES 193 (18% from fat); FAT 3.9g (sat 1.3g, mono 1.8g, poly 0.4g); PROTEIN 24g; CARB 14g; FIBER 0.3g; CHOL 74mg; IRON 1.6mg; SODIUM 274mg; CALC 11mg

Curried Pork over Basmati Rice

- 3½ cups cubed red potato
- 1 cup chopped onion
- 1 cup chopped red bell pepper
- ¼ cup fat-free, less-sodium chicken broth
- 2 tablespoons all-purpose flour (about ½ ounce)
- 2 tablespoons tomato paste
- 1 tablespoon sugar
- 1 tablespoon minced peeled fresh ginger
- 1½ teaspoons salt
- 1 teaspoon Madras curry powder
- 1 teaspoon ground cumin
- 1 (1½-pound) boneless pork loin roast, cubed
- 2 garlic cloves, minced
- ½ cup coconut milk
- 3 cups hot cooked basmati rice

1. Combine first 13 ingredients in an electric slow cooker; stir well to dissolve flour. Cook on LOW 6 to 8 hours or until pork and potatoes are tender. Stir in coconut milk. Serve over rice. Yield: 6 servings (serving size: about 1 cup curried pork and ½ cup rice).

CALORIES 373 (14% from fat); FAT 5.8g (sat 1.9g, mono 2.1g, poly 0.6g); PROTEIN 29.3g; CARB 49.9g; FIBER 3.5g; CHOL 75mg; IRON 3.1mg; SODIUM 731mg; CALC 37mg

Oven-Braised Pork Roast with Apples

- 1 teaspoon salt, divided
- 1 teaspoon garlic powder
- 2 tablespoons brown sugar
- 2 teaspoons ground cumin
- 1 teaspoon ground cinnamon
- ½ teaspoon coarsely ground black pepper
- ¼ teaspoon ground ginger
- ¼ teaspoon ground red pepper
- ¼ teaspoon ground cloves
- 1 (3½-pound) boneless pork loin roast, trimmed
- Cooking spray
- ½ cup chopped onion
- ½ cup chopped dried apricots
- ½ cup thawed orange juice concentrate
- ⅓ cup golden raisins
- 1 (14-ounce) can fat-free, less-sodium chicken broth
- 2 tablespoons butter
- 4 Rome apples, each cut into 8 wedges
- 1 tablespoon balsamic vinegar

1. Combine ¾ teaspoon salt and next 8 ingredients. Rub evenly over pork. Cover and refrigerate 2 hours.
2. Preheat oven to 425°.
3. Heat a large Dutch oven over medium-high heat. Coat pan with cooking spray. Add pork to pan; cook 4 minutes, browning on all sides. Remove pork from pan. Add onion to pan; sauté 1 minute. Return pork to pan. Add apricots, orange juice concentrate, raisins, and broth; bring to a boil. Cover and bake at 425° for 30 minutes. Reduce oven temperature to 325° (do not remove pork from oven); bake 20 minutes or until a thermometer inserted into thickest portion of pork registers 160° (slightly pink). Remove pork from pan, reserving cooking liquid. Place pork on a platter; cover with foil.
4. Remove apricots and raisins from pan. Bring broth mixture to a boil over high heat; cook until reduced to ½ cup (about 5 minutes). Remove from heat.
5. Melt butter in a large nonstick skillet over medium-high heat. Add apples; cook 2 minutes on each side or until lightly browned. Stir in reserved apricots and raisins, reduced broth mixture, vinegar, and remaining ¼ teaspoon salt; cook 3 minutes. Slice pork; serve with apple mixture. Yield: 12 servings (serving size: 3 ounces pork and ½ cup apple mixture).

CALORIES 297 (31% from fat); FAT 10.1g (sat 3.8g, mono 4.1g, poly 1.1g); PROTEIN 29.7g; CARB 21.7g; FIBER 2.6g; CHOL 83mg; IRON 1.9mg; SODIUM 355mg; CALC 43mg

Country Sausage Patties

Sausage patties require some fat to stay moist, which is why Boston butt is a good cut of pork for this recipe. For best results, prepare the mixture a day ahead and refrigerate, which allows the spices to permeate the meat overnight. You can, however, cook the patties right away. Refrigerate cooked sausage up to three days, or freeze up to two months.

- 1 (1½-pound) boneless pork shoulder (Boston butt), trimmed and cut into 1-inch cubes
- ¼ cup cold water
- 1 teaspoon salt
- 1 teaspoon dark brown sugar
- 1 teaspoon minced fresh or ¼ teaspoon dried rubbed sage
- 1 teaspoon minced fresh or ¼ teaspoon dried thyme
- 1 teaspoon crushed red pepper
- 1 teaspoon freshly ground black pepper
- ½ teaspoon ground coriander
- ½ teaspoon hot pepper sauce (such as Tabasco)
- ¼ teaspoon grated whole nutmeg
- Cooking spray

1. Place half of pork in a food processor; pulse until coarsely ground. Place pork in a large bowl. Repeat procedure with remaining pork. Add ¼ cup water and next 9 ingredients. Knead mixture until well blended. Cover and refrigerate mixture 8 hours or overnight.

2. Divide mixture into 16 equal portions, shaping each into a ½-inch-thick patty. Heat a large nonstick skillet over medium-high heat. Coat pan with cooking spray. Add half the patties; cook 6 minutes. Turn patties over; cook 5 minutes or until done. Repeat procedure with remaining patties. Yield: 8 servings (serving size: 2 patties).

CALORIES 111 (42% from fat); FAT 5.2g (sat 1.8g, mono 2.3g, poly 0.6g); PROTEIN 14g; CARB 1.1g; FIBER 0.3g; CHOL 47mg; IRON 1mg; SODIUM 349mg; CALC 15mg

Roast Pork Loin with Savory Fennel Bread Pudding

- 1 cup sugar
- 8 cups water
- ¼ cup kosher salt
- 1 (2-pound) boneless pork loin roast, trimmed
- 1 teaspoon olive oil
- 3 cups thinly sliced fennel (about 1 large bulb)
- 2 cups thinly sliced onion
- 4 garlic cloves, minced and divided
- 2 (14-ounce) cans fat-free, less-sodium chicken broth, divided
- ½ teaspoon freshly ground black pepper, divided
- 8 ounces French bread or other firm white bread, torn into 1-inch pieces
- ¼ cup (1 ounce) shredded fontina cheese
- Cooking spray
- 1 tablespoon ground fennel seeds

1. Combine sugar, water, and salt in a large bowl, stirring until sugar and salt dissolve. Add pork; cover and brine 2 hours to overnight in refrigerator.

2. Preheat oven to 350°.

3. Heat oil in a large nonstick skillet over medium heat. Add sliced fennel, onion, and 2 garlic cloves; cook until golden brown (about 20 minutes), stirring frequently. Add ¼ cup broth; cook until liquid evaporates, scraping pan to loosen browned bits. Stir in ¼ teaspoon pepper. Add remaining broth; bring to a boil. Remove from heat.

4. Combine bread and fennel mixture. Stir in cheese. Spoon mixture into an 11 x 7–inch baking dish coated with cooking spray. Bake at 350° for 1 hour and 10 minutes or until golden brown.

5. While bread pudding bakes, rinse pork and pat dry. Combine fennel seeds, 2 garlic cloves, and ¼ teaspoon pepper; rub evenly over pork.

6. Heat a large ovenproof skillet over medium-high heat. Coat pan with cooking spray. Add pork to pan; cook 5 minutes, browning on all sides. Place pan in oven; bake at 350° for 40 minutes or until a thermometer registers 160° (slightly pink). Let stand 10 minutes before serving. Serve bread pudding with pork. Yield: 8 servings (serving size: about 3 ounces pork and about ½ cup bread pudding).

CALORIES 316 (30% from fat); FAT 10.6g (sat 3.8g, mono 4.6g, poly 1g); PROTEIN 28.2g; CARB 25.8g; FIBER 3.1g; CHOL 68mg; IRON 2.4mg; SODIUM 790mg; CALC 97mg

Roast Pork Loin with Savory Fennel Bread Pudding

Garlic and Fennel Pork Roast

Garlic and Fennel Pork Roast

Fresh rosemary can be substituted for fennel seeds in the rub for this family-style boneless roast. Sliced pickled peppers and steamed chopped kale are great accompaniments.

- 2 tablespoons crushed fennel seeds
- 1 teaspoon salt
- ½ teaspoon freshly ground black pepper
- 5 garlic cloves, minced
- 1 (3½-pound) boneless pork loin roast, trimmed
- Cooking spray
- 1 cup dry white wine

1. Preheat oven to 350°.

2. Combine first 4 ingredients. Make 12 (1½-inch) slits along 1 side of roast; stuff slits with fennel mixture. Place roast, slit side down, on a shallow roasting pan coated with cooking spray. Rub remaining fennel mixture over top of roast.

3. Bake at 350° for 1 hour and 10 minutes or until a thermometer registers 160° (slightly pink). Transfer roast to a serving platter. Add wine to pan, scraping pan to loosen browned bits. Pour wine mixture into a saucepan. Bring to a boil over medium-high heat. Reduce heat; simmer until reduced to ⅔ cup (about 8 minutes), stirring occasionally. Remove from heat. Pour accumulated juices from serving platter into wine mixture. Serve wine mixture with pork. Yield: 10 servings (serving size: about 4 ounces pork and about 1 tablespoon wine mixture).

CALORIES 250 (33% from fat); FAT 9.2g (sat 3.1g, mono 4.2g, poly 1g); PROTEIN 34.4g; CARB 1.5g; FIBER 0.5g; CHOL 94mg; IRON 1.7mg; SODIUM 318mg; CALC 47mg

Mushroom-Prosciutto Pizza

For a crisp crust, bake the prepared pizza crust on the lowest rack in the oven for a few minutes before adding the toppings.

- Cooking spray
- ¼ cup finely chopped shallots
- 1 (8-ounce) package presliced mushrooms
- 1 teaspoon chopped fresh thyme
- 1 garlic clove, minced
- 2 teaspoons sherry vinegar
- 1 (10-ounce) Italian cheese-flavored thin pizza crust (such as Boboli)
- 2 ounces prosciutto, cut into thin strips
- ⅓ cup (about 1½ ounces) shredded fontina cheese

1. Preheat oven to 450°.

2. Heat a 12-inch nonstick skillet over medium-high heat. Coat pan with cooking spray. Add shallots and mushrooms to pan; sauté 7 minutes or until mushrooms are tender. Add thyme and garlic; sauté 1 minute. Stir in vinegar; remove from heat.

3. Place crust on bottom rack of oven. Bake at 450° for 4 minutes.

4. Place crust on a baking sheet. Spread mushroom mixture evenly over crust; sprinkle with prosciutto and fontina cheese. Bake at 450° for 6 minutes or until cheese melts. Yield: 4 servings.

CALORIES 273 (28% from fat); FAT 8.4g (sat 3.7g, mono 2.4g, poly 0.8g); PROTEIN 15.3g; CARB 34.5g; FIBER 0.4g; CHOL 23mg; IRON 2.3mg; SODIUM 723mg; CALC 254mg

Ham and Cheese Hash Browns

Ham and Cheese Hash Browns

This recipe is a great use for leftover ham. Though it resembles a skillet potato hash, it's more easily prepared in the microwave.

3 cups frozen hash brown potatoes with onions and peppers (such as Ore-Ida Potatoes O'Brien)
1/3 cup fat-free, less-sodium chicken broth
1/2 cup drained canned quartered artichoke hearts, chopped
1/4 cup chopped green onions
1/8 teaspoon black pepper
3 ounces smoked ham, cut into bite-sized pieces
1/2 cup (about 2 ounces) shredded Monterey Jack cheese

1. Combine potatoes and chicken broth in a 1-quart microwave-safe casserole. Cover with lid, and microwave at HIGH 12 minutes, stirring after 6 minutes.
2. Uncover dish. Stir in artichoke hearts, green onions, pepper, and ham. Sprinkle with shredded cheese. Microwave, uncovered, at HIGH 1 minute. Yield: 2 servings (serving size: 1 3/4 cups).

CALORIES 378 (30% from fat); FAT 12.5g (sat 6.2g, mono 2.7g, poly 1.4g); PROTEIN 20g; CARB 41.8g; FIBER 6.1g; CHOL 55mg; IRON 1.3mg; SODIUM 817mg; CALC 204mg

Potato, Ham, and Spinach Gratin

2 teaspoons olive oil
1/2 cup thinly sliced shallots
2 garlic cloves, minced
1 cup chopped reduced-fat ham (about 4 ounces)
1 teaspoon salt, divided
3/4 teaspoon freshly ground black pepper, divided
1/8 teaspoon grated whole nutmeg
1 (10-ounce) package frozen chopped spinach, thawed, drained, and squeezed dry
1/3 cup all-purpose flour (about 1 1/2 ounces)
2 cups 1% low-fat milk
7 cups (1/8-inch-thick) Yukon gold potato slices (about 2 1/2 pounds)
Cooking spray
3/4 cup (3 ounces) shredded Gruyère or Swiss cheese

1. Preheat oven to 375°.
2. Heat oil in a small nonstick skillet over medium-high heat. Add shallots and garlic; sauté 2 minutes or until tender. Remove from heat; stir in ham, 1/4 teaspoon salt, 1/4 teaspoon pepper, nutmeg, and spinach.
3. Lightly spoon flour into a dry measuring cup; level with a knife. Combine flour, milk, remaining 1/2 teaspoon pepper, and 1/4 teaspoon salt, stirring with a whisk.
4. Arrange half of potato slices in an 8-inch square baking pan coated with cooking spray; sprinkle potato with 1/4 teaspoon salt. Spread spinach mixture over potato. Arrange remaining potato over spinach mixture; top with milk mixture. Sprinkle with remaining 1/4 teaspoon salt. Cover with foil coated with cooking spray. Bake at 375° for 1 hour and 15 minutes or until potato is tender. Uncover and sprinkle with cheese; bake an additional 15 minutes.
5. Preheat broiler.
6. Broil 2 minutes or until cheese is lightly browned. Yield: 8 servings.

CALORIES 240 (24% from fat); FAT 6.3g (sat 2.9g, mono 2.5g, poly 0.5g); PROTEIN 12.8g; CARB 34g; FIBER 3g; CHOL 22mg; IRON 1.7mg; SODIUM 581mg; CALC 235mg

Fire and Spice Ham

Sweet-hot pepper jelly and tangy pineapple preserves create an easy glaze for the ham.

1 (5 1/2- to 6-pound) 33%-less-sodium smoked, fully cooked ham half
Cooking spray
1/2 cup red pepper jelly
1/2 cup pineapple preserves
1/4 cup packed brown sugar
1/4 teaspoon ground cloves

1. Preheat oven to 425°.
2. Trim fat and rind from ham. Score outside of ham in a diamond pattern. Place ham on a broiler pan coated with cooking spray. Combine jelly and next 3 ingredients, stirring with a whisk until well blended. Brush about one-third of jelly mixture over ham.
3. Bake at 425° for 5 minutes. Reduce oven temperature to 325° (do not remove ham from oven); bake an additional 45 minutes, basting ham with jelly mixture every 15 minutes. Transfer ham to a serving platter; let stand 15 minutes before slicing. Yield: 18 servings (serving size: about 3 ounces).

CALORIES 188 (23% from fat); FAT 4.9g (sat 1.6g, mono 2.3g, poly 0.5g); PROTEIN 18.4g; CARB 16.8g; FIBER 0g; CHOL 47mg; IRON 1.4mg; SODIUM 865mg; CALC 10mg

Ham and Asparagus Frittata

Here, we extended whole eggs with egg whites for a healthier entrée. Serve the frittata with fruit and toasted English muffins for a light supper.

- 2/3 cup chopped 33%-less-sodium ham (about 3 ounces)
- 1/2 cup (2 ounces) shredded low-fat Jarlsberg cheese
- 1/4 teaspoon black pepper
- 1/8 teaspoon salt
- 3 large egg whites
- 2 large eggs
- Cooking spray
- 1/2 cup finely chopped onion
- 1/2 cup finely chopped bell pepper
- 1/2 cup (1-inch) slices asparagus
- 1/4 teaspoon dried Italian seasoning

1. Preheat broiler.
2. Combine first 6 ingredients in a medium bowl, stirring well with a whisk.
3. Heat a 9-inch skillet over medium-high heat. Coat pan with cooking spray. Add onion, bell pepper, and asparagus; sauté 3 minutes. Add egg mixture; reduce heat to medium. Cover and cook 3 minutes or until almost set. Sprinkle with Italian seasoning. Wrap handle of pan with foil; broil 3 minutes or until egg is set. Cut into 4 wedges. Yield: 2 servings (serving size: 2 wedges).

CALORIES 251 (33% from fat); FAT 9.2g (sat 3.4g, mono 3.5g, poly 1.1g); PROTEIN 31.3g; CARB 9.6g; FIBER 2g; CHOL 247mg; IRON 2.1mg; SODIUM 791mg; CALC 373mg

Corn, Bacon, and Green Onion Tart

Refrigerated pizza dough tends to draw up when it's first removed from the can. Let the dough rest a few minutes before you begin to work with it so it will be more pliable.

- 2 slices applewood-smoked bacon (such as Nueske's), chopped
- 2 cups fresh corn kernels (about 4 ears)
- 1/2 cup chopped green onions
- 1 cup 2% reduced-fat milk
- 1/4 cup (1 ounce) grated fresh Parmesan cheese, divided
- 1/2 teaspoon kosher salt
- 1/2 teaspoon freshly ground black pepper
- 2 large egg whites, lightly beaten
- 1 large egg, lightly beaten
- Cooking spray
- 1 (13.8-ounce) can refrigerated pizza crust dough

1. Preheat oven to 375°.
2. Cook bacon in a large nonstick skillet over medium-high heat 3 minutes or until lightly browned. Add corn and green onions; sauté 3 minutes. Place corn mixture in a large bowl. Add milk, 2 tablespoons cheese, salt, pepper, egg whites, and egg; stir until well blended.
3. Coat a 10½-inch round removable-bottom tart pan lightly with cooking spray. Unroll dough onto a lightly floured surface; let rest 5 minutes. Pat dough into bottom and up sides of prepared pan. Place pan on a baking sheet. Pour bacon mixture into dough; sprinkle with remaining 2 tablespoons cheese. Bake at 375° for 25 minutes or until set. Cool in pan 10 minutes on a wire rack. Yield: 4 servings.

CALORIES 419 (22% from fat); FAT 10.1g (sat 3.8g, mono 1.5g, poly 0.7g); PROTEIN 19.1g; CARB 66.1g; FIBER 2.6g; CHOL 67mg; IRON 3.5mg; SODIUM 1,221mg; CALC 150mg

Corn, Bacon, and Green Onion Tart

Oven-Fried Chicken, page 213

Poultry

Pilaf with Chicken, Spinach, and Walnuts

Pilaf has many variations. This Turkish version gains flavor from popcorn-scented basmati rice and fresh dill. Don't stir the rice as it simmers; doing so makes it gummy. Use leftover meat from a roasted chicken, or pick up a rotisserie chicken from your supermarket.

- 1½ tablespoons olive oil, divided
- 1 cup chopped onion
- 1½ cups uncooked basmati rice
- 1 cup diced plum tomato
- ½ teaspoon salt
- 1 (14-ounce) can fat-free, less-sodium chicken broth
- 1 (3-inch) cinnamon stick
- 1 (6-ounce) package fresh baby spinach
- 2 cups chopped roasted skinless, boneless chicken breasts (about 2 breasts)
- ½ cup coarsely chopped walnuts, toasted
- 1 tablespoon finely chopped fresh dill

1. Heat 1 tablespoon oil in a large nonstick skillet over medium-high heat. Add onion; sauté 10 minutes or until lightly browned. Stir in rice; cook 1 minute, stirring constantly. Stir in 1½ teaspoons oil, tomato, salt, broth, and cinnamon stick; bring to a boil. Cover, reduce heat, and simmer 15 minutes or until liquid is absorbed.

2. Stir in spinach; cook 2 minutes or until spinach wilts. Stir in chicken. Sprinkle evenly with walnuts and dill. Discard cinnamon stick. Yield: 6 servings (serving size: 1⅓ cups).

CALORIES 368 (29% from fat); FAT 11.9g (sat 1.8g, mono 4g, poly 5.6g); PROTEIN 19.8g; CARB 47.5g; FIBER 2.1g; CHOL 33mg; IRON 1.5mg; SODIUM 616mg; CALC 58mg

Spicy Chicken Pasta

1 (9-ounce) package fresh angel hair pasta
Cooking spray
1 cup vertically sliced onion
1 tablespoon dried basil
1½ teaspoons bottled minced garlic
½ teaspoon crushed red pepper
1 cup half-and-half
¼ cup reduced-fat sour cream
1 teaspoon all-purpose flour
¼ teaspoon salt
⅛ teaspoon black pepper
1 (6-ounce) package honey-roasted chicken breast cuts (such as Louis Rich)
1 (10-ounce) package frozen chopped spinach, thawed, drained, and squeezed dry
1 tablespoon grated fresh Parmesan cheese

1. Cook pasta according to package directions, omitting salt and fat. Drain in a colander over a bowl, reserving ¼ cup cooking liquid; set aside.
2. While pasta cooks, heat a large nonstick skillet over medium-high heat. Coat pan with cooking spray. Add onion; sauté 2 minutes. Add basil, garlic, and red pepper; sauté 1 minute. Combine half-and-half, sour cream, and flour, stirring with a whisk. Add reserved ¼ cup pasta cooking liquid and half-and-half mixture to pan; bring to a boil. Stir in salt, black pepper, chicken, and spinach; bring to a boil. Stir in cooked pasta; cook 1 minute or until thoroughly heated. Sprinkle with Parmesan. Yield: 4 servings (serving size: about 1¾ cups).

CALORIES 383 (29% from fat); FAT 12.4g (sat 6.2g, mono 3.8g, poly 1.2g); PROTEIN 20.5g; CARB 46.1g; FIBER 6g; CHOL 108mg; IRON 5.3mg; SODIUM 784mg; CALC 253mg

Baked Chiles Rellenos

5 large poblano chiles
Cooking spray
2½ cups thinly sliced zucchini
1 teaspoon minced garlic
1 teaspoon ground cumin, divided
2 jalapeño peppers
1 (14.5-ounce) can diced tomatoes, drained
1 (8-ounce) can tomato sauce
1½ cups (6 ounces) preshredded part-skim mozzarella cheese
1 cup shredded cooked chicken breast
½ teaspoon salt

1. Preheat broiler.
2. Place poblano peppers on a foil-lined baking sheet; broil 3 inches from heat 8 minutes or until blackened and charred, turning after 6 minutes. Place in a zip-top plastic bag; seal. Let stand 15 minutes. Peel and discard skins. Cut a lengthwise slit in each chile; discard seeds, leaving stems intact.
3. Heat a saucepan over medium-high heat. Coat pan with cooking spray. Add zucchini and garlic; cook 4 minutes or until crisp-tender. Stir in ½ teaspoon cumin, jalapeño, tomatoes, and sauce; bring to a boil. Reduce heat; simmer 15 minutes. Discard jalapeño.
4. Preheat oven to 350°.
5. Combine ½ teaspoon cumin, cheese, chicken, and salt in a bowl; toss. Spoon about ½ cup cheese mixture into each chile; secure with a wooden pick. Place stuffed chiles in an 11 x 7–inch baking dish coated with cooking spray; pour tomato mixture over chiles. Cover; bake at 350° for 20 minutes. Uncover; bake an additional 10 minutes. Yield: 5 servings (serving size: 1 stuffed chile and about ⅔ cup tomato mixture).

CALORIES 201 (33% from fat); FAT 7.7g (sat 3.8g, mono 2.2g, poly 0.8g); PROTEIN 20g; CARB 15.4g; FIBER 3.9g; CHOL 43mg; IRON 2mg; SODIUM 795mg; CALC 267mg

Roast Chicken Chimichangas

2½ cups shredded roasted skinless, boneless chicken breasts
1 cup (4 ounces) crumbled queso fresco cheese
¼ cup chopped green onions
1 teaspoon dried oregano
¼ teaspoon ground cumin
1 garlic clove, minced
1 (4.5-ounce) can chopped green chiles, drained
1 (16-ounce) can fat-free refried beans
6 (8-inch) flour tortillas
Cooking spray
½ cup bottled green salsa

1. Preheat oven to 500°.
2. Combine first 7 ingredients in a large bowl; toss well.
3. Spread ¼ cup beans down center of each tortilla. Top each tortilla with ⅔ cup chicken mixture; roll up. Place rolls, seam sides down, on a large baking sheet coated with cooking spray. Coat tops with cooking spray. Bake at 500° for 7 minutes. Serve with salsa. Yield: 6 servings (serving size: 1 chimichanga and about 4 teaspoons salsa).

CALORIES 380 (23% from fat); FAT 9.7g (sat 3.1g, mono 4.1g, poly 1.6g); PROTEIN 28.8g; CARB 42.5g; FIBER 6.5g; CHOL 55mg; IRON 3.8mg; SODIUM 728mg; CALC 157mg

Thai-Style Chicken

The list of ingredients is short, but most have bold flavors that contribute to the dish's great taste. Serve over rice, and garnish with green onion curls.

- 1½ teaspoons canola oil
- 1 medium onion, cut into ¼-inch wedges
- ¾ cup light coconut milk
- ½ teaspoon red curry paste
- ⅛ teaspoon black pepper
- 1 pound chicken breast tenders
- 3 tablespoons chopped fresh cilantro
- 1½ teaspoons fish sauce
- ¼ teaspoon salt
- 1 (7-ounce) bottle roasted red bell peppers, drained and coarsely chopped

1. Heat oil in a large nonstick skillet over medium-high heat. Add onion; cook 4 minutes or until onion is golden, stirring frequently. Stir in coconut milk, curry paste, and black pepper. Add chicken; bring to a simmer. Cook 8 minutes or until chicken is done, stirring frequently. Stir in cilantro and remaining ingredients; cook 1 minute. Yield: 4 servings (serving size: 1 cup).

CALORIES 195 (26% from fat); FAT 5.7g (sat 2.2g, mono 0.8g, poly 1.5g); PROTEIN 27.3g; CARB 6.7g; FIBER 0.9g; CHOL 66mg; IRON 1.2mg; SODIUM 601mg; CALC 26mg

Coconut Curried Chicken

Lush coconut milk and sultry green curry paste let you enjoy authentic Thai flavor in this quick entrée. You can use cooked, peeled, and deveined shrimp instead of chicken. Just add the shrimp at the end to heat it.

- 1½ cups water, divided
- ⅔ cup uncooked couscous
- 1 cup light coconut milk
- 1 tablespoon cornstarch
- 1 tablespoon fish sauce
- 2 teaspoons sugar
- 2 teaspoons bottled minced garlic
- 2 teaspoons bottled minced ginger
- 1 teaspoon green curry paste
- 2 teaspoons canola oil, divided
- 1 pound chicken breast tenders
- ½ teaspoon salt, divided
- 1 cup frozen green peas
- ½ cup prechopped onion
- 1 (8-ounce) package presliced mushrooms
- 1 teaspoon lime juice
- Lime wedges (optional)

1. Bring 1 cup water to a boil in a medium saucepan. Stir in couscous; cover and remove from heat. Let stand 5 minutes. Fluff with a fork.

2. While couscous cooks, combine ½ cup water, coconut milk, and next 6 ingredients, stirring well with a whisk.

3. Heat 1 teaspoon oil in a large nonstick skillet over medium-high heat. Sprinkle chicken with ¼ teaspoon salt. Add chicken to pan; cook 6 minutes or until done, turning once. Remove from pan; keep warm.

4. Add remaining 1 teaspoon oil to pan. Add peas, onion, and mushrooms; cook 3 minutes or until mushrooms are tender. Add coconut milk mixture and remaining ¼ teaspoon salt to pan; bring to a boil. Reduce heat, and simmer 1 minute. Add chicken and lime juice to pan; cook 1 minute or until thoroughly heated. Serve over couscous, and garnish with lime wedges, if desired. Yield: 4 servings (serving size: 1½ cups chicken mixture and ½ cup couscous).

CALORIES 361 (18% from fat); FAT 7.2g (sat 2.6g, mono 1.8g, poly 1.2g); PROTEIN 34.4g; CARB 38.1g; FIBER 4.4g; CHOL 66mg; IRON 2.2mg; SODIUM 778mg; CALC 39mg

Cilantro-Serrano Pesto with Grilled Chicken and Penne

Cotija is an aged Mexican cheese available in many supermarkets and fresh Latin grocery stores. Substitute Parmesan cheese if you can't find cotija. If the sauce is too thick, loosen it by adding a little hot cooking water from the pasta.

- 1½ cups fresh cilantro
- ½ cup fresh mint
- ½ cup cotija cheese
- 3 tablespoons toasted pecan halves
- 1 teaspoon kosher salt
- 2 garlic cloves
- 1 serrano chile, seeded and sliced
- 2 tablespoons extravirgin olive oil
- 2 teaspoons sherry vinegar
- ⅛ teaspoon freshly ground black pepper
- ¾ pound skinless, boneless chicken breast halves
- Cooking spray
- 6 cups hot cooked penne pasta (about 3 ounces uncooked)
- 2 cups cherry tomatoes, halved

1. Place first 7 ingredients in a food processor, and process until well blended. With processor on, slowly pour olive oil through food chute; process until well blended. Place pesto in a large bowl; stir in sherry vinegar and black pepper.

2. Heat a grill pan over medium-high heat. Coat chicken with cooking spray. Add chicken to pan; cook 5 minutes on each side or until done. Cut chicken into bite-sized pieces. Add chicken, pasta, and tomatoes to pesto; toss to combine. Yield: 6 servings (serving size: 1 cup).

CALORIES 429 (29% from fat); FAT 13.8g (sat 3.5g, mono 6.5g, poly 1.9g); PROTEIN 28.2g; CARB 47.1g; FIBER 2.4g; CHOL 60mg; IRON 11.5mg; SODIUM 492mg; CALC 104mg

Chicken and Broccoli Casserole

For crisper broccoli, remove it from the boiling water after three minutes. Serve casserole with a simple green salad.

- 3 quarts water
- 1 (12-ounce) package broccoli florets
- 4 (6-ounce) skinless, boneless chicken breast halves
- 1 (12-ounce) can evaporated fat-free milk
- ¼ cup all-purpose flour (about 1 ounce)
- ¼ teaspoon salt
- ¼ teaspoon freshly ground black pepper
- Dash of nutmeg
- 1 cup fat-free mayonnaise
- ½ cup fat-free sour cream
- ¼ cup dry sherry
- 1 teaspoon Worcestershire sauce
- 1 (10.75-ounce) can condensed 30% reduced-sodium, 98% fat-free cream of mushroom soup, undiluted
- 1 cup (4 ounces) grated fresh Parmesan cheese, divided
- Cooking spray

1. Preheat oven to 400°.

2. Bring water to a boil in a large Dutch oven over medium-high heat. Add broccoli; cook 5 minutes or until crisp-tender. Transfer broccoli to a large bowl with a slotted spoon. Add chicken to boiling water; reduce heat, and simmer 15 minutes or until done. Transfer chicken to a cutting board; cool slightly. Cut chicken into bite-sized pieces; add chicken to bowl with broccoli.

3. Combine evaporated milk, flour, salt, pepper, and nutmeg in a saucepan, stirring with a whisk until smooth. Bring to a boil over medium-high heat; cook 1 minute, stirring constantly. Remove from heat. Add mayonnaise, next 4 ingredients, and ½ cup cheese, stirring until well combined. Add mayonnaise mixture to broccoli mixture; stir gently until combined.

4. Spoon mixture into a 13 x 9–inch baking dish coated with cooking spray. Sprinkle with remaining ½ cup cheese. Bake at 400° for 50 minutes or until mixture bubbles at edges and cheese begins to brown. Remove from oven; let cool on a wire rack 5 minutes. Yield: 8 servings (serving size: about 1 cup).

CALORIES 276 (25% from fat); FAT 7.8g (sat 3.5g, mono 1.8g, poly 1.1g); PROTEIN 31.1g; CARB 18.9g; FIBER 2.1g; CHOL 66mg; IRON 1.6mg; SODIUM 696mg; CALC 365mg

Chicken and Broccoli Casserole

Tarragon Chicken-in-a-Pot Pies

Tarragon Chicken-in-a-Pot Pies

Popular in French cooking, tarragon adds anise flavor to the creamy chicken mixture. Hollowed-out rolls serve as edible, individual bowls that soak up the sauce.

- 2 tablespoons all-purpose flour
- 1 cup 1% low-fat milk
- ½ cup fat-free, less-sodium chicken broth
- ½ cup dry white wine
- 1 tablespoon olive oil
- ⅔ cup chopped sweet onion
- 1 pound skinless, boneless chicken breast, cut into bite-sized pieces
- 1 cup sliced carrot
- 1 cup (⅛-inch-thick) slices zucchini
- ½ teaspoon salt
- ½ teaspoon dried tarragon
- ½ teaspoon black pepper
- 4 (4.5-ounce) country or peasant rolls

1. Place flour in a small bowl; slowly add milk, stirring with a whisk to form a slurry. Add broth and white wine.

2. Heat oil in a large saucepan over medium-high heat; add onion and chicken. Sauté 2 minutes; stir in carrot and next 4 ingredients. Cover, reduce heat, and cook 4 minutes. Stir slurry into chicken mixture, and bring to a boil. Cover, reduce heat, and simmer 10 minutes or until thick, stirring occasionally.

3. Cut rolls horizontally 1 inch from tops. Hollow out bottoms of rolls, leaving ¼-inch-thick shells; reserve torn bread and bread tops for another use. Spoon 1¼ cups chicken mixture into each bread shell. Yield: 4 servings.

CALORIES 413 (17% from fat); FAT 7.8g (sat 2.7g, mono 3g, poly 0.7g); PROTEIN 35.7g; CARB 48.8g; FIBER 3.5g; CHOL 68mg; IRON 4.2mg; SODIUM 865mg; CALC 199mg

Salsa Chicken

Personalize this easy recipe by using your favorite tomato-based salsa. Or try a fruit salsa, such as peach, cranberry, or pineapple. Serve over hot cooked rice.

- 1 pound skinless, boneless chicken breast, cut into bite-sized pieces
- 2 teaspoons taco seasoning
- Cooking spray
- ⅔ cup bottled salsa
- ⅔ cup (about 2½ ounces) reduced-fat shredded Cheddar cheese
- 1 (4-ounce) can whole green chiles, drained and thinly sliced
- ¼ cup fat-free sour cream
- 2 tablespoons sliced ripe olives

1. Preheat oven to 475°.

2. Combine chicken and seasoning in a medium bowl, tossing to coat. Heat a large nonstick skillet over medium-high heat. Coat pan with cooking spray. Add chicken; cook 4 minutes or until browned, stirring occasionally. Arrange chicken in an 8-inch square baking dish coated with cooking spray; top with salsa, cheese, and chiles. Bake at 475° for 8 minutes or until chicken is done and cheese melts. Top each serving with 1 tablespoon sour cream and 1½ teaspoons olives. Yield: 4 servings.

CALORIES 207 (15% from fat); FAT 3.5g (sat 1.4g, mono 1.1g, poly 0.5g); PROTEIN 33.4g; CARB 9.5g; FIBER 2.1g; CHOL 71mg; IRON 1.5mg; SODIUM 587mg; CALC 130mg

Lemon Chicken and Rice with Artichokes

This one-dish meal is ready in less than half an hour. If you want another vegetable side dish, add steamed carrots tossed with a little butter and parsley.

Cooking spray
- 1 pound skinless, boneless chicken breast, cut into ½-inch strips
- 2¼ cups chopped onion
- 1 cup chopped red bell pepper
- 2 cups instant rice
- ¼ cup fresh lemon juice
- ¼ teaspoon salt
- ¼ teaspoon black pepper
- 1 (14-ounce) can fat-free, less-sodium chicken broth
- 1 (14-ounce) can quartered artichoke hearts, drained
- 2 tablespoons grated Romano or Parmesan cheese

1. Heat a Dutch oven over medium-high heat. Coat pan with cooking spray. Add chicken, onion, and bell pepper; sauté 5 minutes. Stir in rice, lemon juice, salt, black pepper, and broth; bring to a boil. Cover, reduce heat, and simmer 15 minutes or until rice is tender. Stir in artichokes; cook 1 minute or until thoroughly heated. Sprinkle with cheese. Yield: 4 servings (serving size: 2 cups).

CALORIES 324 (8% from fat); FAT 2.8g (sat 1g, mono 0.7g, poly 0.5g); PROTEIN 35g; CARB 40.7g; FIBER 8.3g; CHOL 69mg; IRON 3.1mg; SODIUM 773mg; CALC 120mg

8 pts per serving

Rum-Glazed Pineapple, Mango, and Chicken Kebabs

Taste a bit of the Caribbean in every bite of this quick and easy summer barbecue treat. Serve with grilled corn on the cob and basmati or jasmine rice tossed with toasted coconut on the side.

- 3/4 cup pineapple juice
- 1/4 cup sugar
- 1/4 cup dark rum
- 2 tablespoons finely chopped seeded jalapeño pepper
- 1 tablespoon cider vinegar
- 2 teaspoons cornstarch
- 2 tablespoons chopped fresh cilantro
- 1 1/2 teaspoons grated lime rind
- 1 1/2 pounds skinless, boneless chicken breast, cut into 30 cubes
- 2 mangoes, peeled and each cut into 9 (1-inch) cubes
- 18 (1-inch) cubes fresh pineapple
- 1 1/2 tablespoons canola oil
- 1 teaspoon salt
- Cooking spray

1. Prepare grill.
2. Combine first 4 ingredients in a medium saucepan; bring to a boil. Reduce heat; simmer 5 minutes. Combine vinegar and cornstarch in a small bowl. Add cornstarch mixture to pan; bring to a boil. Cook 1 minute, stirring constantly. Let stand 5 minutes. Stir in cilantro and rind.
3. Thread 5 chicken cubes, 3 mango cubes, and 3 pineapple cubes alternately onto each of 6 (12-inch) skewers. Brush kebabs with oil; sprinkle with salt. Place kebabs on grill rack coated with cooking spray; grill 4 minutes. Turn kebabs; brush with half of glaze, and grill 4 minutes. Turn kebabs; brush with remaining glaze. Grill 2 minutes, turning once. Yield: 6 servings (serving size: 1 kebab).

NOTE: If using bamboo skewers, soak them in water 30 minutes beforehand.

CALORIES 313 (30% from fat); FAT 10.4g (sat 2.4g, mono 3.5g, poly 3.5g); PROTEIN 26g; CARB 30g; FIBER 1.8g; CHOL 71mg; IRON 1.3mg; SODIUM 450mg; CALC 28mg

Chicken Pasanda

This traditional Pakistani dish also includes fresh pineapple cubes and pita wedges served on the side to dip into creamy cashew sauce.

- 1/2 cup roasted cashews
- 2 cups plain low-fat yogurt
- 1 cup coarsely chopped onion
- 1/4 cup fresh lemon juice
- 2 tablespoons chopped peeled fresh ginger
- 2 jalapeño peppers, seeded
- 2 1/2 teaspoons ground coriander seeds
- 3/4 teaspoon ground cardamom
- 3/4 teaspoon ground cinnamon
- 1/2 teaspoon black pepper
- 1/4 teaspoon ground cloves
- 1 teaspoon salt, divided
- 4 (6-ounce) skinless, boneless chicken breast halves, each cut into 4 pieces
- 2 teaspoons canola oil
- 1 cup cubed fresh pineapple
- 2 tablespoons chopped cashews, roasted
- 2 tablespoons chopped fresh cilantro
- 4 (6-inch) pitas, each cut into 6 wedges

1. Place 1/2 cup roasted cashews in a food processor; process until smooth (about 2 minutes), scraping sides of bowl once. Add yogurt; process until well blended. Remove from processor; set aside.
2. Combine chopped onion, lemon juice, ginger, and jalapeño in food processor or blender; process until finely chopped.
3. Combine coriander seeds and next 4 ingredients in a large zip-top plastic bag; add 1/2 teaspoon salt and chicken pieces. Seal bag, and shake to coat.
4. Heat oil in a large nonstick skillet over medium-high heat; add chicken pieces. Cook 4 minutes on each side or until done. Remove chicken from pan; keep warm.
5. Add onion mixture to pan. Reduce heat to medium; cook 3 minutes or until liquid evaporates, stirring frequently. Add remaining 1/2 teaspoon salt and yogurt mixture to pan; cook 3 minutes or until heated, stirring frequently.
6. Spoon 1/2 cup yogurt mixture onto each of 6 plates. Top each serving with 4 chicken pieces. Sprinkle each serving with about 2 1/2 tablespoons pineapple, 1 teaspoon chopped cashews, and 1 teaspoon cilantro. Arrange 4 pita wedges on each plate. Yield: 6 servings.

CALORIES 368 (27% from fat); FAT 11g (sat 2.5g, mono 4.5g, poly 2.5g); PROTEIN 27.7g; CARB 40.3g; FIBER 2.9g; CHOL 51mg; IRON 3.2mg; SODIUM 708mg; CALC 206mg

Chicken, Mushroom, and Cheese Quesadillas

Using preshredded cheese and presliced mushrooms makes preparation a snap.

- 1 teaspoon olive oil
- 1 teaspoon ground cumin
- ¼ teaspoon salt, divided
- ¼ teaspoon black pepper, divided
- 12 ounces skinless, boneless chicken breasts, cut into ¼-inch-thick slices
- ¾ cup chopped onion
- 1 (8-ounce) package presliced mushrooms
- 1 garlic clove, minced
- 1 jalapeño pepper, seeded and chopped
- 4 (8-inch) flour tortillas
- 1½ cups (6 ounces) preshredded light Mexican cheese blend (such as Sargento)

1. Heat olive oil in a large nonstick skillet over medium-high heat. Combine cumin, ⅛ teaspoon salt, and ⅛ teaspoon pepper; sprinkle over chicken. Add chicken to pan; sauté 5 minutes or until browned. Remove chicken from pan; set aside. Add onion, mushrooms, garlic, jalapeño, ⅛ teaspoon salt, and ⅛ teaspoon pepper to pan; sauté 5 minutes. Remove from pan; let stand 5 minutes. Wipe pan with paper towels.

2. Heat pan over medium heat. Sprinkle each tortilla with about ⅓ cup cheese. Arrange ½ cup mushroom mixture over one half of each tortilla. Arrange chicken evenly over mushroom mixture. Carefully fold each tortilla in half. Add 2 quesadillas to pan; cook 2 minutes on each side or until lightly browned and cheese melts. Repeat procedure with remaining quesadillas. Serve immediately. Yield: 4 servings (serving size: 1 quesadilla).

CALORIES 388 (29% from fat); FAT 12.5g (sat 5.7g, mono 2.5g, poly 0.9g); PROTEIN 38.5g; CARB 31.3g; FIBER 1.7g; CHOL 65mg; IRON 2.8mg; SODIUM 759mg; CALC 429mg

Chicken Scaloppine with Broccoli Rabe

If you can't find cutlets, pound chicken breast halves between heavy-duty plastic wrap to ¼-inch thickness. Broccoli florets can be substituted for rapini; the cooking time may be a little longer, though. Add a side of roasted potato wedges and carrots, if desired.

- 1 tablespoon olive oil
- ⅓ cup Italian-seasoned breadcrumbs
- ¼ teaspoon black pepper
- 4 (6-ounce) skinless, boneless chicken breast cutlets
- ½ cup dry white wine
- ½ cup fat-free, less-sodium chicken broth
- 3 tablespoons fresh lemon juice
- 1 teaspoon butter
- 1 pound broccoli rabe (rapini), cut into 3-inch pieces
- 2 tablespoons chopped fresh parsley
- 2 tablespoons capers, rinsed and drained
- 4 lemon slices (optional)
- Parsley sprigs (optional)

1. Heat oil in a large nonstick skillet over medium-high heat.

2. Combine breadcrumbs and pepper in a shallow dish; dredge chicken in breadcrumb mixture. Add chicken to pan; cook 3 minutes on each side or until done. Remove from pan; keep warm.

3. Add wine, broth, juice, and butter to pan, scraping pan to loosen browned bits. Stir in broccoli rabe; cover and cook 3 minutes or until tender. Stir in chopped parsley and capers. Garnish with lemon slices and parsley sprigs, if desired. Yield: 4 servings (serving size: 1 chicken cutlet and ½ cup broccoli rabe mixture).

CALORIES 318 (21% from fat); FAT 7.4g (sat 1.7g, mono 3.3g, poly 1g); PROTEIN 44.3g; CARB 14g; FIBER 3.9g; CHOL 101mg; IRON 2.9mg; SODIUM 577mg; CALC 102mg

Chicken Scaloppine with Broccoli Rabe

Southwestern Chicken Roll-Ups

This recipe is fast and easy, and can be prepared in advance. Use toothpicks to secure the chicken before dredging.

6 (6-ounce) skinless, boneless chicken breast halves
6 tablespoons (about 3 ounces) ⅓-less-fat cream cheese
6 tablespoons picante sauce
6 cilantro sprigs
6 tablespoons Italian-seasoned breadcrumbs
Cooking spray

1. Preheat oven to 350°.
2. Place each chicken breast half between 2 sheets of heavy-duty plastic wrap; pound to ¼-inch thickness using a meat mallet or rolling pin. Top each breast half with 1 tablespoon cheese, 1 tablespoon picante sauce, and 1 cilantro sprig. Roll up jelly-roll fashion, beginning at narrow end.
3. Dredge chicken rolls in breadcrumbs. Place rolls, seam sides down, on a baking sheet coated with cooking spray; lightly coat rolls with cooking spray. Bake at 350° for 20 minutes or until chicken is done. Yield: 6 servings (serving size: 1 chicken roll).

CALORIES 257 (20% from fat); FAT 5.8g (sat 2.7g, mono 1.5g, poly 0.6g); PROTEIN 41.7g; CARB 6.9g; FIBER 0.3g; CHOL 109mg; IRON 1.6mg; SODIUM 385mg; CALC 40mg

Easy Schnitzel

This is a simpler, lighter version of the German specialty Wiener schnitzel.

4 (6-ounce) skinless, boneless chicken breast halves
¼ teaspoon salt
¼ teaspoon freshly ground black pepper
2 tablespoons all-purpose flour
2 tablespoons Dijon mustard
1 large egg, lightly beaten
½ cup dry breadcrumbs
1½ tablespoons grated fresh Parmesan cheese
2 teaspoons finely chopped fresh parsley
2 teaspoons chopped fresh chives
1 garlic clove, minced
1 tablespoon olive oil
4 lemon wedges (optional)

1. Preheat oven to 350°.
2. Place each chicken breast half between 2 sheets of heavy-duty plastic wrap; pound to ½-inch thickness using a meat mallet or rolling pin. Sprinkle chicken with salt and pepper.
3. Place flour in a shallow bowl. Combine mustard and egg in a shallow dish. Combine breadcrumbs, cheese, parsley, chives, and garlic in a shallow dish. Dredge 1 chicken breast half in flour, turning to coat; shake off excess flour. Dip in egg mixture; dredge in breadcrumb mixture. Repeat procedure with remaining chicken, flour, egg mixture, and breadcrumb mixture.
4. Heat oil in a large ovenproof nonstick skillet over medium-high heat. Add chicken; sauté 2½ minutes or until browned. Remove from heat. Turn chicken over; place pan in oven. Bake at 350° for 10 minutes or until chicken is done. Serve with lemon wedges, if desired. Yield: 4 servings (serving size: 1 chicken breast half).

CALORIES 328 (22% from fat); FAT 8.1g (sat 1.9g, mono 3.8g, poly 1.3g); PROTEIN 45.3g; CARB 16.7g; FIBER 0.7g; CHOL 153mg; IRON 2.6mg; SODIUM 636mg; CALC 85mg

Greek Chicken with Capers, Raisins, and Feta

For an even faster dish, use packaged crumbled feta cheese.

- 4 (6-ounce) skinless, boneless chicken breast halves
- 2 tablespoons all-purpose flour
- 1 teaspoon dried oregano
- 1 tablespoon olive oil
- 1 cup thinly sliced onion
- 1½ cups fat-free, less-sodium chicken broth
- ⅓ cup golden raisins
- 2 tablespoons lemon juice
- 2 tablespoons capers
- ¼ cup (1 ounce) crumbled feta cheese
- 4 thin lemon slices (optional)

1. Place each chicken breast half between 2 sheets of heavy-duty plastic wrap; flatten to ¼-inch thickness using a meat mallet or rolling pin. Combine flour and dried oregano in a shallow dish, and dredge chicken in flour mixture.

2. Heat oil in a large nonstick skillet over medium-high heat. Add chicken; cook 4 minutes on each side. Remove chicken from pan; keep warm. Add onion to pan; sauté 2 minutes. Stir in broth, raisins, and lemon juice; cook 3 minutes, scraping pan to loosen browned bits. Return chicken to pan. Cover, reduce heat, and simmer 8 minutes or until chicken is done.

3. Place a chicken breast on each of 4 serving plates. Add capers to sauce in pan. Spoon ⅓ cup sauce over each serving; top with 1 tablespoon cheese. Garnish with lemon slices, if desired. Yield: 4 servings.

CALORIES 319 (22% from fat); FAT 7.7g (sat 2.5g, mono 3.4g, poly 1g); PROTEIN 43.1g; CARB 18.5g; FIBER 1.5g; CHOL 107mg; IRON 2.1mg; SODIUM 559mg; CALC 89mg

Herbed Chicken Breasts with Tomatillo Salsa and Queso Fresco

SALSA:

- 2 quarts water
- ½ pound tomatillos (about 10 small), husks and stems removed
- 1 garlic clove
- ½ to 1 serrano chile
- ½ cup chopped fresh cilantro
- ¼ cup coarsely chopped onion
- 1 teaspoon fresh lime juice
- ¼ teaspoon salt

CHICKEN:

- 3 (1-ounce) slices white bread
- 4 (6-ounce) skinless, boneless chicken breast halves
- ½ teaspoon salt
- ½ teaspoon ground cumin
- ¼ teaspoon ground red pepper
- 1 large egg, lightly beaten
- 1 tablespoon olive oil
- ½ cup (2 ounces) crumbled queso fresco cheese
- Cilantro sprigs (optional)
- Lime wedges (optional)

1. Preheat oven to 350°.

2. To prepare salsa, bring water to a boil. Add tomatillos, garlic, and chile; cook 7 minutes. Drain and rinse with cold water. Combine tomatillos, garlic, chile, chopped cilantro, onion, lime juice, and ¼ teaspoon salt in a food processor or blender; pulse 4 or 5 times or until ingredients are coarsely chopped. Set aside.

3. To prepare chicken, place bread in a food processor, and pulse 10 times or until coarse crumbs measure 1½ cups. Arrange crumbs on a baking sheet; bake at 350° for 3 minutes or until lightly browned. Cool completely.

4. Place each chicken breast half between 2 sheets of heavy-duty plastic wrap; pound to ½-inch thickness using a meat mallet or rolling pin. Combine ½ teaspoon salt, cumin, and red pepper; sprinkle evenly over chicken.

5. Place breadcrumbs in a shallow dish. Place egg in another shallow dish. Dip chicken in egg; dredge in breadcrumbs.

6. Heat oil in a large nonstick skillet over medium-high heat. Add chicken; cook 4 minutes on each side or until done. Top chicken with salsa; sprinkle with queso fresco cheese. Garnish with cilantro sprigs and lime wedges, if desired. Yield: 4 servings (serving size: 1 chicken breast half, ¼ cup salsa, and 2 tablespoons cheese).

CALORIES 364 (26% from fat); FAT 10.7g (sat 3.2g, mono 4.5g, poly 1.6g); PROTEIN 47.1g; CARB 17.7g; FIBER 2g; CHOL 162mg; IRON 3mg; SODIUM 770mg; CALC 169mg

Mexican Chicken with Almond-Chile Cream

The almond nut meal, made in the blender, lends a creamy richness to the sauce even with minimal added fat. Look for ground ancho chile pepper in the spice section. If you can't find it, substitute 1½ teaspoons regular chili powder and ½ teaspoon ground chipotle chile pepper. Crema Mexicana is similar to crème fraîche but has a thinner consistency and sweeter flavor. Slice chicken, and serve with flour tortillas and a tossed salad.

3 tablespoons sliced almonds
2 teaspoons ground ancho chile pepper
4 (6-ounce) skinless, boneless chicken breast halves
¼ teaspoon salt, divided
¼ teaspoon freshly ground black pepper
2 teaspoons butter
1 teaspoon canola oil
1 garlic clove, minced
1 cup fat-free, less-sodium chicken broth
2 tablespoons crema Mexicana
Cilantro sprigs (optional)

1. Combine almonds and chile pepper in a blender or food processor; process until mixture resembles coarse meal.
2. Place each chicken breast half between 2 sheets of heavy-duty plastic wrap, and pound to ½-inch thickness using a heavy skillet. Sprinkle with ⅛ teaspoon salt and black pepper.
3. Heat butter and oil in a large nonstick skillet over medium heat. Add chicken; cook 6 minutes on each side or until done. Remove chicken from pan, and keep warm.
4. Add minced garlic to pan; cook 1 minute, stirring constantly. Add almond mixture, remaining ⅛ teaspoon salt, and broth; bring to a boil, scraping pan to loosen browned bits. Cook until broth mixture is reduced to ½ cup (about 3 minutes). Remove from heat. Stir in crema Mexicana. Serve sauce over chicken. Garnish with cilantro sprigs, if desired. Yield: 4 servings (serving size: 1 chicken breast half and 2 tablespoons sauce).

CALORIES 269 (30% from fat); FAT 8.9g (sat 2.8g, mono 3.1g, poly 1.4g); PROTEIN 41.3g; CARB 2.8g; FIBER 1.2g; CHOL 109mg; IRON 1.4mg; SODIUM 387mg; CALC 35mg

Chicken in Cherry Marsala Sauce

If you can't find dried cherries, use dried cranberries. The microwave is ideal for heating small amounts of liquid to rehydrate dried fruit.

⅓ cup dried cherries
⅓ cup Marsala
2 teaspoons olive oil
4 (6-ounce) skinless, boneless chicken breast halves
½ teaspoon salt, divided
½ teaspoon black pepper, divided
1 teaspoon butter
¼ cup finely chopped shallots
1 tablespoon chopped fresh thyme
½ cup fat-free, less-sodium chicken broth

1. Combine dried cherries and Marsala in a small microwave-safe bowl. Microwave at HIGH 45 seconds; set aside.
2. Heat olive oil in a large nonstick skillet over medium-high heat. Add chicken; cook 4 minutes on each side or until done. Remove chicken from pan; sprinkle with ¼ teaspoon salt and ¼ teaspoon pepper. Cover and keep warm.
3. Add butter to pan; cook until butter melts. Add shallots and thyme; sauté 1 minute or until tender. Stir in broth, scraping pan to loosen browned bits. Add cherry mixture, remaining ¼ teaspoon salt, and remaining ¼ teaspoon pepper; bring to a boil. Reduce heat to medium; simmer 2 minutes or until sauce is slightly thick. Serve chicken with sauce. Yield: 4 servings (serving size: 1 chicken breast half and about ¼ cup sauce).

CALORIES 297 (16% from fat); FAT 5.4g (sat 1.4g, mono 2.6g, poly 0.8g); PROTEIN 40.5g; CARB 13.7g; FIBER 1.1g; CHOL 101mg; IRON 2.1mg; SODIUM 464mg; CALC 33mg

Chicken with Summer Squash and Lemon-Chive Sauce

You can serve up a side of quinoa or egg noodles to complete the meal.

- 2 teaspoons canola oil
- 4 (6-ounce) skinless, boneless chicken breast halves
- ¼ teaspoon salt
- ¼ teaspoon black pepper
- 2 cups (½-inch) cubed yellow squash
- 1½ cups (½-inch) cubed zucchini
- 1 cup fat-free, less-sodium chicken broth
- 1 tablespoon chopped fresh chives
- ½ teaspoon grated lemon rind
- 1 tablespoon fresh lemon juice
- 2 teaspoons cornstarch
- 2 teaspoons honey mustard

1. Heat oil in a large nonstick skillet over medium-high heat. Sprinkle chicken with salt and pepper; add chicken to pan. Cook 4 minutes on each side; remove from pan. Keep warm.
2. Reduce heat to medium. Add cubed squash and zucchini to pan, and cook 2 minutes, stirring frequently. Return chicken to pan.
3. Combine broth and next 5 ingredients in a small bowl, stirring with a whisk. Add broth mixture to pan. Cover, reduce heat to medium-low, and cook 3 minutes. Yield: 4 servings (serving size: 1 chicken breast half and ½ cup squash mixture).

CALORIES 237 (17% from fat); FAT 4.6g (sat 0.8g, mono 1.9g, poly 1.3g); PROTEIN 41.3g; CARB 5.8g; FIBER 1.2g; CHOL 99mg; IRON 1.6mg; SODIUM 419mg; CALC 36mg

Chicken with Duxelles

Duxelles is a thick mixture of finely chopped mushrooms, shallots, and seasonings cooked slowly to evaporate the liquid and intensify the mushroom flavor. Drizzling with half-and-half at the end pulls the flavors together. Using the microwave shortens that cooking time significantly. The food processor relieves you of tedious chopping.

- 3 cups fresh parsley leaves (about 1 bunch)
- 2 large shallots, peeled and quartered
- 4 cups coarsely chopped mushrooms (about ¾ pound)
- 1 tablespoon olive oil, divided
- ½ teaspoon salt, divided
- ¼ teaspoon black pepper, divided
- ⅛ teaspoon ground red pepper
- 2 teaspoons bottled minced garlic
- 4 (6-ounce) skinless, boneless chicken breast halves
- ¼ cup half-and-half

1. Place parsley leaves and shallots in a food processor; process until shallots are finely chopped. Add mushrooms, and process until finely chopped, scraping sides of bowl occasionally. Place mushroom mixture in a deep-dish 10-inch pie plate. Microwave at HIGH 12 minutes, stirring every 4 minutes. Stir in 1 teaspoon oil, ¼ teaspoon salt, ⅛ teaspoon black pepper, and red pepper.
2. Combine remaining 2 teaspoons oil, remaining ¼ teaspoon salt, remaining ⅛ teaspoon black pepper, minced garlic, and chicken in a bowl; toss well. Arrange chicken spokelike on top of mushroom mixture. Drizzle with half-and-half. Cover with plastic wrap; vent. Microwave at HIGH 7 minutes or until done. Yield: 4 servings (serving size: 1 chicken breast half and about ½ cup duxelles).

CALORIES 284 (25% from fat); FAT 7.9g (sat 2.1g, mono 3.5g, poly 1g); PROTEIN 43.2g; CARB 8.8g; FIBER 1.4g; CHOL 104mg; IRON 4.6mg; SODIUM 430mg; CALC 101mg

Cuban-Style Chicken

The simple addition of a mojo marinade lends a Latin flair to this easy dish. Look for it in the ethnic-foods aisle.

- 4 (6-ounce) skinless, boneless chicken breast halves
- 3 tablespoons commercial mojo marinade (such as Goya)
- ½ cup finely chopped onion
- ¼ cup finely chopped fresh parsley
- 1 teaspoon canola oil
- 4 teaspoons fresh lime juice
- Lime wedges (optional)

1. Combine chicken and mojo in a large zip-top plastic bag; seal and marinate in refrigerator 2 hours, turning bag occasionally.

2. While chicken marinates, combine onion and parsley; refrigerate.

3. Remove chicken from bag; pat chicken dry. Heat oil in a large nonstick skillet over medium-high heat. Add chicken; cook 4 minutes on each side or until done. Drizzle each breast with 1 teaspoon lime juice; top each serving with 2 tablespoons onion mixture. Serve with lime wedges, if desired. Yield: 4 servings.

CALORIES 212 (14% from fat); FAT 3.3g (sat 0.7g, mono 1.2g, poly 0.8g); PROTEIN 39.6g; CARB 3.3g; FIBER 0.4g; CHOL 99mg; IRON 1.6mg; SODIUM 282mg; CALC 48mg

Spiced Chicken with Black-Eyed Peas and Rice

Spiced Chicken with Black-Eyed Peas and Rice

For juicier chicken, sear it on the stove top first, and then finish the cooking in the oven.

- 1 tablespoon olive oil, divided
- 1 teaspoon paprika
- 1 teaspoon Old Bay seasoning
- ½ teaspoon sugar
- ½ teaspoon salt, divided
- 4 (6-ounce) skinless, boneless chicken breast halves
- 1 cup chopped onion
- 1 garlic clove, minced
- 1½ cups cooked long-grain rice
- 1 teaspoon hot pepper sauce (such as Tabasco)
- 1 (15.8-ounce) can black-eyed peas, undrained
- ¼ cup sliced green onions

1. Preheat oven to 350°.
2. Heat 2 teaspoons olive oil in a large nonstick skillet over medium-high heat. Combine paprika, seasoning, sugar, and ¼ teaspoon salt; sprinkle over chicken. Add chicken to pan; cook 2 minutes on each side. Wrap handle of pan with foil. Place pan in oven. Bake at 350° for 6 minutes or until chicken is done. Cover and keep warm.
3. Heat 1 teaspoon olive oil in a large saucepan over medium-high heat. Add onion and garlic; sauté 3 minutes. Stir in rice, ¼ teaspoon salt, 1 teaspoon hot pepper sauce, and peas; cook 3 minutes or until thoroughly heated, stirring frequently. Spoon about ¾ cup rice mixture into each of 4 bowls; top each serving with 1 chicken breast half. Sprinkle each serving with 1 tablespoon green onions. Yield: 4 servings.

CALORIES 405 (14% from fat); FAT 6.5g (sat 1.3g, mono 3.1g, poly 1.2g); PROTEIN 47g; CARB 37.5g; FIBER 5g; CHOL 99mg; IRON 3.4mg; SODIUM 868mg; CALC 64mg

Maple-Orange Chicken

Use real maple syrup, not pancake syrup, in the pan sauce.

- Cooking spray
- 4 (6-ounce) skinless, boneless chicken breast halves
- 3 tablespoons water
- 3 tablespoons maple syrup
- 2 tablespoons low-sodium soy sauce
- 2 tablespoons cider vinegar
- 1½ teaspoons grated orange rind

1. Heat a large nonstick skillet over medium heat. Coat pan with cooking spray. Add chicken to pan; cook 6 minutes on each side or until done.
2. Combine water and remaining ingredients; add to pan. Cook 1 minute, turning chicken to coat. Yield: 4 servings (serving size: 1 breast half and about 1 tablespoon sauce).

CALORIES 233 (8% from fat); FAT 2.1g (sat 0.6g, mono 0.5g, poly 0.5g); PROTEIN 39.8g; CARB 11.3g; FIBER 0.1g; CHOL 99mg; IRON 1.5mg; SODIUM 415mg; CALC 31mg

Sweet and Sour Chicken

The entire dinner is cooked on the grill in a foil cooking bag.

- 4 (6-ounce) skinless, boneless chicken breast halves
- 2 cups teriyaki marinade, divided
- 2 cups (1-inch) cubed fresh pineapple
- 1½ cups yellow or orange bell pepper strips
- 1½ cups red bell pepper strips
- 2 cups vertically sliced Vidalia onion
- 2 cups cherry tomatoes
- ¼ cup chopped fresh cilantro

1. Place chicken in a large zip-top plastic bag; add 1 cup marinade. Seal bag; toss gently to coat. Place pineapple, bell peppers, and onion in another large zip-top plastic bag; add 1 cup marinade. Seal; toss gently. Refrigerate 2 hours, turning bags occasionally.
2. Prepare grill.
3. Drain pineapple mixture, discarding marinade. Place pineapple mixture and tomatoes in a large foil cooking bag. Drain chicken, discarding marinade. Place chicken on top of pineapple mixture. Seal and cut 6 (½-inch) slits in top of cooking bag. Place bag on grill. Grill 25 minutes or until chicken is done. Cut bag open with a sharp knife or cooking shears. Carefully peel back foil. Sprinkle with cilantro. Yield: 4 servings (serving size: 1 chicken breast half and 1 cup pineapple mixture).

CALORIES 336 (8% from fat); FAT 3.2g (sat 0.7g, mono 0.6g, poly 0.9g); PROTEIN 43g; CARB 35g; FIBER 7g; CHOL 99mg; IRON 3mg; SODIUM 279mg; CALC 72mg

Easy Puebla-Style Chicken Mole

Easy Puebla-Style Chicken Mole

This version of the Mexican classic comes together in minutes. To save time, use an immersion blender to puree the sauce while it's still in the pan. Serve with black beans and yellow rice, or as a filling for enchiladas. Garnish with sliced green onions, if you wish.

- 1 teaspoon olive oil
- 1 cup thinly sliced onion
- 1 teaspoon ground cumin
- 1 teaspoon ground coriander
- ½ teaspoon ground cinnamon
- 2 stemmed dried seeded ancho chiles, torn into 2-inch pieces (about ¼ cup)
- 2 garlic cloves, thinly sliced
- 3 cups fat-free, less-sodium chicken broth
- 1⅓ cups coarsely chopped tomato (about 1 medium)
- ¼ cup golden raisins
- 3 tablespoons sliced almonds, toasted
- 3 (½ x 2–inch) orange rind strips
- ¾ pound skinless, boneless chicken breast halves
- ¾ pound skinless, boneless chicken thighs
- ½ ounce unsweetened chocolate
- ¼ teaspoon salt
- ¼ teaspoon black pepper

1. Heat oil in a Dutch oven over medium-high heat. Add onion; cook 5 minutes or until almost tender. Combine cumin, coriander, and cinnamon in a small bowl; sprinkle over onion in pan. Cook 1 minute. Add chiles and garlic to pan; cook 2 minutes or until chiles soften. Add broth and next 4 ingredients to pan; bring to a boil. Add chicken to pan; cover, reduce heat, and simmer 10 minutes or until chicken is done. Remove chicken from pan; shred with 2 forks. Set aside.

2. Add chocolate to chile mixture; let stand until chocolate melts. Using an immersion blender in pan, puree chocolate mixture until smooth. Cook over medium heat 20 minutes or until reduced to 3½ cups, stirring occasionally. Add chicken to sauce; stir in salt and pepper. Yield: 6 servings (serving size: about 1 cup chicken mixture).

CALORIES 211 (29% from fat); FAT 6.8g (sat 1.8g; mono 2.8g; poly 1.3g); PROTEIN 27.2g; CARB 10.5g; FIBER 2.5g; CHOL 80mg; IRON 2.1mg; SODIUM 380mg; CALC 50mg

Oven-Fried Chicken

(pictured on page 190)

Marinating in buttermilk results in tender, juicy chicken, and double breading gives a crisp crust even without the skin. For a smoky taste, use ground chipotle pepper in place of the ground red pepper.

- ¾ cup low-fat buttermilk
- 2 bone-in chicken breast halves (about 1 pound), skinned
- 2 chicken drumsticks (about ½ pound), skinned
- 2 chicken thighs (about ½ pound), skinned
- ½ cup all-purpose flour (about 2¼ ounces)
- 1 teaspoon salt
- ½ teaspoon ground red pepper
- ¼ teaspoon white pepper
- ¼ teaspoon ground cumin
- Cooking spray

1. Combine first 4 ingredients in a large zip-top plastic bag; seal. Marinate in refrigerator 1 hour, turning occasionally.

2. Preheat oven to 450°.

3. Lightly spoon flour into a dry measuring cup; level with a knife. Combine flour, salt, peppers, and cumin in a second large zip-top plastic bag. Remove chicken from first bag, discarding marinade. Add chicken, one piece at a time, to flour mixture, shaking bag to coat chicken. Remove chicken from bag, shaking off excess flour; lightly coat each chicken piece with cooking spray. Return chicken, one piece at a time, to flour mixture, shaking bag to coat chicken. Remove chicken from bag, shaking off excess flour.

4. Place chicken on a baking sheet lined with parchment paper. Lightly coat chicken with cooking spray. Bake at 450° for 35 minutes or until done, turning after 20 minutes. Yield: 4 servings (serving size: 1 breast half or 1 thigh and 1 drumstick).

CALORIES 263 (15% from fat); FAT 4.4g (sat 1.2g, mono 1.1g, poly 0.9g); PROTEIN 38.4g; CARB 14.9g; FIBER 0.8g; CHOL 110mg; IRON 2.2mg; SODIUM 754mg; CALC 73mg

Slow Cooker Sweet and Sour Chicken

Pork tenderloin can be used in place of chicken thighs.

- 1 cup chopped onion
- ⅓ cup sugar
- ⅓ cup ketchup
- ¼ cup orange juice
- 3 tablespoons cornstarch
- 3 tablespoons cider vinegar
- 2 tablespoons low-sodium soy sauce
- 1 tablespoon grated peeled fresh ginger
- 1 pound skinless, boneless chicken thighs, cut into 1-inch pieces
- 2 (8-ounce) cans pineapple chunks in juice, drained
- 1 large green bell pepper, cut into ¾-inch pieces
- 1 large red bell pepper, cut into ¾-inch pieces
- 3 cups hot cooked white rice

1. Combine first 12 ingredients in an electric slow cooker. Cover and cook on LOW 6 hours or HIGH 4 hours. Serve over rice. Yield: 6 servings (serving size: ⅔ cup chicken mixture and ½ cup rice).

CALORIES 381 (21% from fat); FAT 8.7g (sat 2.3g, mono 3.2g, poly 2g); PROTEIN 23.2g; CARB 51.9g; FIBER 2.1g; CHOL 72mg; IRON 2.5mg; SODIUM 396mg; CALC 29mg

Yakitori

The Japanese term "yakitori" refers to small pieces of marinated chicken that are skewered and grilled. We preferred the dark-meat chicken with the soy-ginger mixture.

- ¼ cup sake (rice wine)
- ¼ cup low-sodium soy sauce
- 3 tablespoons sugar
- 2 tablespoons grated peeled fresh ginger
- ¼ teaspoon crushed red pepper
- 2 garlic cloves, minced
- 1 pound skinless, boneless chicken thighs, cut into 24 bite-sized pieces
- 5 green onions, each cut into 4 (2-inch) pieces
- Cooking spray

1. Combine first 6 ingredients in a small saucepan. Bring to a boil; cook until reduced to ¼ cup (about 2½ minutes). Remove from heat; cool.
2. Combine soy sauce mixture and chicken in a zip-top plastic bag, and seal. Marinate in refrigerator 1 hour.
3. Heat a large grill pan over medium-high heat.
4. Thread 6 chicken pieces and 5 green onion pieces alternately onto each of 4 (10-inch) skewers. Brush kebabs with soy mixture. Coat pan with cooking spray. Place kebabs in pan; cook 4 minutes on each side or until browned and chicken is done. Yield: 4 servings (serving size: 1 kebab).

CALORIES 172 (24% from fat); FAT 4.5g (sat 1.1g, mono 1.4g, poly 1.1g); PROTEIN 22.9g; CARB 6.7g; FIBER 0.3g; CHOL 94mg; IRON 1.5mg; SODIUM 366mg; CALC 19mg

Yakitori

Chicken Paprikash–Topped Potatoes

The traditional Hungarian dish of chicken and onion in creamy paprika sauce makes a hearty topping for baked potatoes. Dark-meat chicken complements the bold flavors.

- 4 baking potatoes (about 1½ pounds)
- 4 skinless, boneless chicken thighs (about 12 ounces), cut into bite-sized pieces
- 2 tablespoons all-purpose flour
- 2 teaspoons paprika
- ¾ teaspoon salt
- ¼ teaspoon ground red pepper
- 1 tablespoon butter
- ½ cup coarsely chopped onion
- 1 (8-ounce) package presliced mushrooms
- 2 garlic cloves, minced
- ½ cup fat-free, less-sodium chicken broth
- ¼ cup reduced-fat sour cream
- 2 tablespoons chopped fresh parsley

1. Pierce potatoes with a fork, and arrange in a circle on paper towels in a microwave oven. Microwave at HIGH 16 minutes or until done, rearranging potatoes after 8 minutes. Wrap each potato in foil; let stand 5 minutes.

2. Combine chicken, flour, paprika, salt, and pepper in a large zip-top plastic bag; seal and shake to coat.

3. Melt butter in a large nonstick skillet over medium-high heat. Add chicken mixture, onion, mushrooms, and garlic; sauté 5 minutes. Add broth; bring to a boil. Cook 6 minutes or until chicken is done and sauce thickens, stirring frequently. Remove from heat; stir in sour cream.

4. Remove foil from potatoes, and split open with a fork. Fluff pulp. Divide chicken mixture evenly over potatoes; sprinkle with parsley. Yield: 4 servings (serving size: 1 potato, ½ cup chicken mixture, and 1½ teaspoons parsley).

CALORIES 311 (25% from fat); FAT 8.6g (sat 3.9g, mono 1.9g, poly 1.2g); PROTEIN 22.9g; CARB 36.3g; FIBER 3.4g; CHOL 86mg; IRON 2.6g; SODIUM 619mg; CALC 56mg

Margarita-Braised Chicken Thighs

Stir chopped cilantro and green onions into steamed rice for an easy side.

- ½ cup flour (about 2¼ ounces)
- 1 tablespoon paprika
- 2 teaspoons garlic powder
- 8 skinless, boneless chicken thighs (about 1½ pounds)
- ½ teaspoon salt
- 1 tablespoon olive oil
- Cooking spray
- 1 cup thinly sliced onion (about 1 medium)
- 5 garlic cloves, minced
- ½ cup dried tropical fruit
- ½ cup orange juice
- ¼ cup tequila
- 1 lime, thinly sliced

1. Preheat oven to 400°.
2. Combine first 3 ingredients in a small baking dish. Sprinkle chicken with salt; dredge chicken in flour mixture.
3. Heat oil in a large nonstick skillet over medium-high heat. Add chicken to pan; cook 4 minutes on each side or until lightly browned. Transfer chicken to an 11 x 7–inch baking dish coated with cooking spray. Add onion to pan; cook 3 minutes. Add garlic to pan; sauté 1 minute.
4. Combine fruit, juice, and tequila in a microwave-safe dish; microwave at HIGH 2 minutes. Pour fruit mixture into pan; bring to a boil, scraping pan to loosen browned bits. Cook 1 minute. Pour onion mixture over chicken; top with lime slices. Bake at 400° for 20 minutes or until chicken is done. Yield: 4 servings (serving size: 2 chicken thighs and about ⅓ cup fruit mixture).

CALORIES 350 (25% from fat); FAT 9.9g (sat 2.2g, mono 4.3g, poly 2.1g); PROTEIN 25.1g; CARB 37.9g; FIBER 2.7g; CHOL 94mg; IRON 2.7mg; SODIUM 416mg; CALC 55mg

Braised Chicken Thighs with Figs and Bay Leaves

Chicken thighs are more succulent than breasts, but you can use the latter if you prefer. Serve this entrée with couscous to capture the tangy sauce.

- 8 chicken thighs (about 2¼ pounds), skinned
- ½ teaspoon salt
- ¼ teaspoon black pepper
- 8 bay leaves
- 2 teaspoons olive oil
- 3 tablespoons water
- ½ cup sliced shallots
- ⅓ cup dry red wine
- 1 tablespoon red wine vinegar
- 1 teaspoon honey
- 16 fresh figs, halved

1. Sprinkle chicken with salt and black pepper. Place 1 bay leaf on each chicken thigh. Heat oil in a heavy 10-inch skillet over medium-high heat. Place chicken, bay leaf sides down, in pan. Cook 5 minutes or until browned. Turn chicken over; cook 3 minutes. Add 3 tablespoons water; cover, reduce heat, and simmer 5 minutes. Remove chicken from pan. Add shallots; cook 2 minutes. Add chicken, wine, vinegar, and honey to pan; bring to a boil. Cook for 1 minute. Cover, reduce heat, and simmer 5 minutes or until chicken is done. Add figs; cover and simmer 5 minutes or until figs are tender. Yield: 4 servings (serving size: 2 chicken thighs, 8 fig halves, and ¼ cup sauce).

CALORIES 393 (26% from fat); FAT 11.4g (sat 2.6g, mono 4.5g, poly 2.5g); PROTEIN 42.4g; CARB 27.4g; FIBER 4.4g; CHOL 163mg; IRON 2.9mg; SODIUM 472mg; CALC 74mg

Lemony Spanish Pepper Chicken

While the chicken simmers, you can roast the green beans and cook the egg noodles.

- 8 chicken thighs (about 2½ pounds), skinned
- 1½ teaspoons dried oregano
- ½ teaspoon salt
- ¼ teaspoon black pepper
- ¼ teaspoon paprika
- Cooking spray
- 1½ cups red bell pepper strips
- 1½ cups green bell pepper strips
- 1 tablespoon grated lemon rind
- ¼ cup fresh lemon juice
- ½ cup fat-free, less-sodium chicken broth
- 2 tablespoons ketchup

1. Sprinkle chicken with oregano, salt, black pepper, and paprika. Heat a large nonstick skillet over medium-high heat. Coat pan with cooking spray. Add chicken; sauté 3 minutes or until lightly browned. Turn chicken over; top with bell peppers, rind, and juice. Cover, reduce heat, and simmer 30 minutes or until chicken is done. Remove chicken from pan. Combine broth and ketchup in a small bowl. Stir ketchup mixture into pan; bring to a boil. Serve pepper mixture with chicken. Yield: 4 servings (serving size: 2 chicken thighs and ½ cup bell pepper mixture).

CALORIES 267 (26% from fat); FAT 7.8g (sat 2g, mono 2.4g, poly 2g); PROTEIN 39.4g; CARB 8.7g; FIBER 1.9g; CHOL 161mg; IRON 2.8mg; SODIUM 609mg; CALC 40mg

Chicken and Shrimp Paella

Paella (pi-ay-ah) is named after a large, shallow, two-handled pan, also called paella, in which it's prepared and served. Since the pan is a specialty cookware purchase, you can use your favorite large nonstick skillet instead. This dish is a bit soupy when first prepared, but the rice quickly absorbs the liquid.

6 chicken thighs (about 1½ pounds), skinned
1 teaspoon chopped fresh or ¼ teaspoon dried rosemary
¾ teaspoon salt, divided
¼ teaspoon freshly ground black pepper
2 teaspoons vegetable oil
1 (4-ounce) link hot turkey Italian sausage
1 cup chopped onion
½ cup chopped red bell pepper
1½ cups uncooked Arborio or Valencia rice
½ cup diced plum tomato
1 teaspoon Hungarian sweet paprika
¼ teaspoon saffron threads, crushed
1 garlic clove, minced
3 cups fat-free, less-sodium chicken broth
¾ pound large shrimp, peeled and deveined
1 cup (1-inch) diagonally cut asparagus
½ cup frozen green peas, thawed

1. Preheat oven to 400°.
2. Sprinkle chicken with rosemary, ½ teaspoon salt, and ¼ teaspoon black pepper. Heat oil in a large nonstick skillet over medium-high heat. Add chicken, and cook 3 minutes on each side or until lightly browned. Remove chicken from pan; cover and keep warm.
3. Remove casings from sausage. Add sausage to pan, and cook 1 minute, stirring to crumble. Add 1 cup onion and ½ cup bell pepper; cook 7 minutes, stirring constantly. Add rice, tomato, paprika, saffron, and garlic; cook 1 minute, stirring constantly. Return chicken to pan. Add 3 cups broth and ¼ teaspoon salt; bring to a boil. Wrap handle of pan with foil, and cover pan with lid or aluminum foil.
4. Bake at 400° for 10 minutes. Remove pan from oven. Add shrimp, asparagus, and peas, stirring gently until combined. Cover and bake an additional 5 minutes or until shrimp are done. Yield: 6 servings (serving size: 1 chicken thigh and about 1 cup rice mixture).

CALORIES 433 (15% from fat); FAT 7g (sat 1.6g, mono 2g, poly 2.5g); PROTEIN 34.8g; CARB 52.8g; FIBER 3g; CHOL 156mg; IRON 3.2mg; SODIUM 787mg; CALC 73mg

Teriyaki-Glazed Chicken with Tangy Apricot Ketchup

Blend the remaining contents of the can of chiles in adobo sauce; store in a freezer container. Just scoop out as much as you need (1 tablespoon equals 1 chile), no need to defrost.

1 chipotle chile, canned in adobo sauce
½ cup low-sodium teriyaki sauce
1 tablespoon minced garlic cloves, divided
8 chicken thighs (about 2½ pounds), skinned
1 tablespoon olive oil
1 cup chopped onion
2 cups chopped apricots (about ¾ pound)
¼ cup apricot preserves
1 tablespoon fresh lime juice
¾ teaspoon salt, divided
Cooking spray
¼ cup chopped fresh cilantro

1. Remove 1 chile from can; mince. Place 1 teaspoon minced chile in a large zip-top plastic bag. Reserve ½ teaspoon minced chile, and set aside. Reserve remaining chiles and sauce for another use. Add teriyaki sauce, 2 teaspoons garlic, and chicken to bag; seal and marinate in refrigerator 3 to 12 hours.
2. Heat oil in a medium nonstick skillet over medium heat. Add remaining 1 teaspoon garlic and onion; cook 5 minutes or until tender, stirring frequently. Add reserved ½ teaspoon minced chile, chopped apricots, preserves, lime juice, and ½ teaspoon salt; cook over medium-high heat 5 minutes or until apricots are very tender. Remove from heat; cool slightly. Place apricot mixture in a blender; process until smooth. Cool to room temperature. Remove ½ cup apricot mixture.
3. Prepare grill.
4. Remove chicken from bag; discard marinade. Sprinkle chicken with remaining ¼ teaspoon salt. Place chicken on grill rack coated with cooking spray, and grill 10 minutes on each side, basting frequently with reserved ½ cup apricot mixture during last 5 minutes. Serve chicken with remaining apricot mixture. Sprinkle with cilantro. Yield: 4 servings (serving size: 2 chicken thighs, ¼ cup apricot ketchup, and 1 tablespoon cilantro).

CALORIES 317 (26% from fat); FAT 9.1g (sat 1.9g, mono 4.3g, poly 1.7g); PROTEIN 29.5g; CARB 30.1g; FIBER 3.1g; CHOL 113mg; IRON 2.4mg; SODIUM 824mg; CALC 52mg

Chicken Thighs with Roasted Apples

Chicken Thighs with Roasted Apples

The roasted apples create a flavorful chunky sauce for this rustic dish. Gala apples are a good substitute for Braeburn.

- 5 cups chopped Braeburn apple (about 1½ pounds)
- 1 teaspoon chopped fresh sage
- ¼ teaspoon ground cinnamon
- ⅛ teaspoon ground nutmeg
- 4 garlic cloves, chopped
- ½ teaspoon salt, divided
- Cooking spray
- 8 chicken thighs (about 2½ pounds), skinned
- ¼ teaspoon black pepper
- Chopped parsley (optional)

1. Preheat oven to 475°.
2. Combine first 5 ingredients in a large bowl. Sprinkle ¼ teaspoon salt over apple mixture; toss well to coat. Spread apple mixture on a jelly-roll pan coated with cooking spray.
3. Sprinkle chicken with ¼ teaspoon salt and pepper; arrange on top of apple mixture. Bake at 475° for 25 minutes or until chicken is done and apple is tender. Remove chicken from pan; set aside, and keep warm.
4. Partially mash apple mixture with a potato masher; serve with chicken. Sprinkle with parsley, if desired. Yield: 4 servings (serving size: 2 chicken thighs and about ⅔ cup roasted apples).

CALORIES 257 (20% from fat); FAT 5.7g (sat 1.4g, mono 1.6g, poly 1.4g); PROTEIN 25.9g; CARB 26.6g; FIBER 3.5g; CHOL 107mg; IRON 1.7mg; SODIUM 405mg; CALC 30mg

Jamaican-Spiced Jerk Chicken

A great hands-off meal—slow cooking chicken thighs in the classic Caribbean seasoning mixture yields tender morsels in a spicy jus. Serve over yellow rice.

- 1 Scotch bonnet chile
- 1 cup chopped green onions
- 2 tablespoons sugar
- 2 tablespoons cider vinegar
- 2 tablespoons low-sodium soy sauce
- 1 teaspoon ground allspice
- ¼ teaspoon ground cinnamon
- ¼ teaspoon dried thyme
- ½ teaspoon salt
- 2 garlic cloves, crushed
- 6 chicken thighs (about 2 pounds), skinned

1. Remove stem from chile; cut chile in half. Combine chile, chopped green onions, and next 8 ingredients in a food processor; process until smooth.
2. Place chicken in an electric slow cooker; top with onion mixture, stirring gently to coat. Cover and cook on LOW 6 hours. Remove chicken thighs from slow cooker with a slotted spoon. Remove meat from bones, and shred meat into bite-sized pieces using 2 forks.
3. Place a zip-top plastic bag inside a 2-cup glass measure. Pour liquid from slow cooker into bag; let stand 10 minutes (fat will rise to the top). Seal bag; carefully snip off 1 bottom corner of bag. Drain drippings into a bowl, stopping before fat layer reaches opening; discard fat. Serve chicken with jus. Yield: 4 servings (serving size: 4 ounces chicken and ¼ cup jus).

CALORIES 317 (26% from fat); FAT 9g (sat 2.3g, mono 2.8g, poly 2.3g); PROTEIN 45.8g; CARB 10.9g; FIBER 1.3g; CHOL 188mg; IRON 3.2mg; SODIUM 763mg; CALC 53mg

Chicken and Dumplings from Scratch

Creating a chicken and dumplings recipe that's creamy, rich, and thick is a challenge, especially thickening the base. Relying solely on cornstarch produced a gluey consistency and thin flavor, and using all flour created pasty results. A little of each achieved the perfect thickness and texture. Toasting the flour, a process similar to making a dry roux, adds richness. Finish the dish with a splash of cream for flavor.

STEW:

- 1 (4-pound) whole chicken
- 3 quarts water
- 3 cups chopped onion
- 1 cup chopped celery
- 1 cup chopped carrot
- 1 teaspoon salt
- ¼ teaspoon freshly ground black pepper
- 10 garlic cloves, peeled
- 4 thyme sprigs
- 2 bay leaves
- ¼ cup all-purpose flour (about 1 ounce)
- 2 teaspoons cornstarch
- 3 tablespoons heavy cream

DUMPLINGS:

- ¾ cup 1% low-fat milk
- 1 large egg
- 1½ cups all-purpose flour (about 6¾ ounces)
- 1 tablespoon baking powder
- 1 tablespoon cornmeal
- ½ teaspoon salt

REMAINING INGREDIENTS:

- 1 tablespoon chopped parsley
- Freshly ground black pepper

1. To prepare stew, remove and discard giblets and neck from chicken. Rinse chicken with cold water; place chicken in an 8-quart stockpot. Add 3 quarts water and next 8 ingredients; bring to a simmer. Reduce heat, and simmer 45 minutes; skim surface occasionally, discarding solids. Remove chicken from pot; cool. Strain stock through a sieve into a large bowl; discard solids. Remove chicken meat from bones; tear chicken meat into 2-inch pieces, and store in refrigerator. Let stock cool to room temperature.

2. Pour stock into 2 zip-top plastic bags. Let stand 15 minutes. Working with one bag at a time, snip off 1 bottom corner of bag; drain liquid into stockpot, stopping before fat layer reaches opening. Discard fat. Repeat procedure with remaining bag. Bring stock to a boil over medium-high heat; reduce heat, and simmer until reduced to 8 cups (about 15 minutes).

3. Heat a cast-iron skillet over medium-high heat 5 minutes. Lightly spoon ¼ cup flour into a dry measuring cup; level with a knife. Add flour to pan; cook 1 minute or until lightly browned, stirring constantly. Combine browned flour and cornstarch in a large bowl; add ⅔ cup stock to flour mixture, stirring with a whisk until smooth. Add flour mixture to remaining stock in pan; bring to a boil over medium-high heat. Cook 2 minutes or until slightly thick. Reduce heat; stir in cream. Add chicken; keep warm over low heat.

4. To prepare dumplings, combine milk and egg in a medium bowl. Lightly spoon 1½ cups flour into dry measuring cups; level with a knife. Combine flour, baking powder, cornmeal, and ½ teaspoon salt. Add flour mixture to milk mixture, stirring with a fork just until dry ingredients are moistened.

5. Drop one-third of dumpling batter by 8 heaping teaspoonfuls onto chicken mixture. Cover and cook 3 minutes or until dumplings are done (do not allow chicken mixture to boil). Remove dumplings with a slotted spoon; place in a large serving bowl or on a deep serving platter. Keep warm. Repeat procedure with remaining dumpling batter.

6. Remove pan from heat; slowly pour stew over dumplings. Sprinkle with parsley and freshly ground black pepper. Serve immediately. Yield: 6 servings (serving size: 1⅓ cups stew and 4 dumplings).

CALORIES 334 (21% from fat); FAT 7.9g (sat 3.2g, mono 2.4g, poly 1.2g); PROTEIN 31.4g; CARB 32.2g; FIBER 1.2g; CHOL 130mg; IRON 3.3mg; SODIUM 755mg; CALC 211mg

Double-Herb Roasted Chicken and Potatoes

The taste and scent of the fresh herbs infuse the meat with flavor that lingers even after removing the skin. Try rosemary, sage, or thyme in place of oregano.

- 1 (6-pound) roasting chicken
- 3 tablespoons chopped fresh oregano, divided
- 2 garlic cloves, minced
- 8 fresh basil leaves
- Cooking spray
- 8 red potatoes, quartered lengthwise
- ¼ teaspoon salt
- ¼ to ½ teaspoon black pepper

1. Preheat oven to 450°.
2. Remove and discard giblets and neck from chicken. Rinse chicken with cold water; pat dry. Trim excess fat. Starting at neck cavity, loosen skin from breast and drumsticks by inserting fingers, gently pushing between skin and meat.
3. Combine 2 tablespoons chopped oregano and garlic cloves. Rub seasoning mixture under loosened skin and drumsticks. Carefully place basil leaves under loosened skin. Tie ends of legs with cord. Lift wing tips up and over back; tuck under chicken.
4. Place chicken, breast side up, on a broiler pan coated with cooking spray. Pierce skin several times with a meat fork. Arrange potatoes on rack around chicken. Coat chicken and potatoes with cooking spray. Sprinkle chicken and potatoes with remaining 1 tablespoon oregano, salt, and pepper. Insert a thermometer into meaty part of thigh, making sure not to touch bone. Bake at 450° for 30 minutes. Reduce oven temperature to 350° (do not remove chicken from oven); bake an additional 45 minutes or until thermometer registers 165°. Cover chicken loosely with foil; let stand 10 minutes. Discard skin. Remove chicken from pan; place on a serving platter. Serve with roasted potatoes. Yield: 8 servings (serving size: 4 ounces chicken and 4 potato wedges).

CALORIES 349 (13% from fat); FAT 5g (sat 1.2g, mono 1.4g, poly 1.2g); PROTEIN 39.4g; CARB 34.4g; FIBER 3.2g; CHOL 113mg; IRON 3.1mg; SODIUM 217mg; CALC 42mg

Chicken with Citrus

Enjoy this simple dish when citrus is at its peak. Free-range chickens are worth the extra expense for their fresh, pure flavor, but this recipe will work with a roasting chicken.

- 1 (3¼-pound) whole free-range chicken
- 2 teaspoons dried oregano, divided
- 1 teaspoon sea salt, divided
- ½ teaspoon freshly ground black pepper
- 1 lemon, cut in half
- 1 orange, cut in half
- 1 tablespoon unsalted butter, softened
- Cooking spray
- 2 cups water, divided

1. Preheat oven to 450°.
2. Remove and discard giblets and neck. Rinse chicken with cold water; pat dry. Sprinkle 1 teaspoon oregano, ½ teaspoon salt, and pepper in body cavity. Place lemon and orange halves in cavity (this will be a tight fit).
3. Combine remaining oregano and butter. Starting at neck cavity, loosen skin from breast and drumsticks by inserting fingers, gently pushing between skin and meat. Rub butter mixture under loosened skin. Lift wing tips up and over back; tuck under chicken. Tie legs together with cord. Place chicken, breast side up, on a rack coated with cooking spray. Place rack in a broiler pan; add 1½ cups water to pan. Insert a thermometer into meaty part of thigh, making sure not to touch bone. Bake at 450° for 50 minutes or until thermometer registers 165°. Let stand 20 minutes. Remove fruit from cavity, and set aside. Remove skin; discard. Sprinkle chicken evenly with remaining ½ teaspoon salt.
4. Place a zip-top plastic bag inside a 2-cup glass measure. Pour drippings from pan into bag; add remaining ½ cup water. Let stand 2 minutes (fat will rise to top). Seal bag; carefully snip off 1 bottom corner of bag. Drain drippings into measuring cup, stopping before fat layer reaches opening; discard remaining fat. Return drippings to broiler pan; cook over medium heat, scraping pan to loosen browned bits. Simmer 8 minutes or until mixture measures ¼ cup. Slice chicken; squeeze juice from reserved lemon and orange over chicken. Serve with sauce. Yield: 4 servings (serving size: about 4 ounces chicken and 1 tablespoon sauce).

CALORIES 287 (39% from fat); FAT 12.4g (sat 4.4g, mono 4.4g, poly 2.3g); PROTEIN 36g; CARB 6.4g; FIBER 1.7g; CHOL 114mg; IRON 2.3mg; SODIUM 711mg; CALC 51mg

Chicken with Citrus

Sage Pesto-Rubbed Roast Chicken

Sage Pesto–Rubbed Roast Chicken

The pestolike mixture rubbed under the skin adds a subtle herb flavor to the chicken.

PESTO:

⅓ cup chopped fresh parsley
¼ cup chopped fresh sage
⅓ cup fat-free, less-sodium chicken broth
2 tablespoons chopped walnuts, toasted
1 teaspoon extravirgin olive oil
½ teaspoon salt
3 garlic cloves, peeled

CHICKEN:

1 (7-pound) roasting chicken
Cooking spray
Sage sprigs (optional)
Parsley sprigs (optional)

1. Preheat oven to 450°.
2. To prepare pesto, combine first 7 ingredients in a blender or food processor; process until smooth.
3. To prepare chicken, remove and discard giblets and neck from chicken. Rinse chicken with cold water; pat dry. Trim excess fat. Starting at neck cavity, loosen skin from breast and drumsticks by inserting fingers, gently pushing between skin and meat. Rub pesto under loosened skin and over breast and drumsticks. Lift wing tips up and over back; tuck under chicken. Place chicken, breast side up, on a broiler pan coated with cooking spray. Insert a thermometer into meaty part of thigh, making sure not to touch bone. Bake at 450° for 30 minutes. Reduce oven temperature to 350° (do not remove chicken from oven); bake an additional 1½ hours or until thermometer registers 165°. Let stand 10 minutes. Discard skin before serving. Garnish with sage and parsley sprigs, if desired. Yield: 9 servings (serving size: about 4 ounces).

CALORIES 219 (27% from fat); FAT 6.5g (sat 1.4g, mono 2.1g, poly 2g); PROTEIN 37.1g; CARB 0.9g; FIBER 0.2g; CHOL 117mg; IRON 2.1mg; SODIUM 287mg; CALC 30mg

Roast Chicken with Cumin, Honey, and Orange

1 (3-pound) roasting chicken
¼ cup honey
1½ tablespoons grated orange rind
1 tablespoon ground cumin
¼ teaspoon salt
⅛ teaspoon black pepper
1 garlic clove, minced

1. Preheat oven to 400°.
2. Remove and discard giblets and neck from chicken. Rinse chicken with cold water; pat dry. Trim excess fat. Starting at neck cavity, loosen skin from breast and drumsticks by inserting fingers, gently pushing between skin and meat.
3. Combine honey and remaining ingredients. Rub honey mixture under loosened skin and over breast and drumsticks. Lift wing tips up and over back; tuck under chicken.
4. Place chicken, breast side up, on a foil-lined broiler pan. Pierce skin several times with a meat fork. Insert a thermometer into meaty part of thigh, making sure not to touch bone. Bake at 400° 30 minutes; cover loosely with foil. Bake an additional 40 minutes or until thermometer registers 165°. Let stand 10 minutes. Discard skin. Yield: 4 servings (serving size: 4 ounces).

CALORIES 273 (27% from fat); FAT 8.2g (sat 2.2g, mono 3g, poly 1.9g); PROTEIN 31.2g; CARB 19g; FIBER 0.2g; CHOL 95mg; IRON 2.4mg; SODIUM 241mg; CALC 37mg

Roasted Chicken with Onions, Potatoes, and Gravy

- 1 (4-pound) roasting chicken
- 1 teaspoon salt, divided
- 3/4 teaspoon freshly ground black pepper, divided
- 4 oregano sprigs
- 1 lemon, quartered
- 1 celery stalk, cut into 2-inch pieces
- Cooking spray
- 2 tablespoons butter, melted
- 2 pounds medium yellow onions, peeled and each cut into 8 wedges
- 2 pounds small red potatoes, quartered
- 1/4 cup all-purpose flour (about 1 ounce)
- 1 (14-ounce) can fat-free, less-sodium chicken broth, divided
- Lemon wedges (optional)
- Fresh oregano sprigs (optional)

1. Preheat oven to 425°.

2. Remove and discard giblets and neck from chicken. Rinse chicken with cold water; pat dry. Trim excess fat. Starting at neck cavity, loosen skin from breast and drumsticks by inserting fingers, gently pushing between skin and meat. Combine 1/2 teaspoon salt and 1/2 teaspoon pepper; rub under loosened skin and over breast and drumsticks. Place oregano, quartered lemon, and celery into body cavity. Lift wing tips up and over back, and tuck under chicken. Tie legs together with string. Place chicken, breast side up, on rack of a broiler pan coated with cooking spray.

3. Combine remaining 1/2 teaspoon salt, remaining 1/4 teaspoon pepper, butter, onions, and potatoes in a large bowl; toss well to coat. Arrange onion mixture around chicken on rack. Place rack in pan. Bake at 425° for 20 minutes. Reduce oven temperature to 325° (do not remove pan from oven); bake an additional 1 hour and 15 minutes or until onions and potatoes are tender and a thermometer inserted into meaty part of thigh registers 165°. Set chicken, onions, and potatoes aside; cover and keep warm.

4. Place a zip-top plastic bag inside a 2-cup glass measure. Pour pan drippings into bag; let stand 10 minutes (fat will rise to the top). Seal bag; carefully snip off 1 bottom corner of bag. Drain drippings into a small saucepan, stopping before fat layer reaches opening; discard fat. Combine flour and 1/2 cup broth in a small bowl, stirring with a whisk. Add flour mixture and remaining broth to saucepan. Bring to a boil over medium-high heat. Reduce heat to medium; cook 5 minutes or until gravy thickens, stirring frequently with a whisk. Serve gravy with chicken and onion mixture. Garnish with lemon wedges and oregano sprigs, if desired. Yield: 5 servings (serving size: about 4 ounces chicken, 1 1/2 cups onion mixture, and 1/3 cup gravy).

CALORIES 475 (19% from fat); FAT 10g (sat 4.2g, mono 2.8g, poly 1.6g); PROTEIN 44.5g; CARB 50.7g; FIBER 5.6g; CHOL 132mg; IRON 3.9mg; SODIUM 881mg; CALC 76mg

Asian Roasted Chicken

- 1 (3-pound) broiler-fryer chicken
- 1/4 cup low-sodium soy sauce
- 1 tablespoon grated peeled fresh ginger
- 2 garlic cloves, minced
- 1 (14-ounce) can fat-free, less-sodium chicken broth
- 1/4 teaspoon dark sesame oil
- 1/2 cup (2-inch) sliced green onions

1. Remove and discard giblets and neck from chicken. Rinse chicken with cold water; pat dry. Trim excess fat. Starting at neck cavity, loosen skin from breast and drumsticks by inserting fingers, gently pushing between skin and meat.

2. Combine soy sauce, ginger, garlic, and broth in a large heavy-duty zip-top plastic bag. Add chicken; seal and marinate in refrigerator 4 to 8 hours, turning bag occasionally. Remove chicken from bag, reserving 1/2 cup marinade.

3. Preheat oven to 375°.

4. Place chicken, breast side up, on rack of a broiler pan or roasting pan. Insert a thermometer into meaty part of thigh, making sure not to touch bone. Bake at 375° for 1 hour and 10 minutes or until thermometer registers 165°. Cover chicken loosely with foil, and let stand 10 minutes for chicken to reabsorb juices. Discard skin.

5. Add 1/2 cup reserved marinade to drippings in pan (you'll have about 1/4 cup drippings), scraping pan to loosen browned bits. Pour marinade mixture into a small saucepan; bring to a boil. Cook 5 minutes. Stir in oil. Cut chicken into quarters. Drizzle with sesame mixture. Sprinkle with onions. Yield: 4 servings (serving size: about 4 ounces chicken and about 1 1/2 tablespoons sauce).

CALORIES 226 (33% from fat); FAT 8.4g (sat 2.2g, mono 3g, poly 2g); PROTEIN 32.2g; CARB 2.3g; FIBER 0.4g; CHOL 95mg; IRON 1.5mg; SODIUM 548mg; CALC 28mg

Roasted Chicken with Onions, Potatoes, and Gravy

Rosemary-Lemon Cornish Hens with Roasted Potatoes

You can easily vary this recipe by using thyme in place of rosemary or sprinkling ground red pepper and garlic powder over the potatoes.

- 2 teaspoons crushed dried rosemary
- ½ teaspoon salt, divided
- ¼ teaspoon black pepper, divided
- 2 (1¼-pound) Cornish hens
- ½ lemon, halved and divided
- Cooking spray
- 2 cups cubed Yukon gold or red potato
- 2 teaspoons olive oil

1. Preheat oven to 375°.

2. Combine rosemary, ¼ teaspoon salt, and ⅛ teaspoon pepper.

3. Remove and discard giblets from hens. Rinse hens with cold water; pat dry. Remove skin; trim excess fat. Working with 1 hen at a time, place 1 lemon piece in cavity of each hen; tie ends of legs together with twine. Lift wing tips up and over back; tuck under hen. Repeat procedure with remaining hen and lemon piece. Rub hens with rosemary mixture. Place hens, breast sides up, on a broiler pan coated with cooking spray.

4. Toss potato with oil; sprinkle with remaining ¼ teaspoon salt and ⅛ teaspoon pepper. Arrange potato around hens.

5. Insert a thermometer into meaty part of thigh, making sure not to touch bone. Remove twine. Bake at 375° for 1 hour or until thermometer registers 165°. Yield: 2 servings (serving size: 1 hen and about ¾ cup potatoes).

CALORIES 372 (28% from fat); FAT 11.4g (sat 2.4g, mono 5.5g, poly 2.1g); PROTEIN 41.8g; CARB 24.1g; FIBER 2.7g; CHOL 180mg; IRON 3mg; SODIUM 702mg; CALC 47mg

Seared Duck Breast with Ginger-Rhubarb Sauce

The sweet, spicy heat from the ginger preserves is balanced by tart rhubarb and wine. Chicken breasts can be substituted for duck, if desired.

- 2 cups dry red wine
- 1 cup finely chopped rhubarb
- 2 tablespoons finely chopped shallots
- 1 bay leaf
- 1 star anise
- ½ cup ginger preserves
- ½ teaspoon kosher salt, divided
- 2 (12-ounce) packages boneless whole duck breast, thawed, skinned, and cut in half
- ½ teaspoon freshly ground black pepper
- 2 teaspoons olive oil

1. Combine first 5 ingredients in a large saucepan; bring to a boil. Cook until reduced to 1 cup (about 18 minutes). Stir in preserves and ¼ teaspoon salt; cook 1 minute. Strain wine mixture through a sieve over a bowl; discard solids.

2. Sprinkle duck with ¼ teaspoon salt and pepper. Heat oil in a large nonstick skillet over medium heat. Add duck; cook 5 minutes on each side or until desired degree of doneness. Cut duck diagonally across grain into thin slices; serve with sauce. Yield: 4 servings (serving size: 1 duck breast half and about 2 tablespoons sauce).

CALORIES 380 (23% from fat); FAT 9.5g (sat 2.6g, mono 3.7g, poly 1.2g); PROTEIN 34.2g; CARB 23.1g; FIBER 0.6g; CHOL 131mg; IRON 8.3mg; SODIUM 347mg; CALC 29mg

Seared Duck Breast with Ginger-Rhubarb Sauce

Turkey-Jasmine Rice Meatballs with Baby Bok Choy

Use a box grater to shred the ginger after you've peeled away the brown outer layer. Jasmine rice has a pleasant aroma that underscores the other Asian ingredients, but any long-grain white rice will work to help keep the meatballs moist and add a bit of texture. Chopped bok choy can substitute for whole baby bok choy.

MEATBALLS:

1 cup water
1/3 cup uncooked jasmine rice
1/4 cup dry breadcrumbs
1/4 cup chopped green onions
3/4 teaspoon salt
1/4 teaspoon freshly ground black pepper
1 1/4 pounds ground turkey
2 large egg whites
1 garlic clove, minced
Cooking spray

BOK CHOY:

6 baby bok choy (about 1 1/3 pounds)
2 teaspoons vegetable oil
1/4 cup chopped green onions
1 tablespoon shredded peeled fresh ginger
1 garlic clove, minced
1 cup water
3/4 cup fat-free, less-sodium chicken broth
3 tablespoons low-sodium soy sauce
1 1/2 teaspoons sugar
1/2 teaspoon crushed red pepper
1 1/2 tablespoons dry sherry
2 teaspoons cornstarch

1. To prepare meatballs, bring 1 cup water to a boil in a small saucepan. Stir in jasmine rice; reduce heat, and simmer 15 minutes or until rice is almost tender. Drain; cool. Combine rice, breadcrumbs, and next 6 ingredients. Shape mixture into 18 meatballs.

2. Heat a large nonstick skillet over medium-high heat. Coat pan with cooking spray. Add meatballs; cook 5 minutes, browning on all sides. Cover, reduce heat to medium, and cook 10 minutes or until done, turning often. Remove pan from heat; keep warm.

3. While meatballs cook, prepare bok choy. Cut each bok choy in half lengthwise. Rinse under cold running water; drain well. Arrange bok choy in a steamer basket, overlapping pieces.

4. Heat oil in a Dutch oven over medium-high heat. Add 1/4 cup onions, ginger, and 1 garlic clove; sauté 30 seconds. Place steamer basket in pan. Combine water and next 4 ingredients; pour over bok choy. Bring to a boil; cover, reduce heat, and steam over medium-low heat 20 minutes or until bok choy is tender, rearranging bok choy after 10 minutes. Remove bok choy and steamer basket from pan; cover and keep warm.

5. Combine 1 1/2 tablespoons sherry and 2 teaspoons cornstarch; add to pan. Bring to a boil; cook 1 minute or until slightly thick. Yield: 6 servings (serving size: 3 meatballs, 2 bok choy halves, and 3 tablespoons sauce).

CALORIES 251 (35% from fat); FAT 9.8g (sat 2.4g, mono 3.4g, poly 2.9g); PROTEIN 21.3g; CARB 18g; FIBER 1.9g; CHOL 75mg; IRON 2.6mg; SODIUM 832mg; CALC 135mg

About Bok Choy

Baby bok choy is a smaller version of bok choy. This Chinese cabbage is sweeter and more flavorful than its "adult" counterpart. You can substitute baby bok choy wherever you would normally use bok choy. Store bok choy in a plastic bag in the refrigerator, and use within a few days.

Joe's Special

This San Francisco specialty turns straightforward scrambled eggs into a distinctive dinner. To stay true to the recipe's roots, serve with toasted sourdough bread.

- ½ teaspoon dried basil
- ¼ teaspoon salt
- 4 large egg whites
- 3 large eggs
- 4 ounces hot turkey Italian sausage
- 2 cups chopped onion
- 6 cups chopped Swiss chard
- 4 (1½-ounce) slices sourdough bread, toasted

1. Combine first 4 ingredients in a medium bowl, stirring with a whisk.

2. Remove casings from sausage. Cook sausage in a large nonstick skillet over medium-high heat until lightly browned; stir to crumble. Add onion; cook 3 minutes or until onion is tender. Stir in chard; cover and cook 3 minutes or until chard wilts, stirring occasionally. Uncover and cook 1 minute or until liquid evaporates. Stir in egg mixture; cook 3 minutes or until eggs are set, stirring frequently. Serve with toast. Yield: 4 servings (serving size: 1 cup egg mixture and 1 toast slice).

CALORIES 335 (23% from fat); FAT 8.6g (sat 2.4g, mono 3.3g, poly 1.8g); PROTEIN 20.9g; CARB 43.2g; FIBER 4.3g; CHOL 183mg; IRON 3.7mg; SODIUM 931mg; CALC 116mg

Breakfast Sausage Casserole

This satisfying recipe is a good choice if you have weekend guests. Assemble and refrigerate the casserole the night before, and just pop it in the oven the next morning. Look for turkey sausage near other breakfast-style sausage in the frozen foods section of your supermarket.

Cooking spray
1 (16-ounce) package frozen turkey sausage, thawed (such as Louis Rich)
8 (1½-ounce) slices sourdough bread, cut into ½-inch cubes (about 8 cups)
⅔ cup (about 2½ ounces) shredded sharp Cheddar cheese
3 cups 1% low-fat milk, divided
1 cup egg substitute
1 tablespoon Dijon mustard
1 (10.75-ounce) can condensed 30% reduced-sodium, 98% fat-free cream of mushroom soup, undiluted

1. Heat a large nonstick skillet over medium-high heat. Coat pan with cooking spray. Add sausage to pan; cook 5 minutes or until browned, stirring well to crumble.
2. Arrange bread in a 13 x 9–inch baking dish coated with cooking spray. Top evenly with cooked turkey sausage and Cheddar cheese. Combine 2½ cups milk, egg substitute, and Dijon mustard, stirring with a whisk. Pour over bread mixture in dish. Cover and refrigerate 8 hours or overnight.
3. Preheat oven to 350°.
4. Uncover casserole. Combine remaining ½ cup milk and cream of mushroom soup, stirring with a whisk. Pour over bread mixture. Bake at 350° for 1 hour and 5 minutes or until set and lightly browned. Let stand 15 minutes before serving. Yield: 8 servings.

CALORIES 321 (30% from fat); FAT 10.8g (sat 5.3g, mono 2.5g, poly 1.1g); PROTEIN 22g; CARB 32.2g; FIBER 1.6g; CHOL 58mg; IRON 2.8mg; SODIUM 968mg; CALC 238mg

Tamale Pie

Once a staple in Northern Italian kitchens, polenta is now a popular item on American tables. Precooked polenta comes ready-packed in 16-ounce tubes and eliminates the need for lengthy preparation. Use a fork or pastry blender to crumble the firm polenta.

1½ (16-ounce) tubes polenta (such as Melissa's), crumbled
Cooking spray
2 (15-ounce) cans low-fat turkey chili
1 cup (4 ounces) preshredded sharp Cheddar cheese
6 tablespoons bottled salsa
6 tablespoons reduced-fat sour cream

1. Preheat oven to 475°.
2. Place polenta in an 11 x 7–inch baking dish coated with cooking spray. Top with chili and cheese. Bake at 475° for 13 minutes or until bubbly. Top each serving with 1 tablespoon salsa and 1 tablespoon sour cream. Yield: 6 servings.

CALORIES 324 (27% from fat); FAT 9.7g (sat 5.5g, mono 2.5g, poly 1g); PROTEIN 18.8g; CARB 40.6g; FIBER 6.6g; CHOL 46mg; IRON 2.8mg; SODIUM 881mg; CALC 223mg

Salads

Grilled Vegetable Salad with Creamy Blue Cheese Dressing, page 255

Melon, Berry, and Pear Salad with Cayenne-Lemon-Mint Syrup

Melon, Berry, and Pear Salad with Cayenne-Lemon-Mint Syrup

Simple and nutrient-packed, this fruit salad is a deliciously healthful way to satisfy a sweet tooth. The ground red pepper provides an unexpected heat that balances the sweetness of the fruit. This recipe makes 15 cups and is a perfect make-ahead dish for summer picnics or other social gatherings. If you don't need that much, you can easily cut the salad ingredients in half. But go ahead and make the whole recipe for the syrup, and just store it in an airtight container in the refrigerator for later use.

SYRUP:

- 1/3 cup sugar
- 1/3 cup water
- 1/4 cup fresh lemon juice
- 3 tablespoons honey
- 1/2 teaspoon ground red pepper
- 1/4 cup chopped fresh mint
- 1 tablespoon grated lemon rind

SALAD:

- 6 cups cubed cantaloupe
- 6 cups cubed honeydew melon
- 2 cups fresh blueberries
- 2 cups quartered fresh strawberries
- 1 1/2 cups cubed ripe pear (about 2 medium)
- 1 cup fresh blackberries
- 1 tablespoon chopped fresh mint
- 1/8 teaspoon freshly ground black pepper

1. To prepare syrup, combine first 5 ingredients in a small saucepan. Bring to a boil; cook 3 minutes or until mixture is slightly syrupy. Remove from heat; stir in 1/4 cup mint and rind. Let stand 30 minutes. Strain syrup through a sieve over a small bowl; discard solids.

2. To prepare salad, combine cantaloupe and next 7 ingredients in a large bowl. Add syrup; toss gently to coat. Cover and refrigerate 2 hours, stirring occasionally. Yield: 10 servings (serving size: about 1 1/2 cups).

CALORIES 168 (4% from fat); FAT 0.7g (sat 0.1g, mono 0.1g, poly 0.3g); PROTEIN 2.3g; CARB 42.6g; FIBER 3.1g; CHOL 0mg; IRON 0.8mg; SODIUM 37mg; CALC 33mg

Salad of Papaya, Mango, and Grapefruit

If pressed for time, use bottled grapefruit sections from the produce department. Combine ingredients a few hours ahead, but stir in mint just before serving.

- 2 cups grapefruit sections (about 2 large grapefruit)
- 2 peeled ripe mangoes, each cut into 12 wedges
- 1 peeled ripe papaya, cut into thin slices
- 2 to 3 tablespoons fresh lime juice
- 2 tablespoons extravirgin olive oil
- 1/4 teaspoon salt
- 1/8 teaspoon black pepper
- 3 tablespoons chopped fresh mint

1. Combine first 3 ingredients in a large bowl. Combine juice, oil, salt, and pepper, stirring with a whisk. Drizzle dressing over fruit; sprinkle with mint. Toss gently to combine. Yield: 12 servings (serving size: about 3/4 cup).

CALORIES 77 (28% from fat); FAT 2.4g (sat 0.3g, mono 1.7g, poly 0.2g); PROTEIN 0.7g; CARB 15.2g; FIBER 3.5g; CHOL 0mg; IRON 0.1mg; SODIUM 50mg; CALC 18mg

Green Salad with Apples and Maple-Walnut Dressing

This salad contains sweet, spicy, nutty, and salty notes. Walnut oil adds depth; you can substitute extravirgin olive oil—albeit with milder results.

- 6 cups gourmet salad greens
- 1 cup (2-inch) julienne-cut Braeburn apple
- 2 tablespoons cider vinegar
- 2 tablespoons maple syrup
- 2 teaspoons whole-grain Dijon mustard
- 1 1/2 teaspoons walnut oil
- 1/8 teaspoon salt
- 1/8 teaspoon ground red pepper

1. Combine salad greens and apple in a large bowl.

2. Combine vinegar and next 5 ingredients, stirring with a whisk. Drizzle over salad; toss gently to coat. Yield: 4 servings (serving size: about 1 1/4 cups).

CALORIES 73 (27% from fat); FAT 2.2g (sat 0.2g, mono 0.5g, poly 1.3g); PROTEIN 1.6g; CARB 13.7g; FIBER 2.5g; CHOL 0mg; IRON 1.4mg; SODIUM 159mg; CALC 58mg

Warm Salad of Grilled Figs, Grapes, and Bitter Greens

Grilling intensifies the sweetness of fresh figs by caramelizing their natural sugars—a nice contrast to the slight bitterness of the radicchio and endive.

- 1½ tablespoons extravirgin olive oil, divided
- 2 tablespoons sherry vinegar or cider vinegar
- ½ teaspoon salt
- ½ teaspoon freshly ground black pepper
- 2 cups torn radicchio
- 2 cups thinly sliced fennel bulb
- 2 cups sliced Belgian endive
- 2 cups seedless red grapes
- 12 medium dark-skinned fresh figs, halved (about 1¼ pounds)
- Cooking spray

1. Prepare grill.
2. Combine 1 tablespoon oil, vinegar, salt, and pepper in a large bowl. Add radicchio, fennel, endive, and grapes; toss gently to coat. Set aside.
3. Brush remaining 1½ teaspoons oil over cut sides of figs. Place figs on grill rack coated with cooking spray; grill 1½ minutes on each side or until lightly browned. Place radicchio mixture on a platter, and top with grilled figs. Yield: 6 servings (serving size: about 1¼ cups).

CALORIES 154 (24% from fat); FAT 4.1g (sat 0.6g, mono 2.6g, poly 0.5g); PROTEIN 1.8g; CARB 31.3g; FIBER 5.2g; CHOL 0mg; IRON 1mg; SODIUM 219mg; CALC 66mg

Arugula Salad with Port-Cooked Pears and Roquefort Cheese

Sweet wine infuses pears with flavor that marries well with the pungent cheese. Serve with pork tenderloin.

- 2 peeled Bartlett pears, cored and quartered
- Cooking spray
- ½ cup port or other sweet red wine
- 1 teaspoon sugar
- 1 tablespoon white wine vinegar
- 1 teaspoon walnut oil
- ¼ teaspoon salt
- ¼ teaspoon freshly ground black pepper
- 8 cups trimmed arugula (about 8 ounces)
- 2 cups (½-inch) slices Belgian endive (about ½ pound)
- ¼ cup (1 ounce) crumbled Roquefort or other blue cheese
- 2 tablespoons chopped walnuts, toasted

1. Preheat oven to 400°.
2. Arrange pears in a 13 x 9–inch baking dish coated with cooking spray, and drizzle with port. Sprinkle evenly with sugar. Cover and bake at 400° for 10 minutes. Uncover and bake an additional 15 minutes or until pears are almost tender. Cool completely, and reserve 1 tablespoon liquid from pan. Thinly slice pears; set aside. Combine reserved 1 tablespoon liquid, vinegar, oil, salt, and pepper, stirring with a whisk.
3. Combine sliced pears, arugula, and endive in a large bowl. Drizzle vinegar mixture over arugula mixture; toss gently to coat. Arrange about 1⅓ cups salad on each of 8 plates. Sprinkle each serving with 1½ teaspoons cheese and ¾ teaspoon nuts. Yield: 8 servings.

CALORIES 88 (31% from fat); FAT 3g (sat 0.9g, mono 0.6g, poly 1.4g); PROTEIN 2g; CARB 11g; FIBER 2.5g; CHOL 3mg; IRON 0.6mg; SODIUM 131mg; CALC 62mg

Autumn Apple, Pear, and Cheddar Salad with Pecans

Serve this classic flavor combination with roast chicken or a pork roast. Double the dressing to have extra on hand.

- 1 cup apple juice
- 2 tablespoons cider vinegar
- 1 teaspoon extravirgin olive oil
- ½ teaspoon salt
- ¼ teaspoon freshly ground black pepper
- 10 cups gourmet salad greens (about 10 ounces)
- 1 cup seedless red grapes, halved
- 1 medium McIntosh apple, cored and cut into 18 wedges
- 1 medium Bartlett pear, cored and cut into 18 wedges
- ¼ cup (1 ounce) finely shredded sharp Cheddar cheese
- 3 tablespoons chopped pecans, toasted

1. Place apple juice in a small saucepan; bring to a boil over medium-high heat. Cook until reduced to about 3 tablespoons (about 10 minutes). Combine reduced apple juice, cider vinegar, olive oil, salt, and black pepper, stirring with a whisk until well blended. Set aside.

2. Combine greens, grapes, apple, and pear in a large bowl. Drizzle with apple juice mixture; toss gently to coat. Arrange salad on individual plates; sprinkle each serving with cheese and nuts. Yield: 6 servings (serving size: about 1⅔ cups salad, 2 teaspoons cheese, and 1½ teaspoons nuts).

CALORIES 134 (36% from fat); FAT 5.4g (sat 1.2g, mono 2.6g, poly 1.1g); PROTEIN 3.4g; CARB 21.1g; FIBER 4.1g; CHOL 5mg; IRON 1.5mg; SODIUM 255mg; CALC 93mg

Pike Place Market Salad

Pike Place Market Salad

This flavorful salad calls for an herb salad mix, which can be found prebagged in the produce section of the supermarket, or use any combination of lettuces and herbs. Any fresh berry or cherry will do nicely. The dressing and caramelized walnuts can be made a day ahead (store the nuts in an airtight container and the dressing in the refrigerator). The salad gets its name from Seattle's Pike Place Market—an icon of fresh, seasonal bounty.

WALNUTS:

1 tablespoon sugar
3 tablespoons coarsely chopped walnuts
Cooking spray

DRESSING:

½ cup apple cider
3 tablespoons water
¼ teaspoon cornstarch
1 tablespoon finely chopped shallots
1 tablespoon champagne vinegar
⅛ teaspoon salt
⅛ teaspoon freshly ground black pepper

REMAINING INGREDIENTS:

8 cups herb salad mix
2 cups fresh blackberries
¼ cup (1 ounce) crumbled blue cheese

1. To prepare nuts, place sugar in a small skillet over medium heat; cook 90 seconds or until sugar dissolves, stirring as needed so sugar dissolves evenly and doesn't burn. Reduce heat; stir in walnuts. Cook over low heat 30 seconds or until golden. Spread mixture onto foil coated with cooking spray. Cool completely; break into small pieces.
2. To prepare dressing, place cider in a small saucepan over medium-high heat; bring to a boil. Cook until reduced to 2 tablespoons (about 5 minutes). Combine 3 tablespoons water and cornstarch; add to pan. Bring cider mixture to a boil, stirring constantly; cook 30 seconds. Remove from heat. Stir in shallots, vinegar, salt, and pepper; cool.
3. To prepare salad, place salad mix in a large bowl. Drizzle with dressing; toss gently to coat. Divide evenly among 4 plates; top with berries, cheese, and walnuts. Serve immediately. Yield: 4 servings (serving size: 2 cups salad, ½ cup berries, 1 tablespoon cheese, and 2¼ teaspoons walnuts).

CALORIES 165 (37% from fat); FAT 6.7g (sat 1.8g, mono 0.7g, poly 3g); PROTEIN 5.2g; CARB 24.6g; FIBER 4.5g; CHOL 6mg; IRON 1.9mg; SODIUM 199mg; CALC 116mg

Mixed Greens Salad with Honey-Orange Dressing

The sweetness in the citrus-based dressing balances the bitterness of the radicchio. This easy, all-purpose salad goes with almost any dinner.

3 tablespoons fresh orange juice
1 tablespoon honey
2 teaspoons minced shallots
2 teaspoons white wine vinegar
½ teaspoon Dijon mustard
¼ teaspoon salt
¼ teaspoon freshly ground black pepper
4 cups chopped romaine lettuce
4 cups torn radicchio
3 cups bagged baby spinach leaves

1. Combine first 7 ingredients in a large bowl, stirring with a whisk. Add romaine lettuce, radicchio, and spinach; toss gently to coat. Yield: 8 servings (serving size: about 1 cup).

CALORIES 24 (8% from fat); FAT 0.2g (sat 0g, mono 0g, poly 0.1g); PROTEIN 1.1g; CARB 5.3g; FIBER 1.1g; CHOL 0mg; IRON 0.8mg; SODIUM 97mg; CALC 26mg

Romaine Salad with Avocado-Lime Vinaigrette

This vinaigrette works wonders in place of olive oil as a salad dressing. For another recipe highlighting this flavored oil, try Spiced Shrimp with Avocado Oil (recipe on page 106). Our favorite brand is Elysian Isle.

- 1 teaspoon fresh lime juice
- ¼ teaspoon salt
- ¼ teaspoon freshly ground black pepper
- 1 tablespoon avocado oil
- 8 cups shredded romaine lettuce (about 15 ounces)
- 1 cup cherry tomatoes, halved
- ¼ cup vertically sliced red onion

1. Combine first 3 ingredients, stirring with a whisk. Gradually add avocado oil, stirring constantly with a whisk.

2. Combine lettuce, tomatoes, and onion in a large bowl, tossing gently. Drizzle juice mixture over lettuce mixture; toss gently to coat. Serve immediately. Yield: 4 servings (serving size: 2 cups).

CALORIES 61 (58% from fat); FAT 3.9g (sat 0.5g, mono 2.5g, poly 0.7g); PROTEIN 2.3g; CARB 5.8g; FIBER 2.6g; CHOL 0mg; IRON 1.5mg; SODIUM 160mg; CALC 45mg

Fall Green Salad

VINAIGRETTE:

- ¼ cup water
- 3 tablespoons fresh lemon juice
- ½ teaspoon cornstarch
- 1 tablespoon honey
- ½ teaspoon white wine vinegar
- ¼ teaspoon salt
- ¼ teaspoon freshly ground black pepper
- ¼ cup (1 ounce) grated fresh Parmesan cheese

SALAD:

- 4 cups torn curly leaf lettuce
- 4 cups torn romaine lettuce
- 3 cups trimmed arugula
- ½ cup thinly sliced red onion

1. To prepare vinaigrette, combine water, juice, and cornstarch in a small saucepan, stirring with a whisk. Bring to a boil over medium-high heat; cook 1 minute, stirring frequently. Remove from heat. Stir in honey, vinegar, salt, and pepper. Place in a blender or food processor. Add cheese; process until well blended. Cool to room temperature.

2. To prepare salad, combine lettuces and red onion in a large bowl. Drizzle with vinaigrette, tossing gently to combine. Serve immediately. Yield: 8 servings (serving size: 1 cup).

CALORIES 38 (24% from fat); FAT 1g (sat 0.6g, mono 0.3g, poly 0.1g); PROTEIN 2.4g; CARB 5.9g; FIBER 1.4g; CHOL 2mg; IRON 0.5mg; SODIUM 145mg; CALC 80mg

Caesar Salad with Peppers

DRESSING:

- 2 large whole garlic heads
- ¼ cup fat-free mayonnaise
- 1½ teaspoons Dijon mustard
- 1 teaspoon anchovy paste
- Dash of black pepper
- 3 tablespoons red wine vinegar
- 1 tablespoon olive oil

SALAD:

- 2 yellow bell peppers
- 2 red bell peppers
- 14 cups torn romaine lettuce
- ¼ cup (1 ounce) finely grated fresh Parmesan cheese, divided
- 4 (1-ounce) slices rye bread, cubed and toasted

1. Preheat oven to 400°.

2. To prepare dressing, remove white papery skin from garlic heads (do not peel or separate cloves). Wrap each head separately in foil. Bake at 400° for 1 hour; cool. Cut crosswise; squeeze to extract garlic pulp to measure 3 tablespoons. Discard skins. Place garlic, mayonnaise, mustard, paste, and black pepper in a food processor; process until smooth. With food processor on, slowly pour vinegar and oil through food chute; process until well blended.

3. Preheat broiler.

4. To prepare salad, cut bell peppers in half lengthwise; discard seeds and membranes. Place halves, skin sides up, on a foil-lined baking sheet; flatten with hand. Broil 15 minutes or until blackened. Place in a zip-top plastic bag; seal. Let stand 15 minutes. Peel; cut into 1-inch strips. Combine dressing, lettuce, 2 tablespoons cheese, and rye bread cubes in a large bowl, tossing gently to coat. Place 2 cups salad mixture on each of 8 plates. Arrange bell pepper strips evenly on top of salads; sprinkle evenly with remaining 2 tablespoons cheese. Yield: 8 servings.

CALORIES 111 (30% from fat); FAT 3.7g (sat 1g, mono 1.7g, poly 0.5g); PROTEIN 5g; CARB 15.3; FIBER 3.4g; CHOL 2mg; IRON 2.2mg; SODIUM 378mg; CALC 98mg

Roasted Fig and Arugula Salad

Roasting figs slightly caramelizes them and creates flavorful browned bits that eventually season the vinaigrette. If you don't have molasses on hand, use honey or maple syrup.

- ⅓ cup sherry vinegar or cider vinegar
- 1 tablespoon molasses
- 2 teaspoons extravirgin olive oil
- ¼ teaspoon salt
- 4 large dark-skinned fresh figs, halved
- Cooking spray
- 5 cups trimmed arugula
- ¼ cup (1 ounce) crumbled goat cheese
- ⅛ teaspoon freshly ground black pepper

1. Preheat oven to 425°.

2. Combine first 4 ingredients in a medium bowl, stirring with a whisk. Add figs; toss to coat. Remove figs with a slotted spoon, reserving vinegar mixture.

3. Place figs in a cast-iron or ovenproof skillet coated with cooking spray. Bake at 425° for 8 to 10 minutes. Remove figs from pan; place on a plate. Immediately add reserved vinegar mixture to hot pan, scraping pan to loosen browned bits. Pour into a small bowl; let figs and vinaigrette cool to room temperature.

4. Place arugula on a platter, and arrange figs over arugula. Sprinkle with cheese and pepper. Drizzle with cooled vinaigrette. Yield: 4 servings (serving size: 1¼ cups).

CALORIES 109 (34% from fat); FAT 4.1g (sat 1.4g, mono 2.1g, poly 0.4g); PROTEIN 2.4g; CARB 18g; FIBER 2.5g; CHOL 3mg; IRON 1.1mg; SODIUM 182mg; CALC 84mg

Escarole Salad with Melons and Crispy Prosciutto

The Italian combination of melon and prosciutto pairs nicely in this first-course salad. Serve alongside pork tenderloin, green beans, and corn custards.

- 4 thin slices prosciutto (about 1½ ounces), coarsely chopped
- 3 tablespoons minced shallots
- 2 tablespoons balsamic vinegar
- 1 tablespoon red wine vinegar
- 1½ teaspoons extravirgin olive oil
- ¼ teaspoon salt
- ¼ teaspoon freshly ground black pepper
- 12 cups torn escarole (about 1¼ pounds)
- 2 cups torn radicchio (about 4 ounces)
- 2 cups cubed honeydew melon
- 2 cups cubed cantaloupe
- 2 tablespoons sliced almonds, toasted

1. Preheat oven to 400°.

2. Arrange prosciutto in a single layer on a baking sheet. Bake at 400° for 6 minutes or until crisp.

3. Combine shallots and next 5 ingredients in a large bowl, stirring with a whisk. Add escarole and radicchio; toss to coat. Add honeydew and cantaloupe; toss well.

4. Place 2 cups escarole mixture on each of 6 plates; top each serving with about 2 teaspoons prosciutto. Sprinkle each serving with 1 teaspoon almonds. Yield: 6 servings.

CALORIES 105 (32% from fat); FAT 3.7g (sat 0.7g, mono 2.1g, poly 0.6g); PROTEIN 3.6g; CARB 16.4g; FIBER 4g; CHOL 4mg; IRON 1.1mg; SODIUM 228mg; CALC 68mg

Field Greens with Mississippi Caviar

Nutritious, inexpensive black-eyed peas have been a southern kitchen staple for three centuries. This salad's bright seasonings make it a good side for grilled meat or chicken.

- ¾ cup water
- 1 garlic clove, minced
- Dash of black pepper
- 4 cups fresh or frozen black-eyed peas
- 1 cup (1-inch) julienne-cut yellow bell pepper
- 1 cup chopped tomato
- ½ cup bottled reduced-calorie Italian dressing
- ⅓ cup chopped fresh parsley
- ¼ cup chopped red onion
- ¼ teaspoon salt
- 6 cups mixed salad greens

1. Combine water, garlic, and black pepper in a large saucepan; bring to a boil. Add peas; cover and cook over medium-low heat 30 minutes or until tender. Drain.

2. Combine peas, bell pepper, and next 5 ingredients in a large bowl; toss gently to combine. Cover and chill 3 hours or overnight. Serve over salad greens. Yield: 6 servings (serving size: 1 cup pea mixture and 1 cup greens).

CALORIES 197 (14% from fat); FAT 3g (sat 0.5g, mono 0.5g, poly 1.7g); PROTEIN 11.2g; CARB 33.5g; FIBER 9.3g; CHOL 1mg; IRON 3.7mg; SODIUM 281mg; CALC 68mg

Tricolor Bitter Greens Salad

Any combination of lettuces can be used, such as romaine, Bibb, and Boston. Thinly slice the greens with a chef's knife just before preparing the salad to keep the edges from turning brown and to give the salad a tidy look.

DRESSING:

1 tablespoon minced shallots
1 tablespoon fresh lemon juice
1 teaspoon Dijon mustard
½ teaspoon salt
⅛ teaspoon freshly ground black pepper
1½ teaspoons walnut oil or extravirgin olive oil

SALAD:

2 cups trimmed arugula
2 cups thinly sliced Belgian endive (about 2 small heads)
2 cups thinly sliced radicchio
2 tablespoons shaved Parmigiano-Reggiano cheese

1. To prepare dressing, combine shallots, lemon juice, mustard, salt, and pepper. Gradually add oil, stirring with a whisk.
2. To prepare salad, combine arugula and 1 tablespoon dressing; toss to coat. Arrange ½ cup arugula mixture on each of 4 salad plates. Combine endive, radicchio, and remaining dressing; toss to coat. Arrange about 1 cup endive mixture evenly over each serving. Top salads evenly with cheese. Serve immediately. Yield: 4 servings.

CALORIES 45 (58% from fat); FAT 2.9g (sat 0.8g, mono 0.7g, poly 1.2g); PROTEIN 2.3g; CARB 3.2g; FIBER 1.2g; CHOL 2mg; IRON 0.6mg; SODIUM 395mg; CALC 78mg

Watermelon, Fennel, and Parsley Salad

The unlikely combination of fennel, parsley, and watermelon is as refreshing as it is surprising. It makes a nice complement to spicy grilled meat.

5 cups cubed seeded watermelon, divided
1 tablespoon fresh lemon juice
½ teaspoon sea salt
¼ teaspoon freshly ground black pepper
4 cups thinly sliced fennel bulb (about 2 medium bulbs)
1½ cups fresh flat-leaf parsley leaves

1. Place 1 cup watermelon in a blender; process until smooth. Strain mixture through a fine sieve over a bowl, reserving ¼ cup watermelon juice; discard solids and remaining watermelon juice. Combine ¼ cup watermelon juice, lemon juice, salt, and pepper in a large bowl, stirring well. Add remaining watermelon, fennel, and parsley; toss gently to combine. Yield: 8 servings (serving size: 1 cup).

CALORIES 49 (2% from fat); FAT 0.6g (sat 0.1g, mono 0.1g, poly 0.2g); PROTEIN 1.5g; CARB 10.9g; FIBER 2.2g; CHOL 0mg; IRON 1.2mg; SODIUM 175mg; CALC 45mg

Radish Slaw with New York Deli Dressing

In this colorful slaw, peppery radishes stand in for cabbage.

4 cups shredded radishes (about 40 radishes)
2 cups finely chopped yellow bell pepper
1½ cups shredded carrot
½ cup white wine vinegar
4 teaspoons sugar
1 tablespoon chopped fresh dill
1 tablespoon mustard oil or olive oil
½ teaspoon salt
½ teaspoon black pepper

1. Combine first 3 ingredients in a large bowl. Combine white wine vinegar and next 5 ingredients, stirring with a whisk. Drizzle dressing over slaw; toss well to combine. Serve immediately. Yield: 10 servings (serving size: ¾ cup).

CALORIES 46 (35% from fat); FAT 1.8g (sat 0.2g, mono 0.9g, poly 0.4g); PROTEIN 0.9g; CARB 7.4g; FIBER 1.6g; CHOL 0mg; IRON 0.5mg; SODIUM 136mg; CALC 20mg

Watermelon, Fennel, and Parsley Salad

Green Bean Salad with Bacon

Mustard and honey emulsify and flavor a warm bacon vinaigrette that coats the beans thoroughly, even after the salad has chilled.

- 2 pounds green beans, trimmed
- 3 bacon slices
- 2 tablespoons finely chopped shallots
- 1/4 cup red wine vinegar
- 1 tablespoon honey
- 1 tablespoon Dijon mustard
- 1/2 teaspoon freshly ground black pepper
- 1/4 teaspoon kosher salt

1. Cook beans in boiling water 5 minutes. Drain and plunge beans into ice water; drain. Place beans in a large bowl.
2. Cook bacon in a large nonstick skillet over medium heat until crisp. Remove bacon from pan, reserving 1 teaspoon drippings in pan. Crumble bacon; set aside. Add shallots to drippings in pan; cook 1 1/2 minutes, stirring frequently. Add vinegar; cook 30 seconds, scraping pan to loosen browned bits. Drizzle mixture over beans.
3. Combine honey, mustard, pepper, and salt, stirring with a whisk. Pour over bean mixture; toss to coat. Sprinkle with crumbled bacon. Yield: 6 servings (serving size: about 1 2/3 cups).

CALORIES 86 (24% from fat); FAT 2.3g (sat 0.7g, mono 0.7g, poly 0.2g); PROTEIN 3.3g; CARB 13.1g; FIBER 5.6g; CHOL 4mg; IRON 1mg; SODIUM 217mg; CALC 80mg

Summer Bean Salad

Scarlett runner peas take a bit longer to cook than other shelled peas, so if you use them, allow a few extra minutes of cooking time before adding the green and wax beans. Savory is a slightly bitter, minty herb. If you can't find it, increase the amount of thyme from 2 teaspoons to 1 1/2 tablespoons.

- 1 1/4 cups fresh shelled peas (such as black-eyed, lima, or scarlett runner; about 3 pounds unshelled)
- 3/4 pound green beans, trimmed and cut in half crosswise
- 3/4 pound wax beans, trimmed and cut in half crosswise
- 1/4 cup minced shallots
- 3 tablespoons chopped fresh chives
- 1 1/2 tablespoons chopped fresh savory
- 3 tablespoons white wine vinegar
- 2 tablespoons extravirgin olive oil
- 2 teaspoons chopped fresh thyme
- 3/4 teaspoon salt
- 1/4 teaspoon freshly ground black pepper
- 1 garlic clove, minced

1. Cook peas in boiling water 15 minutes. Add beans; cook 5 minutes or until crisp-tender. Drain and rinse with cold water. Drain; place bean mixture in a large bowl.
2. Combine shallots and next 8 ingredients. Pour over bean mixture; toss well. Serve at room temperature or chilled. Yield: 8 servings (serving size: about 1 cup).

CALORIES 118 (31% from fat); FAT 4g (sat 0.6g, mono 2.7g, poly 0.5g); PROTEIN 5.2g; CARB 16.8g; FIBER 6.5g; CHOL 0mg; IRON 2.6mg; SODIUM 226mg; CALC 61mg

Southwestern Corn and Black Bean Salad

SALAD:

1 pound dried black beans
11½ cups water, divided
1 teaspoon olive oil
2 teaspoons cumin seeds
2 garlic cloves, minced
2 cups fresh corn kernels (about 4 ears)
2 cups chopped seeded tomato
1 cup finely chopped Vidalia or other sweet onion
1 cup chopped red bell pepper
1 cup chopped green bell pepper

DRESSING:

½ cup fresh lime juice (about 3 limes)
1 tablespoon chili powder
3 tablespoons olive oil
2 teaspoons salt
1½ teaspoons ground cumin
2 teaspoons honey
2 jalapeño peppers, seeded and minced
3 garlic cloves, minced
⅓ cup chopped fresh cilantro

1. To prepare salad, sort and wash beans. Combine beans and 5½ cups water in a 6-quart pressure cooker. Close lid securely; bring to high pressure over high heat. Adjust heat to medium or level needed to maintain high pressure; cook 1 minute. Remove from heat; place cooker under cold running water. Remove lid. Drain beans; rinse with cold water. Drain and cool.

2. Heat 1 teaspoon oil in cooker over medium heat. Add cumin seeds and 2 garlic cloves; cook 1 minute, stirring frequently. Add black beans and remaining 6 cups water. Close lid securely; bring to high pressure over high heat. Adjust heat to medium or level needed to maintain high pressure; cook 12 minutes. Remove from heat; place cooker under cold running water. Remove lid. Drain bean mixture; rinse with cold water. Drain and cool. Combine bean mixture, corn, tomato, onion, and bell peppers in a large bowl.

3. To prepare dressing, combine juice and next 7 ingredients, stirring with a whisk. Stir in cilantro. Pour dressing over bean mixture; stir gently to combine. Cover and refrigerate at least 30 minutes. Yield: 12 servings (serving size: 1 cup).

CALORIES 216 (21% from fat); FAT 5g (sat 0.7g, mono 3g, poly 0.8g); PROTEIN 10g; CARB 35.7g; FIBER 8g; CHOL 0mg; IRON 2.8mg; SODIUM 408mg; CALC 65mg

Beet and Red Onion Salad with Ricotta-Provolone Topping

Cooking the beets in a plastic bag in the microwave saves on cleanup and preparation time. To avoid ruby-red hands, peel beets under running water. You can prepare and chill this salad a day in advance to allow the flavors to meld. Let stand at room temperature for 15 minutes, and prepare cheese mixture and chop basil right before serving.

2½ pounds small beets
2 tablespoons red wine vinegar
2 teaspoons extravirgin olive oil
½ teaspoon salt
¼ teaspoon freshly ground black pepper
1½ cups thinly sliced red onion
½ serrano chile, seeded and thinly sliced
½ cup part-skim ricotta cheese
¼ cup (1 ounce) finely shredded sharp provolone cheese
2 teaspoons hot water
⅓ cup thinly sliced fresh basil

1. Leave root and 1 inch of stems on beets; scrub with a brush. Pierce each beet 2 times with a sharp knife. Place beets in a large zip-top plastic bag; seal halfway. Microwave at HIGH 20 minutes or until tender, rotating bag every 5 minutes. Remove bag from microwave; cool to room temperature. Remove beets from bag; reserve liquid in bag. Peel beets; cut into ¼-inch-thick slices.

2. Combine reserved beet liquid, vinegar, oil, salt, and pepper in a large bowl, stirring with a whisk. Add beets, onion, and serrano; toss gently to coat.

3. Combine ricotta, provolone, and hot water, stirring well. Arrange 1 cup salad on each of 6 serving plates; top each serving with 1 tablespoon basil and about 1 tablespoon cheese mixture. Yield: 6 servings.

CALORIES 159 (29% from fat); FAT 5.1g (sat 2.1g, mono 1.7g, poly 0.3g); PROTEIN 7.2g; CARB 23.2g; FIBER 6.2g; CHOL 11mg; IRON 1.9mg; SODIUM 424mg; CALC 135mg

Beet and Leek Salad with Peanut Dressing

Beet and Leek Salad with Peanut Dressing

2 medium beets (about 3/4 pound)
Cooking spray
4 cups thinly sliced leek (about 1 pound)
1/2 teaspoon olive oil
1/2 teaspoon salt, divided
1/4 cup water
1 tablespoon fresh lime juice
1 tablespoon creamy peanut butter
1 1/2 teaspoons minced peeled fresh ginger
2 cups alfalfa sprouts

1. Preheat oven to 425°.
2. Leave root and 1 inch of stem on beets; scrub with a brush. Place beets on a small baking sheet coated with cooking spray. Bake at 425° for 1 hour or until tender when pierced with a fork. Cool. Trim off beet roots and stems; rub off skins. Cut each beet in half lengthwise; slice each beet half crosswise into 1/4-inch-thick slices.
3. Combine sliced leek, olive oil, and 1/4 teaspoon salt on a baking sheet coated with cooking spray; toss well to coat. Bake at 425° for 15 minutes or until tender and just beginning to turn golden brown; stir after 8 minutes.
4. Combine water, lime juice, peanut butter, ginger, and 1/4 teaspoon salt, stirring well with a whisk until mixture is smooth.
5. Arrange 1/3 cup sprouts on each of 6 salad plates; divide beets and leek evenly among servings. Drizzle about 2 teaspoons dressing over each serving. Yield: 6 servings.

CALORIES 84 (23% from fat); FAT 2.1g (sat 0.4g, mono 1g, poly 0.5g); PROTEIN 2.9g; CARB 15.1g; FIBER 3.1g; CHOL 0mg; IRON 1.9mg; SODIUM 266mg; CALC 49mg

German-Style Potato Salad

2 pounds red potatoes, cut into 1/8-inch-thick slices (about 5 cups)
8 bacon slices, cut into 1/2-inch pieces
1/3 cup cider vinegar
2 1/2 teaspoons sugar
3/4 teaspoon salt
1/4 teaspoon black pepper
1/2 cup finely chopped onion
1/4 cup finely chopped red bell pepper
1/4 cup finely chopped fresh parsley

1. Steam potatoes, covered, 10 minutes or until tender.
2. Cook bacon in a nonstick skillet over medium heat until crisp. Remove bacon from pan; reserve 2 teaspoons drippings.
3. Combine drippings, vinegar, sugar, salt, and black pepper in a large bowl; stir well with a whisk. Add potatoes, onion, and bell pepper; toss gently to coat. Cover and let stand 1 hour, stirring occasionally. Add bacon and parsley; toss gently. Yield: 11 servings (serving size: 1/2 cup).

CALORIES 108 (30% from fat); FAT 3.6g (sat 1.3g, mono 1.6g, poly 0.5g); PROTEIN 3.6g; CARB 15.9g; FIBER 1.7g; CHOL 5mg; IRON 1.3mg; SODIUM 253mg; CALC 14mg

Stacked Heirloom Tomato Salad with Ricotta Salata Cream

Substitute feta cheese for ricotta salata, if you prefer.

6 (1-ounce) slices country peasant loaf bread
Cooking spray
1 garlic clove, halved
1/2 cup (2 ounces) crumbled ricotta salata cheese
1/2 cup (4 ounces) reduced-fat silken tofu
2 tablespoons water
2 tablespoons fresh lemon juice
1 garlic clove, minced
6 medium tomatoes, cut into 1/3-inch-thick slices (about 3 1/4 pounds)
1/4 cup thinly sliced fresh basil
1 teaspoon coarsely ground black pepper

1. Prepare grill or grill pan.
2. Place bread on grill rack or grill pan coated with cooking spray; grill 2 minutes on each side or until lightly browned. Remove from grill. Rub cut sides of halved garlic clove over one side of each bread slice. Set aside.
3. Combine cheese, tofu, 2 tablespoons water, juice, and minced garlic in a blender; process until smooth.
4. Place 1 bread slice on each of 6 plates; divide tomato slices evenly among servings. Spoon about 1 tablespoon cheese mixture on each serving; sprinkle evenly with basil and pepper. Yield: 6 servings.

CALORIES 168 (26% from fat); FAT 4.9g (sat 2.3g, mono 1.8g, poly 0.6g); PROTEIN 7.6g; CARB 26.7g; FIBER 3.7g; CHOL 10mg; IRON 2mg; SODIUM 339mg; CALC 49mg

Creole Tomato Salad

Creole Tomato Salad

SALAD:

3 ripe tomatoes, cut into 1/4-inch-thick slices (about 2 pounds)
1 Vidalia or other sweet onion, thinly sliced and separated into rings
1/4 teaspoon salt
1 tablespoon thinly sliced fresh mint
2 teaspoons chopped fresh chives

VINAIGRETTE:

4 teaspoons olive oil
4 teaspoons red wine vinegar
1 teaspoon Dijon mustard
1/2 teaspoon minced fresh garlic

1. To prepare salad, alternate tomato and onion slices on a platter. Sprinkle with salt. Top with mint and chives.

2. To prepare vinaigrette, combine olive oil, vinegar, mustard, and garlic in a jar. Cover tightly; shake vigorously. Drizzle vinaigrette over salad. Serve at room temperature. Yield: 4 servings.

CALORIES 73 (55% from fat); FAT 4.8g (sat 0.7g, mono 3.4g, poly 0.6g); PROTEIN 1.4g; CARB 7.5g; FIBER 1.5g; CHOL 0mg; IRON 0.6mg; SODIUM 185mg; CALC 13mg

Grilled Vegetable Salad with Creamy Blue Cheese Dressing

(pictured on page 236)

DRESSING:

1/3 cup low-fat mayonnaise
1/3 cup plain low-fat yogurt
1/4 cup (1 ounce) crumbled blue cheese
1/4 cup 1% low-fat milk
1/4 teaspoon freshly ground black pepper
1/8 teaspoon salt

SALAD:

1/4 pound green beans, trimmed
1/4 pound sugar snap peas, trimmed
1/4 pound carrots, peeled and cut diagonally into 1/2-inch-thick pieces
1 cup (1/2-inch-thick) slices red onion
Cooking spray
1/2 teaspoon freshly ground black pepper
1/4 teaspoon garlic salt
6 cups torn romaine lettuce
1/2 cup thinly sliced radishes

1. To prepare dressing, combine first 6 ingredients, stirring with a whisk until blended. Cover and chill.

2. Prepare grill.

3. To prepare salad, cook beans, peas, and carrots in boiling water 3 minutes or until crisp-tender. Drain and plunge into ice water; drain. Place mixture in a large bowl; add onion slices. Lightly coat vegetable mixture with cooking spray. Sprinkle with 1/2 teaspoon black pepper and garlic salt; toss gently to coat.

4. Place vegetable mixture in a wire grilling basket coated with cooking spray. Place grilling basket on grill rack; grill 7 minutes on each side or until lightly browned. Arrange 1 1/2 cups lettuce on each of 4 salad plates. Divide grilled vegetables and radishes evenly among servings. Serve 1/4 cup dressing with each salad. Yield: 4 servings.

CALORIES 144 (29% from fat); FAT 4.7g (sat 2g, mono 0.8g, poly 0.3g); PROTEIN 6.8g; CARB 20.4g; FIBER 5.2g; CHOL 8mg; IRON 2.4mg; SODIUM 497mg; CALC 187mg

Marinated-Vegetable Salad

The herbs and seasonings in the salad dressing go well with whatever vegetables are in season.

3 cups diagonally sliced carrot (about 1 pound)
2 cups (2-inch) julienne-cut zucchini
1 cup vertically sliced red onion
1/2 cup (2-inch) julienne-cut red bell pepper
1/4 cup red wine vinegar
2 tablespoons finely grated fresh Parmesan cheese
1 tablespoon chopped fresh parsley
1 tablespoon water
1 tablespoon olive oil
1/4 teaspoon dried basil
1/4 teaspoon dried oregano
1/4 teaspoon salt
1/8 teaspoon black pepper

1. Place carrot in a microwave-safe dish; cover with plastic wrap. Microwave at HIGH 4 minutes or until crisp-tender; cool.

2. Place zucchini in a microwave-safe dish; cover with plastic wrap. Microwave at HIGH 1 1/2 minutes or until crisp-tender; cool.

3. Combine carrot, zucchini, onion, and bell pepper in a large bowl. Combine vinegar and next 8 ingredients in a small bowl, stirring with a whisk. Pour vinegar mixture over vegetables, tossing to coat. Cover and marinate in refrigerator 2 hours. Yield: 7 servings (serving size: 1 cup).

CALORIES 59 (40% from fat); FAT 2.6g (sat 0.6g, mono 1.6g, poly 0.3g); PROTEIN 1.8g; CARB 8.1g; FIBER 2.2g; CHOL 1mg; IRON 0.6mg; SODIUM 129mg; CALC 44mg

Grilled Zucchini and Summer Squash Salad with Citrus Splash Dressing

The sweet and tart fresh fruit flavors of the salad dressing add just the right amount of zest to complement but not overwhelm the mild summer squash.

- 2 tablespoons grated orange rind
- ¾ cup fresh orange juice (about 3 oranges)
- ½ cup fresh lime juice (about 3 limes)
- 3 tablespoons honey
- 2 teaspoons olive oil
- ½ teaspoon salt
- ¼ teaspoon crushed red pepper
- 2 red onions
- 4 zucchini, each halved lengthwise (about 1¼ pounds)
- 4 yellow squash, each halved lengthwise (about 1 pound)
- Cooking spray
- 3 tablespoons thinly sliced fresh basil

1. Combine first 7 ingredients in a large zip-top plastic bag. Peel onions, leaving root intact; cut each onion into 4 wedges. Add onion, zucchini, and yellow squash to bag. Seal and marinate in refrigerator 1 hour, turning bag occasionally.
2. Prepare grill.
3. Drain vegetables in a colander over a bowl, reserving marinade. Place vegetables on grill rack coated with cooking spray. Grill 8 minutes or until tender; turn and baste occasionally with ¾ cup marinade. Place vegetables on a serving platter; sprinkle with basil. Serve vegetables with remaining marinade. Yield: 4 servings (serving size: 2 zucchini halves, 2 squash halves, 2 onion wedges, and 3 tablespoons citrus dressing).

CALORIES 168 (16% from fat); FAT 3g (sat 0.4g, mono 1.8g, poly 0.5g); PROTEIN 4g; CARB 36.1g; FIBER 4g; CHOL 0mg; IRON 1.3mg; SODIUM 302mg; CALC 70mg

Three-Grain Summer-Vegetable Salad

Quinoa (*KEEN-wah*) is not only high in fiber but also higher in protein than any other grain. Millet, usually found in health-food stores, is a tiny, delicate grain that's also rich in protein. The pressure cooker frees you from watching and waiting for the grains to cook completely on the stove top.

- Cooking spray
- ¼ cup minced fresh onion
- 1 cup uncooked basmati rice
- ½ cup uncooked millet
- ½ cup uncooked quinoa
- 2 cups water
- 1 cup apple juice
- 1 (3-inch) cinnamon stick
- 1 cup diced peeled Granny Smith apple (about 1 pound)
- ½ cup raisins
- ½ cup sliced green onions
- ½ cup chopped red bell pepper
- ⅓ cup light mayonnaise
- ¼ cup minced fresh cilantro
- 2 tablespoons lemon juice
- 2 teaspoons curry powder
- ½ teaspoon salt

1. Place a 6-quart pressure cooker over medium-high heat. Coat pan with cooking spray. Add onion; sauté 1 minute. Add rice, millet, and quinoa; sauté 30 seconds. Stir in 2 cups water, apple juice, and cinnamon stick. Close lid securely; bring to high pressure over medium-high heat (about 4 minutes). Adjust heat to low or level needed to maintain high pressure; cook 5 minutes. Remove from heat; place pressure cooker under cold running water. Let stand 7 minutes; remove lid. Discard cinnamon stick; fluff mixture with a fork. Spoon mixture into a large bowl; cool 5 minutes.
2. Stir in apple and remaining ingredients. Serve chilled or at room temperature. Yield: 9 servings (serving size: 1 cup).

CALORIES 212 (15% from fat); FAT 3.6g (sat 0.5g, mono 1g, poly 1.7g); PROTEIN 4.2g; CARB 42.5g; FIBER 2.9g; CHOL 3mg; IRON 3mg; SODIUM 207mg; CALC 30mg

Nectarine-and-Chickpea Couscous Salad with Honey-Cumin Dressing

Try this as a summer lunch side dish. The spices in the honey-lime dressing complement pork or ham.

1¼ cups water
1 cup uncooked couscous
2 tablespoons fresh lime juice
1 tablespoon olive oil
1 tablespoon honey
½ teaspoon salt
½ teaspoon ground cumin
½ teaspoon ground coriander
1½ cups coarsely chopped nectarines (about 3 medium)
½ cup coarsely chopped spinach
¼ cup thinly sliced green onions
1 (15½-ounce) can chickpeas (garbanzo beans), drained
Nectarine slices (optional)

1. Bring 1¼ cups water to a boil in a medium saucepan; stir in couscous. Remove from heat; cover and let stand 5 minutes. Fluff with a fork; cool.

2. Combine lime juice and next 5 ingredients in a large bowl; stir well with a whisk. Add cooked couscous, chopped nectarines, spinach, onions, and chickpeas; toss well. Garnish with nectarine slices, if desired. Yield: 6 servings (serving size: 1 cup).

CALORIES 213 (16% from fat); FAT 3.9g (sat 0.5g, mono 2g, poly 0.8g); PROTEIN 7.8g; CARB 38.8g; FIBER 3.6g; CHOL 0mg; IRON 2.2mg; SODIUM 297mg; CALC 36mg

Rice Noodle Salad with Vegetables and Tofu

Rice Noodle Salad with Vegetables and Tofu

The addition of sautéed summer squash, red bell pepper, and tofu gives this noodle salad added texture and flavor. Look for baked tofu in health-food stores or in the produce section of large supermarkets.

- 4 ounces rice sticks
- 1/4 cup chopped fresh mint
- 1/4 cup low-sodium soy sauce
- 3 tablespoons sugar
- 2 tablespoons chopped dry-roasted peanuts
- 6 tablespoons rice wine vinegar
- 2 serrano chiles, halved lengthwise, seeded, and thinly sliced
- 2 garlic cloves, minced
- 2 teaspoons dark sesame oil
- 1 large yellow squash (about 8 ounces), halved lengthwise and thinly sliced
- 2 cups thinly sliced red bell pepper rings
- 1 medium zucchini (about 6 ounces), halved lengthwise and thinly sliced
- 3 cups sliced green cabbage
- 2 cups fresh bean sprouts
- 1/2 cup chopped green onions
- 12 ounces baked tofu, cubed

1. Cook noodles according to package directions.
2. Combine mint and next 6 ingredients. Combine half of mint mixture and rice noodles in a large bowl.
3. Heat oil in a large nonstick skillet over medium-high heat. Add squash, bell pepper, and zucchini; sauté 4 minutes. Add green cabbage and next 3 ingredients; sauté 3 minutes. Arrange noodle mixture on a platter, and top with cabbage mixture. Drizzle with remaining mint mixture. Yield: 6 servings (serving size: 1 2/3 cups).

CALORIES 253 (23% from fat); FAT 6.6g (sat 1.1g, mono 1.9g, poly 2.6g); PROTEIN 11.7g; CARB 37.9g; FIBER 4.9g; CHOL 0mg; IRON 2.9mg; SODIUM 540mg; CALC 252mg

Tabbouleh with Oranges and Sunflower Seeds

Fresh mint balances the grassy herb flavor of parsley.

- 3/4 cup uncooked bulgur or cracked wheat
- 2 cups boiling water
- 2 navel oranges
- 1 tablespoon sugar
- 1 1/2 tablespoons olive oil
- 1/4 teaspoon salt
- 1/4 teaspoon black pepper
- 1 cup chopped fresh parsley
- 3/4 cup chopped fresh mint
- 3/4 cup diced seeded peeled cucumber
- 1/2 cup coarsely chopped red onion
- 2 navel oranges, each cut crosswise into 10 (1/4-inch-thick) slices
- 2 tablespoons sunflower seeds

1. Combine bulgur and 2 cups boiling water in a large bowl. Cover and let stand 30 minutes; drain.
2. Peel and section 2 oranges over a bowl; squeeze membranes to extract juice. Set orange sections aside; reserve 1/4 cup juice. Discard membranes. Combine reserved orange juice, sugar, oil, salt, and pepper; stir well with a whisk.
3. Add orange sections, parsley, mint, cucumber, and onion to bulgur mixture; stir well. Add orange juice mixture, and toss gently to coat. Cover and chill at least 2 hours.
4. Arrange 4 orange slices on each of 5 serving plates; top with tabbouleh. Sprinkle evenly with sunflower seeds. Yield: 5 servings.

CALORIES 204 (28% from fat); FAT 6.3g (sat 0.8g, mono 3.4g, poly 1.7g); PROTEIN 5.3g; CARB 35.2g; FIBER 10g; CHOL 0mg; IRON 1.8mg; SODIUM 131mg; CALC 83mg

Lemony Rice Salad with Carrots and Radishes

2 tablespoons water
1 teaspoon grated lemon rind
2 tablespoons fresh lemon juice
1 tablespoon olive oil
2 teaspoons chopped fresh thyme
½ teaspoon salt
¼ teaspoon black pepper
2 cups hot cooked long-grain rice
¾ cup shredded carrot
¾ cup shredded radish
¼ cup golden raisins
3 tablespoons chopped walnuts, toasted

1. Combine first 7 ingredients in a small bowl.
2. Combine rice and next 4 ingredients. Drizzle with lemon mixture; toss. Yield: 4 servings (serving size: 1 cup).

CALORIES 223 (28% from fat); FAT 7g (sat 0.7g, mono 3.3g, poly 2.5g); PROTEIN 4.2g; CARB 37.5g; FIBER 2.2g; CHOL 0mg; IRON 1.6mg; SODIUM 307mg; CALC 33mg

Orzo-Bell Pepper Salad

DRESSING:

2 tablespoons fresh lemon juice
2½ teaspoons extravirgin olive oil
2 teaspoons red wine vinegar
½ teaspoon salt
¼ teaspoon freshly ground black pepper
3 garlic cloves, minced

SALAD:

1 cup uncooked orzo (rice-shaped pasta)
⅓ cup finely chopped red bell pepper
⅓ cup finely chopped green bell pepper
⅓ cup finely chopped yellow bell pepper
1 cup finely chopped tomato
½ cup (2 ounces) diced fresh marinated mozzarella cheese (such as Cappiello)
¼ cup minced fresh parsley
¼ cup finely chopped red onion
¼ cup chopped pitted kalamata olives

1. To prepare dressing, whisk first 6 ingredients.
2. To prepare salad, cook pasta in boiling water 6 minutes or until al dente. Add bell peppers; cook 10 seconds. Drain. Combine pasta mixture and half of dressing in a large bowl; cool to room temperature. Add remaining dressing, tomato, and next 4 ingredients; toss gently to coat. Cover; chill at least 1 hour. Yield: 4 servings (serving size: 1 cup).

CALORIES 351 (29% from fat); FAT 11.3g (sat 3.4g, mono 5.8g, poly 1g); PROTEIN 11.6g; CARB 48.6g; FIBER 3.4g; CHOL 8mg; IRON 2.7mg; SODIUM 619mg; CALC 134mg

Southwestern Salad Bar

1 tablespoon fajita seasoning
2 cups fresh corn kernels (about 4 ears)
5 teaspoons fresh lime juice, divided
2 teaspoons minced fresh cilantro
⅔ cup chopped red onion
2 garlic cloves, minced
2 (15-ounce) cans black beans, rinsed and drained
1 (7-ounce) bottle roasted red bell peppers, drained and chopped
½ cup diced peeled avocado
¾ cup light ranch dressing
1½ teaspoons minced canned chipotle chiles in adobo sauce
12 cups packaged chopped romaine lettuce
3 cups chopped skinless, boneless rotisserie chicken
1½ cups (6 ounces) preshredded reduced-fat Cheddar cheese
1½ cups unsalted baked tortilla chips, crumbled
1 cup chopped peeled mango
1 cup sliced green onions
½ cup thinly sliced radishes

1. Cook fajita seasoning in a large saucepan over medium heat 2 minutes or until toasted, stirring frequently. Combine seasoning, corn, 1 tablespoon juice, and cilantro in a medium serving bowl.
2. Combine onion, garlic, beans, and bell peppers in a medium serving bowl. Combine avocado and remaining 2 teaspoons juice in a small serving bowl, tossing gently to coat. Combine dressing and chipotle in a small serving bowl.
3. Place lettuce in a large serving bowl. Place chicken in a medium serving bowl. Place cheese, chips, mango, green onions, and radishes in individual serving bowls. Arrange bowls, buffet-style, beginning with lettuce and ending with dressing. Yield: 8 servings (serving size: 1½ cups lettuce, ¾ cup bean mixture, ¼ cup corn mixture, about ⅓ cup chicken, 3 tablespoons chips, 3 tablespoons cheese, 2 tablespoons mango, 2 tablespoons onions, 1 tablespoon radishes, 1 tablespoon avocado, and 1½ tablespoons dressing).

CALORIES 411 (29% from fat); FAT 12.7g (sat 2.5g, mono 4.6g, poly 4.2g); PROTEIN 32g; CARB 45.9g; FIBER 11.3g; CHOL 55mg; IRON 3.7mg; SODIUM 822mg; CALC 179mg

Southwestern Salad Bar

Chicken, Red Potato, and Green Bean Salad

Red potatoes work well and add a nice color to this salad, but you can use any waxy potato, such as fingerling or white. If the potatoes aren't about golf ball–sized, cut each into eight wedges before cooking.

DRESSING:

- ⅓ cup coarsely chopped fresh parsley
- 3 tablespoons red wine vinegar
- 1 tablespoon fresh lemon juice
- 1 tablespoon whole-grain Dijon mustard
- 1 tablespoon extravirgin olive oil
- ½ teaspoon salt
- ¼ teaspoon freshly ground black pepper
- 1 garlic clove, minced

SALAD:

- 1 pound small red potatoes
- 1 teaspoon salt
- ½ pound diagonally cut green beans
- 2 cups cubed cooked chicken (about 8 ounces)
- 2 tablespoons chopped red onion
- 1 (10-ounce) package gourmet salad greens (about 6 cups)

1. To prepare dressing, combine first 8 ingredients, stirring well with a whisk.

2. To prepare salad, place potatoes in a saucepan; cover with water. Add 1 teaspoon salt; bring to a boil. Reduce heat; simmer 10 minutes or until almost tender. Add beans; cook 4 minutes or until crisp-tender. Drain. Rinse with cold water; drain well.

3. Quarter potatoes. Place potatoes, beans, chicken, onion, and greens in a large bowl. Drizzle with dressing; toss gently to coat. Serve immediately. Yield: 4 servings (serving size: about 1¾ cups).

CALORIES 269 (29% from fat); FAT 8.8g (sat 1.8g, mono 4.4g, poly 1.6g); PROTEIN 22.4g; CARB 26.1g; FIBER 5.8g; CHOL 53mg; IRON 3.8mg; SODIUM 761mg; CALC 96mg

Cherry-Pecan Chicken Salad

Use either vacuum-packed soft or firm silken tofu in the dressing for this salad. When pureed it gives the dressing a creamy, thick consistency.

SALAD:

- 3 cups chopped roasted skinless, boneless chicken breasts (about 3 breasts)
- 2 cups pitted sweet cherries (about ¾ pound)
- 1 cup chopped peeled English cucumber
- ½ cup frozen green peas, thawed
- ¼ cup chopped celery
- ¼ cup chopped red onion
- ¼ cup chopped carrot
- 3 tablespoons chopped pecans, toasted
- 2 tablespoons sliced green onions
- 2 teaspoons chopped fresh or ½ teaspoon dried tarragon

DRESSING:

- ½ pound soft silken tofu
- ¼ cup red wine vinegar
- 1 tablespoon fresh thyme leaves
- ½ teaspoon salt
- ¼ teaspoon freshly ground black pepper
- ⅛ teaspoon ground red pepper

1. To prepare salad, combine first 10 ingredients in a large bowl.

2. To prepare dressing, combine tofu and next 5 ingredients in a blender; process until smooth. Pour over chicken mixture; toss gently to coat. Cover and chill 1 hour. Yield: 4 servings (serving size: 1½ cups).

CALORIES 277 (29% from fat); FAT 8.9g (sat 1.4g, mono 3.6g, poly 2.9g); PROTEIN 26g; CARB 25g; FIBER 2.5g; CHOL 54mg; IRON 2.4mg; SODIUM 361mg; CALC 76mg

Sesame Chicken Salad

Serve this delicious salad soon after mixing, or it will wilt and lose its bright color. For quicker prep, substitute bagged shredded cabbage for the napa.

VINAIGRETTE:

- ¼ cup rice vinegar
- ¼ cup low-sodium soy sauce
- 2 tablespoons creamy peanut butter
- 1 teaspoon dark sesame oil
- 1 teaspoon bottled minced fresh ginger
- 1 teaspoon bottled minced garlic

SALAD:

- 2½ cups chopped cooked chicken breast
- 2 cups thinly sliced napa (Chinese) cabbage
- 1 cup red bell pepper strips
- 1 cup fresh bean sprouts
- 1 cup grated carrot
- 2 tablespoons chopped green onions
- 1 teaspoon sesame seeds, toasted

1. To prepare vinaigrette, combine first 6 ingredients in a small bowl, stirring with a whisk.

2. To prepare salad, combine chicken and next 5 ingredients in a large bowl. Drizzle with vinaigrette, tossing gently to coat. Sprinkle with sesame seeds. Yield: 4 servings (serving size: 1½ cups).

CALORIES 256 (31% from fat); FAT 8.8g (sat 2g, mono 3.6g, poly 2.5g); PROTEIN 31.9g; CARB 12.1g; FIBER 3g; CHOL 74mg; IRON 2mg; SODIUM 654mg; CALC 54mg

Chicken Salad with Peas and Fresh Herb Vinaigrette

Fresh parsley and thyme in the vinaigrette and sweet frozen peas in the chicken salad render a lighter flavor than the traditional mayonnaise-based chicken salads.

- ½ cup fresh parsley
- ½ cup chopped green onions
- 3 tablespoons rice vinegar
- 1 tablespoon stone-ground mustard
- 1 teaspoon sugar
- 1 to 2 teaspoons chopped fresh thyme
- 2 teaspoons extravirgin olive oil
- ¼ teaspoon salt
- 1 garlic clove
- 1½ cups chopped cooked chicken breast
- ¾ cup chopped celery
- 1 (10-ounce) package frozen green peas, thawed
- 2 tablespoons sliced almonds, toasted

1. Combine first 9 ingredients in a food processor; process until smooth. Combine parsley mixture, chicken, celery, and peas in a large bowl, tossing well. Sprinkle each serving with toasted almonds. Yield: 4 servings (serving size: 1 cup chicken salad and 1½ teaspoons almonds).

CALORIES 209 (29% from fat); FAT 6.8g (sat 1.1g, mono 3.8g, poly 1.3g); PROTEIN 21.8g; CARB 14.8g; FIBER 4.9g; CHOL 45mg; IRON 2.7mg; SODIUM 364mg; CALC 70mg

Chicken and Strawberries over Mixed Greens

Chicken and Strawberries over Mixed Greens

Using precooked chicken makes this dish even quicker to prepare. Serve with focaccia topped with coarse salt and rosemary to complement the sweet strawberries and raisins in the salad.

- 2 cups chopped roasted skinless, boneless chicken breasts (about 2 breasts)
- 2 cups quartered small strawberries (about 1 pint)
- ⅓ cup finely chopped celery
- ⅓ cup finely chopped red onion
- 2 tablespoons golden raisins
- 1 tablespoon sesame seeds, toasted
- 1 tablespoon chopped fresh or 1 teaspoon dried tarragon
- 1 tablespoon extravirgin olive oil
- 1 tablespoon balsamic vinegar
- ½ teaspoon paprika
- ⅛ teaspoon salt
- ⅛ teaspoon black pepper
- 4 cups gourmet salad greens

1. Combine first 5 ingredients in a large bowl. Combine sesame seeds and next 6 ingredients in a small bowl, stirring well with a whisk. Pour over chicken mixture; toss well to coat. Cover and chill 1 hour. Serve over salad greens. Yield: 4 servings (serving size: 1¼ cups chicken mixture and 1 cup greens).

CALORIES 164 (35% from fat); FAT 6.3g (sat 1.2g, mono 3.4g, poly 1.3g); PROTEIN 15.3g; CARB 13.3g; FIBER 3.5g; CHOL 35mg; IRON 1.7mg; SODIUM 376mg; CALC 78mg

Chicken Salad with Garden Herbs

This recipe leaves you with a bonus: homemade chicken stock.

- 1 (3½-pound) whole chicken
- ¼ cup chopped fresh chives
- 3 tablespoons white wine vinegar
- 2 tablespoons capers
- 2 teaspoons chopped fresh thyme
- 1 teaspoon chopped fresh oregano
- 4 teaspoons extravirgin olive oil
- ½ teaspoon salt
- ½ teaspoon freshly ground black pepper
- 1 garlic clove, minced

1. Place chicken in a stockpot. Cover with water; bring to a boil. Reduce heat, and simmer 50 minutes or until tender. Drain, reserving broth for another use. Cool chicken completely. Remove skin from chicken; discard skin. Remove chicken from bones; discard bones and fat. Chop chicken into bite-sized pieces.

2. Combine chives and next 8 ingredients in a large bowl. Add chicken; toss well to coat. Yield: 6 servings (serving size: ⅔ cup).

CALORIES 172 (29% from fat); FAT 5.6g (sat 1.1g, mono 2.9g, poly 0.9g); PROTEIN 28.4g; CARB 0.5g; FIBER 0.3g; CHOL 83mg; IRON 1.2mg; SODIUM 392mg; CALC 23mg

Grilled Chicken Salad with Feta and Cucumbers

This dish is bright with lemon juice, mint, and dill.

- 8 (6-ounce) skinless, boneless chicken breast halves
- 1 tablespoon olive oil
- ¾ teaspoon salt, divided
- ¼ teaspoon freshly ground black pepper
- Cooking spray
- 4 cups (½-inch) cubed peeled English cucumber (about 2 large)
- 2 cups chopped red onion
- 2 cups (8 ounces) crumbled feta cheese
- 1 tablespoon grated lemon rind
- ¼ cup fresh lemon juice
- 6 tablespoons chopped fresh mint
- 6 tablespoons chopped fresh dill
- Mint sprigs (optional)

1. Prepare grill or broiler.

2. Brush chicken with olive oil; sprinkle with ½ teaspoon salt and pepper. Place chicken on grill rack or broiler pan coated with cooking spray; grill 5 minutes on each side or until done. Place chicken on platter; let cool 5 minutes. Slice each chicken breast half in half lengthwise; slice chicken pieces crosswise into thin slices.

3. Combine chicken, cucumber, and next 6 ingredients in a large bowl. Sprinkle with remaining ¼ teaspoon salt; toss to combine. Garnish with mint sprigs, if desired. Yield: 12 servings (serving size: 1⅓ cups).

CALORIES 202 (30% from fat); FAT 6.7g (sat 3.4g, mono 2.1g, poly 0.6g); PROTEIN 29.5g; CARB 4.9g; FIBER 1g; CHOL 83mg; IRON 1.2mg; SODIUM 433mg; CALC 121mg

Chicken Salad with Nectarines in Mint Vinaigrette

The mint adds a refreshing note to the dressing, which would also work well in a fresh fruit salad. Use any curly lettuce leaves in place of red leaf.

DRESSING:

1 cup loosely packed fresh mint leaves
⅓ cup sugar
¼ cup white wine vinegar
1 tablespoon fresh lemon juice
¼ teaspoon salt
¼ teaspoon freshly ground black pepper

SALAD:

2 cups chopped cooked chicken breast
1 cup chopped seeded cucumber
⅓ cup chopped pecans, toasted
2 tablespoons minced red onion
3 nectarines, peeled, pitted, and chopped
5 red leaf lettuce leaves

1. To prepare dressing, place mint and sugar in a food processor; process until finely chopped, scraping sides of bowl. Add vinegar, lemon juice, salt, and black pepper; process 30 seconds to combine.

2. To prepare salad, combine chicken, cucumber, pecans, onion, and nectarines in a medium bowl. Drizzle dressing over salad; toss well to coat. Place 1 lettuce leaf on each of 5 plates; top each serving with ¾ cup salad. Yield: 5 servings.

CALORIES 241 (28% from fat); FAT 7.4g (sat 1g, mono 3.6g, poly 2.1g); PROTEIN 16.7g; CARB 29g; FIBER 3.6g; CHOL 39mg; IRON 3.4mg; SODIUM 163mg; CALC 71mg

Salmon and Edamame Pasta Salad

Using edamame (soybeans) in a familiar dish is an easy way to incorporate soy into your diet. Fresh dill is a popular herb commonly paired with salmon, but you could also use parsley or basil.

1½ cups uncooked farfalle (about 4 ounces bow tie pasta)
⅔ cup shelled edamame
Cooking spray
1 (4-ounce) salmon fillet, skinned
2 teaspoons olive oil
1 cup finely chopped red onion
4 ounces baby spinach (about 6 cups)
¼ cup chopped fresh dill
4 teaspoons whole-grain Dijon mustard
½ teaspoon salt
¼ teaspoon freshly ground black pepper

1. Cook pasta in boiling water 5 minutes. Add edamame; cook 6 minutes or until tender. Drain and rinse with cold water. Drain and place pasta mixture in a large bowl.

2. Heat a nonstick skillet over medium-high heat. Coat pan with cooking spray. Add salmon; cook 7 minutes or until fish flakes easily when tested with a fork or until desired degree of doneness, turning once. Coarsely chop salmon. Add to pasta mixture; toss gently to combine.

3. Heat olive oil in pan over medium-high heat. Add onion; sauté 4 minutes or until tender. Add spinach; cook 2 minutes or just until wilted, stirring frequently. Add spinach mixture and dill to pasta mixture; toss gently to combine. Add mustard, salt, and pepper; toss gently to coat. Yield: 4 servings (serving size: 1 cup).

CALORIES 262 (27% from fat); FAT 8g (sat 1.3g, mono 3.2g, poly 2.2g); PROTEIN 17.1g; CARB 31.5g; FIBER 4.8g; CHOL 14mg; IRON 3.6mg; SODIUM 418mg; CALC 137mg

Shellfish and Bacon Spinach Salad

Gently rinse mussels under cold running water, and discard any opened mussels before you cook them. After cooking, be sure to discard any unopened mussels.

2 thick slices applewood-smoked bacon, diced (such as Neuske's)
2 garlic cloves, minced
¼ cup riesling or other dry white wine
⅛ teaspoon crushed red pepper
3 pounds mussels, scrubbed and debearded
⅓ cup thinly sliced red onion, separated into rings
2 (6-ounce) packages baby spinach, thoroughly washed

1. Cook bacon in a Dutch oven over medium heat until crisp. Remove bacon from pan, reserving 1 tablespoon drippings in pan. Crumble bacon, and set aside.

2. Add minced garlic to drippings in pan; cook over medium heat 1 minute. Add wine and pepper. Add mussels to pan; cover and cook 6 minutes or until shells open. Remove from heat; discard any unopened shells. Place mussels in a bowl. Add onion and spinach to wine mixture in pan; cook 1 minute or until spinach wilts. Divide spinach mixture among 4 plates, and sprinkle evenly with bacon. Arrange mussels over spinach mixture, and drizzle evenly with any remaining wine mixture. Yield: 4 servings (serving size: about 2 dozen mussels, 2 cups spinach mixture, and 1 tablespoon bacon).

CALORIES 165 (25% from fat); FAT 4.6g (sat 1.5g, mono 0.6g, poly 0.7g); PROTEIN 16.7g; CARB 14.9g; FIBER 4.2g; CHOL 37mg; IRON 7.3mg; SODIUM 586mg; CALC 96mg

Mediterranean Salad with Shrimp

Mediterranean Salad with Shrimp

Use shredded rotisserie chicken in place of the shrimp, if you'd prefer.

- 4 quarts water
- 1½ pounds large shrimp, peeled and deveined
- 1½ cups halved cherry tomatoes
- 1 cup (¼-inch-thick) slices red onion, separated into rings
- 1 cup (¼-inch-thick) slices cucumber, halved
- 1 (10-ounce) package torn romaine lettuce (about 6 cups)
- 1 tablespoon chopped fresh flat-leaf parsley
- 3 tablespoons red wine vinegar
- 2 teaspoons Dijon mustard
- 1 teaspoon extravirgin olive oil
- ¾ teaspoon dried oregano
- ¼ teaspoon salt
- ¼ teaspoon black pepper
- 2 garlic cloves, minced
- ½ cup (2 ounces) crumbled feta cheese
- 8 kalamata olives, pitted and halved
- 4 pepperoncini peppers

1. Bring water to a boil in a large saucepan. Add shrimp; cook 2 minutes or until done. Drain and rinse with cold water. Place shrimp in a bowl; cover and chill.
2. Place tomatoes, onion, cucumber, and lettuce in a large bowl; toss to combine. Combine parsley and next 7 ingredients, stirring with a whisk. Spoon 1 tablespoon dressing over shrimp; toss to combine. Add shrimp mixture and remaining dressing to lettuce mixture, and toss gently to coat.
3. Spoon about 2¾ cups salad onto each of 4 plates. Top each serving with 2 tablespoons cheese, 4 olive halves, and 1 pepperoncini pepper. Yield: 4 servings.

CALORIES 296 (30% from fat); FAT 9.8g (sat 3.2g, mono 3.6g, poly 1.8g); PROTEIN 39.4g; CARB 12.1g; FIBER 3.2g; CHOL 271mg; IRON 6mg; SODIUM 849mg; CALC 219mg

Mediterranean Potato Salad with Shrimp and Feta

"Baking" the potatoes in the microwave instead of in the oven cuts the cook time in half.

DRESSING:

- 1½ tablespoons chopped fresh basil
- 1 tablespoon fresh lemon juice
- 2 teaspoons extravirgin olive oil
- ¾ teaspoon sugar
- ¼ teaspoon freshly ground black pepper
- ¼ teaspoon Dijon mustard

SALAD:

- 5 cups small red potatoes, quartered (about 1½ pounds)
- ½ teaspoon salt
- ¼ teaspoon freshly ground black pepper
- 1 pound medium shrimp, cooked and peeled
- 3 cups thinly sliced romaine lettuce
- 1 cup red bell pepper, cut into ¼-inch strips
- 1 cup yellow bell pepper, cut into ¼-inch strips
- 1 cup thinly sliced red onion
- ½ cup (2 ounces) crumbled feta cheese
- 2 tablespoons chopped pitted kalamata olives

1. To prepare dressing, combine first 6 ingredients, stirring well with a whisk.
2. To prepare salad, arrange potatoes in a single layer on a microwave-safe dish, and sprinkle with ½ teaspoon salt and ¼ teaspoon pepper. Microwave at HIGH 15 minutes or until potatoes are tender. Place potatoes in a large bowl.
3. Add shrimp and 1 tablespoon dressing to potatoes in bowl; toss gently to combine. Add remaining dressing, lettuce, bell peppers, onion, and cheese; toss gently to coat. Top each serving with 1½ teaspoons kalamata olives. Yield: 4 servings (serving size: 2½ cups).

CALORIES 362 (23% from fat); FAT 9.4g (sat 3.1g, mono 3.8g, poly 1.4g); PROTEIN 30.3g; CARB 39.4g; FIBER 5.5g; CHOL 185mg; IRON 5.1mg; SODIUM 740mg; CALC 183mg

Summer Shrimp Salad with Cilantro

If you don't have cilantro, this light summer salad is just as good with fresh basil.

DRESSING:

½ cup vegetable broth
1½ teaspoons cornstarch
3 tablespoons fresh lime juice
2 teaspoons extravirgin olive oil
¾ teaspoon sugar
¼ teaspoon ground cumin
½ teaspoon salt
¼ teaspoon freshly ground black peppercorns

SALAD:

1 pound medium shrimp, cooked and peeled
1½ cups julienne-cut yellow squash
1½ cups julienne-cut zucchini
1½ cups cherry tomatoes, halved
1 cup fresh corn kernels (about 2 ears)
2 tablespoons minced fresh cilantro

1. To prepare dressing, combine vegetable broth and cornstarch in a small saucepan, stirring with a whisk; bring to a boil. Cook 1 minute, stirring constantly. Remove from heat; stir in juice and next 5 ingredients. Cool.

2. To prepare salad, combine shrimp and next 5 ingredients in a large bowl. Add dressing mixture to shrimp mixture, tossing well. Yield: 4 servings (serving size: 1¾ cups).

CALORIES 198 (22% from fat); FAT 4.8g (sat 0.7g, mono 2.1g, poly 1.2g); PROTEIN 20.4g; CARB 20.9g; FIBER 3.8g; CHOL 129mg; IRON 3.1mg; SODIUM 559mg; CALC 72mg

Coconut-Rice Salad with Mango and Shrimp

You can also cook the shrimp on the grill and arrange them on top of the rice salad.

5¾ cups water, divided
1 pound medium shrimp, peeled and deveined
¾ cup light coconut milk
1¼ cups uncooked long-grain rice
¼ teaspoon salt
2 cups cubed peeled ripe mango (about 2 large)
1 cup diced seeded peeled cucumber
¼ cup chopped fresh cilantro
¼ cup thinly sliced green onions
¼ cup fresh lime juice
3 tablespoons chopped fresh mint
2 tablespoons minced seeded jalapeño pepper
½ teaspoon salt

1. Bring 4 cups water to a boil in a large saucepan. Add shrimp; cook 1½ minutes or until done. Drain and rinse with cold water. Cover and chill.

2. Combine 1¾ cups water and coconut milk in pan; bring to a boil. Add rice and ¼ teaspoon salt; cover, reduce heat, and simmer 20 minutes or until liquid is absorbed. Remove from heat; fluff with a fork. Spoon rice mixture into a large bowl; cool.

3. Add shrimp, mango, and next 7 ingredients to rice mixture, tossing well. Cover and chill. Yield: 4 servings (serving size: 2 cups).

CALORIES 396 (10% from fat); FAT 4.4g (sat 2g, mono 0.8g, poly 1g); PROTEIN 22.4g; CARB 65.8g; FIBER 2.6g; CHOL 130mg; IRON 5mg; SODIUM 574mg; CALC 86mg

Grilled Steak Salad with Caper Vinaigrette

This salad is great with leftover beef. If watercress is unavailable, use mixed salad greens. Substitute artichoke hearts for the hearts of palm, or just omit them. Serve with herbed focaccia.

SALAD:

- 1 pound beef tenderloin, trimmed
- Cooking spray
- 4 cups water
- 3 cups (1-inch) cut green beans (about ½ pound)
- 4 cups trimmed watercress (about 1 bunch)
- 1 cup grape tomatoes, halved
- ¾ cup thinly sliced red onion
- 1 (8-ounce) package presliced mushrooms
- 1 (7.75-ounce) can hearts of palm, rinsed and drained

DRESSING:

- ¼ cup red wine vinegar
- 1½ tablespoons fresh lemon juice
- 1 tablespoon capers
- 1 tablespoon honey mustard
- 2 teaspoons extravirgin olive oil
- ½ teaspoon sugar
- ½ teaspoon salt
- ⅛ teaspoon freshly ground black pepper

1. Prepare grill or broiler.

2. To prepare salad, place beef on grill rack or broiler pan coated with cooking spray; grill 7 minutes on each side or until desired degree of doneness. Let stand 10 minutes. Cut steak diagonally across grain into thin slices. Place beef in a large bowl.

3. Bring water to a boil in a saucepan; add beans. Cover and cook 3 minutes or until crisp-tender. Rinse with cold water; drain well. Add beans, watercress, tomatoes, onion, mushrooms, and hearts of palm to beef; toss gently to combine.

4. To prepare dressing, combine vinegar, lemon juice, capers, honey mustard, olive oil, sugar, salt, and black pepper, stirring well with a whisk. Drizzle dressing over salad, and toss gently to coat. Yield: 4 servings (serving size: 2 cups).

CALORIES 224 (29% from fat); FAT 7.3g (sat 2g, mono 3.3g, poly 0.5g); PROTEIN 27.3g; CARB 16.8g; FIBER 5.2g; CHOL 60mg; IRON 5.7mg; SODIUM 699mg; CALC 114mg

Grilled Sirloin Salad

Flank steak can be substituted for sirloin.

- 1 tablespoon chili powder
- 2 teaspoons dried oregano
- 1 teaspoon dried thyme
- ½ teaspoon salt
- ½ teaspoon onion powder
- ½ teaspoon garlic powder
- ¼ teaspoon black pepper
- 1 pound boneless sirloin steak, trimmed
- 8 cups mixed salad greens
- 1½ cups red bell pepper strips
- 1 cup vertically sliced red onion
- 1 tablespoon chopped fresh parsley
- 1 tablespoon red wine vinegar
- 1 teaspoon olive oil
- 1 teaspoon fresh lemon juice
- 1 (8¾-ounce) can whole-kernel corn, rinsed and drained

1. Combine first 7 ingredients; rub over both sides of steak. Heat a nonstick grill pan over medium-high heat. Add steak; cook 5 minutes on each side or until desired degree of doneness. Cut steak diagonally across grain into thin slices.

2. Combine salad greens and next 7 ingredients in a large bowl; toss well to coat. Top with steak. Yield: 4 servings (serving size: 3 cups salad and 3 ounces steak).

CALORIES 278 (28% from fat); FAT 8.7g (sat 2.7g, mono 3.7g, poly 1g); PROTEIN 30.4g; CARB 22g; FIBER 6.1g; CHOL 76mg; IRON 6.1mg; SODIUM 530mg; CALC 106mg

How to Slice a Steak

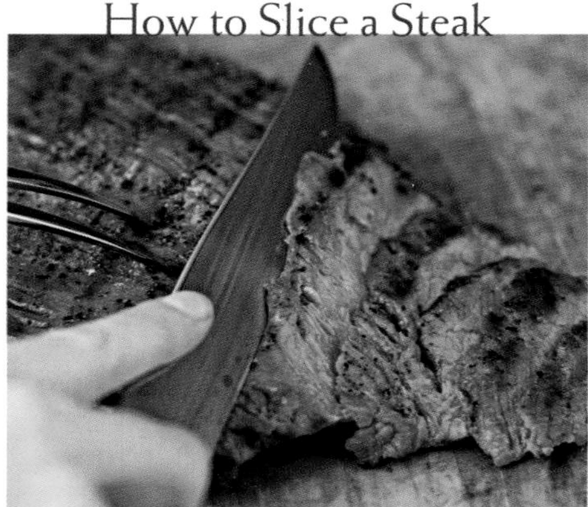

Before slicing meat, allow it to stand 10 minutes. Then cut across the grain into ⅛- to ¼-inch-thick slices for maximum tenderness. Tilting your knife diagonally and slicing away from you ensures the largest surface area possible for each piece.

Thai Beef and Radish Salad

Southeast Asian salads are traditionally eaten out of hand, with lettuce leaves for wrappers. To make the job of cutting the steak diagonally into thin slices easier, chill the meat in the freezer 10 minutes.

- 1 tablespoon chile paste with garlic (such as sambal oelek)
- 2 teaspoons minced peeled fresh ginger
- 1 garlic clove, minced
- 1 pound (½-inch-thick) boneless sirloin steak, cut diagonally across grain into thin slices
- 1½ tablespoons fresh lime juice
- 1 tablespoon fish sauce
- 2 teaspoons sugar
- Cooking spray
- 2 cups sliced radishes
- ¼ cup chopped fresh cilantro
- 2 tablespoons chopped fresh mint
- 1 serrano chile, seeded and finely chopped
- 8 Bibb lettuce leaves

1. Combine chile paste, ginger, and garlic in a large zip-top plastic bag; add steak, tossing well to coat. Marinate in refrigerator 30 minutes, turning once.

2. Combine lime juice, fish sauce, and sugar, stirring with a whisk; set aside.

3. Heat a large nonstick skillet over medium-high heat. Coat pan with cooking spray. Remove steak from bag; discard marinade. Add steak to pan; cook 2 minutes or until desired degree of doneness, turning once. Remove steak from pan. Cut steak into 1-inch pieces; place in a medium bowl. Add radishes, cilantro, mint, and serrano chile. Pour lime juice mixture over beef mixture, tossing to coat. Spoon about ⅓ cup salad mixture into each lettuce leaf. Serve immediately. Yield: 4 servings (serving size: 2 filled lettuce leaves).

CALORIES 223 (41% from fat); FAT 10.2g (sat 3.9g, mono 4.2g, poly 0.4g); PROTEIN 25.7g; CARB 6.8g; FIBER 1.4g; CHOL 76mg; IRON 3.1mg; SODIUM 471mg; CALC 35mg

Grilled Jamaican Pork Tenderloin Salad

Butterflying the pork helps it cook faster. If you can't find papaya, use an extra cup of chopped pineapple.

DRESSING:

- 2 tablespoons fresh or 2 teaspoons dried thyme leaves
- 2 tablespoons fresh lime juice
- 1 tablespoon olive oil
- 1 tablespoon minced fresh ginger
- 2 teaspoons brown sugar
- ½ teaspoon salt
- ½ teaspoon ground allspice
- ½ teaspoon ground cinnamon
- ¼ teaspoon freshly ground black pepper
- ¼ teaspoon ground nutmeg
- 1 garlic clove, minced

SALAD:

- 1 (1-pound) pork tenderloin
- Cooking spray
- 4 cups mixed salad greens
- 2 cups chopped peeled fresh pineapple
- 1 cup chopped peeled papaya

1. Prepare grill or broiler.

2. To prepare dressing, combine first 11 ingredients in a food processor; process until smooth.

3. To prepare pork, slice pork lengthwise, cutting to, but not through, other side. Open halves, laying pork flat. Rub 2 tablespoons dressing on pork, and reserve remaining dressing. Place pork on grill rack or broiler pan coated with cooking spray; cook 10 minutes on each side or until a thermometer registers 160° (slightly pink). Let pork stand 5 minutes. Cut pork into ¼-inch-thick slices; toss with reserved dressing.

4. Place 1 cup salad greens on each of 4 plates; top with 3 ounces pork, ½ cup pineapple, and ¼ cup papaya. Yield: 4 servings.

CALORIES 263 (30% from fat); FAT 8.7g (sat 2.3g, mono 4.8g, poly 0.9g); PROTEIN 28.4g; CARB 18.3g; FIBER 3.2g; CHOL 69mg; IRON 2.7mg; SODIUM 371mg; CALC 78mg

Salad Niçoise in Pita Pockets, page 280

Sandwiches

Southwestern Falafel with Avocado Spread

Inspired by the traditional Middle Eastern sandwich of chickpea patties in pita bread, this southwestern version features cumin-flavored pinto bean patties and a spread that is much like guacamole. Serve with tomato soup.

PATTIES:

- 1 (15-ounce) can pinto beans, rinsed and drained
- ½ cup (2 ounces) shredded Monterey Jack cheese
- ¼ cup finely crushed baked tortilla chips (about ¾ ounce)
- 2 tablespoons finely chopped green onions
- 1 tablespoon finely chopped cilantro
- ⅛ teaspoon ground cumin
- 1 large egg white
- 1½ teaspoons canola oil

AVOCADO SPREAD:

- ¼ cup mashed peeled avocado
- 2 tablespoons finely chopped plum tomato
- 1 tablespoon finely chopped red onion
- 2 tablespoons fat-free sour cream
- 1 teaspoon fresh lime juice
- ⅛ teaspoon salt
- 2 (6-inch) pitas, each cut in half crosswise

1. To prepare patties, place pinto beans in a medium bowl; partially mash with a fork. Add Monterey Jack cheese and next 5 ingredients; stir until well combined. Form into 4 (½-inch-thick) oval patties.

2. Heat oil in a large nonstick skillet over medium-high heat. Add patties; cook 3 minutes on each side or until patties are browned and thoroughly heated.

3. To prepare avocado spread, while patties cook, combine avocado, tomato, red onion, sour cream, juice, and salt. Place 1 patty in each pita half. Spread about 2 tablespoons avocado spread over patty in each pita half. Yield: 4 servings (serving size: 1 stuffed pita half).

CALORIES 281 (30% from fat); FAT 9.5g (sat 3.4g, mono 3.9g, poly 1.5g); PROTEIN 12.2g; CARB 37.4g; FIBER 5.9g; CHOL 13mg; IRON 2.4mg; SODIUM 625mg; CALC 188mg

Grilled Vegetable and Mozzarella Sandwich

You can use a grilling basket to make it easier to handle the vegetables as they cook. If you can't find a loaf of ciabatta, use focaccia.

- 3 cups (⅛-inch-thick) diagonally cut zucchini (about 1 pound)
- 3 (⅛-inch-thick) slices red onion
- 1 red bell pepper, seeded and cut into 4 pieces
- 2 tablespoons balsamic vinegar
- 1 teaspoon extravirgin olive oil
- ½ teaspoon salt
- ¼ teaspoon freshly ground black pepper
- Cooking spray
- 1 (1-pound) loaf ciabatta, cut in half horizontally
- 1 cup gourmet salad greens
- 5 ounces fresh mozzarella cheese, sliced
- 8 fresh basil leaves

1. Prepare grill.
2. Combine first 7 ingredients in a large bowl, tossing to coat. Remove vegetables from bowl, reserving vinegar mixture. Place onion and bell pepper on grill rack coated with cooking spray; grill 7 minutes on each side or until tender. Grill zucchini 3 minutes on each side or until tender.
3. Hollow out bottom half of bread, leaving a ½-inch-thick shell; reserve torn bread for another use. Layer vegetables, greens, cheese, and basil in loaf; drizzle reserved vinegar mixture on top. Cover with top of bread; press lightly.
4. Place filled loaf on grill rack; grill 4 minutes on each side or until cheese melts. Cut into quarters. Yield: 4 servings (serving size: 1 sandwich quarter).

CALORIES 338 (30% from fat); FAT 11.1g (sat 5.7g, mono 3.5g, poly 1g); PROTEIN 14.3g; CARB 44.8g; FIBER 4.4g; CHOL 28mg; IRON 2.9mg; SODIUM 785mg; CALC 287mg

Eggplant-and-Portobello Mushroom Melts

- 4 portobello mushrooms (about 10 ounces)
- 4 (½-inch-thick) slices peeled eggplant (about 8 ounces)
- ¼ cup balsamic vinaigrette (such as Wish-Bone), divided
- ¼ cup chopped bottled roasted red bell peppers
- 2 tablespoons chopped fresh basil
- 4 (½-ounce) slices provolone cheese
- 4 (2-ounce) onion rolls, halved
- ½ cup spinach leaves

1. Preheat broiler.
2. Remove stems from mushrooms; discard stems. Remove brown gills from undersides of mushrooms using a sharp knife, and discard gills. Place mushrooms and eggplant on a broiler pan; brush vegetables with 1 tablespoon vinaigrette. Broil 6 minutes. Turn vegetables over, and brush with 1 tablespoon vinaigrette. Broil an additional 5 minutes or until tender.
3. Combine bell peppers and basil. Spoon 1 tablespoon pepper mixture over each eggplant slice. Top each mushroom with 1 cheese slice. Broil 1 minute or until cheese melts. Brush 2 tablespoons vinaigrette evenly over cut sides of onion rolls. Arrange spinach evenly on bottom halves of rolls. Top each roll half with 1 mushroom and 1 eggplant slice; cover with roll tops. Yield: 4 servings.

CALORIES 276 (30% from fat); FAT 9.3g (sat 3.5g, mono 2.5g, poly 2.5g); PROTEIN 12g; CARB 39.6g; FIBER 3.9g; CHOL 15mg; IRON 2.9mg; SODIUM 564mg; CALC 205mg

Ham and Cheese Breakfast Sandwich with Mango Chutney

This sandwich packs protein from egg and soy ham, calcium from cheese, and fiber and B vitamins from the whole-grain muffin. If you can't find soy ham, use Canadian bacon or ham.

- Cooking spray
- 8 (½-ounce) slices soy ham (such as Lightlife) or Canadian bacon
- 4 large eggs
- 4 whole-grain English muffins, split and toasted
- 8 teaspoons mango chutney
- ¾ cup (3 ounces) reduced-fat shredded sharp Cheddar cheese

1. Preheat broiler.

2. Heat a large nonstick skillet over medium-high heat. Coat pan with cooking spray. Add ham; cook 2 minutes on each side or until lightly browned. Remove from pan; keep warm. Reduce heat to medium; recoat pan with cooking spray. Break eggs into hot pan; cook 1 minute on each side or until desired degree of doneness.

3. Place muffin halves, cut sides up, on a baking sheet. Spread 2 teaspoons chutney over bottom half of each muffin; top with 2 ham slices, 1 egg, and 1 tablespoon cheese. Sprinkle 2 tablespoons cheese over top half of each muffin. Broil 1½ minutes or until bubbly. Place top halves of muffins over bottom halves. Yield: 4 servings (serving size: 1 sandwich).

CALORIES 334 (30% from fat); FAT 11g (sat 4.8g, mono 3.7g, poly 1.5g); PROTEIN 24.8g; CARB 34.7g; FIBER 4.7g; CHOL 228mg; IRON 3.4mg; SODIUM 865mg; CALC 380mg

Pepperoni, Provolone, and Pesto Stromboli

This sandwich uses meatless pepperoni, which is thicker and less chewy than regular pepperoni.

- 1 cup warm water (100° to 110°)
- 1 package dry yeast (about 2¼ teaspoons)
- 3 cups plus 2 tablespoons all-purpose flour, divided
- 1 tablespoon sugar
- ¼ teaspoon salt
- Cooking spray
- ⅓ cup commercial pesto (such as DiGiorno)
- 1½ cups (6 ounces) shredded provolone cheese
- ¼ cup chopped pitted kalamata olives
- 1 (7-ounce) bottle roasted red bell peppers, drained and chopped
- 1 (4-ounce) package meatless fat-free pepperoni (such as Lightlife Smart Deli)

1. Combine warm water and yeast in a large bowl; let stand 5 minutes. Lightly spoon flour into dry measuring cups; level with a knife. Add 3 cups flour, sugar, and salt to yeast mixture; stir to form a dough. Turn dough out onto a floured surface. Knead until smooth and elastic (about 5 minutes); add enough of remaining flour, 1 tablespoon at a time, to prevent dough from sticking to hands (dough will feel sticky). Place dough in a large bowl coated with cooking spray, turning to coat top. Cover and let rise in a warm place (85°), free from drafts, 1 hour or until doubled in size. (Gently press two fingers into dough. If indentation remains, dough has risen enough.) Punch dough down; cover and let rest 5 minutes.

2. Preheat oven to 350°.

3. Press dough into a 15 x 10–inch jelly-roll pan coated with cooking spray. Spread pesto over dough, leaving a 1-inch border; top with cheese, olives, peppers, and pepperoni, pressing gently into dough. Beginning with a long side, roll up jelly-roll fashion. Press seam firmly to seal. Place roll, seam side down, on pan. Cut 4 slits across top of dough using a sharp knife; let rise 30 minutes. Lightly coat dough with cooking spray. Bake at 350° for 40 minutes. Let stand 10 minutes before slicing. Cut crosswise into 16 slices. Yield: 8 servings (serving size: 2 slices).

CALORIES 361 (32% from fat); FAT 13g (sat 4.4g, mono 3.6g, poly 2.4g); PROTEIN 16.8g; CARB 44.7g; FIBER 2.4g; CHOL 18mg; IRON 3.2mg; SODIUM 708mg; CALC 167mg

Salad Niçoise in Pita Pockets

(pictured on page 274)

Fresh green beans give this tuna sandwich, inspired by the classic Mediterranean salad, an interesting crunch. Cooking the beans in the microwave saves time.

- 1 cup (1-inch) cut fresh green beans (about 4 ounces)
- 1 tablespoon water
- ¼ cup niçoise olives, pitted and chopped (about 18 olives)
- 1 tablespoon capers
- 1 (12-ounce) can solid white tuna in water, drained
- 1 tablespoon extravirgin olive oil
- 1 tablespoon fresh lemon juice
- ½ teaspoon salt
- 2 (6-inch) whole wheat pitas, cut in half
- 4 curly leaf lettuce leaves

1. Combine beans and water in a small microwave-safe bowl; cover. Microwave at HIGH 1½ minutes or until beans are crisp-tender; drain. Rinse with cold water. Drain; cool. Combine beans, olives, capers, and tuna.

2. Combine oil, juice, and salt, stirring with a whisk. Pour oil mixture over tuna mixture, and toss gently to coat.

3. Line each pita half with 1 lettuce leaf; spoon about ½ cup tuna mixture into each pita half. Yield: 4 servings (serving size: 1 stuffed pita half).

CALORIES 253 (30% from fat); FAT 8.3g (sat 1.5g, mono 4.4g, poly 1.7g); PROTEIN 24.1g; CARB 21.6g; FIBER 4.2g; CHOL 36mg; IRON 2.6mg; SODIUM 702mg; CALC 48mg

Grilled Tuna Sandwiches with Onions, Bell Peppers, and Chile-Cilantro Mayonnaise

The tangy citrus quality of the mayonnaise pairs well with the grilled tuna.

- 2 tablespoons chopped fresh cilantro
- 6 tablespoons low-fat mayonnaise
- 1 teaspoon ground ancho chile pepper
- 1 teaspoon grated lime rind
- 1 teaspoon fresh lime juice
- ¼ teaspoon ground chipotle chile pepper
- 5 teaspoons olive oil, divided
- 4 (¼-inch-thick) slices Oso Sweet or other sweet onion
- 1 red bell pepper, seeded and quartered
- ½ teaspoon salt, divided
- 4 (5-ounce) tuna steaks (about ¾ inch thick)
- ¼ teaspoon ground cumin
- ¼ teaspoon freshly ground black pepper
- 4 (2-ounce) sandwich buns
- 4 red leaf lettuce leaves

1. Heat a grill pan over medium-high heat.

2. Combine first 6 ingredients in a small bowl.

3. Brush 3 teaspoons oil evenly over onion and bell pepper; sprinkle with ¼ teaspoon salt. Place onion and bell pepper on grill pan; cook 3½ minutes on each side or until tender. Remove from pan.

4. Brush 2 teaspoons oil evenly over tuna; sprinkle with remaining ¼ teaspoon salt, cumin, and black pepper. Place tuna on grill pan; cook 3½ minutes on each side or until medium-rare or desired degree of doneness.

5. Split each bun in half horizontally. Spread mayonnaise mixture evenly over cut sides of buns. Top bottom half of each bun with 1 lettuce leaf, 1 bell pepper quarter, 1 onion slice, and 1 tuna steak. Cover with top halves of buns. Yield: 4 servings (serving size: 1 sandwich).

CALORIES 434 (24% from fat); FAT 11.7g (sat 1.8g, mono 5.8g, poly 1.6g); PROTEIN 38.9g; CARB 41.8g; FIBER 3.4g; CHOL 64mg; IRON 3.4mg; SODIUM 888mg; CALC 119mg

Grilled Tuna Sandwiches with Onions, Bell Peppers, and Chile-Cilantro Mayonnaise

Shrimp Po'boy with Spicy Ketchup

A New Orleans specialty, this sandwich is often made with deep-fried shrimp. Oven-frying the shrimp, which are coated in garlicky breadcrumbs, delivers big flavor without the fat.

- 3 tablespoons dry breadcrumbs
- ¼ teaspoon salt
- ¼ teaspoon black pepper
- 1 garlic clove, minced
- 1 tablespoon olive oil
- 1 pound large shrimp, peeled and deveined
- ¼ cup ketchup
- 1½ teaspoons fresh lemon juice
- ½ teaspoon Worcestershire sauce
- ¼ teaspoon chili powder
- ¼ teaspoon hot sauce
- 2 (10-inch) submarine rolls, split
- 2 cups torn curly leaf lettuce
- ½ cup thinly sliced red onion

1. Prepare broiler.

2. Line a large baking sheet with heavy-duty foil. Combine first 4 ingredients in a medium bowl, stirring with a fork. Combine oil and shrimp; toss well. Place half of shrimp in breadcrumb mixture; toss well to coat. Place breaded shrimp in a single layer on prepared baking sheet. Repeat procedure with remaining shrimp and breadcrumb mixture. Broil 4 minutes or until shrimp are done.

3. Combine ketchup, juice, Worcestershire, chili powder, and hot sauce in a small bowl, stirring with a whisk.

4. Spread 2 tablespoons ketchup mixture over cut sides of each roll half. Place 1 cup lettuce over bottom half of each roll, and top with ¼ cup onion. Arrange 1 cup shrimp on each roll half; top with remaining roll half. Cut sandwiches in half. Yield: 4 servings (serving size: 1 sandwich half).

CALORIES 401 (20% from fat); FAT 9.1g (sat 1.7g, mono 4.6g, poly 1.7g); PROTEIN 30g; CARB 48.9g; FIBER 3g; CHOL 172mg; IRON 5.3mg; SODIUM 864mg; CALC 183mg

Gyros

A Greek specialty, gyros are traditionally made from spiced, spit-roasted lamb. In this recipe, we mold a ground beef and lamb mixture into loaves. The yogurt-cucumber sauce is a variation on another traditional Greek favorite, tzatziki.

LOAVES:

1 teaspoon onion powder
1 teaspoon garlic powder
1 teaspoon dried oregano
2 teaspoons fresh lemon juice
1/4 teaspoon salt
3 garlic cloves, minced
6 ounces ground sirloin
6 ounces ground lamb
Cooking spray
1/8 teaspoon ground red pepper

SAUCE:

1 cup peeled shredded cucumber
1/4 cup vertically sliced red onion
1 tablespoon chopped fresh mint
1/2 teaspoon garlic powder
1/2 teaspoon fresh lemon juice
1/8 teaspoon salt
1/8 teaspoon black pepper
1 (8-ounce) carton plain fat-free yogurt

REMAINING INGREDIENT:

4 pocketless pitas

1. Preheat broiler.

2. To prepare loaves, combine first 8 ingredients. Divide mixture in half, forming each half into a 6 x 3–inch loaf. Place each loaf on a broiler pan coated with cooking spray; broil 7 minutes on each side or until done.

3. Sprinkle loaves with ground red pepper. Cut each loaf crosswise into 1/8-inch slices.

4. To prepare sauce, place cucumber and red onion onto several layers of heavy-duty paper towels. Cover with additional paper towels, and let stand 5 minutes.

5. Combine cucumber mixture, mint, and next 5 ingredients, stirring well. Divide meat slices among pitas; top each serving with about 1/4 cup sauce. Yield: 4 servings (serving size: 1 sandwich).

CALORIES 375 (28% from fat); FAT 11.6g (sat 4.4g, mono 4.7g, poly 1g); PROTEIN 25g; CARB 42.4g; FIBER 2.3g; CHOL 61mg; IRON 3.5mg; SODIUM 627mg; CALC 158mg

Grilled Vidalia Onion and Steak Sandwiches

Grilled Vidalia Onion and Steak Sandwiches

The cola in the marinade tenderizes the flank steak.

STEAK:

¾ cup cola
2 tablespoons red wine vinegar
1 teaspoon coarsely ground black pepper
½ teaspoon salt
½ teaspoon ground chipotle chile pepper
4 garlic cloves, crushed
1 bay leaf, crushed
1 (1½-pound) flank steak, trimmed

DRESSING:

¾ cup minced arugula
½ cup low-fat mayonnaise

REMAINING INGREDIENTS:

Cooking spray
6 (½-inch-thick) slices Vidalia onion
6 (2-ounce) Kaiser rolls
12 (¼-inch-thick) slices tomato

1. To prepare steak, combine first 7 ingredients in a large zip-top plastic bag. Add steak; seal and marinate in refrigerator 2 hours, turning bag occasionally. Remove steak from bag, reserving marinade. Pour marinade into a microwave-safe bowl; microwave at HIGH 2 minutes or until mixture comes to a boil. Set aside.

2. Prepare grill or broiler.

3. To prepare dressing, combine arugula and mayonnaise; set aside.

4. Place steak on grill rack or broiler pan coated with cooking spray; grill 8 minutes on each side or until steak is medium-rare or desired degree of doneness. Remove steak from grill; cover and let stand 5 minutes. Place onion slices on grill rack; grill 4 minutes on each side, basting occasionally with reserved marinade. Place rolls on grill rack, cut sides down; grill 2 minutes or until lightly browned.

5. Cut steak diagonally across grain into thin slices. Spread 2 tablespoons dressing on bottom half of each roll. Divide steak, tomato, and onion evenly among bottom halves of rolls. Top with top halves of rolls. Yield: 6 servings (serving size: 1 sandwich).

CALORIES 417 (24% from fat); FAT 11g (sat 3.3g, mono 3.8g, poly 2.2g); PROTEIN 30.5g; CARB 49.1g; FIBER 3.2g; CHOL 38mg; IRON 3.9mg; SODIUM 747mg; CALC 104mg

Barbecue Brisket Sandwiches

Most meats, especially tough cuts, take well to pressure cooking and become much more tender. The shredded meat mixture can be refrigerated and reheated for dinners later in the week.

1 cup sliced onion, separated into rings
¾ cup bottled chili sauce
½ cup beer
1 tablespoon Worcestershire sauce
1 (2½-pound) beef brisket, trimmed
1 teaspoon black pepper
4 garlic cloves, minced
¼ cup packed brown sugar
8 (2½-ounce) submarine rolls

1. Combine sliced onion, chili sauce, beer, and Worcestershire sauce in a 6-quart pressure cooker. Bring to a boil; reduce heat, and simmer 5 minutes. Remove ½ cup chili sauce mixture from pressure cooker.

2. Cut brisket in half crosswise. Rub brisket with pepper and garlic. Place in pressure cooker. Spoon ½ cup chili sauce mixture over brisket. Close lid securely; bring to high pressure over high heat (about 5 minutes). Adjust heat to medium or level needed to maintain high pressure, and cook 1 hour. Remove from heat; place pressure cooker under cold running water. Remove lid.

3. Remove brisket from pressure cooker, and set aside. Add brown sugar to chili sauce mixture in pressure cooker; bring to a boil. Reduce heat, and simmer, uncovered, 5 minutes, stirring frequently. Shred brisket using 2 forks. Return meat to sauce in pressure cooker; cook until thoroughly heated. Spoon 1 cup meat with sauce over bottom of each roll; cover with tops of rolls. Yield: 8 servings.

CALORIES 494 (28% from fat); FAT 15.2g (sat 4g, mono 4.9g, poly 0.4g); PROTEIN 33.2g; CARB 54.2g; FIBER 0.9g; CHOL 79mg; IRON 5.9mg; SODIUM 886mg; CALC 43mg

Pressed Cubano with Bacon

Garlic oil gives these sandwiches a crisp, flavorful crust. Hawaiian rolls provide a slightly sweet contrast to the salty ham, pickles, and mustard. To make this easy supper even quicker to prepare, use precooked bacon. Serve with banana peppers.

- 1 teaspoon extravirgin olive oil
- 1 garlic clove, minced
- 4 (3-ounce) Hawaiian rolls, sliced in half horizontally
- 2 tablespoons yellow mustard
- 8 (½-ounce) slices reduced-fat Swiss cheese, divided
- 4 bacon slices, cooked and halved
- 12 dill pickle slices
- 2 teaspoons minced fresh cilantro
- 6 ounces thinly sliced 33%-less-sodium ham
- 2 ounces thinly sliced deli oven-roasted turkey breast

1. Combine oil and garlic.
2. Spread cut sides of rolls evenly with mustard. Place 1 cheese slice, 2 bacon halves, 3 pickle slices, and ½ teaspoon cilantro on bottom half of each roll. Divide ham and turkey evenly among bottom halves of rolls; top each serving with 1 cheese slice and top half of roll. Brush garlic oil evenly over outside of rolls.
3. Heat a large nonstick skillet over medium heat. Add 2 sandwiches to pan. Place a cast-iron or heavy skillet on top of sandwiches, and press gently to flatten. Cook 3 minutes on each side or until cheese melts and bread is toasted (leave cast-iron skillet on sandwiches while they cook). Repeat with remaining sandwiches. Yield: 4 servings (serving size: 1 sandwich).

CALORIES 432 (30% from fat); FAT 14.5g (sat 6.3g, mono 4.1g, poly 1.2g); PROTEIN 27.1g; CARB 47.6g; FIBER 2.8g; CHOL 49mg; IRON 3.1mg; SODIUM 1,053mg; CALC 292mg

Chipotle Pulled-Pork Barbecue Sandwiches

Sweet-and-sour pickles are a tasty balance to the smoky barbecue sauce in this updated southern-style sandwich. Serve with coleslaw.

- 1 (7-ounce) can chipotle chiles in adobo sauce
- ¼ cup barbecue sauce
- 1 teaspoon garlic powder
- 1½ teaspoons ground cumin
- 1 (1-pound) pork tenderloin, trimmed and cut into ½-inch cubes
- 1 (14.5-ounce) can diced tomatoes, undrained
- 1 tablespoon olive oil
- 3 cups thinly sliced onion
- 2 teaspoons chopped fresh thyme
- 1 teaspoon sugar
- 6 (½-ounce) slices provolone cheese
- 12 sandwich-cut bread-and-butter pickles
- 6 (2½-ounce) Kaiser rolls

1. Remove 1 chile from can; reserve remaining chiles and sauce for another use. Finely chop chile.
2. Place chopped chile, barbecue sauce, and next 4 ingredients in a medium saucepan; bring to a boil over medium-high heat. Cover, reduce heat, and simmer 45 minutes, stirring occasionally. Uncover and cook 10 minutes or until sauce thickens and pork is very tender; remove from heat. Remove pork from sauce; shred pork. Return pork to sauce.
3. Heat oil in a large nonstick skillet over medium-high heat. Add onion, thyme, and sugar; cook 10 minutes or until golden, stirring occasionally.
4. Heat a large nonstick skillet over medium heat. Place 1 cheese slice, ½ cup pork mixture, about 2 tablespoons onions, and 2 pickle slices on bottom half of each roll. Cover with top halves of rolls. Add 3 sandwiches to pan. Place a cast-iron or heavy skillet on top of sandwiches; press gently to flatten. Cook 2 minutes on each side or until cheese melts and bread is toasted (leave cast-iron skillet on sandwiches while they cook). Repeat procedure with remaining sandwiches. Yield: 6 servings (serving size: 1 sandwich).

CALORIES 431 (26% from fat); FAT 12.4g (sat 3.9g, mono 3.7g, poly 1.8g); PROTEIN 28.3g; CARB 51.4g; FIBER 4.7g; CHOL 59mg; IRON 4.1mg; SODIUM 910mg; CALC 207mg

Chipotle Pulled-Pork Barbecue Sandwiches

Cashew Chicken Salad Sandwiches

Cashew Chicken Salad Sandwiches

This sandwich goes together as fast as making a turkey sandwich but is much more interesting. Add lettuce and tomato, if you'd like.

- ¼ cup fat-free sour cream
- 1 tablespoon light mayonnaise
- ¼ teaspoon curry powder
- 2 cups chopped roasted skinless, boneless chicken breast (about 2 breasts)
- ⅓ cup chopped celery
- 2 tablespoons chopped dry-roasted cashews
- 1 tablespoon finely chopped green onions
- 2 (2-ounce) whole wheat hamburger buns

1. Combine first 3 ingredients in a large bowl, stirring until well blended. Add chicken, celery, cashews, and green onions; stir well. Serve on buns. Yield: 2 servings (serving size: ⅔ cup chicken salad and 1 bun).

CALORIES 353 (26% from fat); FAT 10.3g (sat 2.6g, mono 1.5g, poly 1.8g); PROTEIN 31.6g; CARB 35.8g; FIBER 4.8g; CHOL 69mg; IRON 1.8mg; SODIUM 925mg; CALC 115mg

Smoky Bacon and Blue Cheese Chicken Salad Pitas

You can make the chicken salad ahead; place it in pita halves just before serving.

- ¾ cup plain fat-free yogurt
- ¼ cup (1 ounce) crumbled blue cheese
- 2 tablespoons light mayonnaise
- ½ teaspoon freshly ground black pepper
- 3 cups shredded romaine lettuce
- 1½ cups shredded cooked chicken (about 6 ounces)
- 4 bacon slices, cooked and crumbled
- 2 medium tomatoes, seeded and chopped
- 4 (6-inch) whole wheat pitas, cut in half

1. Combine first 4 ingredients, stirring well. Combine lettuce, chicken, bacon, and tomatoes in a medium bowl, stirring well. Drizzle yogurt mixture over chicken mixture; toss gently to coat. Spoon ½ cup salad into each pita half. Serve immediately. Yield: 4 servings (serving size: 2 stuffed pita halves).

CALORIES 375 (29% from fat); FAT 12.1g (sat 3.7g, mono 3.6g, poly 3.1g); PROTEIN 26.1g; CARB 43.8g; FIBER 6.3g; CHOL 55mg; IRON 3.5mg; SODIUM 696mg; CALC 130mg

Balsamic-Glazed Chicken Sandwiches with Red Onions and Goat Cheese

You'll need less than half an hour to prepare this tangy chicken sandwich.

- ¾ cup balsamic vinegar
- ½ cup dry red wine
- 2 teaspoons brown sugar
- 1 teaspoon low-sodium soy sauce
- 2 (6-ounce) skinless, boneless chicken breast halves
- ½ teaspoon salt
- ¼ teaspoon freshly ground black pepper
- Cooking spray
- 1 tablespoon olive oil
- 1½ cups thinly vertically sliced red onion
- 1 (3-ounce) package goat cheese
- 4 (2-ounce) hoagie or Kaiser rolls
- 1 cup trimmed arugula

1. Combine first 4 ingredients in a small saucepan over medium heat. Bring mixture to a boil, stirring until sugar dissolves. Cook until reduced to ⅓ cup (about 12 minutes). Remove from heat; cool slightly.

2. Heat a large nonstick skillet over medium-high heat. Sprinkle chicken with salt and pepper. Coat pan with cooking spray. Add chicken to pan; cook 4 minutes on each side or until done. Remove chicken from pan; thinly slice. Cover and keep warm.

3. Add oil to pan; reduce temperature to medium-low. Add onion; cook 5 minutes or until onion is soft and beginning to brown, stirring frequently. Remove from heat.

4. Spread about 1½ tablespoons goat cheese evenly over bottom half of each roll; divide sliced chicken and onion evenly over rolls. Drizzle each serving with about 1 tablespoon balsamic mixture; top with ¼ cup trimmed arugula and top halves of rolls. Serve immediately. Yield: 4 servings (serving size: 1 sandwich).

CALORIES 424 (25% from fat); FAT 11.6g (sat 4.2g, mono 4.4g, poly 1.7g); PROTEIN 30.1g; CARB 43.9g; FIBER 2.2g; CHOL 59mg; IRON 3.7mg; SODIUM 796mg; CALC 129mg

Spicy Chicken and Arugula Sandwich

We found plain focaccia, perfect for this sandwich, at the deli counter. The arugula adds a peppery bite, but any other salad green will work.

- 2 teaspoons olive oil
- 2 (6-ounce) skinless, boneless chicken breast halves
- 1 tablespoon fajita seasoning
- ¼ cup light mayonnaise
- 3 tablespoons chopped fresh cilantro
- 1 teaspoon grated lime rind
- 1 tablespoon fresh lime juice
- 1 (9-ounce) round loaf focaccia, halved horizontally
- 1 medium ripe tomato, thinly sliced (about 4 ounces)
- 1½ cups trimmed arugula

1. Heat oil in a large nonstick skillet over medium-high heat. Place heavy-duty plastic wrap over chicken; pound each piece to a ¼-inch thickness using a meat mallet or rolling pin. Sprinkle both sides of chicken with fajita seasoning. Add chicken to pan; cook 2 minutes on each side or until done. Cut into (1-inch-thick) slices.

2. While chicken cooks, combine mayonnaise, cilantro, rind, and juice; spread evenly over cut sides of bread. Arrange chicken on bottom half of bread; top with tomato and arugula. Cover with top half of bread. Cut into 4 wedges. Yield: 4 servings (serving size: 1 wedge).

CALORIES 341 (26% from fat); FAT 9.9g (sat 2.3g, mono 2.7g, poly 4.4g); PROTEIN 24.9g; CARB 37.6g; FIBER 1.7g; CHOL 53mg; IRON 2.5mg; SODIUM 545mg; CALC 35mg

Turkey and Cheese Panini

In Italian, "panini" means small bread and refers to a pressed sandwich. Using a grill pan gives the sandwich impressive grill marks, but the recipe works just as well in a regular nonstick skillet. If you don't have provolone cheese, you can use mozzarella.

2 tablespoons fat-free mayonnaise
4 teaspoons basil pesto
8 (1-ounce) thin slices sourdough bread
8 ounces sliced cooked turkey breast
2 ounces thinly sliced provolone cheese
8 (1/8-inch-thick) slices tomato
Cooking spray

1. Combine mayonnaise and pesto, stirring well. Spread 1 tablespoon mayonnaise mixture on each of 4 bread slices; top each slice with 2 ounces turkey, 1/2 ounce cheese, and 2 tomato slices. Top with remaining bread slices.
2. Heat a grill pan over medium heat. Coat pan with cooking spray. Add sandwiches to pan; top with a heavy skillet. Cook 3 minutes on each side or until golden brown. Yield: 4 servings (serving size: 1 sandwich).

CALORIES 257 (29% from fat); FAT 8.2g (sat 2.9g, mono 0.2g, poly 0.1g); PROTEIN 18.4g; CARB 30.4g; FIBER 4.1g; CHOL 30mg; IRON 2.4mg; SODIUM 1,208mg; CALC 204mg

Hot Turkey Sandwiches

Serve these quick-to-make hearty sandwiches for lunch or any time you have turkey leftovers or a rotisserie chicken on hand. Cranberry-shallot chutney adds a sweet tanginess. Bottled chicken gravy will work fine in this recipe.

8 (1-ounce) slices French bread
2 tablespoons light mayonnaise
1/4 cup turkey gravy
4 reduced-sodium bacon slices, cooked and cut in half
12 ounces sliced cooked turkey breast
2 slices provolone cheese, halved
1 cup arugula
1 tablespoon cranberry-shallot chutney

1. Preheat oven to 400°.
2. Place French bread slices on a baking sheet. Spread light mayonnaise evenly over 4 bread slices. Spread turkey gravy evenly over remaining 4 bread slices. Top mayonnaise-spread slices evenly with bacon slices, turkey, and provolone cheese. Bake at 400° for 10 minutes or until cheese melts. Top cheese evenly with arugula. Drizzle with cranberry-shallot chutney. Top with gravy-spread bread slices, and press sandwiches together. Yield: 4 servings (serving size: 1 sandwich).

CALORIES 402 (25% from fat); FAT 11g (sat 4.5g, mono 3.5g, poly 1.2g); PROTEIN 38.2g; CARB 35.1g; FIBER 2.1g; CHOL 89mg; IRON 3.3mg; SODIUM 787mg; CALC 174mg

Barbecue Turkey Burgers

As long as you have the grill pan out, add Spicy Grilled Sweet Potatoes (recipe on page 317) for an easy side.

1/4 cup chopped onion
1/4 cup barbecue sauce, divided
2 tablespoons dry breadcrumbs
2 teaspoons prepared mustard
3/4 teaspoon chili powder
1/2 teaspoon garlic powder
1/4 teaspoon salt
1 pound ground turkey
Cooking spray
4 large leaf lettuce leaves
4 (1/4-inch-thick) slices tomato
4 (1 1/2-ounce) hamburger buns

1. Combine onion, 2 tablespoons barbecue sauce, breadcrumbs, and next 5 ingredients in a medium bowl. Divide turkey mixture into 4 equal portions, shaping each portion into a 1 1/2-inch-thick patty.
2. Heat a grill pan over medium-high heat. Coat pan with cooking spray. Place patties in pan; cook 7 minutes on each side or until done.
3. Place 1 lettuce leaf, 1 tomato slice, and 1 patty on bottom half of each bun. Spread each patty with 1 1/2 teaspoons barbecue sauce. Cover with top halves of buns. Yield: 4 servings (serving size: 1 burger).

CALORIES 310 (22% from fat); FAT 7.6g (sat 2.1g, mono 1.7g, poly 2.8g); PROTEIN 29.9g; CARB 28.5g; FIBER 2.1g; CHOL 65mg; IRON 3.5mg; SODIUM 642mg; CALC 102mg

Barbecue Turkey Burgers

Jamaican Jerk Turkey Burgers with Papaya-Mango Salsa

Fruity salsa is a good match for these spicy burgers. Be sure to coat the burgers and the grill rack with cooking spray to prevent sticking. Prepare the salsa up to a day in advance; refrigerate in a covered container.

SALSA:

- ⅔ cup diced peeled mango
- ⅔ cup diced peeled papaya
- ¼ cup finely chopped red bell pepper
- ¼ cup finely chopped red onion
- 2 tablespoons chopped fresh cilantro
- ½ teaspoon grated lime rind
- 2 tablespoons fresh lime juice

BURGERS:

- 1 cup finely chopped red onion
- ½ cup dry breadcrumbs
- ⅓ cup bottled sweet-and-sour sauce
- ¼ cup finely chopped red bell pepper
- 1 tablespoon Jamaican jerk seasoning (such as Spice Islands)
- 1 large egg white
- 1 pound ground turkey
- Cooking spray
- 4 (2-ounce) Kaiser rolls or hamburger buns, split

1. To prepare salsa, combine first 7 ingredients. Let stand at room temperature at least 30 minutes.

2. Prepare grill.

3. To prepare burgers, combine 1 cup onion and next 5 ingredients, stirring well. Add turkey, and mix well to combine. Divide turkey mixture into 4 equal portions, shaping each into a 1-inch-thick patty. Cover and refrigerate patties 20 minutes.

4. Lightly coat both sides of patties with cooking spray, and place patties on a grill rack coated with cooking spray. Grill 7 minutes on each side or until done.

5. Place Kaiser rolls, cut sides down, on grill rack; grill 1 minute or until lightly toasted. Place 1 patty on bottom half of each roll; top with ½ cup salsa and top half of roll. Yield: 4 servings (serving size: 1 burger).

CALORIES 424 (22% from fat); FAT 10.4g (sat 2.5g, mono 3.7g, poly 2.9g); PROTEIN 24.1g; CARB 58g; FIBER 3.9g; CHOL 67mg; IRON 4mg; SODIUM 818mg; CALC 121mg

California Burgers

Alfalfa sprouts and avocados crown these juicy burgers. A combination of regular ground turkey and ground turkey breast offers superior texture. If you don't need this many burgers, wrap individual patties in plastic wrap and again in foil; freeze. Thaw as many as you need in the refrigerator; cook as directed. The sauce can also be made ahead; cover and chill.

SAUCE:

½ cup ketchup
1 tablespoon Dijon mustard
1 tablespoon fat-free mayonnaise

PATTIES:

½ cup finely chopped shallots
¼ cup dry breadcrumbs
1 teaspoon salt
1 teaspoon Worcestershire sauce
¼ teaspoon freshly ground black pepper
3 garlic cloves, minced
1¼ pounds ground turkey breast
1¼ pounds ground turkey
Cooking spray

REMAINING INGREDIENTS:

10 (2-ounce) hamburger buns
10 red leaf lettuce leaves
20 bread-and-butter pickles
10 (¼-inch-thick) slices red onion, separated into rings
2 peeled avocados, each cut into 10 slices
3 cups alfalfa sprouts

1. Prepare grill or broiler.
2. To prepare sauce, combine first 3 ingredients; set aside.
3. To prepare patties, combine shallots and next 7 ingredients, mixing well. Divide mixture into 10 equal portions, shaping each into a ½-inch-thick patty. Place patties on grill rack or broiler pan coated with cooking spray; grill 4 minutes on each side or until done.
4. Spread 1 tablespoon sauce on top half of each hamburger bun. Layer bottom half of each bun with 1 lettuce leaf, 1 patty, 2 pickles, 1 onion slice, 2 avocado slices, and about ⅓ cup of sprouts. Cover with top halves of buns. Yield: 10 servings (serving size: 1 burger).

CALORIES 384 (29% from fat); FAT 12.4g (sat 2.6g, mono 5.1g, poly 2.8g); PROTEIN 31.4g; CARB 37.5g; FIBER 3.9g; CHOL 68mg; IRON 4mg; SODIUM 828mg; CALC 94mg

Sausage and Egg Burrito

Use two beaten large eggs in place of the egg substitute, if desired. Keep in mind however, that this will increase the total fat to 14.6 grams per serving.

Cooking spray
½ cup chopped red bell pepper
¼ cup chopped onion
3 ounces turkey breakfast sausage
½ cup egg substitute
¼ cup (1 ounce) reduced-fat shredded Cheddar cheese
6 tablespoons bottled salsa, divided
2 (8-inch) fat-free flour tortillas
¼ cup reduced-fat sour cream

1. Heat a medium skillet over medium-high heat. Coat pan with cooking spray. Add bell pepper, onion, and sausage; cook 4 minutes or until browned, stirring to crumble sausage. Add egg substitute; cook 2 minutes, stirring frequently. Remove from heat; stir in cheese and 2 tablespoons salsa. Remove from heat. Cover and let stand 2 minutes.
2. Heat tortillas according to package directions. Spoon half of egg mixture down center of each tortilla; roll up. Serve with remaining salsa and sour cream. Yield: 2 servings (serving size: 1 burrito, 2 tablespoons salsa, and 2 tablespoons sour cream).

CALORIES 314 (28% from fat); FAT 9.6g (sat 4.4g, mono 3.1g, poly 1.8g); PROTEIN 20.7g; CARB 26.9g; FIBER 3.9g; CHOL 50mg; IRON 2.6mg; SODIUM 915mg; CALC 148mg

Boston Baked Beans, page 300

Sides

Baked Apples

Serve these juicy baked apples as a topping for oatmeal or pancakes, or as a side with pork. Any sweet-tart apple such as Ida Red and McIntosh will also work well in place of Galas.

2 cups dried cranberries
1 ¼ cups coarsely chopped walnuts
1 cup packed brown sugar
1 cup water
2 teaspoons ground cinnamon
6 Gala apples, cored and chopped (about 3 pounds)

1. Combine all ingredients in a large microwave-safe dish. Microwave at HIGH 20 minutes or until apples are soft, stirring occasionally. Yield: 6 cups (serving size: ¼ cup).

CALORIES 126 (29% from fat); FAT 4.1g (sat 0.4g, mono 0.6g, poly 3g); PROTEIN 1g; CARB 23.7g; FIBER 2.3g; CHOL 0mg; IRON 0.5mg; SODIUM 4mg; CALC 16mg

Baked Apples

Rum-Spiked Grilled Pineapple

Grilling caramelizes the natural sugars in the fresh pineapple. Serve this as a side dish with barbecued chicken or pork for summer cookouts.

1 pineapple, peeled, cored, halved lengthwise, and sliced lengthwise into 12 wedges (about 1 ½ pounds)
2 tablespoons butter, melted
¼ cup packed light brown sugar
¼ cup dark rum
¼ teaspoon ground cinnamon
Cooking spray
Lime wedges

1. Prepare grill.
2. Brush pineapple with 2 tablespoons butter. Combine brown sugar, rum, and ¼ teaspoon cinnamon in a microwave-safe bowl. Microwave at HIGH 1 ½ minutes or until sugar dissolves. Brush rum mixture evenly over pineapple wedges. Place pineapple on grill rack coated with cooking spray. Grill 3 minutes on each side or until grill marks form and pineapple is thoroughly heated. Serve with lime wedges. Yield: 6 servings (serving size: 2 pineapple wedges).

CALORIES 146 (25% from fat); FAT 4g (sat 2.4g, mono 1g, poly 0.2g); PROTEIN 0.7g; CARB 23.4g; FIBER 1.6g; CHOL 10mg; IRON 0.5mg; SODIUM 32g; CALC 25mg

Raspberry-Asparagus Medley

1 tablespoon white wine vinegar
2 tablespoons raspberry preserves
1 ½ teaspoons Dijon mustard
⅛ teaspoon salt
½ teaspoon grated lemon rind
2 ½ cups (1-inch) slices asparagus (about 1 pound)
1 ½ cups fresh raspberries
2 tablespoons finely chopped pecans, toasted

1. Combine first 4 ingredients in a small saucepan; bring to a boil. Remove from heat; stir in rind.
2. Cook asparagus in boiling water 2 minutes or until crisp-tender. Drain and plunge into ice water, and drain. Combine preserves mixture, asparagus, and raspberries in a bowl; toss gently to coat. Sprinkle with pecans. Yield: 6 servings (serving size: about ½ cup).

CALORIES 65 (30% from fat); FAT 2.2g (sat 0.2g, mono 1.1g, poly 0.7g); PROTEIN 2.3g; CARB 10.8g; FIBER 3.9g; CHOL 0mg; IRON 1mg; SODIUM 82mg; CALC 27mg

Rum-Spiked Grilled Pineapple

Haricots Verts and Grape Tomato Salad with Crème Fraîche Dressing

Haricots verts (ah-ree-koh VEHR) are tender, young French green beans. If not labeled as such in your market, look for slim, petite green beans. Crème fraîche adds a nutty flavor and rich texture to the dressing; look for it near the gourmet cheeses in your supermarket. Whole sour cream is an acceptable substitute.

- 1 pound haricots verts, trimmed
- ¼ cup finely chopped fresh basil
- 2 tablespoons minced shallots
- 2 tablespoons fresh lemon juice
- 2 tablespoons crème fraîche or whole sour cream
- 1 tablespoon honey
- ½ teaspoon salt
- 1 pint grape or cherry tomatoes, halved
- 1 tablespoon pine nuts, toasted

1. Cook haricots verts in boiling water 2 minutes or until crisp-tender. Drain. Rinse with cold water; drain.
2. Combine basil and next 5 ingredients in a large bowl, stirring with a whisk. Add haricots verts and grape tomatoes; toss gently to coat. Divide salad mixture evenly among 6 plates, and sprinkle with nuts. Yield: 6 servings (serving size: about ¾ cup salad and ½ teaspoon nuts).

CALORIES 74 (34% from fat); FAT 2.8g (sat 1.1g, mono 0.8g, poly 0.6g); PROTEIN 1.7g; CARB 11.4g; FIBER 3.5g; CHOL 7mg; IRON 0.7mg; SODIUM 203mg; CALC 47mg

Green Beans with Roasted Onion Vinaigrette

Serve these as a side with a rotisserie chicken for a simple summer meal. To simplify things, you can make and refrigerate the vinaigrette and steam and chill the green beans a day ahead.

- 2 pounds green beans, trimmed
- 2 red onions, peeled (about 1 pound)
- 4 teaspoons olive oil, divided
- ¼ teaspoon salt
- ¼ teaspoon black pepper
- 2 sprigs fresh thyme
- 1 tablespoon chopped fresh dill
- 3 tablespoons Champagne vinegar or white wine vinegar
- 1 tablespoon stone-ground mustard

1. Preheat oven to 400°.
2. Cook green beans in boiling water 5 minutes. Drain and plunge beans into ice water; drain. Place beans in a large bowl.
3. Cut onions in half vertically. Drizzle cut side of each onion half with ¼ teaspoon oil. Sprinkle halves evenly with salt and pepper. Place 1 thyme sprig on 1 onion half; top with other half. Wrap in foil. Repeat procedure with remaining thyme and onion halves. Bake wrapped onions at 400° for 1 hour or until tender. Cool to room temperature. Discard thyme; chop onions.
4. Combine remaining 1 tablespoon olive oil, onions, dill, vinegar, and mustard in a small bowl. Toss beans with onion mixture. Yield: 8 servings (serving size: about 4 ounces green beans and ¼ cup onion vinaigrette).

CALORIES 83 (29% from fat); FAT 2.7g (sat 0.4g, mono 1.7g, poly 0.4g); PROTEIN 2.9g; CARB 14g; FIBER 4.8g; CHOL 0mg; IRON 1.6mg; SODIUM 109mg; CALC 65mg

Green Beans with Roasted Onion Vinaigrette

Boston Baked Beans

(pictured on page 294)

Molasses was first shipped to Boston from the West Indies in the late 1600s and soon became a signature flavor in this New England recipe.

- 1 cup chopped onion
- ½ cup ketchup
- ½ cup maple syrup
- 2 tablespoons light brown sugar
- 2 tablespoons molasses
- 1 teaspoon dry mustard
- ½ teaspoon salt
- ¼ teaspoon ground allspice
- ⅛ teaspoon ground ginger
- 3 (15-ounce) cans small white beans, rinsed and drained
- 4 bacon slices, uncooked and chopped

1. Combine all ingredients in an electric slow cooker. Cover and cook on LOW 5 hours. Yield: 10 servings (serving size: ½ cup).

CALORIES 141 (7% from fat); FAT 1.1g (sat 0.2g, mono 0.2g, poly 0.2g); PROTEIN 5.8g; CARB 32.4g; FIBER 4g; CHOL 2mg; IRON 1.5mg; SODIUM 531mg; CALC 64mg

Country Lima Beans

Humble ingredients create a flavorful, satisfying dish. Oven cooking works well and makes preparation a snap. Serve as a side with roast beef, pork, or chicken; or you can even enjoy this as a main dish with a simple green salad.

- 2 cups dried lima beans (about 1 pound)
- 1 teaspoon salt
- ½ teaspoon freshly ground black pepper
- 3 bacon slices, chopped
- 1 cup chopped onion
- 1 cup finely chopped carrot
- 2 cups water
- 2 tablespoons butter, softened

1. Sort and wash beans; place in a large Dutch oven. Cover with water to 2 inches above beans; cover and let stand 8 hours or overnight. Drain beans. Return beans to pan; stir in salt and black pepper.

2. Preheat oven to 300°.

3. Cook bacon slices in a large nonstick skillet over medium heat until crisp. Remove bacon from pan with a slotted spoon; set bacon aside. Add onion and carrot to drippings in pan; sauté 5 minutes or until golden. Add onion mixture, bacon, 2 cups water, and butter to bean mixture in Dutch oven; stir well. Cover and bake at 300° for 2½ hours or until beans are tender, stirring every hour. Yield: 8 cups (serving size: 1 cup).

CALORIES 248 (26% from fat); FAT 7.2g (sat 2.8g, mono 2.9g, poly 0.8g); PROTEIN 11.8g; CARB 35.4g; FIBER 11.2g; CHOL 13mg; IRON 3.3mg; SODIUM 404mg; CALC 53mg

Broccoli with Pan-Roasted Peppers

This colorful side dish is a fine way to perk up a weeknight rotisserie chicken dinner.

- 4 cups broccoli florets (about 1½ pounds)
- 1 tablespoon olive oil
- 1¾ cups (1-inch) red bell pepper strips (2 medium)
- 1¾ cups (1-inch) yellow bell pepper strips (2 medium)
- ¼ cup red wine vinegar
- 1 teaspoon sugar
- ¾ teaspoon salt
- ¼ teaspoon freshly ground black pepper

1. Cook broccoli in boiling water 4 minutes or until crisp-tender, and drain. Rinse with cold water; drain.

2. Heat oil in a large nonstick skillet over medium-high heat. Add bell peppers and red wine vinegar. Cover, reduce heat to medium, and cook 15 minutes or until peppers are tender, stirring frequently. Uncover; sprinkle with sugar. Increase heat to medium-high; cook 2 minutes or until liquid evaporates and bell peppers begin to brown, stirring constantly. Add broccoli; cook 2 minutes or until thoroughly heated, tossing to combine. Remove from heat, and stir in salt and black pepper. Yield: 6 servings (serving size: 1 cup).

CALORIES 65 (39% from fat); FAT 2.8g (sat 0.4g, mono 1.7g, poly 0.5g); PROTEIN 2.5g; CARB 9.9g; FIBER 1.4g; CHOL 0mg; IRON 1mg; SODIUM 311mg; CALC 31mg

Broccoli, Cheese, and Rice Casserole

This family favorite is versatile because it works equally well for potluck suppers or Sunday dinner. It's also easy to prepare; all of the ingredients are combined at once.

- 1 cup uncooked instant rice
- ½ cup chopped onion
- ¼ cup fat-free milk
- 4 ounces light processed cheese, cubed (such as Velveeta Light)
- 2 tablespoons butter, softened
- 2 (10-ounce) packages frozen chopped broccoli, thawed and drained
- 1 (10.75-ounce) can condensed 30% reduced-sodium, 98% fat-free cream of mushroom soup, undiluted (such as Campbell's)

1. Preheat oven to 350°.

2. Combine all ingredients in a large bowl, and spoon into a 2-quart casserole. Bake at 350° for 45 minutes. Yield: 8 servings (serving size: ½ cup).

CALORIES 137 (29% from fat); FAT 4.4g (sat 1.7g, mono 1.4g, poly 0.9g); PROTEIN 6.6g; CARB 19.2g; FIBER 2.2g; CHOL 8mg; IRON 1.1mg; SODIUM 410mg; CALC 160mg

Corn Fritter Casserole

Corn Fritter Casserole

This moist, sweet-savory side dish is a cross between corn bread and corn pudding.

3 tablespoons butter, softened
3 large egg whites
1 (8-ounce) block fat-free cream cheese, softened
½ cup finely chopped onion
½ cup finely chopped red bell pepper
1 (15¼-ounce) can whole-kernel corn, drained
1 (14¾-ounce) can cream-style corn
1 (8½-ounce) package corn muffin mix (such as Jiffy)
¼ teaspoon black pepper
Cooking spray

1. Preheat oven to 375°.
2. Combine first 3 ingredients in a large bowl, stirring with a whisk until smooth. Stir in onion, bell pepper, whole-kernel corn, and cream-style corn; mix well. Add muffin mix and black pepper, stirring until well combined. Pour into an 11 x 7–inch baking dish coated with cooking spray. Bake at 375° for 50 minutes or until a wooden pick inserted in center comes out clean. Yield: 9 servings (serving size: about ⅔ cup).

CALORIES 247 (31% from fat); FAT 8.4g (sat 3.7g, mono 2.7g, poly 0.7g); PROTEIN 8.6g; CARB 36.7g; FIBER 1.9g; CHOL 31mg; IRON 1.3mg; SODIUM 629mg; CALC 72mg

Roasted Cauliflower with Fresh Herbs and Parmesan

Use any fresh herbs you have on hand for this recipe. While parsley, tarragon, and thyme make a nice combination, you can also try sage, chives, and rosemary. The recipe can easily be halved.

12 cups cauliflower florets (about 2 heads)
1½ tablespoons olive oil
1 tablespoon chopped fresh parsley
2 teaspoons chopped fresh thyme
2 teaspoons chopped fresh tarragon
3 garlic cloves, minced
¼ cup (1 ounce) grated fresh Parmesan cheese
2 tablespoons fresh lemon juice
½ teaspoon salt
¼ teaspoon pepper

1. Preheat oven to 450°.
2. Place cauliflower in a large roasting pan or jelly-roll pan. Drizzle with oil; toss well to coat. Bake at 450° for 20 minutes or until tender and browned, stirring every 5 minutes. Sprinkle with parsley, thyme, tarragon, and garlic. Bake an additional 5 minutes. Combine cauliflower mixture, Parmesan cheese, and remaining ingredients in a large bowl; toss well to combine. Yield: 8 servings (serving size: about 1 cup).

CALORIES 89 (35% from fat); FAT 3.5g (sat 0.8g, mono 2.1g, poly 0.4g); PROTEIN 5.2g; CARB 12.1g; FIBER 5.4g; CHOL 2mg; IRON 1.1mg; SODIUM 251mg; CALC 83mg

Fresh Corn Bread Pudding

Simple ingredients render this side dish versatile enough for breakfast with country ham or an elegant dinner with filet mignon and asparagus.

1 (¾-pound) loaf country-style bread (such as Pepperidge Farm Hearty Country White)
2 teaspoons butter
3 cups fresh corn kernels (about 6 ears)
3 garlic cloves, minced
3 cups fat-free milk
1 cup egg substitute
1 teaspoon salt
¼ teaspoon freshly ground black pepper
1¼ cups (5 ounces) shredded sharp Cheddar cheese
Cooking spray

1. Preheat oven to 300°.
2. Trim crust from bread; discard crust. Cut bread into 2-inch cubes. Place bread cubes on a baking sheet. Bake at 300° for 30 minutes or until bread is toasted, turning occasionally.
3. Increase oven temperature to 425°.
4. Heat butter in a large nonstick skillet over medium-high heat. Add corn and garlic to pan; cook 4 minutes or until lightly browned, stirring occasionally. Combine milk, egg substitute, 1 teaspoon salt, and ¼ teaspoon black pepper in a large bowl, stirring with a whisk.
5. Add corn mixture and cheese to milk mixture; stir to combine. Fold in bread cubes.
6. Pour corn mixture into a 2-quart baking dish coated with cooking spray; let stand 10 minutes. Bake at 425° for 40 minutes or until puffed and set. Yield: 8 servings (serving size: 1 cup).

CALORIES 254 (30% from fat); FAT 8.5g (sat 4.5g, mono 2.2g, poly 0.5g); PROTEIN 15g; CARB 32.5g; FIBER 3.3g; CHOL 23mg; IRON 1.6mg; SODIUM 691mg; CALC 272mg

Grilled Corn with Creamy Chipotle Sauce

Grilled Corn with Creamy Chipotle Sauce

Instead of butter, try this smoky, spicy sauce—it's a savory complement to the sweet corn. To remove the silks from an ear of corn, rub with a damp paper towel or a damp, soft-bristled toothbrush. Though the corn needs to be grilled at the last minute, the sauce can be prepared a day ahead.

- ¼ teaspoon salt
- 1 chipotle chile, canned in adobo sauce
- 1 garlic clove
- ½ cup 2% reduced-fat cottage cheese
- 2 tablespoons light mayonnaise
- 2 tablespoons plain fat-free yogurt
- 6 ears shucked corn
- Cooking spray

1. Prepare grill.
2. Place first 3 ingredients in a food processor; process until minced. Add cottage cheese; process until smooth, scraping sides of bowl occasionally. Add mayonnaise and yogurt; process until blended. Spoon sauce into a bowl; cover and chill.
3. Place corn on grill rack coated with cooking spray. Grill 10 minutes, turning frequently. Serve corn with sauce. Yield: 6 servings (serving size: 1 ear of corn and 2 tablespoons sauce).

CALORIES 116 (25% from fat); FAT 3.2g (sat 0.7g, mono 0.7g, poly 1.5g); PROTEIN 5.7g; CARB 19g; FIBER 2.5g; CHOL 3.3mg; IRON 0.5mg; SODIUM 245mg; CALC 23mg

Basic Lentils

Try this simple yet versatile dish with chicken, fish, or as part of a vegetable plate. You can substitute low-sodium vegetable broth for a vegetarian version.

- 2 cups dried lentils
- 1½ cups chopped onion
- 1½ cups water
- 1 cup chopped celery
- 1 cup chopped carrot
- 1 tablespoon extravirgin olive oil
- 1 teaspoon salt
- ½ teaspoon freshly ground black pepper
- 2 (14-ounce) cans fat-free, less-sodium chicken broth
- 2 bay leaves

1. Combine all ingredients in an electric slow cooker. Cover and cook on LOW 5 hours or until tender. Discard bay leaves. Yield: 12 servings (serving size: ½ cup).

CALORIES 143 (10% from fat); FAT 1.6g (sat 0.2g, mono 1g, poly 0.3g); PROTEIN 9.3g; CARB 22.9g; FIBER 10.8g; CHOL 0mg; IRON 2.7mg; SODIUM 319mg; CALC 34mg

New Orleans Okra

Onion, celery, and green bell pepper are used so often in Louisiana that locals call them "the trinity." Here they're combined with another local staple: okra.

- 1 tablespoon olive oil
- 2 cups chopped onion
- ½ cup minced celery
- ½ cup minced green bell pepper
- 1 tablespoon tomato paste
- 2 (14.5-ounce) cans diced tomatoes, undrained
- ½ teaspoon ground red pepper
- 1½ pounds small okra pods, trimmed and cut into ½-inch slices
- ¼ teaspoon salt

1. Heat oil in a Dutch oven over medium-high heat. Add onion; sauté 5 minutes. Add celery, bell pepper, and tomato paste; cook 2 minutes. Stir in diced tomatoes and red pepper; cook 10 minutes or until sauce thickens. Add okra pods. Cover, reduce heat, and simmer 20 minutes or until okra pods are tender. Stir in salt. Yield: 8 servings (serving size: ¾ cup).

CALORIES 101 (16% from fat); FAT 1.9g (sat 0.3g, mono 1.3g, poly 0.2g); PROTEIN 4g; CARB 20.3g; FIBER 5.2g; CHOL 0mg; IRON 1.2mg; SODIUM 499mg; CALC 149mg

Fresh Peas with Pancetta

Fresh Peas with Pancetta

Avoid the temptation to substitute regular bacon for the pancetta because bacon's smoky quality will overwhelm the delicate flavor of the peas. The season for fresh baby peas is short; if you miss it, frozen will work in this dish.

- 3 slices pancetta, chopped (about 1 ounce)
- ¾ cup finely chopped white onion
- 1 garlic clove, minced
- 3 cups shelled green peas or frozen petite green peas
- 1 cup fat-free, less-sodium chicken broth
- 2 teaspoons sugar
- ¼ teaspoon salt
- ¼ cup chopped fresh flat-leaf parsley

1. Heat a large nonstick skillet over medium-high heat. Add pancetta; sauté 5 minutes or until crispy. Remove pancetta from pan, reserving drippings in pan. Add onion and garlic to pan; sauté 2 minutes or until tender. Add peas, broth, sugar, and salt to pan. Simmer 5 minutes or until peas are tender, stirring occasionally. Stir in pancetta and chopped parsley. Yield: 6 servings (serving size: ½ cup).

CALORIES 153 (23% from fat); FAT 3.9g (sat 1.6g, mono 0.1g, poly 0.2g); PROTEIN 8.4g; CARB 21.6g; FIBER 6.4g; CHOL 8mg; IRON 2mg; SODIUM 425mg; CALC 44mg

Okra-Pepper Sauté

- 2 teaspoons butter
- 1 cup yellow bell pepper strips
- 1 cup red bell pepper strips
- 3 cups okra pods, cut in half diagonally (about ½ pound)
- 2 tablespoons chopped fresh cilantro
- ¼ teaspoon salt
- ¼ teaspoon black pepper

1. Heat butter in a large nonstick skillet over medium heat. Add bell peppers, and sauté 4 minutes. Add okra; cover, reduce heat, and cook 15 minutes or until okra is tender. Stir in cilantro, ¼ teaspoon salt, and black pepper. Yield: 4 servings (serving size: ¾ cup).

CALORIES 52 (38% from fat); FAT 2.2g (sat 1.3g, mono 0.6g, poly 0.2g); PROTEIN 1.6g; CARB 7.2g; FIBER 1.4g; CHOL 5mg; IRON 1.2mg; SODIUM 173mg; CALC 53mg

Sherry-Braised Roasted Peppers

Serve this versatile side dish with flank steak or chicken, or toss it with pasta. Keep leftovers in the refrigerator for a few days. Reheat in the microwave, or serve at room temperature.

- 2 large green bell peppers (about 1 pound)
- 2 large red bell peppers (about 1 pound)
- 2 large yellow bell peppers (about 1 pound)
- 1 tablespoon olive oil
- 2 tablespoons capers
- 1 teaspoon minced fresh rosemary
- 1 teaspoon minced fresh thyme
- 2 large garlic cloves, minced
- 2 tablespoons medium dry sherry
- ¼ teaspoon salt

1. Preheat broiler.

2. Cut peppers in half lengthwise; discard seeds and membranes. Place pepper halves, skin sides up, on a foil-lined baking sheet; flatten with hand. Broil 15 minutes or until blackened. Place in a zip-top plastic bag; seal. Let stand 15 minutes. Peel and cut pepper halves into ½-inch-wide strips.

3. Heat oil in a large nonstick skillet over medium-high heat. Add capers, rosemary, thyme, and garlic; sauté 1 minute. Reduce heat to medium. Add sherry; cook 1 minute. Add pepper strips and salt; cook 2 minutes or until thoroughly heated. Serve warm or at room temperature. Yield: 6 servings (serving size: ½ cup).

CALORIES 70 (33% from fat); FAT 2.6g (sat 0.4g, mono 1.7g, poly 0.4g); PROTEIN 1.6g; CARB 11.1g; FIBER 2.3g; CHOL 0mg; IRON 0.9mg; SODIUM 186mg; CALC 19mg

Camembert Mashed Potatoes

Camembert Mashed Potatoes

The buttery taste and creamy texture of Camembert cheese glorifies these potatoes. The rind is easiest to remove if the cheese is well chilled.

- 1½ (8-ounce) rounds Camembert cheese
- 11 cups cubed peeled Yukon gold potato (about 4½ pounds)
- ½ cup 1% low-fat milk
- ¾ teaspoon salt
- ¾ teaspoon freshly ground black pepper
- Chopped fresh chives (optional)
- Freshly ground black pepper (optional)

1. Cut cheese into 6 wedges. Carefully remove rind from cheese; discard rind. Chop cheese; let stand at room temperature while potato cooks.
2. Place potato in a large Dutch oven; cover with water. Bring to a boil. Reduce heat; simmer 12 minutes or until tender. Drain in a colander; return potato to pan. Add cheese, milk, salt, and ¾ teaspoon pepper; mash with a potato masher to desired consistency. Garnish with chives and additional pepper, if desired. Yield: 12 servings (serving size: about ⅔ cup).

CALORIES 198 (20% from fat); FAT 4.4g (sat 2.8g, mono 1.3g, poly 0.1g); PROTEIN 7.9g; CARB 30.7g; FIBER 2g; CHOL 13mg; IRON 1.5mg; SODIUM 310mg; CALC 82mg

Mashed Potatoes with Green Onions

Using a slow cooker to prepare the potatoes reduces the chance of them boiling over on the stove top, and there is less chance of them overcooking.

- ¾ cup water
- 3 tablespoons butter, divided
- 2 pounds baking potatoes, peeled and cut into ½-inch cubes (about 4½ cups)
- ¾ cup fat-free milk
- ½ cup chopped green onions
- 1 teaspoon salt
- ⅛ teaspoon freshly ground black pepper

1. Combine ¾ cup water, 2 tablespoons butter, and potato in an electric slow cooker. Cover and cook on HIGH 3 hours or until tender.
2. Stir in remaining 1 tablespoon butter and remaining ingredients; mash with a potato masher to desired consistency. Yield: 10 servings (serving size: ½ cup).

CALORIES 123 (26% from fat); FAT 3.5g (sat 2.2g, mono 0.9g, poly 0.2g); PROTEIN 2.4g; CARB 20.9g; FIBER 1.6g; CHOL 9mg; IRON 0.3mg; SODIUM 274mg; CALC 33mg

How to Mash Potatoes

Whether you prefer your potatoes chunky or silky, potato mashers give you a multitude of options. They're your best bet if you like the texture of the skin in your potatoes.

Spicy Roasted Potatoes and Asparagus

We've simplified cooking for two by combining menu items in one dish. Move the potatoes to one side of the dish before you add the asparagus so the spears can cook in a single, even layer. Watch the spears closely, especially if they're thin.

- 2 teaspoons olive oil, divided
- ¼ teaspoon sea salt, divided
- ¼ teaspoon chopped fresh or ⅛ teaspoon dried thyme
- ⅛ teaspoon freshly ground black pepper
- ⅛ teaspoon crushed red pepper
- 6 small red potatoes (about ¾ pound), quartered
- Cooking spray
- 2 tablespoons grated fresh Parmesan cheese
- 1 teaspoon minced garlic, divided
- ½ pound asparagus spears

1. Preheat oven to 450°.
2. Combine 1 teaspoon oil, ⅛ teaspoon salt, thyme, peppers, and potato in an 11 x 7–inch baking dish coated with cooking spray. Bake at 450° for 20 minutes, stirring occasionally. Stir in cheese and ½ teaspoon garlic.
3. Snap off tough ends of asparagus. Combine remaining 1 teaspoon oil, ⅛ teaspoon salt, ½ teaspoon garlic, and asparagus. Add asparagus mixture to dish. Bake 10 minutes or until asparagus is crisp-tender. Yield: 2 servings.

CALORIES 223 (27% from fat); FAT 6.8g (sat 1.9g, mono 3.9g, poly 0.6g); PROTEIN 9.1g; CARB 34.2g; FIBER 4.6g; CHOL 5mg; IRON 3.6mg; SODIUM 419mg; CALC 136mg

Walnut-Crusted Potato and Blue Cheese Cakes

To avoid dirtying another dish, mash the potatoes in the same pot you use to cook them. The cakes can be shaped a few hours ahead, covered, and chilled until you're ready to eat. After chilling, cook them in the pan for an extra minute to make sure the insides of the cakes are thoroughly heated.

- 2 pounds small red potatoes, halved
- 1 garlic clove, peeled
- ⅓ cup (about 1½ ounces) crumbled blue cheese
- ¼ cup 1% low-fat milk
- 1 tablespoon chopped fresh parsley
- ¾ teaspoon salt
- ¼ teaspoon freshly ground black pepper
- 3 tablespoons chopped walnuts
- 2 (1½-ounce) slices sourdough bread
- 1 tablespoon olive oil, divided

1. Place potato halves and garlic in a large saucepan; cover with water. Bring to a boil; reduce heat, and simmer 20 minutes or until tender. Drain. Return potato halves and garlic to pan. Add blue cheese and next 4 ingredients; mash with a potato masher until desired consistency. Cool slightly. Shape potato mixture into 12 (½-inch-thick) cakes; set aside.
2. Place walnuts and bread in a food processor; pulse 10 times or until coarse crumbs form. Place in a shallow bowl or pie plate. Dredge cakes in breadcrumb mixture.
3. Heat 1½ teaspoons oil in a large nonstick skillet over medium heat. Add 6 cakes; cook 2 minutes on each side or until browned. Remove cakes from pan; cover and keep warm. Repeat procedure with remaining 1½ teaspoons oil and 6 cakes. Yield: 6 servings (serving size: 2 potato cakes).

CALORIES 219 (30% from fat); FAT 7.4g (sat 2g, mono 2.6g, poly 2.2g); PROTEIN 6.7g; CARB 32.5g; FIBER 3.3g; CHOL 6mg; IRON 1.9mg; SODIUM 489mg; CALC 84mg

Potato-Peanut Cakes

Fresh corn teams with buttery Yukon gold potatoes and chopped peanuts in these patties. Serve with a grilled steak and coleslaw. Preheat the griddle before coating with cooking spray so the patties will brown nicely.

- 3/4 pound Yukon gold potatoes
- 1 bacon slice
- 1 cup fresh corn kernels (about 2 ears)
- 1/4 cup finely chopped onion
- 1/4 cup finely chopped red bell pepper
- 1 teaspoon chopped fresh thyme
- 1/4 cup sliced green onions
- 1/4 cup chopped peanuts
- 1/2 teaspoon salt
- 1 large egg, lightly beaten
- Cooking spray
- Chopped fresh thyme (optional)

1. Place potatoes in a saucepan; cover with water. Bring to a boil; reduce heat, and simmer 15 minutes or until tender. Drain and cool. Shred potatoes into a large bowl.

2. Cook bacon in a large nonstick skillet over medium heat until crisp. Remove bacon from pan; crumble. Add corn, onion, bell pepper, and 1 teaspoon thyme to drippings in pan; cook 4 minutes or until onion is tender.

3. Combine potato, bacon, corn mixture, green onions, peanuts, salt, and egg; stir with a fork until well blended.

4. Heat a nonstick griddle or skillet over medium-high heat. Coat griddle with cooking spray. Spoon about 1/3 cup potato mixture onto hot griddle; flatten slightly with a spatula. Cook 5 minutes on each side or until golden brown. Garnish with thyme, if desired. Yield: 8 servings (serving size: 1 cake).

CALORIES 110 (40% from fat); FAT 4.9g (sat 1.1g, mono 2.2g, poly 1.2g); PROTEIN 3.9g; CARB 14g; FIBER 1.9g; CHOL 28mg; IRON 1mg; SODIUM 183mg; CALC 16mg

Two-Potato Latkes

Two-Potato Latkes

You can use a food processor's shredding blade for fast preparation. Serve latkes with applesauce and sour cream. Even though these are traditionally served during Hanukkah, you'll want to enjoy them year-round.

2 tablespoons olive oil
¼ cup grated fresh onion
1 pound shredded peeled baking potato
½ pound shredded peeled sweet potato
½ cup all-purpose flour (about 2¼ ounces)
⅓ cup finely chopped green onions
½ teaspoon salt
¼ teaspoon freshly ground black pepper
1 garlic clove, minced
1 large egg, lightly beaten
Cooking spray
Green onion strips (optional)

1. Preheat oven to 425°.
2. Drizzle a jelly-roll pan evenly with olive oil, tilting pan to coat.
3. Combine grated onion and potato in a sieve; squeeze out excess moisture. Lightly spoon flour into a dry measuring cup; level with a knife. Combine potato mixture, flour, and next 5 ingredients in a large bowl. Divide mixture into 8 equal portions, squeezing out excess liquid. Shape each portion into a ¼-inch-thick patty; place on prepared pan. Lightly coat tops of patties with cooking spray. Bake at 425° for 12 minutes. Carefully turn patties over; cook 30 minutes or until lightly browned, turning every 10 minutes. Garnish with green onion strips, if desired. Yield: 4 servings (serving size: 2 latkes).

CALORIES 256 (29% from fat); FAT 8.3g (sat 1.4g, mono 5.5g, poly 1g); PROTEIN 5.7g; CARB 40g; FIBER 4g; CHOL 53mg; IRON 1.7mg; SODIUM 337mg; CALC 38mg

Hash Brown Casserole with Bacon, Onions, and Cheese

Though filling enough as a main dish, you can also serve smaller portions of this creamy, cheesy casserole as a tasty side to scrambled eggs. We enjoyed the way the preshredded cheese blend melted over the casserole; substitute sharp Cheddar cheese, if you wish.

6 bacon slices
1 cup chopped onion
2 garlic cloves, minced
1 (32-ounce) package frozen southern-style hash brown potatoes
1 cup (4 ounces) preshredded Classic Melts Four Cheese blend, divided
½ cup chopped green onions
½ cup fat-free sour cream
½ teaspoon salt
¼ teaspoon freshly ground black pepper
1 (10.75-ounce) can condensed 30% reduced-sodium, 98% fat-free cream of mushroom soup, undiluted (such as Campbell's)
Cooking spray

1. Cook bacon slices in a large nonstick skillet over medium heat until crisp. Remove bacon from pan, and crumble. Discard drippings in pan. Add 1 cup onion and garlic to pan; cook 5 minutes or until tender, stirring frequently. Stir in potato; cover and cook 15 minutes, stirring occasionally.
2. Combine crumbled bacon, ¼ cup cheese, green onions, sour cream, salt, pepper, and soup in a large bowl. Add potato mixture; toss gently to combine. Spoon mixture into an 11 x 7–inch baking dish coated with cooking spray. Sprinkle with remaining ¾ cup cheese. Cover with foil coated with cooking spray. Refrigerate 8 hours or overnight.
3. Preheat oven to 350°.
4. Remove baking dish from refrigerator; let stand at room temperature 15 minutes. Bake casserole, covered, at 350° for 30 minutes. Uncover and bake an additional 30 minutes or until bubbly around edges and cheese begins to brown. Yield: 6 servings (serving size: about 1 cup).

CALORIES 293 (31% from fat); FAT 10g (sat 4.8g, mono 3.3g, poly 0.7g); PROTEIN 12.2g; CARB 41.4g; FIBER 4.7g; CHOL 31mg; IRON 0.2mg; SODIUM 720mg; CALC 214mg

Mashed Sweet Potatoes with Pecan Butter

This side dish tastes like the traditional streusel-topped sweet potato casserole but is much simpler to prepare with the help of the microwave. It can easily be multiplied to serve more.

- 2 medium sweet potatoes (about 1 pound)
- 3 tablespoons 1% low-fat milk
- 2 tablespoons brown sugar, divided
- ⅛ teaspoon salt
- 1 tablespoon butter, softened
- 1 tablespoon chopped pecans, toasted
- ⅛ teaspoon ground cinnamon

1. Pierce potatoes with a fork; arrange on paper towels in microwave oven. Microwave potatoes at HIGH 10 minutes, rearranging potatoes after 5 minutes. Wrap potatoes in a towel; let stand 5 minutes. Scoop out pulp; discard skins. Combine pulp, milk, 1 tablespoon brown sugar, and salt in a medium bowl; mash.

2. Combine remaining 1 tablespoon brown sugar, butter, pecans, and cinnamon in a small bowl. Top each serving with pecan mixture. Yield: 2 servings (serving size: ¾ cup potatoes and 1 tablespoon pecan mixture).

CALORIES 299 (27% from fat); FAT 9g (sat 4.1g, mono 3.3g, poly 1.1g); PROTEIN 3.9g; CARB 52g; FIBER 5.4g; CHOL 16mg; IRON 1.4mg; SODIUM 237mg; CALC 78mg

Asiago, Potato, and Bacon Gratin

Remember this secret when cooking potatoes: Instead of salting the water they boil in, sprinkle the potatoes with salt after draining for the most pronounced flavor.

- 1½ pounds peeled Yukon gold potatoes, cut into ¼-inch-thick slices
- 1 teaspoon salt, divided
- Cooking spray
- 2 tablespoons minced shallots
- ¼ cup all-purpose flour (about 1 ounce)
- 2 cups 1% low-fat milk, divided
- ¾ cup (3 ounces) grated Asiago cheese
- ¼ cup chopped fresh chives
- ¼ teaspoon freshly ground black pepper
- 4 bacon slices, cooked and crumbled
- ¼ cup (1 ounce) grated fresh Parmesan cheese

1. Preheat oven to 350°.

2. Place potato in a large saucepan; cover with water. Bring to a boil. Reduce heat, and simmer 5 minutes or until almost tender. Drain. Sprinkle potatoes evenly with ¼ teaspoon salt; set aside, and keep warm.

3. Heat a medium saucepan over medium heat. Coat pan with cooking spray. Add shallots; cook 2 minutes or until tender, stirring frequently. Lightly spoon flour into a dry measuring cup; level with a knife. Sprinkle flour over shallots. Gradually add ½ cup milk, stirring with a whisk until well blended. Gradually add remaining 1½ cups milk, stirring with a whisk. Cook over medium heat 9 minutes or until thick, stirring frequently. Remove from heat; stir in ¾ teaspoon salt, Asiago, chives, pepper, and bacon.

4. Arrange half of potato slices in an 8-inch square baking dish coated with cooking spray. Pour half of cheese sauce over potato slices. Top with remaining potato slices and cheese sauce; sprinkle with Parmesan cheese. Bake at 350° for 35 minutes or until cheese is bubbly and lightly browned. Yield: 6 servings.

CALORIES 250 (30% from fat); FAT 8.2g (sat 4.6g, mono 2.7g, poly 0.5g); PROTEIN 12.3g; CARB 31.9g; FIBER 2.3g; CHOL 23mg; IRON 0.9mg; SODIUM 618mg; CALC 306mg

Wild Mushroom–and–Sweet Potato Gratin

Chanterelle mushrooms and fontina cheese contribute a delicate, nutty flavor that contrasts nicely with the sweet potatoes in this dish. Serve with roasted pork loin or ham.

- 2 teaspoons olive oil
- 4 cups (¼-inch-thick) slices cremini mushrooms (about 8 ounces)
- 3½ cups (¼-inch-thick) slices chanterelle mushrooms (about 8 ounces)
- ⅓ cup finely chopped shallots
- ½ teaspoon kosher salt, divided
- ½ teaspoon black pepper, divided
- 1½ tablespoons finely chopped fresh parsley, divided
- 1½ tablespoons chopped fresh chives, divided
- 4 cups peeled sweet potatoes, cut into ¼-inch-thick slices (about 1½ pounds)
- Cooking spray
- 1 cup (4 ounces) shredded fontina cheese
- ½ cup fat-free, less-sodium chicken broth

1. Preheat oven to 425°.

2. Heat oil in a large skillet over medium-high heat. Add mushrooms, shallots, ¼ teaspoon salt, and ¼ teaspoon pepper; sauté 5 minutes or until moisture evaporates, stirring frequently. Remove from heat; stir in 1 tablespoon parsley and 1 tablespoon chives.

3. Arrange half of potato slices in a single layer in an 11 x 7–inch baking dish coated with cooking spray; sprinkle with ⅛ teaspoon salt and ⅛ teaspoon pepper. Spoon half of mushroom mixture over potato slices; sprinkle with half of cheese. Repeat layers, ending with cheese; add broth to dish. Cover and bake at 425° for 30 minutes. Uncover and bake an additional 20 minutes or until potato is tender. Sprinkle with remaining parsley and chives. Yield: 8 servings.

CALORIES 193 (28% from fat); FAT 6.1g (sat 3g, mono 2.3g, poly 0.6g); PROTEIN 8g; CARB 26.8g; FIBER 4.7g; CHOL 17mg; IRON 1.6mg; SODIUM 282mg; CALC 110mg

Spicy Grilled Sweet Potatoes

Spicy Grilled Sweet Potatoes

Fast, easy, and economical, this recipe is nice as an "out of the ordinary" side dish. It has good zesty flavor.

- ¾ teaspoon ground cumin
- ½ teaspoon garlic powder
- ¼ teaspoon salt
- ⅛ teaspoon ground red pepper
- 1 tablespoon olive oil
- 1 pound peeled sweet potatoes, cut into ¼-inch-thick slices
- Cooking spray
- 2 tablespoons chopped fresh cilantro

1. Combine first 4 ingredients in a small bowl.
2. Combine olive oil and sliced sweet potatoes in a medium bowl; toss to coat. Heat a large grill pan over medium heat. Coat pan with cooking spray. Add potato; cook 10 minutes, turning occasionally. Place potato in a bowl; sprinkle with cumin mixture and cilantro, tossing gently to coat. Yield: 4 servings (serving size: ½ cup).

CALORIES 157 (25% from fat); FAT 4.3g (sat 0.6g, mono 2.7g, poly 0.7g); PROTEIN 2g; CARB 28.1g; FIBER 3.5g; CHOL 0mg; IRON 1.1mg; SODIUM 163mg; CALC 31mg

Sweet Potatoes in Picante Sauce

This Latin American dish is often made using a tropical sweet potato known as a boniato.

- 1 tablespoon olive oil
- ½ cup minced celery
- ½ teaspoon crushed fennel seeds
- 2 garlic cloves, minced
- ¾ cup finely chopped onion
- 1 teaspoon salt
- ½ teaspoon ground turmeric
- ¼ teaspoon paprika
- 1 dried red chile, crumbled (about ¼ ounce)
- 6 cups (1½-inch) cubed peeled sweet potatoes (about 2 pounds)
- ½ cup water
- 1 tablespoon chopped fresh cilantro

1. Heat oil in a Dutch oven over medium heat. Add celery, fennel, and garlic; cook 1 minute, stirring constantly. Add chopped onion and next 4 ingredients; cook 10 minutes, stirring frequently. Add potato and water; bring to a boil. Cover, reduce heat, and simmer 35 minutes or until potato is tender. Sprinkle with cilantro. Yield: 10 servings (serving size: 1 cup).

CALORIES 105 (15% from fat); FAT 1.7g (sat 0.3g, mono 1g, poly 0.3g); PROTEIN 1.7g; CARB 21.5g; FIBER 3g; CHOL 0mg; IRON 0.7mg; SODIUM 252mg; CALC 26mg

Sweet Potato Hash

To save time, precook the sweet potatoes in the microwave, then add them to the skillet for last-minute browning with the sausage and onions.

- 1½ pounds sweet potatoes, peeled and diced
- ⅓ cup water
- 1½ teaspoons olive oil
- 2 (1-ounce) links turkey breakfast sausage
- 1¼ cups chopped onion
- ¾ teaspoon salt, divided
- 1½ tablespoons maple syrup
- 1 tablespoon water
- ¼ teaspoon black pepper
- ⅛ teaspoon ground nutmeg

1. Place sweet potato and ⅓ cup water in a large microwave-safe bowl. Cover with plastic wrap; microwave at HIGH 10 minutes or until tender. Carefully uncover; drain and keep warm.
2. Heat oil in a large nonstick skillet over medium-high heat. Remove casings from sausage. Add onion to pan; sauté 6 minutes or until tender. Add sausage and ¼ teaspoon salt; cook 4 minutes or until sausage is done, stirring to crumble. Stir in sweet potato, ½ teaspoon salt, and remaining ingredients. Cook until liquid is absorbed and sweet potato begins to brown (about 5 minutes). Yield: 4 servings (serving size: about 1 cup).

CALORIES 200 (16% from fat); FAT 3.6g (sat 0.8g, mono 1.8g, poly 0.7g); PROTEIN 5.2g; CARB 37.8g; FIBER 4.5g; CHOL 11mg; IRON 1.2mg; SODIUM 571mg; CALC 43mg

Honey-Roasted Root Vegetables

Honey amplifies the natural sweetness of the oven-caramelized vegetables.

- 2 cups coarsely chopped peeled sweet potato (about 1 large)
- 1½ cups coarsely chopped peeled turnip (about 2 medium)
- 1½ cups coarsely chopped parsnip (about 2 medium)
- 1½ cups coarsely chopped carrot (about 2 medium)
- ¼ cup honey
- 2 tablespoons olive oil
- ½ teaspoon salt
- 3 shallots, halved
- Cooking spray

1. Preheat oven to 450°.

2. Combine first 8 ingredients in a large bowl; toss to coat. Place vegetable mixture in a jelly-roll pan coated with cooking spray. Bake at 450° for 35 minutes or until vegetables are tender and begin to brown, stirring every 15 minutes. Yield: 8 servings (serving size: ½ cup).

CALORIES 118 (27% from fat); FAT 3.5g (sat 0.5g, mono 2.5g, poly 0.4g); PROTEIN 1.3g; CARB 21.7g; FIBER 2.3g; CHOL 0mg; IRON 0.5mg; SODIUM 171mg; CALC 33mg

Spinach and Parmesan Fallen Soufflé

Cooking spray
2 tablespoons dry breadcrumbs
2 garlic cloves, minced
1 (10-ounce) package fresh spinach
1 cup 1% low-fat milk
1 tablespoon cornstarch
⅓ cup (about 1½ ounces) grated fresh Parmigiano-Reggiano cheese
¼ teaspoon salt
⅛ teaspoon freshly ground black pepper
⅛ teaspoon grated whole nutmeg
3 large egg whites
1 large egg

1. Preheat oven to 375°.
2. Lightly coat an 11 x 7–inch baking dish with cooking spray; dust with breadcrumbs. Set aside.
3. Heat a large nonstick skillet over medium heat. Coat pan with cooking spray. Add garlic; cook 20 seconds, stirring constantly. Add spinach; cook 3 minutes or until spinach wilts, stirring occasionally. Remove from heat; cool slightly. Place spinach mixture on several layers of heavy-duty paper towels; squeeze until barely moist. Place spinach mixture, milk, and cornstarch in a blender; process until smooth. Add cheese, salt, pepper, and nutmeg; pulse until well blended. Pour into a large bowl.
4. Place egg whites and egg in a large bowl; beat with a mixer at high speed 5 minutes or until tripled in volume. Gently fold one-fourth of mixture into spinach mixture; gently fold in remaining egg mixture (mixture will seem slightly thin). Spoon into baking dish; smooth top with a spatula. Bake at 375° for 35 minutes or until set in center. Cool 5 minutes on a wire rack before serving. Yield: 6 servings.

CALORIES 92 (34% from fat); FAT 3.5g (sat 1.8g, mono 1g, poly 0.3g); PROTEIN 8.5g; CARB 7.3g; FIBER 1.2g; CHOL 42mg; IRON 1.7mg; SODIUM 326mg; CALC 193mg

Yellow Squash Ribbons with Red Onion and Parmesan

4 medium yellow squash (about 1½ pounds)
1 teaspoon olive oil
1 cup thinly vertically sliced red onion
1 garlic clove, minced
¼ teaspoon salt
¼ to ½ teaspoon crushed red pepper
¼ teaspoon freshly ground black pepper
¼ cup (1 ounce) shaved fresh Parmesan cheese

1. Using a sharp vegetable peeler, shave each yellow squash lengthwise into long ribbons to measure about 5 cups. Discard seeds and core of squash.
2. Heat olive oil in a large nonstick skillet over medium heat. Add squash ribbons, red onion, and garlic; cook 4 minutes or until onion is tender, gently stirring occasionally. Remove from heat. Add salt, red pepper, and black pepper, and toss gently to combine. Sprinkle with Parmesan cheese. Yield: 4 servings (serving size: about ¾ cup).

CALORIES 84 (36% from fat); FAT 3.4g (sat 1.4g, mono 1.4g, poly 0.3g); PROTEIN 4.5g; CARB 10.4g; FIBER 3.8g; CHOL 5mg; IRON 1mg; SODIUM 266mg; CALC 128mg

Yellow Squash Gratin

Cooking spray
2 cups chopped onion
3 garlic cloves, minced
3 pounds yellow squash, halved lengthwise and cut into ¼-inch-thick slices (about 12 cups)
½ cup chopped fresh flat-leaf parsley
1½ teaspoons salt
1 teaspoon chopped fresh thyme
½ teaspoon freshly ground black pepper
3 cups cooked long-grain rice
¾ cup (3 ounces) grated Gruyère or Swiss cheese
3 large eggs, lightly beaten
1 (1-ounce) slice white bread
¼ cup (1 ounce) grated fresh Parmesan cheese
1 tablespoon butter, melted

1. Preheat oven to 375°.
2. Heat a Dutch oven over medium-high heat. Coat pan with cooking spray. Add onion; sauté 5 minutes or until tender. Add garlic; sauté 30 seconds. Add yellow squash; sauté 7 minutes or just until tender. Remove from heat; stir in parsley, salt, thyme, and pepper. Add cooked rice, Gruyère, and eggs to squash mixture, stirring until well combined. Spoon squash mixture into a 13 x 9–inch baking dish coated with cooking spray.
3. Place bread in a food processor; pulse 10 times or until fine crumbs measure ½ cup. Combine breadcrumbs, Parmesan, and butter, tossing to combine. Sprinkle breadcrumb mixture over squash mixture. Bake at 375° for 30 minutes or until topping is lightly browned and filling is set. Let stand 5 minutes before serving. Yield: 8 servings.

CALORIES 247 (29% from fat); FAT 8g (sat 4.1g, mono 2.5g, poly 0.6g); PROTEIN 11.2g; CARB 32.4g; FIBER 4.9g; CHOL 98mg; IRON 2.4mg; SODIUM 599mg; CALC 220mg

Double-Squash Basmati Gratin

Basmati rice and feta cheese distinguish this updated squash-rice casserole from its classic counterpart.

- 4 cups zucchini, halved lengthwise and thinly sliced (about 1 ¼ pounds)
- 4 cups yellow squash, halved lengthwise and thinly sliced (about 1 ¼ pounds)
- 2 cups thinly sliced leek (about 2 large)
- ¼ cup fat-free, less-sodium chicken broth
- 1 teaspoon salt, divided
- 1 teaspoon freshly ground black pepper, divided
- 3 garlic cloves, minced
- 1 cup fat-free sour cream
- ⅔ cup 1% low-fat milk
- 2 large egg whites
- 3 cups cooked basmati rice
- 1 cup (4 ounces) crumbed feta cheese
- ½ cup (2 ounces) grated fresh Parmesan cheese
- ¼ cup chopped fresh parsley
- 2 teaspoons chopped fresh oregano
- Cooking spray
- 25 onion or garlic melba snack crackers
- 2 tablespoons butter, melted

1. Preheat oven to 375°.
2. Combine zucchini, squash, leek, broth, ½ teaspoon salt, ½ teaspoon pepper, and garlic in a Dutch oven. Cover and cook over medium-high heat 20 minutes or until squash is very tender, stirring occasionally. Uncover and remove from heat; cool slightly.
3. Combine remaining ½ teaspoon salt, remaining ½ teaspoon pepper, sour cream, milk, and egg whites in a large bowl, stirring with a whisk. Add squash mixture, basmati rice, cheeses, parsley, and oregano; stir well to combine. Pour mixture into a 13 x 9–inch baking dish coated with cooking spray.
4. Place crackers in a food processor; process until coarsely ground. Drizzle with butter; pulse 3 times or until moist. Sprinkle crumb mixture evenly over rice mixture. Bake at 375° for 25 minutes or until bubbly around edges. Let stand 10 minutes. Yield: 9 servings (serving size: about 1 cup).

CALORIES 251 (29% from fat); FAT 8.1g (sat 4.7g, mono 2.3g, poly 0.5g); PROTEIN 11g; CARB 34.1g; FIBER 2.4g; CHOL 25mg; IRON 2.1mg; SODIUM 656mg; CALC 246mg

Swiss Chard with Pine Nuts and Raisins

- 1 ¼ pounds Swiss chard, trimmed
- 2 tablespoons fresh lemon juice
- 1 ½ teaspoons extravirgin olive oil
- ½ teaspoon salt
- ⅛ teaspoon freshly ground black pepper
- ½ cup golden raisins
- 2 tablespoons pine nuts

1. Slice Swiss chard leaves crosswise into thin strips; place in a large bowl. Combine lemon juice, olive oil, salt, and pepper, stirring with a whisk. Drizzle juice mixture over chard; toss to coat. Add raisins and pine nuts; toss to combine. Let stand 15 minutes before serving. Yield: 4 servings (serving size: 1 cup).

CALORIES 111 (29% from fat); FAT 3.6g (sat 0.5g, mono 1.9g, poly 0.9g); PROTEIN 3.5g; CARB 19.8g; FIBER 2.7g; CHOL 0mg; IRON 2.7mg; SODIUM 391mg; CALC 69mg

Roasted Tomatoes with Shallots and Herbs

- 4 medium tomatoes, cut in half horizontally (about 2 pounds)
- ½ teaspoon salt, divided
- Cooking spray
- ¼ cup minced shallots
- 1 tablespoon chopped fresh flat-leaf parsley
- 1 teaspoon chopped fresh or ¼ teaspoon dried oregano
- 1 teaspoon chopped fresh or ¼ teaspoon dried thyme
- ½ teaspoon chopped fresh or ⅛ teaspoon dried rosemary
- ¼ teaspoon freshly ground black pepper
- 2 teaspoons olive oil

1. Preheat oven to 350°.
2. Core and seed tomato halves. Sprinkle cut sides of tomato halves with ¼ teaspoon salt. Place tomato halves, cut sides down, on paper towels. Let stand 20 minutes.
3. Place tomato halves, cut sides up, in a 13 x 9–inch baking dish coated with cooking spray. Sprinkle with remaining ¼ teaspoon salt, shallots, and next 5 ingredients. Drizzle with oil. Bake at 350° for 1 hour and 15 minutes or until tomatoes soften. Yield: 8 servings (serving size: 1 tomato half).

CALORIES 38 (36% from fat); FAT 1.5g (sat 0.2g, mono 0.9g, poly 0.3g); PROTEIN 1.1g; CARB 6.2g; FIBER 1.3g; CHOL 0mg; IRON 0.6mg; SODIUM 121mg; CALC 10mg

Roasted Tomatoes with Shallots and Herbs

Creamy Parmesan Orzo

1 tablespoon butter
1 cup orzo
1¼ cups fat-free, less-sodium chicken broth
1¼ cups water
¼ cup (1 ounce) grated fresh Parmesan cheese
2 tablespoons chopped fresh basil
¼ teaspoon salt
¼ teaspoon freshly ground black pepper
4 teaspoons pine nuts, toasted

1. Heat butter in a medium saucepan over medium heat. Add orzo, and cook 3 minutes, stirring constantly. Stir in broth and water; bring to a boil. Reduce heat, and simmer until liquid is absorbed and orzo is done (about 15 minutes). Remove from heat; stir in cheese, basil, salt, and pepper. Sprinkle with pine nuts. Serve immediately. Yield: 4 servings (serving size: ½ cup).

CALORIES 236 (24% from fat); FAT 6.4g (sat 3.2g, mono 1.8g, poly 0.8g); PROTEIN 9.9g; CARB 34.8g; FIBER 1.7g; CHOL 12mg; IRON 1.8mg; SODIUM 412mg; CALC 82mg

Basmati Rice with Basil and Mint

This foolproof cooking method also works with long-grain white rice and jasmine rice.

1 cup uncooked basmati rice
2 teaspoons canola oil
2 teaspoons minced peeled fresh ginger
2 garlic cloves, minced
2¼ cups fat-free, less-sodium chicken broth
1 tablespoon chopped fresh basil
2 teaspoons chopped fresh mint
¼ teaspoon freshly ground black pepper

1. Preheat oven to 350°.
2. Place rice in a fine-mesh strainer. Rinse with cold water; drain.
3. Heat oil in a large saucepan over medium-high heat. Add ginger and garlic; cook 30 seconds, stirring constantly. Stir in rice; cook 1 minute, stirring constantly. Add broth and remaining ingredients, stirring to combine; bring to a boil. Cover; wrap handle of pan with foil. Bake at 350° for 25 minutes, stirring once. Remove rice from oven; fluff rice with a fork. Yield: 4 servings (serving size: about ¾ cup).

CALORIES 215 (10% from fat); FAT 2.3g (sat 0.3g, mono 0.5g, poly 1.3g); PROTEIN 4.5g; CARB 46.7g; FIBER 1.5g; CHOL 0mg; IRON 1.5mg; SODIUM 254mg; CALC 5mg

Pistachio Rice

A quality pistachio oil gives a robust flavor. This dish is excellent with lamb or chicken.

2 cups water
1 cup basmati rice
¾ teaspoon salt, divided
2 tablespoons dried currants or golden raisins
1½ tablespoons chopped pistachios
1 tablespoon chopped fresh flat-leaf parsley
2 tablespoons pistachio oil
¼ teaspoon freshly ground black pepper
Fresh flat-leaf parsley sprigs (optional)

1. Bring water to a boil in a medium saucepan; add rice and ¼ teaspoon salt. Cover, reduce heat, and simmer 18 minutes or until liquid is absorbed and rice is done. Remove from heat; fluff with a fork. Add ½ teaspoon salt, currants, and next 4 ingredients. Cover and let stand 5 minutes. Garnish with parsley sprigs, if desired. Yield: 6 servings (serving size: about ½ cup).

CALORIES 186 (29% from fat); FAT 5.9g (sat 0.8g, mono 3.8g, poly 1.3g); PROTEIN 2.4g; CARB 33.1g; FIBER 1.3g; CHOL 0mg; IRON 1.2mg; SODIUM 294mg; CALC 8mg

Rice Pilaf with Shallots and Parmesan

We used basmati rice, but any long-grain rice works well in this recipe.

2 teaspoons butter
2 tablespoons minced shallots
1 garlic clove, minced
½ cup uncooked basmati rice
1 cup fat-free, less-sodium chicken broth
¼ cup dry white wine
2 tablespoons grated fresh Parmesan cheese
2 tablespoons minced fresh parsley
⅛ teaspoon freshly ground black pepper
Dash of sea salt

1. Melt butter in a small saucepan over medium-high heat. Add shallots and garlic; sauté 1 minute. Stir in rice; sauté 1 minute. Stir in broth and wine; bring to a boil. Cover, reduce heat, and simmer 15 minutes.
2. Remove from heat; stir in cheese, parsley, pepper, and salt. Yield: 2 servings (serving size: about ¾ cup).

CALORIES 266 (21% from fat); FAT 6.3g (sat 3.8g, mono 1.8g, poly 0.4g); PROTEIN 8.4g; CARB 43.9g; FIBER 0.6g; CHOL 15mg; IRON 0.8mg; SODIUM 455mg; CALC 100mg

Pistachio Rice

Sausage and Mushroom Stuffing

This herbed bread stuffing is a welcome addition to a roast chicken dinner.

- 5 cups (1-inch) cubed white bread (about 7 [1-ounce] slices)
- 5 cups (1-inch) cubed whole wheat bread (about 7 [1-ounce] slices)
- 1 pound turkey Italian sausage
- Cooking spray
- 1 teaspoon canola oil
- 3 cups finely chopped onion
- 1½ cups finely chopped celery
- 1 (8-ounce) package presliced mushrooms
- 1 teaspoon dried thyme
- 1 teaspoon dried rubbed sage
- 1 teaspoon dried rosemary
- ½ teaspoon dried marjoram
- ½ teaspoon black pepper
- ⅓ cup chopped fresh parsley
- 1½ cups fat-free, less-sodium chicken broth

1. Preheat oven to 250°.
2. Place bread in a single layer on 2 baking sheets. Bake at 250° for 1 hour or until dry.
3. Remove casings from sausage. Cook sausage in a large nonstick skillet coated with cooking spray over medium heat until browned, stirring to crumble. Place sausage in a large bowl.
4. Heat canola oil in pan over medium heat. Add onion, celery, and mushrooms; cover and cook 10 minutes or until vegetables are tender, stirring occasionally. Remove from heat; stir in thyme and next 4 ingredients. Add onion mixture, bread, and parsley to sausage; toss gently to combine. Add broth; stir until moist.
5. Increase oven temperature to 350°.
6. Spoon bread mixture into a 13 x 9–inch baking dish coated with cooking spray. Cover and bake at 350° for 15 minutes. Uncover and bake an additional 20 minutes or until top is crusty. Yield: 12 servings (serving size: about ¾ cup).

CALORIES 187 (28% from fat); FAT 5.9g (sat 1.6g, mono 2g, poly 1.5g); PROTEIN 12.4g; CARB 21.6g; FIBER 2.9g; CHOL 38mg; IRON 2.5mg; SODIUM 460mg; CALC 52mg

Sourdough Stuffing with Pears and Sausage

Sourdough bread gives the stuffing a tangier flavor than French or Italian bread, but you can use the latter in a pinch.

- 8 cups (½-inch) cubed sourdough bread (about 12 ounces)
- 1 pound turkey Italian sausage
- Cooking spray
- 5 cups chopped onion (about 2 pounds)
- 2 cups chopped celery
- 1 cup chopped carrot
- 1 (8-ounce) package presliced mushrooms
- 2 cups (½-inch) cubed peeled Bartlett pear (about 2 medium)
- 1½ tablespoons chopped fresh basil
- 2 teaspoons chopped fresh tarragon
- 1 teaspoon salt
- 1½ cups fat-free, less-sodium chicken broth
- ½ teaspoon freshly ground black pepper

1. Preheat oven to 425°.
2. Arrange bread in a single layer on a baking sheet. Bake at 425° for 9 minutes or until golden. Place in a large bowl.
3. Remove casings from sausage. Heat a large nonstick skillet over medium-high heat. Coat pan with cooking spray. Add sausage; cook 8 minutes or until browned, stirring to crumble. Add sausage to bread cubes, tossing to combine. Set aside.
4. Return pan to medium-high heat. Add onion, celery, and carrot; sauté 10 minutes or until onion begins to brown. Stir in mushrooms; cook 4 minutes. Stir in pear, basil, tarragon, and salt; cook 4 minutes or until pear begins to soften, stirring occasionally. Add pear mixture to bread mixture, tossing gently to combine. Stir in broth and pepper.
5. Place bread mixture in a 13 x 9–inch baking dish coated with cooking spray; cover with foil. Bake at 425° for 20 minutes. Uncover; bake an additional 15 minutes or until top is crisp. Yield: 12 servings (serving size: about ¾ cup).

CALORIES 199 (24% from fat); FAT 5.2g (sat 1.6g, mono 1.5g, poly 1g); PROTEIN 10.7g; CARB 28.6g; FIBER 3.4g; CHOL 23mg; IRON 1.8mg; SODIUM 684mg; CALC 54mg

Sourdough Stuffing with Pears and Sausage

Slow-Cooker Sausage-and-Vegetable Chili, page 346

Soups

Chilled Vegetable Basil Soup with Vegetable Confetti

Chilled Vegetable Basil Soup with Vegetable Confetti

To make a spicier version of this gazpacho-style soup, use a spicy or hot variety of tomato or vegetable juice. For the best texture and freshest flavor, chill the soup several hours ahead. Don't stir in zucchini and remaining vegetables until you're ready to serve.

- 2 teaspoons olive oil
- ½ teaspoon fennel seeds
- 2 garlic cloves, minced
- 1 (46-ounce) can no-salt-added tomato juice
- 1 cup basil leaves
- 1 teaspoon hot pepper sauce (such as Tabasco)
- ¼ teaspoon salt
- ½ cup finely chopped zucchini
- ½ cup finely chopped cucumber
- ½ cup chopped yellow bell pepper
- 1 cup halved cherry tomatoes
- ½ cup chopped green onions
- ¼ cup chopped fresh basil
- 2 tablespoons reduced-fat sour cream

1. Heat olive oil in a large saucepan over medium heat. Add fennel seeds and garlic; cook 1 minute, stirring frequently. Add juice, and bring to a boil. Reduce heat, and simmer 2 minutes. Remove from heat; stir in 1 cup basil, hot pepper sauce, and ¼ teaspoon salt. Place soup in a large bowl; cover and chill 6 hours or overnight.

2. Strain mixture through a sieve over a bowl; discard solids. Stir in zucchini and next 5 ingredients. Spoon 1 cup into each of 6 shallow bowls; top each serving with 1 teaspoon sour cream. Serve immediately. Yield: 6 servings.

CALORIES 69 (25% from fat); FAT 1.9g (sat 0.3g, mono 1.2g, poly 0.3g); PROTEIN 2.7g; CARB 12.9g; FIBER 2.2g; CHOL 0mg; IRON 1.7mg; SODIUM 130mg; CALC 54mg

Radish Vichyssoise

Chilled overnight, this soup is refreshing on a warm day. Radishes add an earthy, turniplike flavor. Use white pepper to keep the soup creamy white. You can cut the recipe in half if you're not serving a crowd.

- 1 tablespoon butter
- 1½ cups thinly sliced onion
- 20 radishes, halved (about 1 pound)
- 1½ pounds baking potatoes, peeled and cut into 1-inch pieces
- 3 cups fat-free, less-sodium chicken broth
- 2 cups 2% reduced-fat milk
- ¾ cup reduced-fat sour cream
- 1 teaspoon salt
- ¼ teaspoon black pepper
- ⅛ teaspoon ground nutmeg
- ¼ cup chopped fresh chives

1. Melt 1 tablespoon butter in a large saucepan over medium heat. Add onion, and cook 5 minutes or until tender, stirring frequently. Add radishes and potatoes, tossing to coat with butter. Stir in broth and 2 cups milk; bring to a boil. Cover, reduce heat, and simmer 15 minutes or until potatoes are tender. Cool 10 minutes.

2. Place half of radish mixture in a blender. Remove center piece of blender lid (to allow steam to escape); secure blender lid on blender. Place a clean towel over opening in blender lid (to avoid spills). Blend until smooth. Pour pureed soup into a large bowl. Repeat procedure with remaining radish mixture. Cover and chill at least 2 hours.

3. Add sour cream, salt, pepper, and nutmeg, stirring with a whisk. Cover and chill at least 4 hours or overnight. Sprinkle with chives. Yield: 12 servings (serving size: ¾ cup).

CALORIES 119 (29% from fat); FAT 3.9g (sat 2.3g, mono 1.1g, poly 0.2g); PROTEIN 4.2g; CARB 17.2g; FIBER 1.9g; CHOL 13mg; IRON 0.4mg; SODIUM 359mg; CALC 91mg

Celery-Celeriac Soup with Roquefort Croutons

This deliciously earthy, creamy vegetable soup is complemented by crunchy croutons topped with pungent blue cheese. Celeriac tastes like a cross between celery and parsley.

SOUP:

- 1 tablespoon butter
- 1 cup thinly sliced leek (about 1 large)
- ½ cup chopped shallots
- 4 cups chopped peeled celeriac (celery root; about 2 medium)
- 1½ cups cubed peeled Yukon gold potato
- 1 cup water
- 2 (14-ounce) cans fat-free, less-sodium chicken broth
- 2 thyme sprigs
- 2 bay leaves
- 2 cups thinly sliced celery
- 1 cup 2% reduced-fat milk
- ½ teaspoon salt
- ½ teaspoon coarsely ground black pepper
- ¼ cup half-and-half

CROUTONS:

- 8 (½-inch-thick) slices French bread baguette
- Cooking spray
- ½ cup (2 ounces) crumbled Roquefort cheese

1. To prepare soup, melt butter in a large Dutch oven over medium heat. Add leek and shallots; cook 5 minutes or until tender, stirring frequently. Stir in celeriac and next 5 ingredients; bring to a boil. Cover, reduce heat, and simmer 15 minutes or until vegetables are tender. Stir in celery, milk, salt, and pepper; simmer 10 minutes (do not boil). Remove from heat; let stand 5 minutes. Discard bay leaves and thyme.
2. Place half of celery mixture in a blender. Remove center piece of blender lid (to allow steam to escape); secure lid on blender. Place a clean towel over opening in blender lid (to avoid spills); process until smooth. Pour pureed celery mixture into a large bowl. Repeat procedure with remaining celery mixture. Stir in half-and-half; keep warm.
3. Preheat broiler.
4. To prepare croutons, arrange bread slices in a single layer on a baking sheet; lightly coat with cooking spray. Broil 1 minute or until lightly browned. Turn bread slices over; sprinkle each bread slice with 1 tablespoon cheese. Broil 1 minute or until cheese melts; cool 1 minute on baking sheet. Place bread on a cutting board or work surface; cut each bread slice into 6 wedges to form croutons. Ladle about 1 cup soup into each of 8 small bowls; top each serving with 6 croutons. Serve immediately. Yield: 8 servings.

CALORIES 178 (28% from fat); FAT 5.6g (sat 3.3g, mono 1.6g, poly 0.4g); PROTEIN 7.3g; CARB 25g; FIBER 3g; CHOL 16mg; IRON 1.4mg; SODIUM 585mg; CALC 161mg

Melanie's Garden-Tomato Soup

A grilled cheese is the quintessential partner for tomato soup; however, for fun, serve it with a cheese crouton instead. Broil baguette slices topped with Gruyère cheese.

- 2 teaspoons olive oil
- ¾ cup chopped onion
- 1 tablespoon chopped fresh basil
- 1 teaspoon chopped fresh thyme
- 2 garlic cloves, chopped
- 5 cups diced tomato (about 2 pounds)
- 1½ cups water
- 2½ tablespoons tomato paste
- 2 teaspoons sugar
- ¼ teaspoon salt
- ¼ teaspoon black pepper
- Thinly sliced fresh basil (optional)

1. Heat olive oil in a large saucepan over medium heat. Add onion, basil, thyme, and garlic; cook 4 minutes, stirring frequently. Stir in tomato and next 5 ingredients. Bring to a boil. Reduce heat, and simmer 15 minutes. Place half of soup in a blender. Remove center piece of blender lid (to allow steam to escape); secure blender lid on blender. Place a clean towel over opening of blender lid (to avoid spills). Blend until smooth. Pour into a large bowl. Repeat procedure with remaining soup. Serve warm or chilled. Sprinkle with fresh basil, if desired. Yield: 5 servings (serving size: 1 cup).

CALORIES 81 (29% from fat); FAT 2.6g (sat 0.4g, mono 1.4g, poly 0.5g); PROTEIN 2.3g; CARB 14.6g; FIBER 2.9g; CHOL 0mg; IRON 1.3mg; SODIUM 140mg; CALC 29mg

Creamy Potato-Mushroom Soup

Leek and Lima Bean Soup with Bacon

- 3 bacon slices
- 2 cups chopped leek (about 2 leeks)
- 4 cups fresh baby lima beans
- 4 cups fat-free, less-sodium chicken broth
- 1 cup water
- 2 tablespoons fresh lemon juice
- ½ teaspoon salt
- ¼ teaspoon freshly ground black pepper
- ½ cup thinly sliced green onions
- ½ cup reduced-fat sour cream

1. Cook bacon in a large saucepan over medium heat until crisp. Remove bacon from pan, reserving 1 tablespoon drippings in pan. Crumble bacon; set aside. Add leek to drippings in pan; cook 7 minutes or until tender, stirring frequently. Stir in beans, broth, and water; bring to a boil. Reduce heat, and simmer 10 minutes or until beans are tender.

2. Place half of bean mixture in a blender. Remove center piece of blender lid (to allow steam to escape); secure lid on blender. Place a clean towel over opening in blender lid (to avoid spills); process until smooth. Pour pureed bean mixture into a large bowl. Repeat procedure with remaining bean mixture. Stir in lemon juice, salt, and pepper. Ladle about 1 cup soup into each of 8 bowls; top each serving with 1 tablespoon onions, 1 tablespoon sour cream, and about 1 teaspoon bacon. Yield: 8 servings.

CALORIES 170 (26% from fat); FAT 5g (sat 2.4g, mono 1.8g, poly 0.5g); PROTEIN 8.9g; CARB 22.6g; FIBER 6.1g; CHOL 10mg; IRON 2.3mg; SODIUM 440mg; CALC 55mg

Creamy Potato-Mushroom Soup

- 2 bacon slices
- 4 cups chopped cremini mushrooms
- ½ cup chopped shallots
- 3½ cups cubed Yukon gold or baking potato
- 1 (14-ounce) can fat-free, less-sodium chicken broth
- 2 cups 1% low-fat milk
- 2 tablespoons sherry
- ½ teaspoon salt
- ¼ teaspoon black pepper

1. Cook bacon in a Dutch oven over medium heat until crisp. Remove bacon from pan; crumble and set aside. Add mushrooms and shallots to bacon drippings in pan; sauté 5 minutes or until mushrooms are soft. Remove from pan; set aside.

2. Add potato and broth to pan; bring to a boil. Cover, reduce heat, and simmer 12 minutes or until potato is very tender. Place potato mixture in a food processor or blender, and process until smooth. Return potato mixture to pan.

3. Add low-fat milk, mushroom mixture, sherry, salt, and pepper; cook over low heat 10 minutes or until thoroughly heated. Ladle soup into bowls, and top with crumbled bacon. Yield: 4 servings (serving size: 1½ cups).

CALORIES 236 (13% from fat); FAT 3.5g (sat 1.5g, mono 1.2g, poly 0.4g); PROTEIN 13.2g; CARB 39.4g; FIBER 3.3g; CHOL 9mg; IRON 2.4mg; SODIUM 521mg; CALC 172mg

Golden Potato-Leek Soup with Cheddar Toasts

Golden Potato-Leek Soup with Cheddar Toasts

Yukon gold potatoes are key to the rich, buttery flavor.

SOUP:

1 tablespoon butter
3 cups thinly sliced leek (about 3 medium)
6 cups cubed peeled Yukon gold potato (about 2¼ pounds)
2 cups water
½ teaspoon salt
2 (14-ounce) cans organic vegetable broth (such as Swanson Certified Organic)
2 thyme sprigs

CHEDDAR TOASTS:

8 (¼-inch-thick) slices diagonally cut sourdough French bread baguette
Cooking spray
½ cup (2 ounces) shredded sharp Cheddar cheese
⅛ teaspoon ground red pepper

REMAINING INGREDIENTS:

⅓ cup whipping cream
¼ teaspoon freshly ground black pepper
Thyme sprigs (optional)

1. Preheat oven to 375°.
2. To prepare soup, melt butter in a Dutch oven over medium heat. Add leek; cook 10 minutes or until tender, stirring occasionally (do not brown).
3. Add potato, water, salt, broth, and 2 thyme sprigs. Bring to a boil; reduce heat, and simmer 20 minutes or until potatoes are very tender.
4. To prepare Cheddar toasts, place baguette slices in a single layer on a baking sheet. Bake at 375° for 7 minutes or until toasted. Turn slices over; coat with cooking spray, and sprinkle 1 tablespoon cheese over each slice. Bake 5 minutes or until cheese melts. Sprinkle evenly with red pepper.
5. Remove pan from heat; discard thyme sprigs. Partially mash potatoes with a potato masher; stir in cream. Sprinkle with black pepper. Serve with Cheddar toasts. Garnish with thyme sprigs, if desired. Yield: 8 servings (serving size: about 1 cup soup and 1 toast).

CALORIES 299 (25% from fat); FAT 8.6g (sat 4.7g, mono 2.7g, poly 0.6g); PROTEIN 7.5g; CARB 48.4g; FIBER 3.9g; CHOL 25mg; IRON 2mg; SODIUM 660mg; CALC 113mg

Golden Corn Chowder with Roasted Chiles

With sweet corn, potatoes, and tomatoes at their garden best, corn chowder is certainly the soup for the season. Roast the peppers ahead to save time later.

6 jalapeño peppers
3 cups cubed peeled Yukon gold or red potato (about 1 pound)
2 tablespoons butter
1 cup chopped onion
⅔ cup diced orange or yellow bell pepper
3 tablespoons chopped celery
3 cups fresh corn kernels (about 6 ears)
3 cups 1% low-fat milk
2 cups chopped seeded yellow tomato (about 1 pound)
¾ teaspoon salt
¼ teaspoon white pepper
6 tablespoons (1½ ounces) reduced-fat shredded Monterey Jack cheese
2 tablespoons chopped fresh cilantro

1. Preheat broiler.
2. Place jalapeño peppers on a foil-lined baking sheet; broil 10 minutes or until blackened, turning occasionally. Place in a zip-top plastic bag; seal. Let stand 15 minutes. Peel peppers; cut in half lengthwise, discarding seeds and membranes. Finely chop jalapeño peppers; set aside.
3. Place potato in a medium saucepan, and cover with water; bring to a boil. Reduce heat, and simmer 15 minutes or until tender. Drain; partially mash potato with a potato masher.
4. Melt butter in a Dutch oven over medium heat. Add onion, bell pepper, and celery; cook 10 minutes, stirring frequently. Add jalapeño peppers, potato, corn, milk, tomato, salt, and white pepper; cook until thick (about 30 minutes), stirring occasionally. Ladle soup into each of 6 bowls, and sprinkle with cheese and cilantro. Yield: 6 servings (serving size: 1⅓ cups soup, 1 tablespoon cheese, and 1 teaspoon cilantro).

CALORIES 265 (26% from fat); FAT 7.8g (sat 4.2g, mono 2.3g, poly 0.8g); PROTEIN 11.4g; CARB 41.5g; FIBER 5.4g; CHOL 20mg; IRON 1.8mg; SODIUM 466mg; CALC 230mg

Navy Bean Soup

Ham hocks create a rich stock, and their smoky flavor permeates every spoonful.

- 2¼ cups dried navy beans (about 1 pound)
- 6 cups warm water
- 1 small yellow onion, peeled
- 3 whole cloves
- ⅔ cup chopped celery
- 3 thyme sprigs
- 3 parsley sprigs
- 3 smoked ham hocks (about 1⅓ pounds)
- 1 bay leaf
- 3 cups chopped kale
- 2 cups cubed peeled Yukon gold potato
- 1½ cups chopped Vidalia or other sweet onion
- ⅔ cup thinly sliced carrot
- 1 teaspoon salt
- ¾ teaspoon freshly ground black pepper
- 2 tablespoons chopped fresh parsley

1. Sort and wash beans; place in a large Dutch oven. Cover with water to 2 inches above beans; bring to a boil. Cook 2 minutes; remove from heat. Cover and let stand 1 hour. Drain beans; rinse and drain.

2. Return beans to pan; cover with 6 cups warm water. Stud whole onion with cloves; place in pan. Add celery, thyme, parsley sprigs, ham hocks, and bay leaf; bring to a boil. Cover, reduce heat, and simmer 45 minutes.

3. Discard onion, thyme, parsley sprigs, and bay leaf. Remove ham hocks from pan; cool slightly. Remove meat from bones; finely chop meat to yield ⅓ cup. Discard bones, skin, and fat. Add meat, kale, potato, chopped onion, carrot, salt, and pepper to pan; stir well. Cover and simmer 30 minutes or until beans and vegetables are tender. Stir in parsley. Yield: 6 servings (serving size: about 1⅔ cups).

CALORIES 396 (13% from fat); FAT 5.5g (sat 1.8g, mono 1.8g, poly 1.1g); PROTEIN 22.7g; CARB 67g; FIBER 21.7g; CHOL 12mg; IRON 6.2mg; SODIUM 455mg; CALC 194mg

White Bean, Artichoke, and Chard Ragout with Fennel Relish

RAGOUT:

- 1 tablespoon olive oil
- 3 cups thinly sliced leek (about 2 large)
- 1 cup (½-inch-thick) slices carrot
- 3 garlic cloves, minced
- 2½ cups chopped fennel bulb (about 1 large)
- 2 cups (½-inch) cubed red potatoes
- 1 cup chopped red bell pepper
- ¾ cup water
- 1 teaspoon dried basil
- ¼ teaspoon salt
- ¼ teaspoon dried oregano
- ¼ teaspoon black pepper
- 2 (15-ounce) cans cannellini beans, rinsed and drained
- 1 (14.5-ounce) can diced tomatoes with basil, garlic, and oregano, drained
- 1 (14-ounce) can vegetable broth
- 1 (9-ounce) package frozen artichoke hearts, thawed
- 2 cups chopped Swiss chard

RELISH:

- 1 cup boiling water
- 6 sun-dried tomatoes, packed without oil
- 3 cups shredded fennel bulb (about 1 large)
- 1 cup diced yellow bell pepper
- ¼ cup chopped fresh parsley
- 1 tablespoon fresh lemon juice
- 2 teaspoons olive oil
- ½ teaspoon sugar
- ¼ teaspoon salt
- ⅛ teaspoon black pepper

1. To prepare ragout, heat 1 tablespoon oil in a large nonstick skillet over medium heat. Add leek, carrot, and garlic; cover and cook 5 minutes or until tender.

2. Place leek mixture in an electric slow cooker. Add fennel and next 11 ingredients. Cover and cook on HIGH 8 hours or until vegetables are tender. Add chard; stir until chard wilts.

3. To prepare relish, combine 1 cup boiling water and sun-dried tomatoes; let stand 15 minutes. Drain; chop. Combine sun-dried tomatoes and next 8 ingredients; let stand 30 minutes. Yield: 6 servings (serving size: 2 cups ragout and ½ cup relish).

CALORIES 290 (16% from fat); FAT 5.3g (sat 0.8g, mono 2.8g, poly 0.7g); PROTEIN 13.6g; CARB 52.4g; FIBER 15.6g; CHOL 0mg; IRON 5.5mg; SODIUM 1,088mg; CALC 191mg

White Bean, Artichoke, and Chard Ragout with Fennel Relish

Red Lentil Stew with Yogurt Sauce

An immersion blender is used in both mixtures, first to blend the yogurt sauce and again to roughly puree the lentils in the saucepan. The yogurt sauce tastes best chilled.

- 1 cup plain yogurt
- ¼ cup packed cilantro leaves
- 2 teaspoons canola oil
- 3 cups coarsely chopped onion (about 1 large)
- 2 cups coarsely chopped red bell pepper
- 6 garlic cloves, coarsely chopped
- 1 tablespoon curry powder
- 5¼ cups organic vegetable broth (such as Swanson Certified Organic)
- 1 (14.5-ounce) can whole tomatoes, undrained
- 1 pound dried small red lentils
- 1 tablespoon finely grated peeled fresh ginger
- ⅛ teaspoon ground red pepper
- Cilantro sprigs (optional)

1. Combine yogurt and cilantro in beaker of an immersion blender; blend until cilantro is finely chopped. Cover sauce, and refrigerate.
2. Heat oil in a large saucepan over medium heat. Add onion, bell pepper, and garlic; sauté 8 minutes or until tender. Add curry powder; cook 1 minute, stirring constantly. Add broth and tomatoes to pan; bring to a boil. Stir in lentils. Cover, reduce heat, and simmer 30 minutes or until lentils are very soft. Stir in ginger.
3. Using an immersion blender in pan, coarsely puree lentil mixture. Stir in ground red pepper. Ladle 1 cup lentil mixture into each of 8 individual soup bowls, and top each with 1 tablespoon yogurt sauce. Garnish with cilantro sprigs, if desired. Yield: 8 servings.

CALORIES 265 (10% from fat); FAT 3.1g (sat 0.9g, mono 0.6g, poly 0.8g); PROTEIN 17.5g; CARB 45.1g; FIBER 9.9g; CHOL 4mg; IRON 4.4mg; SODIUM 757mg; CALC 119mg

Smoked Onion and Garlic Soup

Mellow smoked onions and garlic give body and depth to this delightfully fragrant twist on a classic. Fresh thyme sprigs are an aromatic garnish. Heavy-duty foil creates a disposable "tray" for the onions and garlic, exposing them to lots of smoke. For added sturdiness, keep the foil tray on a baking sheet when transporting the onion mixture to and from the grill.

- 2 cups wood chips (such as apple or pecan)
- Cooking spray
- 6 cups thinly vertically sliced yellow onion
- 15 garlic cloves
- 1½ teaspoons chopped fresh or ½ teaspoon dried thyme
- 2 teaspoons tomato paste
- ½ teaspoon freshly ground black pepper
- ¼ cup dry sherry
- 3 (14-ounce) cans less-sodium beef broth
- 12 (½-ounce) slices French bread baguette, toasted
- ¾ cup (3 ounces) shredded Gruyère cheese

1. Soak wood chips in water 30 minutes; drain.
2. Prepare grill for indirect grilling, heating one side to low and leaving one side with no heat. Maintain temperature at 200° to 225°.
3. Place prepared wood chips on hot coals. Place a disposable aluminum foil pan on unheated side of grill. Pour 2 cups water in pan. Place grill rack on grill. Fold a 24 x 12–inch sheet of heavy-duty foil in half crosswise to form a 12-inch square. Fold edges of foil up to form a rim. Coat foil with cooking spray. Place foil tray on a baking sheet; arrange onion and garlic on foil tray. Carefully place foil tray on grill rack over foil pan on unheated side. Close lid; cook 1 hour and 15 minutes. Carefully remove foil tray from grill; place on baking sheet.
4. Heat a large Dutch oven over medium-high heat. Add onion mixture, thyme, tomato paste, and pepper; cook 1 minute, stirring constantly. Add sherry and broth; bring to a boil. Cover, reduce heat, and simmer 1 hour.
5. Preheat broiler.
6. Ladle about 1 cup soup into each of 6 ovenproof soup bowls. Top each serving with 2 toast slices and 2 tablespoons cheese. Broil 3 minutes or until cheese melts. Serve immediately. Yield: 6 servings.

CALORIES 189 (22% from fat); FAT 4.7g (sat 2.7g, mono 1.4g, poly 0.3g); PROTEIN 9.6g; CARB 27.5g; FIBER 1.9g; CHOL 16mg; IRON 1.3mg; SODIUM 601mg; CALC 175mg

Smoked Onion and Garlic Soup

French Onion Soup

French Onion Soup

Allowing the soup to simmer for a couple of hours tenderizes each piece of onion until it's perfectly infused with the broth.

- 2 teaspoons olive oil
- 4 cups thinly vertically sliced Walla Walla or other sweet onion
- 4 cups thinly vertically sliced red onion
- ½ teaspoon sugar
- ½ teaspoon freshly ground black pepper
- ¼ teaspoon salt
- ¼ cup dry white wine
- 8 cups less-sodium beef broth
- ¼ teaspoon chopped fresh thyme
- 8 (1-ounce) slices French bread, cut into 1-inch cubes
- 8 (1-ounce) slices reduced-fat, reduced-sodium Swiss cheese (such as Alpine Lace)

1. Heat olive oil in a Dutch oven over medium-high heat. Add onions to pan; sauté 5 minutes or until tender. Stir in sugar, pepper, and ¼ teaspoon salt. Reduce heat to medium; cook 20 minutes, stirring frequently. Increase heat to medium-high, and sauté 5 minutes or until onion is golden brown. Stir in wine, and cook 1 minute. Add broth and thyme; bring to a boil. Cover, reduce heat, and simmer 2 hours.

2. Preheat broiler.

3. Place bread cubes in a single layer on a baking sheet; broil 2 minutes or until toasted, turning cubes after 1 minute.

4. Place 8 ovenproof soup bowls on a jelly-roll pan. Ladle 1 cup soup into each bowl. Divide bread evenly among bowls, and top each serving with 1 cheese slice. Broil 3 minutes or until cheese begins to brown. Yield: 8 servings.

CALORIES 290 (30% from fat); FAT 9.6g (sat 4.8g, mono 1.9g, poly 0.7g); PROTEIN 16.8g; CARB 33.4g; FIBER 3.1g; CHOL 20mg; IRON 1.6mg; SODIUM 359mg; CALC 317mg

Quick Fall Minestrone

This easy soup brims with fresh vegetables; canned beans and orzo make it hearty and filling. Use a vegetable peeler to quickly remove the skin from the squash.

- 1 tablespoon vegetable oil
- 1 cup chopped onion
- 2 garlic cloves, minced
- 6 cups vegetable broth
- 2½ cups (¾-inch) cubed peeled butternut squash
- 2½ cups (¾-inch) cubed peeled baking potato
- 1 cup (1-inch) cut green beans (about ¼ pound)
- ½ cup diced carrot
- 1 teaspoon dried oregano
- ¼ teaspoon black pepper
- ¼ teaspoon salt
- 4 cups chopped kale
- ½ cup uncooked orzo (rice-shaped pasta)
- 1 (16-ounce) can cannellini beans or other white beans, rinsed and drained
- ½ cup (2 ounces) grated fresh Parmesan cheese

1. Heat oil in a large Dutch oven over medium-high heat. Add onion and garlic; sauté 2½ minutes. Add broth and next 7 ingredients; bring to a boil. Reduce heat; simmer 3 minutes. Add kale, orzo, and cannellini beans; cook 5 minutes or until vegetables are tender. Sprinkle with cheese. Yield: 8 servings (serving size: 1½ cups soup and 1 tablespoon cheese).

CALORIES 212 (21% from fat); FAT 5g (sat 1.6g, mono 1g, poly 1.2g); PROTEIN 9.6g; CARB 36g; FIBER 3.9g; CHOL 5mg; IRON 1.9mg; SODIUM 961mg; CALC 164mg

Spicy Shrimp and Rice Soup

Fine-tune the taste of this filling soup as you wish with the optional toppings.

- 4 cups fat-free, less-sodium chicken broth
- 2 cups water
- 1 cup instant long-grain rice (such as Minute brand)
- 1 tablespoon canola oil
- 1 teaspoon bottled minced garlic
- ½ teaspoon crushed red pepper
- 1½ pounds large shrimp, peeled and deveined
- 4 lime wedges
- Bean sprouts (optional)
- Sliced green onions (optional)
- Chopped fresh cilantro (optional)
- Sliced jalapeño pepper (optional)

1. Combine chicken broth and water in a large saucepan; bring to a boil. Stir in instant long-grain rice; bring to a boil. Remove from heat, and let stand 5 minutes.

2. Heat oil in a large nonstick skillet over medium-high heat. Add garlic, red pepper, and shrimp; sauté 3 minutes or until shrimp are done. Stir shrimp mixture into broth mixture. Divide soup evenly among 4 bowls; serve with lime wedges. Top each serving with sprouts, onions, cilantro, and jalapeño, if desired. Yield: 4 servings (serving size: about 1½ cups soup and 1 lime wedge).

CALORIES 315 (20% from fat); FAT 6.9g (sat 1.1g, mono 3.1g, poly 1.6g); PROTEIN 38.8g; CARB 21.1g; FIBER 1.6g; CHOL 259mg; IRON 5.2mg; SODIUM 644mg; CALC 113mg

Bistro Bouillabaisse

Featuring a tempting variety of seafood, this recipe can easily be doubled to serve four.

- 1 tablespoon olive oil
- ½ cup vertically sliced onion
- ¼ cup julienne-cut leek
- ¼ cup thinly sliced celery
- 1 garlic clove, minced
- ¾ cup diced plum tomato
- ½ teaspoon fennel seeds
- ¼ teaspoon dried thyme
- ⅛ teaspoon dried tarragon
- Dash of crushed saffron threads
- ½ cup dry white wine
- 1 tablespoon Pernod or sambuca (licorice-flavored liqueur)
- 1 cup bottled clam juice
- ½ cup tomato juice
- ⅛ teaspoon freshly ground black pepper
- 8 littleneck clams
- 4 ounces grouper or other firm white fish fillet, cut into 1-inch pieces
- 6 medium mussels, scrubbed and debearded
- 6 large shrimp, peeled and deveined
- 1 (5-ounce) lobster tail, split in half lengthwise
- 2 tablespoons chopped fresh flat-leaf parsley

1. Heat olive oil in a large saucepan over medium heat. Add onion and next 3 ingredients; cook 5 minutes, stirring frequently. Add tomato, fennel seeds, thyme, tarragon, and saffron; cook 1 minute. Stir in wine and liqueur; bring to a boil. Reduce heat, and simmer 5 minutes. Add juices and pepper; bring to a simmer. Cook 10 minutes.

2. Add clams and grouper; cook over medium heat 3 minutes or until clams begin to open. Add mussels, shrimp, and lobster; cook 4 minutes or until mussels open. Discard any unopened clams or mussels. Ladle stew into shallow bowls; sprinkle with chopped fresh parsley. Yield: 2 servings (serving size: 2 cups stew and 1 tablespoon parsley).

CALORIES 399 (27% from fat); FAT 11.9g (sat 2.2g, mono 6g, poly 1.8g); PROTEIN 50.2g; CARB 18.1g; FIBER 2.4g; CHOL 203mg; IRON 9.8mg; SODIUM 977mg; CALC 171mg

Chicken and Barley Stew

Frozen chopped onion makes this dish even quicker to prepare. If you use it, add it with the frozen mixed vegetables. This stew is perfect on a cold winter's night.

- 1 cup uncooked quick-cooking barley
- 3 (14-ounce) cans fat-free, less-sodium chicken broth
- 1 tablespoon olive oil
- 1¾ cups chopped onion
- 1 (10-ounce) package frozen mixed vegetables
- 1 cup chopped cooked chicken
- ¼ teaspoon salt
- ¼ teaspoon dried thyme
- ¼ teaspoon black pepper

1. Bring barley and broth to a boil in a large saucepan. Reduce heat, and simmer 5 minutes.

2. While barley cooks, heat oil in a large nonstick skillet over medium-high heat. Add onion; sauté 3 minutes. Add mixed vegetables; sauté 2 minutes. Add vegetable mixture, chicken, salt, thyme, and pepper to barley mixture; simmer 4 minutes. Yield: 4 servings (serving size: about 1¾ cups).

CALORIES 356 (19% from fat); FAT 7.5g (sat 1.5g, mono 1.9g, poly 3.3g); PROTEIN 22.7g; CARB 50.7g; FIBER 12.1g; CHOL 31mg; IRON 3.1mg; SODIUM 763mg; CALC 54mg

Chicken and Rosemary Dumplings

Chicken and Rosemary Dumplings

Spoonfuls of seasoned buttermilk biscuit dough form light, fluffy dumplings in this classic American dish.

SOUP:

4 cups fat-free, less-sodium chicken broth
3 cups water
1 pound chicken drumsticks, skinned
1 pound skinless, boneless chicken breast halves
2 thyme sprigs
2 teaspoons olive oil
1½ cups diced carrots
1½ cups chopped celery
1 cup diced onion
2 garlic cloves, minced
½ teaspoon salt

DUMPLINGS:

1¼ cups all-purpose flour (about 5½ ounces)
1 tablespoon chopped fresh or ½ teaspoon dried rosemary
2 teaspoons baking powder
¼ teaspoon salt
2 tablespoons butter, softened
½ cup low-fat buttermilk
1 large egg
¼ cup all-purpose flour (about 1 ounce)
¼ cup water

REMAINING INGREDIENT:

Freshly ground black pepper

1. Combine first 5 ingredients in a large Dutch oven over medium-high heat; bring to a boil. Reduce heat, and simmer, uncovered, 15 minutes or until chicken is done. Remove pan from heat. Remove chicken pieces from broth; cool slightly. Strain broth through a sieve into a large bowl; discard solids. Remove chicken from bones. Discard bones; chop chicken into bite-sized pieces. Set chicken aside.

2. Heat oil in pan over medium-high heat. Add carrots, celery, onion, and garlic; sauté 6 minutes or until onion is tender. Add reserved broth mixture and ½ teaspoon salt; simmer 10 minutes. Discard thyme sprigs. Keep warm.

3. To prepare dumplings, lightly spoon flour into dry measuring cups; level with a knife. Combine 1¼ cups flour, rosemary, baking powder, and ¼ teaspoon salt in a large bowl. Cut in butter with a pastry blender or 2 knives until mixture resembles coarse meal. Combine buttermilk and egg, stirring with a whisk. Add buttermilk mixture to flour mixture, stirring just until combined.

4. Return chopped chicken to broth mixture; bring to a simmer over medium-high heat. Combine ¼ cup flour and ¼ cup water, stirring with a whisk until well blended to form a slurry. Add flour mixture to pan; simmer 3 minutes. Drop dumpling dough, 1 tablespoon per dumpling, onto chicken mixture to form 12 dumplings. Cover and cook 7 minutes (do not boil). Sprinkle with black pepper. Yield: 6 servings (serving size: 1⅓ cups soup and 2 dumplings).

CALORIES 366 (24% from fat); FAT 9.7g (sat 3.8g, mono 3.5g, poly 1.3g); PROTEIN 32.5g; CARB 35.1g; FIBER 2.9g; CHOL 115mg; IRON 3.3mg; SODIUM 936mg; CALC 169mg

Southwestern Chicken Soup

This popular dish is perfect for family suppers and is simple to put together if you use a rotisserie chicken.

Cooking spray
1 cup chopped onion
3 garlic cloves, minced
6 cups fat-free, less-sodium chicken broth
¼ cup uncooked white rice
1 teaspoon ground cumin
1 (16-ounce) can Great Northern beans, rinsed and drained
3 cups chopped skinless, boneless rotisserie chicken breast
½ cup coarsely chopped fresh cilantro
½ teaspoon black pepper
¼ teaspoon salt
1 cup chopped seeded tomato
¾ cup diced peeled avocado (about 1 medium)
1 tablespoon fresh lime juice
6 lime wedges

1. Heat a large sauté pan over medium-high heat. Coat pan with cooking spray. Add onion and garlic; sauté 3 minutes. Add broth, rice, cumin, and beans; bring to a boil. Reduce heat; simmer 15 minutes. Stir in chicken, cilantro, pepper, and salt; simmer 5 minutes or until chicken is thoroughly heated.

2. Remove from heat; stir in tomato, avocado, and juice. Serve with lime wedges. Yield: 6 servings (serving size: 1⅔ cups soup and 1 lime wedge).

CALORIES 274 (25% from fat); FAT 7.7g (sat 1.5g, mono 3.9g, poly 1.3g); PROTEIN 28.4g; CARB 23.1g; FIBER 6g; CHOL 60mg; IRON 2.6mg; SODIUM 516mg; CALC 65mg

White Chicken Chili

Cooking spray
- 2 pounds skinless, boneless chicken breast, cut into bite-sized pieces
- 2 cups finely chopped onion
- 2 garlic cloves, minced
- 2 teaspoons ground cumin
- ½ teaspoon dried oregano
- 1 teaspoon ground coriander
- 2 (4.5-ounce) cans chopped green chiles, undrained
- 1 cup water
- 2 (15.5-ounce) cans cannellini beans, rinsed and drained
- 1 (14-ounce) can fat-free, less-sodium chicken broth
- ½ teaspoon hot pepper sauce
- 1 cup (4 ounces) shredded Monterey Jack cheese
- ½ cup chopped fresh cilantro
- ½ cup chopped green onions

1. Heat a large nonstick skillet over medium-high heat. Coat pan with cooking spray. Add chicken to pan; cook 10 minutes or until browned on all sides.

2. Heat a large Dutch oven over medium-high heat. Coat pan with cooking spray. Add onion to pan; sauté 6 minutes or until tender, stirring frequently. Add garlic, and sauté 2 minutes, stirring frequently. Stir in cumin, dried oregano, and coriander; sauté 1 minute. Stir in chiles; reduce heat to low, and cook 10 minutes, partially covered. Add chicken, water, beans, and broth; bring to a simmer. Cover and simmer 10 minutes. Stir in hot sauce. Ladle 1 cup chili into each of 8 bowls; sprinkle each serving with 2 tablespoons cheese, 1 tablespoon cilantro, and 1 tablespoon green onions. Yield: 8 servings.

CALORIES 233 (23% from fat); FAT 5.9g (sat 3.1g, mono 1.6g, poly 0.5g); PROTEIN 32.7g; CARB 11.7g; FIBER 3.4g; CHOL 78mg; IRON 3.2mg; SODIUM 694mg; CALC 180mg

Tuscan Chicken Soup

- 1 cup chopped onion
- 2 tablespoons tomato paste
- ¼ teaspoon salt
- ¼ teaspoon freshly ground black pepper
- 1 (15-ounce) can cannellini beans, rinsed and drained
- 1 (14-ounce) can fat-free, less-sodium chicken broth
- 1 (7-ounce) bottle roasted red bell peppers, rinsed and drained, and cut into ½-inch pieces
- 1 pound skinless, boneless chicken thighs, cut into 1-inch pieces
- 3 garlic cloves, minced
- ½ teaspoon chopped fresh rosemary
- 1 (6-ounce) package fresh baby spinach
- 8 teaspoons grated Parmesan cheese

1. Combine first 9 ingredients in an electric slow cooker. Cover and cook on HIGH 1 hour; reduce heat to low, and cook 3 hours. Stir in rosemary and spinach; cook on LOW 10 minutes. Ladle 1½ cups soup into each of 4 bowls; top each serving with 2 teaspoons cheese. Yield: 4 servings.

CALORIES 239 (17% from fat); FAT 5.8g (sat 1.8g, mono 1.7g, poly 1.4g); PROTEIN 28.6g; CARB 16.3g; FIBER 4.6g; CHOL 97mg; IRON 3.9mg; SODIUM 768mg; CALC 126mg

Chicken-Vegetable Soup with Orzo

This homey soup shows just how quickly you can make chicken broth in the microwave. It also shows off the microwave's fabulous way with vegetables; they not only keep more color but they also retain more vitamins.

- 5 cups water
- 2 pounds chicken drumsticks, skinned
- 2 cups small broccoli florets
- 2 cups presliced mushrooms
- 1½ cups sliced carrot
- 1 cup chopped onion
- ¼ cup chopped fresh basil
- ¼ cup uncooked orzo (rice-shaped pasta)
- 1 teaspoon salt
- ⅛ teaspoon black pepper
- 6 tablespoons (1½ ounces) grated fresh Parmesan cheese

1. Combine 5 cups water and chicken in a 3-quart casserole. Cover with lid, and microwave at HIGH 30 minutes or until chicken is done, stirring after 15 minutes. Drain in a colander over a bowl, reserving cooking liquid. Cool chicken slightly. Remove chicken from bones; discard bones. Shred chicken with 2 forks to measure 2½ cups.

2. Combine broccoli and next 4 ingredients in casserole. Cover; microwave at HIGH 8 minutes or until tender, stirring after 4 minutes. Add reserved cooking liquid, chicken, pasta, salt, and pepper. Cover; microwave at HIGH 6 minutes or until pasta is tender. Ladle 1 cup soup into each of 6 bowls; sprinkle each serving with 1 tablespoon cheese. Yield: 6 servings.

CALORIES 277 (24% from fat); FAT 7.5g (sat 2.6g, mono 2.2g, poly 1.5g); PROTEIN 36.9g; CARB 14.5g; FIBER 3g; CHOL 121mg; IRON 2.8mg; SODIUM 658mg; CALC 134mg

Italian Sausage Soup

This soup has that simmered-all-day flavor but takes just minutes to prepare. Serve it with hot crusty bread.

- 8 ounces hot or sweet turkey Italian sausage
- 2 cups fat-free, less-sodium chicken broth
- 1 (14.5-ounce) can diced tomatoes with basil, garlic, and oregano
- ½ cup uncooked small shell pasta
- 2 cups bagged baby spinach leaves
- 2 tablespoons grated fresh Parmesan or Romano cheese
- 2 tablespoons chopped fresh basil

1. Heat a large saucepan over medium heat. Remove casings from sausage. Add sausage to pan; cook about 5 minutes or until browned, stirring to crumble. Drain; return to pan.

2. Add broth, tomatoes, and pasta to pan; bring to a boil over high heat. Cover, reduce heat, and simmer 10 minutes or until pasta is done. Remove from heat; stir in spinach until wilted. Sprinkle each serving with cheese and basil. Yield: 4 servings (serving size: 1⅓ cups soup, 1½ teaspoons cheese, and 1½ teaspoons basil).

CALORIES 216 (30% from fat); FAT 7.1g (sat 2.6g, mono 2.5g, poly 1.8g); PROTEIN 17.4g; CARB 20g; FIBER 1.6g; CHOL 52mg; IRON 3.2mg; SODIUM 1,020mg; CALC 153mg

Slow-Cooker Sausage-and-Vegetable Chili

(pictured on page 326)

With the help of ready-to-use convenience products and a little creativity, preparing a healthful meal just got easier.

CHILI:

- 1¼ cups bottled salsa
- 1 cup (1-inch) pieces red bell pepper
- 1 cup (1-inch) pieces yellow bell pepper
- 1 tablespoon chili powder
- 1 (15.5-ounce) can whole-kernel corn, drained
- 1 (12-ounce) package chicken sausages with habanero chiles and tequila (such as Gerhard's), cut into ½-inch pieces

REMAINING INGREDIENTS:

- 2 cups hot cooked long-grain rice
- ¼ cup crushed baked tortilla chips
- ¼ cup chopped fresh cilantro
- ¼ cup chopped green onions
- ¼ cup fat-free sour cream

1. To prepare chili, combine salsa, peppers, chili powder, corn, and sausages in an electric slow cooker. Cover with lid; cook on LOW 8 hours.

2. Spoon ½ cup rice into each of 4 bowls; top each serving with about 1¼ cups chili, 1 tablespoon crushed tortilla chips, 1 tablespoon fresh cilantro, 1 tablespoon onions, and 1 tablespoon sour cream. Yield: 4 servings.

NOTE: Smoked turkey sausage can be substituted for the chicken sausage.

CALORIES 412 (23% from fat); FAT 10.6g (sat 2.7g, mono 3.8g, poly 3.2g); PROTEIN 18.1g; CARB 63.1g; FIBER 9.6g; CHOL 66mg; IRON 4mg; SODIUM 1,111mg; CALC 85mg

All-American Beef Stew

- 2 tablespoons uncooked granulated tapioca
- 1 tablespoon sugar
- 1 tablespoon garlic powder
- 1 teaspoon salt
- 3 (5.5-ounce) cans tomato juice
- 4 cups chopped onion
- 3 cups chopped celery
- 2½ cups (¼-inch-thick) slices carrot
- 2 (8-ounce) packages presliced mushrooms
- 2 pounds beef stew meat

1. Place first 5 ingredients in a blender; process until smooth.

2. Combine onion, celery, carrot, mushrooms, and beef in an electric slow cooker; add juice mixture. Cover and cook on HIGH 5 hours or until beef is tender. Yield: 6 servings (serving size: about 1¾ cups).

CALORIES 345 (29% from fat); FAT 11.1g (sat 4g, mono 4.7g, poly 0.7g); PROTEIN 34.1g; CARB 28.8g; FIBER 5.9g; CHOL 95mg; IRON 5.3mg; SODIUM 811mg; CALC 81mg

Udon-Beef Noodle Bowl

This entrée falls somewhere between a soup and a noodle dish. You can eat it with chopsticks, but be sure to have a spoon to catch the broth.

- 8 ounces uncooked udon noodles (thick, round fresh Japanese wheat noodles) or spaghetti
- 1½ teaspoons bottled minced garlic
- ½ teaspoon crushed red pepper
- 2 (14-ounce) cans less-sodium beef broth
- 3 tablespoons low-sodium soy sauce
- 3 tablespoons sake (rice wine) or dry sherry
- 1 tablespoon honey
- Cooking spray
- 2 cups sliced shiitake mushroom caps (about 4 ounces)
- ½ cup thinly sliced carrot
- 8 ounces top round, thinly sliced
- ¾ cup diagonally cut green onions
- 1 (6-ounce) package fresh baby spinach

1. Cook noodles according to package directions; drain.

2. Place garlic, pepper, and broth in a large saucepan. Bring to a boil; reduce heat, and simmer 10 minutes.

3. Combine soy sauce, sake, and honey in a small bowl; stir with a whisk.

4. Heat a large nonstick skillet over medium-high heat. Coat pan with cooking spray. Add mushrooms and carrot, and sauté 2 minutes. Stir in soy sauce mixture; cook 2 minutes, stirring constantly. Add vegetable mixture to broth mixture. Stir in beef; cook 2 minutes or until beef loses its pink color. Stir in noodles, green onions, and spinach. Serve immediately. Yield: 5 servings (serving size: about 1½ cups).

CALORIES 306 (16% from fat); FAT 5.6g (sat 1.8g, mono 2g, poly 0.4g); PROTEIN 22.4g; CARB 36.6g; FIBER 2.4g; CHOL 39mg; IRON 3.4mg; SODIUM 707mg; CALC 59mg

Chunky Minestrone with Beef

Stir in the cooked pasta at the end to help the shells keep their shape. A slow cooker makes this a versatile hands-off recipe.

- 1 pound beef stew meat, trimmed
- 1 cup chopped onion
- ½ cup chopped carrot
- 2 (14.5-ounce) cans no-salt-added diced tomatoes with roasted garlic, undrained
- 2 (14-ounce) cans fat-free, less-sodium chicken broth
- 1 teaspoon dried Italian seasoning
- ½ teaspoon salt
- ¼ teaspoon black pepper
- 2 cups chopped cabbage
- 1 cup thinly sliced yellow squash
- 1 (15½-ounce) can chickpeas (garbanzo beans), rinsed and drained
- 2 cups cooked seashell pasta
- 6 tablespoons (1½ ounces) grated fresh Parmesan cheese

1. Combine first 8 ingredients in an electric slow cooker. Cover and cook on HIGH 1 hour. Reduce heat to LOW, and cook 5 hours or until meat is tender.

2. Stir in cabbage, squash, and chickpeas. Cook on HIGH 45 minutes or until vegetables are tender. Stir in cooked pasta. Top each serving with 1 tablespoon cheese. Yield: 6 servings (serving size: 1½ cups soup and 1 tablespoon cheese).

CALORIES 253 (29% from fat); FAT 8.2g (sat 3.2g, mono 2.3g, poly 0.3g); PROTEIN 22.1g; CARB 21.8g; FIBER 3.7g; CHOL 53mg; IRON 3.1mg; SODIUM 590mg; CALC 136mg

Wild Mushroom and Beef Stew

Wild Mushroom and Beef Stew

Roasted red onions give this stew its robust flavor.

- 5 cups water
- 3 cups fat-free, less-sodium chicken broth
- 1 cup dried porcini mushrooms (about 1 ounce)
- 2 tablespoons all-purpose flour
- 1 teaspoon salt
- 2 garlic cloves, minced
- 2 pounds beef stew meat
- 1 tablespoon canola oil, divided
- Cooking spray
- 2 (8-ounce) packages presliced button mushrooms
- 1 pound cremini mushrooms, sliced (about 10 cups)
- ¼ cup tomato paste
- 4 cups coarsely chopped red onion
- 2 teaspoons chopped fresh or ½ teaspoon dried rosemary
- ½ teaspoon freshly ground black pepper
- 2 tablespoons chopped fresh flat-leaf parsley

1. Bring water and broth to a boil in a saucepan. Add porcini; remove from heat, and let stand 15 minutes. Drain in a colander over a bowl, reserving liquid. Chop porcini; set aside.

2. Combine flour, salt, garlic, and beef, tossing well to coat. Heat 1 teaspoon oil in a large Dutch oven over medium-high heat. Add half of beef mixture; sauté 4 minutes or until browned. Remove from pan. Repeat procedure with 1 teaspoon oil and remaining beef mixture. Wipe pan clean with a paper towel; coat with cooking spray. Add button and cremini mushrooms; cover, reduce heat to medium, and cook 10 minutes or until mushrooms release liquid. Stir in reserved porcini liquid, chopped porcini, beef mixture, and tomato paste; bring to a boil. Cover, reduce heat, and simmer 45 minutes.

3. Preheat oven to 450°.

4. Combine remaining 1 teaspoon oil and onion on a foil-lined jelly-roll pan; toss well to coat. Bake at 450° for 25 minutes, stirring twice.

5. Add roasted onion, rosemary, and pepper to stew. Cover and simmer 30 minutes or until beef is tender. Sprinkle each serving with parsley. Yield: 8 servings (serving size: 1½ cups soup and ¾ teaspoon parsley).

CALORIES 324 (30% from fat); FAT 10.7g (sat 3.3g, mono 4.8g, poly 1.2g); PROTEIN 32.6g; CARB 25.2g; FIBER 6.1g; CHOL 71mg; IRON 7.4mg; SODIUM 509mg; CALC 51mg

Lamb and Lager Stew

Any light or amber lager or ale would be good; a true stout might be too bitter. Serve stew over mashed potatoes or rice with a green salad.

- 1½ cups frozen pearl onions
- 1½ cups (½-inch) diagonally cut celery
- 1 cup (½-inch) diagonally cut carrot
- 2 tablespoons Dijon mustard
- 1 teaspoon salt
- 1 teaspoon dried oregano
- ¼ teaspoon freshly ground black pepper
- 2 pounds boneless leg of lamb, trimmed and cut into 1-inch cubes
- 1 pound baking potatoes, peeled and cut into ¾-inch cubes
- 1 (12-ounce) bottle amber lager
- 4 garlic cloves, crushed
- 3 thyme sprigs
- ½ cup fat-free, less-sodium beef broth
- 3 tablespoons cornstarch

1. Combine first 12 ingredients in an electric slow cooker. Combine broth and cornstarch. Add to lamb mixture; stir well. Cover and cook on HIGH 1 hour; reduce heat to LOW, and cook 6 hours or until meat is tender. Discard thyme sprigs. Yield: 8 servings (serving size: ¾ cup).

CALORIES 331 (23% from fat); FAT 8.3g (sat 2.8g, mono 3.3g, poly 0.9g); PROTEIN 34.4g; CARB 28.2g; FIBER 2.8g; CHOL 100mg; IRON 4.1mg; SODIUM 57mg; CALC 679mg

Asian Pork-and-Noodle Soup

Save time by cooking the pork while the broth mixture simmers.

- 2 cups water
- ½ cup drained, sliced water chestnuts
- ¼ cup thinly sliced fresh shiitake mushroom caps
- 1 teaspoon minced peeled fresh ginger
- 1 teaspoon low-sodium soy sauce
- 2 green onions, cut into 2-inch pieces
- 2 garlic cloves, thinly sliced
- 1 (14-ounce) can less-sodium beef broth
- 1 (3-inch) cinnamon stick
- 6 ounces pork tenderloin
- ⅛ teaspoon black pepper
- Cooking spray
- 2 ounces uncooked soba (buckwheat noodles), broken in half
- 1 tablespoon rice vinegar
- ½ teaspoon dark sesame oil

1. Bring first 9 ingredients to a boil in a large saucepan; reduce heat, and simmer 30 minutes.
2. Preheat broiler.
3. Sprinkle pork with pepper; place on a broiler pan coated with cooking spray. Broil 7 minutes on each side or until done. Cool slightly; cut pork into strips.
4. Bring broth mixture to a boil; add soba noodles. Cook 6 minutes or until tender. Stir in pork, vinegar, and oil. Discard cinnamon stick. Yield: 2 servings (serving size: 2 cups).

CALORIES 277 (17% from fat); FAT 5.2g (sat 1.2g, mono 1.8g, poly 0.9g); PROTEIN 23.4g; CARB 29.8g; FIBER 1g; CHOL 59mg; IRON 2.7mg; SODIUM 137mg; CALC 39mg

Pork Posole

There are three main versions of this hominy stew, each representing a color of the Mexican flag. Red posole, like this version, is made from dried chiles; ours features ancho chiles. The green version is made from fresh chiles, and white posole has no chiles.

- 4 ancho chiles, stemmed and seeded
- 2 cups boiling water
- 1 tablespoon cumin seeds
- 1 tablespoon peanut oil
- 1½ pounds boneless pork loin, trimmed and cut into (½-inch) pieces
- 1½ cups chopped onion
- 4 garlic cloves, minced
- 4 cups fat-free, less-sodium chicken broth
- 2 tablespoons sugar
- ¾ teaspoon salt
- 2 (15.5-ounce) cans white hominy, undrained
- 6 tablespoons sliced radishes
- 6 tablespoons chopped green onions
- 6 tablespoons minced fresh cilantro
- 6 lime slices

1. Heat a cast-iron skillet over high heat. Place chiles in pan; flatten with a spatula. Cook 10 seconds on each side or until blackened. Combine toasted chiles and 2 cups boiling water in a bowl; let stand 10 minutes or until soft. Place chile mixture in a blender or food processor; process until smooth.
2. Cook cumin seeds in a large Dutch oven over medium heat 1 minute or until toasted and fragrant. Place in a spice or coffee grinder; process until finely ground.
3. Heat oil in Dutch oven over medium-high heat. Add pork; cook 5 minutes, browning on all sides. Remove pork from pan. Reduce heat to medium. Add onion and garlic to pan; cook 8 minutes or until onion is browned, stirring frequently. Stir in pork, pureed chiles, toasted ground cumin, broth, sugar, salt, and hominy; bring to a simmer. Cook 30 minutes or until pork is tender. Spoon 1⅔ cups posole into each of 6 bowls; top each serving with 1 tablespoon radishes, 1 tablespoon green onions, and 1 tablespoon cilantro. Serve with lime slices. Yield: 6 servings.

CALORIES 376 (27% from fat); FAT 11.2g (sat 2.9g, mono 4.5g, poly 2.6g); PROTEIN 30.7g; CARB 37.4g; FIBER 7.4g; CHOL 67mg; IRON 4mg; SODIUM 971mg; CALC 67mg

Pork Posole

Desserts

Lemon-Blueberry Bundt Cake, page 360

Red Raspberry Velvet Cake

Red Raspberry Velvet Cake

This classic red-tinted layer cake is believed to have originated at New York's Waldorf-Astoria Hotel.

Cooking spray
3 cups sifted cake flour (about 12 ounces)
2 tablespoons unsweetened cocoa
1 teaspoon baking soda
1 teaspoon baking powder
½ teaspoon salt
1⅔ cups granulated sugar
½ cup butter, softened
4 large egg whites
2 cups fat-free buttermilk
1 (1-ounce) bottle red food coloring
1 teaspoon vanilla extract

FROSTING:

7 ounces ⅓-less-fat cream cheese
1 teaspoon vanilla extract
2¾ cups powdered sugar

REMAINING INGREDIENTS:

½ cup seedless raspberry jam
White chocolate curls (optional)

1. Preheat oven to 350°.
2. Coat 2 (9-inch) round cake pans with cooking spray; line bottoms of pans with wax paper.
3. Lightly spoon 3 cups flour into dry measuring cups; level with a knife. Combine flour, cocoa, and next 3 ingredients. Set aside.
4. Beat granulated sugar and butter with a mixer at medium speed 4 minutes or until well blended. Add egg whites; beat at medium speed 5 minutes or until fluffy. Combine buttermilk, food coloring, and 1 teaspoon vanilla in a small bowl; stir well with a whisk. Add flour mixture to sugar mixture alternately with buttermilk mixture, beginning and ending with flour mixture; mix just until moistened.
5. Pour batter into pans. Tap pans once on counter to remove air bubbles. Bake at 350° for 30 minutes or until a wooden pick inserted in center comes out clean. Do not overbake. Cool in pans 10 minutes; remove from pans. Cool completely on wire racks.
6. To prepare frosting, combine cream cheese and 1 teaspoon vanilla in a medium bowl; beat at high speed 3 minutes or until fluffy. Add powdered sugar; beat at low speed just until blended (do not overbeat).
7. Place 1 cake layer on a plate. Spread with jam; top with second layer. Spread frosting over cake. Garnish with chocolate curls, if desired. Store loosely covered in refrigerator. Yield: 18 servings (serving size: 1 slice).

CALORIES 308 (23% from fat); FAT 7.9g (sat 4.9g, mono 2.1g, poly 0.3g); PROTEIN 3.9g; CARB 56.7g; FIBER 0.5g; CHOL 22mg; IRON 1.3mg; SODIUM 269mg; CALC 29mg

Frosted Pumpkin Cake

Sheet cakes travel well, even ones with frosting. Position toothpicks about one inch into top of cake before covering with foil or plastic wrap.

CAKE:

Cooking spray
1 tablespoon all-purpose flour
¾ cup egg substitute
⅓ cup granulated sugar
⅓ cup applesauce
1 (15-ounce) can pumpkin
2 teaspoons pumpkin-pie spice
1 (18.25-ounce) package yellow cake mix (such as Betty Crocker)

FROSTING:

⅔ cup (6 ounces) tub-style light cream cheese
1¼ teaspoons vanilla extract
3½ cups powdered sugar

1. Preheat oven to 350°.
2. Coat a 13 x 9–inch baking pan with cooking spray; dust with flour.
3. To prepare cake, place egg substitute, granulated sugar, applesauce, and pumpkin in a large bowl; beat with a mixer at high speed 1 minute. Add pumpkin-pie spice and cake mix, beating at high speed 2 minutes. Pour batter into prepared pan. Bake at 350° for 35 minutes or until a wooden pick inserted in center comes out clean. Cool cake completely on a wire rack.
4. To prepare frosting, place cream cheese and vanilla in a large bowl; beat with a mixer at medium speed until smooth. Gradually add powdered sugar, beating just until blended (do not overbeat). Spread frosting evenly over top of cake. Cover and store cake in refrigerator. Yield: 24 servings (serving size: 1 piece).

CALORIES 202 (16% from fat); FAT 3.7g (sat 1.2g, mono 1.1g, poly 1g); PROTEIN 2.6g; CARB 40g; FIBER 1g; CHOL 4mg; IRON 1mg; SODIUM 236mg; CALC 47mg

Pumpkin-Orange Cake

You can also prepare this in a 13 x 9–inch pan (bake 40 minutes, and cool in pan 10 minutes) or a tube pan (bake 55 minutes, and cool in pan 20 minutes).

- ½ cup granulated sugar
- ½ cup butter, softened
- 1 (15-ounce) can pumpkin
- ¼ cup egg substitute
- ½ teaspoon vanilla extract
- 2¾ cups sifted cake flour (about 11 ounces)
- 1 teaspoon baking soda
- ½ teaspoon salt
- ½ teaspoon baking powder
- ½ teaspoon ground cinnamon
- ¼ teaspoon ground ginger
- ¼ teaspoon ground nutmeg
- 1 (12-ounce) can evaporated fat-free milk
- Cooking spray
- 3 cups sifted powdered sugar, divided
- ¾ cup (6 ounces) ⅓-less-fat cream cheese, softened
- 1 teaspoon grated orange rind
- 2 cups mandarin oranges in light syrup, drained
- 1 cup pomegranate seeds (about 2)

1. Preheat oven to 350°.

2. Place granulated sugar and butter in a large bowl; beat with a mixer at medium speed until well blended. Add pumpkin; beat well. Add egg substitute and vanilla; beat until well blended.

3. Lightly spoon flour into dry measuring cups; level with a knife. Combine flour and next 6 ingredients, stirring with a whisk. Add flour mixture and milk alternately to butter mixture, beginning and ending with flour mixture. Pour batter into 2 (9-inch) round cake pans coated with cooking spray; sharply tap pans once on counter to remove air bubbles. Bake at 350° for 30 minutes or until a wooden pick inserted in center comes out clean. Cool in pans 10 minutes on a wire rack; remove from pans. Cool completely on wire rack.

4. Place 1 cup powdered sugar and cream cheese in a large bowl; beat with a mixer at medium speed until well blended. Add remaining powdered sugar and rind; beat until fluffy.

5. Place 1 cake layer on a plate. Spread ⅔ cup cream cheese frosting evenly over top of cake. Top with remaining cake layer; spread remaining cream cheese frosting over top, but not sides, of cake. Arrange orange slices in a ring around outer edge of top cake layer. Sprinkle pomegranate seeds over center of top cake layer. Store cake loosely covered in refrigerator. Yield: 14 servings (serving size: 1 slice).

CALORIES 338 (26% from fat); FAT 9.6g (sat 5.9g, mono 2g, poly 0.4g); PROTEIN 5.9g; CARB 58.5g; FIBER 1.2g; CHOL 28mg; IRON 2.3mg; SODIUM 354mg; CALC 102mg

Yellow Sheet Cake with Chocolate Frosting

This moist, buttery sheet cake is great for any occasion or celebration. Fresh edible flowers, such as chrysanthemums, make an easy, pretty decoration that can be removed before eating the cake. If you offer the cake at an informal gathering, serve it right from the pan.

CAKE:

- Cooking spray
- 1 tablespoon all-purpose flour
- ½ cup butter, melted
- 1 (8-ounce) carton fat-free sour cream
- 1½ cups granulated sugar
- 2 teaspoons vanilla extract
- ½ cup egg substitute
- 2 cups all-purpose flour (about 9 ounces)
- 1 teaspoon baking soda
- ½ teaspoon salt
- ¾ cup low-fat buttermilk

FROSTING:

- ½ cup (4 ounces) block-style fat-free cream cheese, softened
- ¼ cup butter, softened
- 1 teaspoon vanilla extract
- ⅓ cup unsweetened cocoa
- 1 to 2 tablespoons evaporated fat-free milk
- ⅛ teaspoon salt
- 3 cups powdered sugar, divided

1. Preheat oven to 350°.

2. To prepare cake, coat bottom of a 13 x 9–inch baking pan with cooking spray (do not coat sides of pan); line bottom of pan with wax paper. Coat wax paper with cooking spray; dust with 1 tablespoon flour. Set aside.

3. Combine ½ cup melted butter and sour cream in a large bowl, stirring with a whisk until well blended. Add granulated sugar and 2 teaspoons vanilla. Beat with a mixer at medium speed 3 minutes or until well blended. Add egg substitute; beat 2 minutes or until well blended.

Yellow Sheet Cake with Chocolate Frosting

4. Lightly spoon 2 cups flour into dry measuring cups; level with a knife. Combine 2 cups flour, baking soda, and ½ teaspoon salt, stirring well with a whisk. Add flour mixture and buttermilk alternately to sugar mixture, beginning and ending with flour mixture; mix after each addition. Pour batter into prepared pan. Sharply tap pan once on counter to remove air bubbles. Bake at 350° for 30 minutes or until a wooden pick inserted in center comes out clean. Cool in pan 10 minutes on a wire rack; remove from pan. Carefully peel off wax paper; cool completely on wire rack.

5. To prepare frosting, place cream cheese, ¼ cup butter, and 1 teaspoon vanilla in a large bowl; beat with a mixer at high speed until fluffy. Add cocoa, milk, and ⅛ teaspoon salt; beat at low speed until well blended. Gradually add 1½ cups powdered sugar; beat at low speed until creamy. Gradually add remaining 1½ cups powdered sugar. Place cake on a serving platter. Spread frosting over top and sides of cake. Store cake loosely covered in refrigerator. Yield: 18 servings (serving size: 1 piece).

CALORIES 291 (25% from fat); FAT 8.1g (sat 4.1g, mono 3.3g, poly 0.4g); PROTEIN 4.3g; CARB 51.6g; FIBER 0.9g; CHOL 22mg; IRON 1mg; SODIUM 285mg; CALC 54mg

Carrot Sheet Cake with Cream Cheese Frosting

We call for a metal baking pan for the cake; if you select a glass baking dish, you'll want to decrease the baking temperature to 325° and begin checking for doneness after 25 minutes.

CAKE:

Cooking spray
- 9 tablespoons butter, softened
- ⅔ cup packed brown sugar
- ½ cup granulated sugar
- 2 large eggs
- 2 large egg whites
- 2 teaspoons vanilla extract
- 2 cups all-purpose flour (about 9 ounces)
- 2 teaspoons baking soda
- 1 teaspoon ground cinnamon
- ¼ teaspoon salt
- ¾ cup low-fat buttermilk
- 2 cups finely shredded carrot

FROSTING:

- ½ cup (4 ounces) block-style fat-free cream cheese
- ¼ cup butter, softened
- 2 teaspoons vanilla extract
- ⅛ teaspoon salt
- 2¾ cups powdered sugar, divided
- 1 tablespoon orange sugar sprinkles

1. Preheat oven to 350°.

2. To prepare cake, coat a 13 x 9–inch baking pan with cooking spray; line bottom of pan with wax paper. Coat wax paper with cooking spray; set aside.

3. Place 9 tablespoons butter, brown sugar, and granulated sugar in a large bowl; beat with a mixer at medium speed 5 minutes or until well blended. Add eggs and egg whites, 1 at a time, beating well after each addition until pale and fluffy. Beat in 2 teaspoons vanilla.

4. Lightly spoon flour into dry measuring cups; level with a knife. Combine flour, baking soda, cinnamon, and ¼ teaspoon salt, stirring with a whisk. Add flour mixture and buttermilk alternately to sugar mixture, beginning and ending with flour mixture; mix after each addition. Stir in carrot. Spoon batter into prepared pan. Sharply tap pan once on counter to remove air bubbles. Bake at 350° for 30 minutes or until a wooden pick inserted in center comes out clean. Cool in pan 10 minutes on a wire rack; remove from pan. Carefully peel off wax paper; cool completely on wire rack.

5. To prepare frosting, place cream cheese, ¼ cup butter, 2 teaspoons vanilla, and ⅛ teaspoon salt in a large bowl; beat with a mixer at medium speed until smooth. Gradually add 2 cups powdered sugar, beating at low speed until smooth (do not overbeat). Stir in remaining ¾ cup powdered sugar. Cover and chill 30 minutes. Spread frosting over top of cake. Garnish with sprinkles. Store cake loosely covered in refrigerator. Yield: 16 servings (serving size: 1 piece).

CALORIES 309 (30% from fat); FAT 10.3g (sat 5g, mono 4.1g, poly 0.5g); PROTEIN 4.5g; CARB 50.2g; FIBER 0.9g; CHOL 52mg; IRON 1.1mg; SODIUM 358mg; CALC 49mg

Sweet Corn Bread with Mixed Berries and Berry Coulis

SAUCE:

½ cup fresh raspberries
½ cup fresh blueberries
½ cup fresh blackberries
2 tablespoons water
2½ teaspoons granulated sugar

TOPPING:

1 cup fresh raspberries
1 cup fresh blueberries
1 cup fresh blackberries
2 tablespoons dark brown sugar
⅛ teaspoon grated orange rind

CORN BREAD:

¾ cup all-purpose flour (about 3⅓ ounces)
¾ cup yellow cornmeal
⅓ cup granulated sugar
2 teaspoons baking powder
½ teaspoon salt
¾ cup 2% reduced-fat milk
2 tablespoons butter, melted
1 tablespoon canola oil
1 large egg
Cooking spray
½ cup frozen fat-free whipped topping, thawed

1. To prepare sauce, combine first 5 ingredients in a food processor; process until smooth. Strain berry mixture through a fine sieve over a bowl, reserving liquid; discard solids. Cover and chill.

2. To prepare topping, combine 1 cup each raspberries, blueberries, and blackberries in a large bowl. Add brown sugar and orange rind; toss gently to combine. Cover and chill.

3. Preheat oven to 425°.

4. To prepare corn bread, lightly spoon flour and cornmeal into dry measuring cups; level with a knife. Combine flour, cornmeal, ⅓ cup granulated sugar, baking powder, and salt in a large bowl, stirring with a whisk. Add milk, butter, oil, and egg; stir with a whisk.

5. Pour batter into an 8-inch square baking pan coated with cooking spray. Bake at 425° for 15 minutes or until corn bread is lightly browned and a wooden pick inserted in center comes out clean. Cool in pan 10 minutes on a wire rack; remove from pan. Cool completely on wire rack. Cut corn bread into 9 squares.

6. Spoon about 1 tablespoon sauce onto each of 9 plates; top with 1 corn bread square. Top each corn bread square with about ¼ cup berry topping. Spoon about 1 tablespoon whipped topping over each serving. Yield: 9 servings.

CALORIES 218 (24% from fat); FAT 5.6g (sat 2.3g, mono 1.5g, poly 1.3g); PROTEIN 4g; CARB 38g; FIBER 2.5g; CHOL 32mg; IRON 1.2mg; SODIUM 286mg; CALC 106mg

Honeyed Apple Torte

⅓ cup honey
2 tablespoons fresh lemon juice
3 Granny Smith apples, peeled and each cut into 8 wedges (about 1¼ pounds)
¾ cup granulated sugar
6 tablespoons butter, softened
¼ cup packed brown sugar
1 teaspoon vanilla extract
2 large eggs
1 teaspoon grated lemon rind
1 cup all-purpose flour (about 4½ ounces)
1 teaspoon baking powder
¼ teaspoon salt
Cooking spray
1 tablespoon granulated sugar
½ teaspoon ground cinnamon

1. Preheat oven to 350°.

2. Combine honey and juice in a large nonstick skillet; bring to a simmer over medium heat. Add apples; cook 14 minutes or until almost tender, stirring frequently. Remove from heat; set aside.

3. Beat ¾ cup granulated sugar, butter, brown sugar, and vanilla with a mixer at medium speed until well blended (about 4 minutes). Add eggs, 1 at a time, beating well after each addition. Beat in lemon rind. Lightly spoon flour into a dry measuring cup; level with a knife. Combine flour, baking powder, and salt, stirring well with a whisk. Gradually add flour mixture to sugar mixture, beating at low speed until blended. Pour batter into a 9-inch springform pan coated with cooking spray.

4. Remove apples from pan with a slotted spoon, and discard remaining liquid. Arrange apple slices, spokelike, on top of batter, pressing slices gently into batter. Combine 1 tablespoon granulated sugar and cinnamon; sprinkle evenly over apples. Bake at 350° for 1 hour or until cake springs back when touched lightly in center. Cool in pan on a wire rack. Cut into wedges using a serrated knife. Yield: 10 servings (serving size: 1 wedge).

CALORIES 272 (27% from fat); FAT 8.3g (sat 4.6g, mono 2.4g, poly 0.5g); PROTEIN 2.7g; CARB 48.7g; FIBER 1.4g; CHOL 63mg; IRON 1mg; SODIUM 194mg; CALC 46mg

Warm Chocolate Soufflé Cakes with Raspberry Sauce

(pictured on cover)

SAUCE:

- ⅔ cup granulated sugar
- ¼ cup fresh orange juice
- 1 (12-ounce) package frozen unsweetened raspberries, thawed

CAKES:

- Cooking spray
- 2 tablespoons granulated sugar
- ¾ cup fat-free milk
- ¼ cup half-and-half
- 2 ounces unsweetened chocolate, chopped
- ¼ cup unsweetened cocoa
- 1 teaspoon vanilla extract
- 1¼ cups granulated sugar, divided
- ¼ cup butter, softened
- 3 large egg yolks
- ¼ cup all-purpose flour (about 1 ounce)
- ¼ teaspoon cream of tartar
- 5 large egg whites
- 1 tablespoon powdered sugar
- Raspberries and mint sprigs (optional)

1. To prepare sauce, combine first 3 ingredients in a food processor; process until smooth. Strain through a sieve into a bowl; discard solids. Cover and chill.

2. To prepare cakes, coat 12 (6-ounce) ramekins with cooking spray; sprinkle evenly with 2 tablespoons granulated sugar. Set aside.

3. Combine milk and half-and-half in a small saucepan. Bring to a simmer over medium-high heat (do not boil). Remove from heat; add chocolate, stirring until chocolate melts. Add cocoa and vanilla; stir with a whisk. Pour into a bowl; cool completely.

4. Preheat oven to 325°.

5. Place 1 cup granulated sugar and butter in a medium bowl; beat with a mixer at high speed until light and fluffy. Beat in egg yolks. Add cooled chocolate mixture, and beat until blended. Lightly spoon flour into a dry measuring cup; level with a knife. Stir into chocolate mixture.

6. Place cream of tartar and egg whites in a large bowl; beat with a mixer at high speed until soft peaks form. Gradually add remaining ¼ cup granulated sugar, 1 tablespoon at a time, beating until stiff peaks form. Gently stir one-fourth egg white mixture into chocolate mixture; gently fold in remaining egg white mixture. Spoon into prepared ramekins.

7. Place ramekins in 2 (13 x 9–inch) baking pans; add hot water to pans to a depth of 1 inch. Bake at 325° for 35 minutes or until puffy and set. Loosen cakes from sides of ramekins using a narrow metal spatula. Invert onto 12 plates. Sprinkle evenly with powdered sugar; serve with sauce. Garnish with raspberries and mint, if desired. Yield: 12 servings (serving size: 1 cake and 2 tablespoons sauce).

CALORIES 273 (27% from fat); FAT 8.1g (sat 4.3g, mono 2.3g, poly 0.4g); PROTEIN 4.5g; CARB 48.1g; FIBER 2.5g; CHOL 64mg; IRON 1.2mg; SODIUM 63mg; CALC 54mg

Lemon-Blueberry Bundt Cake

(pictured on page 352)

CAKE:

- Cooking spray
- 2 tablespoons granulated sugar
- 3 cups all-purpose flour (about 13½ ounces)
- 1½ teaspoons baking powder
- ½ teaspoon baking soda
- ¼ teaspoon salt
- 1¾ cups granulated sugar
- ¼ cup butter, softened
- 1 tablespoon grated lemon rind
- 4 large eggs
- ½ teaspoon vanilla extract
- 1 (16-ounce) carton reduced-fat sour cream
- 2 cups fresh blueberries

GLAZE:

- 1 cup powdered sugar
- 2 tablespoons fresh lemon juice

1. Preheat oven to 350°.

2. To prepare cake, coat a 12-cup Bundt pan with cooking spray; dust with 2 tablespoons sugar.

3. Lightly spoon flour into dry measuring cups; level with a knife. Combine flour, baking powder, baking soda, and salt, stirring with a whisk.

4. Place 1¾ cups granulated sugar, butter, and rind in a large bowl; beat with a mixer at medium speed until well blended. Add eggs, 1 at a time, beating well after each addition. Beat in vanilla and sour cream. Add flour mixture; beat at medium speed just until combined. Gently fold in blueberries. Spoon batter into prepared pan. Bake at 350° for 1 hour or until a wooden pick inserted in center comes out clean. Cool in pan 15 minutes on a wire rack; remove from pan. Cool completely on wire rack.

5. To prepare glaze, combine powdered sugar and juice, stirring well with a whisk. Drizzle over cake. Yield: 16 servings (serving size: 1 slice).

CALORIES 299 (23% from fat); FAT 7.8g (sat 4g, mono 2.7g, poly 0.5g); PROTEIN 5g; CARB 53.2g; FIBER 1.1g; CHOL 71mg; IRON 1.5mg; SODIUM 172mg; CALC 68mg

Sour Cream Pound Cake with Rum Glaze

Drizzle the brown sugar–rum glaze over the cake while it's still warm so the glaze soaks in nicely.

CAKE:

Cooking spray
3 tablespoons dry breadcrumbs
3 cups cake flour (about 12 ounces)
1 teaspoon baking powder
¼ teaspoon baking soda
¼ teaspoon salt
¾ cup butter, softened
2 cups granulated sugar
3 large eggs
¼ cup fat-free milk
1 tablespoon dark rum
2 teaspoons vanilla extract
1 cup fat-free sour cream

GLAZE:

½ cup packed brown sugar
2 tablespoons dark rum
2 tablespoons water
1½ tablespoons butter

1. Preheat oven to 350°.

2. To prepare cake, coat a 10-inch tube pan with cooking spray; dust with breadcrumbs. Set aside.

3. Lightly spoon flour into dry measuring cups, and level with a knife. Combine flour, baking powder, baking soda, and salt, stirring well with a whisk. Place butter and granulated sugar in a large bowl, and beat with a mixer at medium speed until light and fluffy. Add eggs, 1 at a time, beating well after each addition. Add milk, 1 tablespoon rum, and vanilla, and beat until combined. Beating at low speed, add flour mixture and sour cream alternately to sugar mixture, beginning and ending with flour mixture, and beat just until combined.

4. Spoon batter into prepared pan. Bake at 350° for 1 hour or until a wooden pick inserted in center comes out clean. Cool in pan 10 minutes. Loosen cake from sides of pan using a narrow metal spatula. Place a plate upside down on top of cake; invert onto plate. Invert cake again. Pierce cake liberally with a wooden pick.

5. While cake bakes, prepare glaze. Combine brown sugar, 2 tablespoons rum, and water in a small saucepan; bring to a boil, stirring until sugar dissolves. Add 1½ tablespoons butter, stirring until butter melts. Drizzle half of warm glaze evenly over warm cake; allow mixture to absorb into cake. Drizzle remaining glaze over cake. Cool cake completely. Store loosely covered. Yield: 16 servings (serving size: 1 slice).

CALORIES 325 (30% from fat); FAT 11g (sat 6.3g, mono 3.2g, poly 0.5g); PROTEIN 3.6g; CARB 52.8g; FIBER 0.6g; CHOL 68mg; IRON 1.5mg; SODIUM 232mg; CALC 58mg

Cherry-Almond Upside-Down Cake

Cherry-Almond Upside-Down Cake

If you're pitting the cherries, be sure to work over a bowl and save any accumulated juice, which should be added to the recipe with the cherries.

- 1¼ cups sugar, divided
- ¼ cup dry red wine
- 2 pounds dark sweet cherries, pitted
- 1 teaspoon fresh lemon juice
- Cooking spray
- ¾ cup whole blanched almonds, toasted
- 2 large eggs
- 2 large egg whites
- 1 cup all-purpose flour (about 4½ ounces)
- ½ teaspoon salt

1. Preheat oven to 375°.

2. Combine ¼ cup sugar and red wine in a large saucepan over low heat; stir until sugar dissolves. Increase heat to medium-high; bring to a boil. Stir in cherries. Reduce heat to low; cook 5 minutes or until cherries just begin to soften, stirring frequently. Remove cherries from pan with a slotted spoon, reserving liquid in pan. Place cherries in a bowl; stir in lemon juice. Arrange cherries in an even layer in bottom of a 9-inch square baking pan coated with cooking spray.

3. Cook wine mixture over medium-high heat 3 minutes or until reduced to ¼ cup. Remove from heat; drizzle over cherries in prepared pan.

4. Place almonds and 2 tablespoons sugar in a food processor, and process until finely ground (do not process to a paste).

5. Place eggs and egg whites in a large bowl. Beat with a mixer at high speed until foamy; slowly add remaining ¾ cup plus 2 tablespoons sugar. Beat until thick and lemon-colored (about 2 minutes).

6. Lightly spoon flour into a dry measuring cup; level with a knife. Combine flour and salt. Gradually sift flour mixture over egg mixture; fold in. Fold in ground almond mixture. Carefully spoon batter over cherries in prepared pan. Bake at 375° for 30 minutes or until golden brown. Cool in pan on a wire rack 15 minutes. Place a plate upside down on top of cake; invert onto plate. Yield: 9 servings (serving size: 1 slice).

CALORIES 322 (23% from fat); FAT 8.3g (sat 1.1g, mono 4.6g, poly 2g); PROTEIN 7.5g; CARB 57.8g; FIBER 3.9g; CHOL 47mg; IRON 1.7mg; SODIUM 163mg; CALC 51mg

Apricot-Cherry Upside-Down Mini Cakes

You can also make these treats with nectarines or peaches; just be sure to use small ones (about the size of apricots) so they won't crowd the custard cups.

- Cooking spray
- 1 tablespoon butter, cut into 4 equal pieces
- 4 teaspoons brown sugar
- 2 apricots, halved and pitted
- 16 sweet cherries, pitted and halved
- ⅔ cup all-purpose flour (about 3 ounces)
- ½ teaspoon baking soda
- ¼ teaspoon salt
- ⅓ cup granulated sugar
- 2 tablespoons butter, softened
- ¼ teaspoon vanilla extract
- 1 large egg, lightly beaten
- ⅓ cup fat-free milk
- 6 tablespoons frozen fat-free whipped topping, thawed

1. Preheat oven to 350°.

2. Coat 4 (8-ounce) custard cups or ramekins with cooking spray. Place 1 butter piece in bottom of each cup. Sprinkle 1 teaspoon brown sugar over butter in each cup. Arrange 1 apricot half, cut side up, over brown sugar in each ramekin. Arrange 8 cherry halves, cut sides up, around outside edge of each apricot; set aside.

3. Lightly spoon flour into a dry measuring cup; level with a knife. Combine flour, baking soda, and salt, stirring with a whisk. Place granulated sugar and 2 tablespoons butter in a medium bowl; beat with a mixer at medium speed until well blended. Add vanilla and egg; beat well. Add flour mixture to sugar mixture alternately with milk, beginning and ending with flour mixture; beat well after each addition. Divide batter evenly over fruit in each cup. Place cups on a baking sheet.

4. Bake at 350° for 30 minutes or until a wooden pick inserted in center comes out clean. Cool in cups 5 minutes on a wire rack. Loosen edges of cakes with a knife. Place a dessert plate, upside down, on top of each cup; invert onto serving plates. Drizzle any remaining caramelized syrup evenly over cakes. Serve cakes warm with whipped topping. Yield: 4 servings (serving size: 1 cake and 1½ tablespoons whipped topping).

CALORIES 299 (31% from fat); FAT 10.3g (sat 5.8g, mono 3.1g, poly 0.7g); PROTEIN 5.1g; CARB 46.9g; FIBER 1.6g; CHOL 77mg; IRON 1.5mg; SODIUM 423mg; CALC 48mg

Triple-Layer Strawberry Cake

- 1 (10½-ounce) loaf angel food cake
- 2 cups sliced fresh strawberries, divided
- 3 cups strawberry fat-free frozen yogurt, softened
- 1 tablespoon sugar
- 1 tablespoon orange juice

1. Split cake in thirds horizontally using a serrated knife; place bottom cake layer, cut side up, on a platter. Arrange ½ cup strawberries on cake; spread with 1½ cups yogurt, and top with middle cake layer. Repeat procedure with ½ cup strawberries and 1½ cups yogurt. Top with remaining cake layer; freeze 2 hours.

2. Combine remaining 1 cup strawberries, sugar, and orange juice in a blender, and process until smooth. Cover and chill. Serve sauce with cake. Yield: 8 servings (serving size: 1 slice and 1½ tablespoons sauce).

CALORIES 182 (1% from fat); FAT 0.3g (sat 0g, mono 0g, poly 0.1g); PROTEIN 5.4g; CARB 41.4g; FIBER 0.9g; CHOL 0mg; IRON 0.2mg; SODIUM 240mg; CALC 144mg

Blueberry Cheesecake

CRUST:

- ⅔ cup graham cracker crumbs (about 5 cookie sheets)
- ⅔ cup reduced-fat vanilla wafer crumbs (about 20 cookies)
- 3 tablespoons sugar
- 3 tablespoons butter, melted
- Cooking spray

FILLING:

- 2½ cups fresh or frozen blueberries, thawed
- 3 tablespoons cornstarch, divided
- 2 (8-ounce) blocks fat-free cream cheese, softened
- 1 (8-ounce) block ⅓-less-fat cream cheese, softened
- 1 cup sugar
- ¼ teaspoon salt
- 5 large eggs

TOPPING:

- 1½ cups fat-free sour cream
- 2 tablespoons sugar
- ½ teaspoon vanilla extract

SAUCE:

- ¼ cup sugar
- ¼ cup water
- 1 cup fresh or frozen blueberries, thawed

1. Preheat oven to 325°.

2. To prepare crust, combine first 3 ingredients in a medium bowl. Drizzle with butter, and toss with a fork until moist. Firmly press mixture into bottom of a 9-inch springform pan coated with cooking spray. Bake at 325° for 10 minutes, and cool on a wire rack.

3. To prepare filling, combine 2½ cups blueberries and 1 tablespoon cornstarch in a food processor; process until smooth. Place puree in a small saucepan; bring to a boil. Cook 6 minutes or until slightly thick, stirring constantly. Cool slightly. Reserve ½ cup blueberry puree for sauce; refrigerate. Set aside remaining 1 cup blueberry puree.

4. Place cream cheeses in a large bowl; beat with a mixer at high speed 3 minutes or until smooth. Combine 2 tablespoons cornstarch, 1 cup sugar, and salt. Add sugar mixture to cream cheese mixture; beat well. Add eggs, 1 at a time, beating well after each addition. Pour batter over prepared crust. Pour 1 cup blueberry puree over batter; gently swirl with a knife. Bake at 325° for 1 hour and 10 minutes or until cheesecake center barely moves when pan is touched. Remove cheesecake from oven (do not turn oven off); place cheesecake on a wire rack.

5. To prepare topping, combine sour cream, 2 tablespoons sugar, and vanilla in a small bowl, stirring well. Spread sour cream mixture evenly over cheesecake. Bake at 325° for 10 minutes. Remove cheesecake from oven; run a knife around outside edge. Cool to room temperature. Cover and chill at least 8 hours. Remove sides of springform pan.

6. To prepare sauce, combine reserved ½ cup blueberry puree, ¼ cup sugar, and water in a small saucepan. Cook over medium heat 8 minutes or until sauce is thick, stirring constantly. Gently fold in 1 cup blueberries. Remove from heat, and cool. Serve sauce with cheesecake. Yield: 16 servings (serving size: 1 slice and 1½ tablespoons sauce).

CALORIES 257 (30% from fat); FAT 8.7g (sat 4.6g, mono 2.6g, poly 0.7g); PROTEIN 9.2g; CARB 36.4g; FIBER 1g; CHOL 89mg; IRON 0.6mg; SODIUM 340mg; CALC 110mg

Blueberry Cheesecake

Triple Hazelnut Cheesecake

Use the food processor to prepare the crust and combine the filling ingredients. The hazelnut-chocolate spread is sold next to the peanut butter in your supermarket. Frangelico, a hazelnut liqueur, enhances the nutty flavor of the cheesecake. If you don't have it, the dessert is still delicious without it.

- ½ cup chopped hazelnuts, toasted and divided
- 1 tablespoon light brown sugar
- 15 chocolate wafer cookies
- 1 tablespoon canola oil
- Cooking spray
- 1 tablespoon instant coffee granules
- 1 tablespoon hot water
- ¾ cup unsweetened cocoa
- ¾ cup packed brown sugar
- ½ cup granulated sugar
- 2 tablespoons cornstarch
- 1 (16-ounce) container fat-free cottage cheese
- 1 (8-ounce) block fat-free cream cheese
- ½ cup hazelnut-chocolate spread (such as Nutella)
- 2 tablespoons Frangelico (optional)
- ¼ teaspoon salt
- 3 large eggs, lightly beaten

1. Preheat oven to 325°.
2. Place ¼ cup hazelnuts, 1 tablespoon brown sugar, and chocolate wafers in a food processor; process until finely ground. Add oil; process until crumbs are moist. Firmly press crumb mixture into bottom of a 9-inch springform pan coated with cooking spray. Wrap outside of pan with a double layer of aluminum foil.
3. Dissolve coffee granules in 1 tablespoon hot water in a small bowl. Combine cocoa and next 3 ingredients. Place cheeses in food processor; process until smooth. Add coffee mixture, cocoa mixture, spread, liqueur, and salt; process until smooth. Add eggs, and process until smooth. Pour into pan.
4. Place pan in a large baking pan; add hot water to baking pan to a depth of 1 inch. Bake at 325° for 1 hour or until cheesecake center barely moves when pan is touched.
5. Remove cheesecake from oven, and run a knife around outside edge. Cool to room temperature. Cover and chill at least 8 hours. Remove sides from pan, and sprinkle with remaining ¼ cup hazelnuts. Yield: 12 servings (serving size: 1 slice).

CALORIES 317 (30% from fat); FAT 10.6g (sat 2.4g, mono 6g, poly 1.7g); PROTEIN 12.3g; CARB 44.8g; FIBER 3.2g; CHOL 58mg; IRON 2mg; SODIUM 354mg; CALC 105mg

Cappuccino Cheesecake with Fudge Sauce

Simply swirling the chocolate and espresso mixtures gives this dessert a bit of glamour.

- 1½ cups reduced-fat chocolate wafer crumbs (about 50 cookies)
- 3 tablespoons butter, melted
- 2 tablespoons sugar
- Cooking spray
- 1 cup sugar
- 3 tablespoons all-purpose flour
- 2 (8-ounce) blocks fat-free cream cheese
- 2 (8-ounce) blocks ⅓-less-fat cream cheese
- 2 large eggs
- 2 large egg whites
- 2 tablespoons instant espresso or ¼ cup instant coffee granules
- 1 teaspoon vanilla extract
- ½ teaspoon ground cinnamon
- 1½ cups fat-free hot fudge topping, divided

1. Preheat oven to 325°.
2. Combine first 3 ingredients; firmly press mixture into bottom of a 9-inch springform pan coated with cooking spray. Bake at 325° for 10 minutes; cool in pan on a wire rack.
3. Preheat oven to 450°.
4. Place 1 cup sugar, flour, and cream cheeses in a large bowl; beat with a mixer at medium speed or until smooth. Add eggs and egg whites, 1 at a time, beating well after each addition. Add espresso, vanilla, and cinnamon; beat well. Pour cream cheese mixture into prepared crust. Spoon 4 mounds of fudge topping (2 tablespoons each) onto cheese mixture; swirl mixtures together using a knife. Bake at 450° for 10 minutes. Reduce oven temperature to 250° (do not remove cheesecake from oven); bake an additional 1 hour or until almost set. Remove cheesecake from oven; cool to room temperature. Cover and chill at least 8 hours. Remove sides of springform pan.
5. Drizzle 1 tablespoon fudge topping onto each of 16 plates, and top each with 1 cheesecake wedge. Yield: 16 servings (serving size: 1 slice and 1 tablespoon fudge topping).

CALORIES 313 (30% from fat); FAT 10.3g (sat 5.9g, mono 3g, poly 0.7g); PROTEIN 9.9g; CARB 44.1g; FIBER 1.1g; CHOL 60mg; IRON 0.7mg; SODIUM 468mg; CALC 130mg

Cappuccino Cheesecake with Fudge Sauce

Ricotta Cheesecake with Fresh Berry Topping

Ricotta Cheesecake with Fresh Berry Topping

You'll need at least 1½ batches of Homemade Ricotta Cheese for this cheesecake, but it's well worth the effort. If made in advance, cover and refrigerate, then let it stand at room temperature 30 minutes before serving. While a shiny metal pan makes a delicious cheesecake, a dark metal or nonstick pan yields a taller, lightly browned cake.

CHEESECAKE:

4 cups (2 pounds) Homemade Ricotta Cheese (recipe at right)
1 cup granulated sugar
1 teaspoon grated lemon rind
2 teaspoons vanilla extract
¼ teaspoon salt
4 large eggs
Cooking spray
1 tablespoon powdered sugar

TOPPING:

2 cups quartered strawberries
1 pint fresh raspberries
1 pint fresh blueberries
2 tablespoons granulated sugar
2 tablespoons fresh lemon juice

1. Preheat oven to 350°.

2. To prepare cheesecake, place Homemade Ricotta Cheese, 1 cup granulated sugar, lemon rind, vanilla, and salt in a large bowl; beat with a mixer at medium speed 2 minutes or until smooth. Add eggs, 1 at a time, beating well after each addition. Pour batter into a 10-inch springform pan coated with cooking spray. Bake at 350° for 1 hour or until cheesecake center barely moves when pan is touched. Remove cheesecake from oven; run a knife around outside edge. Cool slightly; remove sides from pan. Sprinkle cheesecake evenly with powdered sugar.

3. To prepare topping, combine berries, 2 tablespoons granulated sugar, and juice; toss gently to combine. Let stand 5 minutes. Serve berry mixture with cheesecake. Yield: 12 servings (serving size: 1 slice and about ½ cup topping).

CALORIES 286 (32% from fat); FAT 10.2g (sat 5.6g, mono 3.1g, poly 0.7g); PROTEIN 18g; CARB 31.7g; FIBER 2.5g; CHOL 101mg; IRON 0.6mg; SODIUM 328mg; CALC 353mg

Homemade Ricotta Cheese

As the milk mixture heats to 170°, be sure to stir gently and occasionally; if you stir too vigorously or too frequently (more than every few minutes), the curds may not separate as effectively from the whey. And don't stir after the milk mixture reaches 170°, or the cheese will become grainy and thin. If your kitchen sink has a gooseneck faucet, it might be difficult to hang the cheesecloth bag on it. If so, lay a long wooden spoon across one corner of the sink, and hang the bag on the handle.

1 gallon 2% reduced-fat milk
5 cups low-fat buttermilk
½ teaspoon fine sea salt

1. Line a large colander or sieve with 5 layers dampened cheesecloth, allowing cheesecloth to extend over outside edges of colander; place colander in a large bowl.

2. Combine milk and buttermilk in a large, heavy stockpot. Attach a candy thermometer to edge of pan so thermometer extends at least 2 inches into milk mixture. Cook over medium-high heat until candy thermometer registers 170° (about 20 minutes), gently stirring occasionally. As soon as milk mixture reaches 170°, stop stirring (whey and curds will begin separating). Continue to cook, without stirring, until thermometer registers 190°. (Be sure not to stir, or curds will break apart.) Immediately remove pan from heat. (Bottom of pan may be slightly scorched.)

3. Using a slotted spoon, gently spoon curds into cheesecloth-lined colander; discard whey, or reserve it for another use. Drain over bowl 5 minutes. Gather edges of cheesecloth together; tie securely. Hang cheesecloth bundle from kitchen faucet; drain 15 minutes or until whey stops dripping. Scrape ricotta into a bowl. Sprinkle with salt; toss gently with a fork to combine. Cool to room temperature. Yield: about 3 cups (serving size: ¼ cup).

CALORIES 115 (48% from fat); FAT 6.1g (sat 3.8g, mono 1.8g, poly 0.2g); PROTEIN 11.5g; CARB 3.5g; FIBER 0g; CHOL 23mg; IRON 0mg; SODIUM 191mg; CALC 250mg

Streusel-Topped Pear Pie

Streusel-Topped Pear Pie

Here the pie dough is made in the food processor, which takes the guesswork out of mixing by hand. Part of the pastry becomes the bottom crust, and the rest, with the addition of oats and brown sugar, becomes the streusel topping. Keep the peels on the pears so they maintain their shape; the skins also give the pie a rustic quality. You can bake the pie up to 2 days ahead, and serve at room temperature.

2 cups all-purpose flour (about 9 ounces)
¾ teaspoon salt, divided
½ cup chilled butter, cut into small pieces
⅓ cup ice water
Cooking spray
½ cup regular oats
⅓ cup packed dark brown sugar
7 cups thinly sliced ripe Bartlett pears (about 6 pears)
½ cup granulated sugar
3 tablespoons all-purpose flour
3 tablespoons finely chopped crystallized ginger
1 teaspoon ground cinnamon

1. Lightly spoon 2 cups flour into dry measuring cups, and level with a knife. Combine 2 cups flour and ½ teaspoon salt in a food processor; pulse 2 times to combine. Add butter; pulse 6 times or until mixture resembles coarse meal. With processor on, slowly pour ice water through food chute, processing just until blended (do not allow dough to form a ball).
2. Remove two-thirds of dough, and press into a 4-inch circle on 2 overlapping sheets of plastic wrap. (Leave remaining dough in processor.) Cover dough with 2 additional sheets of overlapping plastic wrap. Roll dough, still covered, into an 11-inch circle. Place dough in freezer 5 minutes or until plastic wrap can be easily removed.
3. Remove top sheets of plastic wrap; fit dough, plastic wrap side up, into a 9-inch pie plate coated with cooking spray. Remove remaining plastic wrap. Fold edges under, and flute. Refrigerate until ready to use.
4. Add oats and brown sugar to dough in food processor; pulse 4 times or until crumbly. Place oat mixture in a small bowl; cover and chill.
5. Preheat oven to 375°.
6. Combine pears, granulated sugar, 3 tablespoons flour, ginger, cinnamon, and remaining ¼ teaspoon salt; toss well. Spoon pear mixture into crust. Bake at 375° for 25 minutes. Sprinkle oat mixture over pear mixture. Bake an additional 25 minutes or until topping is browned. Cool at least 2 hours on a wire rack. Yield: 10 servings (serving size: 1 wedge).

CALORIES 325 (28% from fat); FAT 10g (sat 5.8g, mono 2.8g, poly 0.6g); PROTEIN 3.9g; CARB 57.1g; FIBER 3.6g; CHOL 25mg; IRON 2mg; SODIUM 273mg; CALC 31mg

Cinnamon Streusel–Topped Pumpkin Pie

FILLING:
¾ teaspoon ground cinnamon
¼ teaspoon ground allspice
¼ teaspoon ground ginger
¼ teaspoon ground nutmeg
⅛ teaspoon ground cloves
2 large eggs
1 (15-ounce) can unsweetened pumpkin
1 (14-ounce) can fat-free sweetened condensed milk

CRUST:
½ (15-ounce) package refrigerated pie dough (such as Pillsbury)
Cooking spray

STREUSEL:
⅓ cup all-purpose flour (about 1½ ounces)
⅓ cup packed dark brown sugar
¼ cup regular oats
¼ cup chopped pecans
¾ teaspoon ground cinnamon
⅛ teaspoon ground ginger
2 tablespoons chilled butter, cut into small pieces
2 to 3 teaspoons water

1. Preheat oven to 375°.
2. To prepare filling, combine first 8 ingredients in a large bowl; stir with a whisk.
3. To prepare crust, roll dough into an 11-inch circle. Fit dough into a 9-inch pie plate coated with cooking spray. Fold edges under; flute.
4. To prepare streusel, lightly spoon flour into a dry measuring cup; level with a knife. Combine flour and next 5 ingredients in a bowl. Cut in butter with a fork or fingertips until crumbly. Sprinkle with water, tossing with a fork just until lightly moistened.
5. Pour pumpkin mixture into crust; sprinkle with streusel. Place pie on a baking sheet. Bake at 375° for 50 minutes or until a knife inserted in center comes out clean. Remove from baking sheet; cool completely on a wire rack. Yield: 12 servings (serving size: 1 wedge).

CALORIES 273 (31% from fat); FAT 9.4g (sat 3.7g, mono 1.9g, poly 0.8g); PROTEIN 5.9g; CARB 41.8g; FIBER 1.7g; CHOL 46mg; IRON 1.1mg; SODIUM 117mg; CALC 118mg

Sweet Potato Pie

Making this fall favorite is reason enough to invite over a friend or two. You can bake it up to two days ahead; cool it completely, cover with plastic wrap, and chill. Before serving, reheat it for about 15 minutes at 325° to bring back its silky texture.

PASTRY:

1¼ cups all-purpose flour (about 5½ ounces)
2 tablespoons granulated sugar
½ teaspoon salt
5 tablespoons chilled butter, cut into small pieces
4 to 5 tablespoons ice water
Cooking spray

FILLING:

1 cup mashed cooked sweet potatoes
1 cup evaporated fat-free milk
¾ cup packed light brown sugar
2 tablespoons all-purpose flour
1 large egg white
½ cup 1% low-fat milk
1 tablespoon butter, melted
1 teaspoon vanilla extract
½ teaspoon ground cinnamon
¼ teaspoon ground nutmeg
Dash of salt

1. To prepare pastry, lightly spoon 1¼ cups flour into dry measuring cups; level with a knife. Place 1¼ cups flour, granulated sugar, and ½ teaspoon salt in a food processor. Process 10 seconds. Add butter; pulse 4 times or until mixture resembles coarse meal. Place flour mixture in a bowl. Sprinkle surface with ice water, 1 tablespoon at a time; toss with a fork until moist. Place pastry on a lightly floured surface; knead lightly 3 or 4 times. Gently press mixture into a 4-inch circle on plastic wrap; cover. Chill 30 minutes.

2. Slightly overlap 2 sheets of plastic wrap on a slightly damp surface. Unwrap and place chilled dough on plastic wrap. Cover with 2 additional sheets of overlapping plastic wrap. Roll dough, still covered, into an 11-inch circle. Place dough in freezer 5 minutes or until plastic wrap can be easily removed.

3. Preheat oven to 350°.

4. Remove top sheets of plastic wrap; fit dough, plastic wrap side up, into a 9-inch pie plate. Remove remaining plastic wrap. Fold edges under; flute. Line bottom of dough with a piece of foil coated with cooking spray; arrange pie weights or dried beans on piece of foil. Bake at 350° for 15 minutes. Remove pie weights and foil; cool pastry on a wire rack.

5. To prepare filling, combine sweet potatoes and next 4 ingredients in a food processor; process until blended. Spoon into a large bowl. Add 1% low-fat milk and next 5 ingredients; stir well. Pour filling into pastry. Bake at 350° for 50 minutes or until a knife inserted in center comes out clean. Cool completely on a wire rack. Yield: 8 servings (serving size: 1 wedge).

CALORIES 302 (27% from fat); FAT 9g (sat 5.6g, mono 2.3g, poly 0.5g); PROTEIN 6.2g; CARB 49.4g; FIBER 1.5g; CHOL 24mg; IRON 1.7mg; SODIUM 295mg; CALC 147mg

Plum Tatin

Use red, purple, green, or a combination of plums in this upside-down tart.

½ (15-ounce) package refrigerated pie dough (such as Pillsbury)
¼ cup packed brown sugar
1 tablespoon all-purpose flour
¼ teaspoon ground cinnamon
¼ teaspoon ground nutmeg
10 small plums, pitted and cut in half (about 2½ pounds)
½ cup granulated sugar
1 teaspoon lemon juice
1 tablespoon chopped pecans

1. Preheat oven to 425°.

2. Roll dough into a 10-inch circle on a lightly floured surface; set aside.

3. Combine brown sugar and next 4 ingredients. Combine granulated sugar and lemon juice in a 10-inch cast-iron skillet; cook sugar mixture over medium-high heat just until it begins to turn golden.

4. Remove from heat; stir until completely golden. Add pecans and plum mixture. Place dough over plum mixture, tucking dough around plums.

5. Bake at 425° for 25 minutes or until bubbly. Immediately place a plate over pan. Carefully invert tart onto plate. Yield: 6 servings.

CALORIES 328 (30% from fat); FAT 11.1g (sat 3.8g, mono 4.6g, poly 1.3g); PROTEIN 2.4g; CARB 57g; FIBER 1.9g; CHOL 7mg; IRON 0.3mg; SODIUM 136mg; CALC 8mg

Cherry-Apricot Turnovers

Layers of phyllo are brushed with a mixture of melted butter and oil, then sprinkled with graham cracker crumbs and brown sugar. The crumbs help keep the phyllo, which envelops the moist filling, dry and crisp.

- 1 cup apricot nectar
- ½ cup chopped dried apricots
- ⅓ cup packed brown sugar
- ¼ teaspoon grated lemon rind
- 2 tablespoons fresh lemon juice
- 3 (3-ounce) bags dried sweet cherries
- 2 tablespoons chopped almonds
- ½ teaspoon vanilla extract
- 2 tablespoons butter, melted
- 2 tablespoons canola oil
- 6 (18 x 14–inch) sheets frozen phyllo dough, thawed
- ¼ cup graham cracker crumbs
- 2 tablespoons brown sugar
- Cooking spray

1. Combine first 6 ingredients in a saucepan; bring to a boil. Reduce heat, and simmer 20 minutes or until liquid is absorbed, stirring occasionally. Stir in almonds and vanilla. Cool completely.

2. Preheat oven to 375°.

3. Combine butter and oil. Place 1 phyllo sheet on a large cutting board or work surface (cover remaining dough to prevent drying). Lightly brush phyllo sheet with 1 tablespoon butter mixture. Sprinkle with 1 tablespoon crumbs and 1½ teaspoons brown sugar. Repeat layers once. Top with 1 phyllo sheet. Gently press layers together. Lightly coat top phyllo sheet with cooking spray. Cut stack lengthwise into 4 (3½-inch-wide) strips. Cut each strip in half crosswise. Spoon 2 tablespoons cherry mixture onto 1 short end of each rectangle, leaving a 1-inch border. Fold 1 corner of edge with 1-inch border over mixture, forming a triangle; continue folding back and forth into a triangle to end of rectangle. Tuck edges under triangle. Place triangles, seam side down, on a large baking sheet coated with cooking spray; lightly coat triangles with cooking spray. Repeat procedure with remaining phyllo, butter mixture, crumbs, brown sugar, cherry mixture, and cooking spray.

4. Bake at 375° for 15 minutes or until golden brown. Remove from baking sheet; cool on a wire rack. Yield: 16 servings (serving size: 1 turnover).

CALORIES 155 (25% from fat); FAT 4.3g (sat 1.2g, mono 2.1g, poly 0.8g); PROTEIN 1.9g; CARB 27g; FIBER 1.9g; CHOL 4mg; IRON 0.8mg; SODIUM 62mg; CALC 21mg

Maple Fruit Crisps

- ½ cup all-purpose flour (about 2¼ ounces)
- ½ cup regular oats
- ⅓ cup packed brown sugar
- 1 teaspoon baking powder
- ½ teaspoon ground cinnamon
- ¼ teaspoon ground nutmeg
- 2 tablespoons slivered almonds
- 1 large egg
- 2½ cups fresh blackberries
- ⅓ cup maple syrup
- 4 nectarines, each peeled and cut into 8 wedges
- 1½ cups vanilla low-fat frozen yogurt

1. Preheat oven to 350°.
2. Lightly spoon flour into a dry measuring cup; level with a knife. Place flour and next 5 ingredients in a food processor; pulse 2 times or until blended. Add almonds; pulse 3 times or until almonds are chopped. Add egg; pulse 5 times or until mixture resembles coarse meal.
3. Combine blackberries, maple syrup, and nectarines in a bowl; toss to coat. Divide fruit mixture evenly among 6 (10-ounce) ramekins or custard cups; crumble oat mixture evenly over fruit mixture. Bake at 350° for 35 minutes or until bubbly. Serve with frozen yogurt. Yield: 6 servings (serving size: 1 ramekin and ¼ cup frozen yogurt).

NOTE: This recipe can also be made in a 1½-quart casserole and baked 35 minutes.

CALORIES 289 (12% from fat); FAT 3.9g (sat 1g, mono 1.3g, poly 1.1g); PROTEIN 5.8g; CARB 61.2g; FIBER 6.4g; CHOL 40mg; IRON 2.1mg; SODIUM 111mg; CALC 141mg

Harvest Pear Crisp

Cinnamon-spiced pears bake under a crunchy streusel topping in this homey dessert. You can assemble the dish ahead and put it in the oven to suit your convenience. Or bake it early in the day and serve it with a scoop of vanilla ice cream. Pulse the streusel mixture in the food processor for an even, crumbly texture.

- 6 cups Anjou or Bartlett pears, cored and cut lengthwise into ½-inch-thick slices (about 3 pounds)
- 1 tablespoon fresh lemon juice
- ⅓ cup granulated sugar
- 1 tablespoon cornstarch
- 1½ teaspoons ground cinnamon, divided
- ⅓ cup all-purpose flour (about 1½ ounces)
- ½ cup packed brown sugar
- ½ teaspoon salt
- 3 tablespoons chilled butter, cut into small pieces
- ⅓ cup regular oats
- ¼ cup coarsely chopped walnuts

1. Preheat oven to 375°.
2. Combine pear slices and lemon juice in a 2-quart baking dish; toss gently to coat. Combine granulated sugar, cornstarch, and 1 teaspoon cinnamon; stir with a whisk. Add cornstarch mixture to pear mixture; toss well to coat.
3. Lightly spoon flour into a dry measuring cup; level with a knife. Place flour, ½ teaspoon cinnamon, brown sugar, and salt in a food processor; pulse 2 times or until combined. Add chilled butter, and pulse 6 times or until mixture resembles coarse meal. Add oats and walnuts; pulse 2 times. Sprinkle flour mixture evenly over pear mixture.
4. Bake at 375° for 40 minutes or until pears are tender and topping is golden brown. Cool 20 minutes on a wire rack. Serve crisp warm or at room temperature. Yield: 8 servings.

CALORIES 285 (24% from fat); FAT 7.7g (sat 3g, mono 1.8g, poly 2.2g); PROTEIN 2.4g; CARB 55.5g; FIBER 5.1g; CHOL 12mg; IRON 1.2mg; SODIUM 197mg; CALC 42mg

Harvest Pear Crisp

Mango Macadamia Crisp

Mango Macadamia Crisp

The tangy-sweet taste and velvety texture of the mango contrast nicely with the crunchy nut topping. A bottled refrigerated mango can be substituted for fresh.

FILLING:

- ¼ cup granulated sugar
- 2 teaspoons cornstarch
- 4 cups chopped peeled ripe mango (about 4 pounds)
- 3 tablespoons fresh lime juice
- 2 teaspoons butter, melted
- Cooking spray

TOPPING:

- ⅓ cup all-purpose flour (about 1½ ounces)
- 3 tablespoons granulated sugar
- 1½ teaspoons brown sugar
- ½ teaspoon ground ginger
- 3 tablespoons butter
- 3 tablespoons chopped macadamia nuts

1. Preheat oven to 400°.

2. Combine ¼ cup granulated sugar and cornstarch, stirring well with a whisk. Add mango, juice, and 2 teaspoons butter; toss gently to combine. Place mango mixture in an 8-inch square baking dish coated with cooking spray.

3. To prepare topping, lightly spoon flour into a dry measuring cup; level with a knife. Combine flour, 3 tablespoons granulated sugar, brown sugar, and ginger, stirring well. Cut in 3 tablespoons butter with a pastry blender or 2 knives until mixture resembles coarse meal. Stir in nuts. Sprinkle flour mixture evenly over mango mixture. Bake at 400° for 40 minutes or until browned. Yield: 8 servings (serving size: about ½ cup).

CALORIES 238 (31% from fat); FAT 8.1g (sat 3.1g, mono 4.2g, poly 0.3g); PROTEIN 1.7g; CARB 43.7g; FIBER 3.3g; CHOL 14mg; IRON 0.6mg; SODIUM 49mg; CALC 21mg

Orange Crisp with Coconut Topping

This delicious dessert is sure to please guests of any occasion. The juicy citrus filling is crowned with a buttery layer of crunchy coconut crumbs. Use a shallow baking dish to better distribute the topping.

FILLING:

- 6 large navel oranges
- 1½ tablespoons uncooked quick-cooking tapioca
- 1 tablespoon Grand Marnier (orange-flavored liqueur)
- Cooking spray

TOPPING:

- ⅔ cup all-purpose flour (about 3 ounces)
- ⅔ cup sugar
- ½ teaspoon salt
- ¼ cup chilled butter, cut into small pieces
- ⅔ cup flaked sweetened coconut

1. Preheat oven to 375°.

2. To prepare filling, peel and section oranges over a large bowl, reserving ¼ cup juice. Add tapioca and liqueur to reserved juice; stir until well blended. Add orange sections; stir gently. Let stand 20 minutes, stirring occasionally.

3. Place filling in an 11 x 7–inch baking dish or shallow 2-quart baking dish coated with cooking spray.

4. To prepare topping, lightly spoon flour into a dry measuring cup; level with a knife. Combine flour, sugar, and salt in a large bowl, stirring with a whisk. Cut in butter with a pastry blender or 2 knives until mixture resembles coarse meal. Add coconut; toss well. Sprinkle topping evenly over filling. Bake at 375° for 35 minutes or until crisp is golden and bubbly. Yield: 8 servings.

CALORIES 231 (31% from fat); FAT 7.9g (sat 5.3g, mono 1.8g, poly 0.3g); PROTEIN 2.2g; CARB 40g; FIBER 2.5g; CHOL 15mg; IRON 0.7mg; SODIUM 221mg; CALC 38mg

Apple Crumble with Golden Raisins

Apple Crumble with Golden Raisins

Baked apple—sweetened with raisins, orange juice, and cinnamon—is graced with a simple crumb topping. For a sweeter flavor, try Braeburn apples.

- 2 tablespoons all-purpose flour
- 2 tablespoons granulated sugar, divided
- 1 tablespoon brown sugar
- 1 tablespoon chilled butter, cut into small pieces
- 1½ cups diced peeled Granny Smith apple
- 1 tablespoon golden raisins
- 2 tablespoons fresh orange juice
- ½ teaspoon fresh lemon juice
- ⅛ teaspoon ground cinnamon
- Cooking spray

1. Preheat oven to 375°.
2. Combine flour, 1 tablespoon granulated sugar, and brown sugar in a medium bowl. Cut in butter with a pastry blender or 2 knives until mixture resembles coarse meal.
3. Combine 1 tablespoon granulated sugar, apple, and next 4 ingredients, tossing well. Divide apple mixture evenly between 2 (6-ounce) ramekins coated with cooking spray. Sprinkle evenly with flour mixture. Bake at 375° for 30 minutes or until golden brown. Yield: 2 servings.

CALORIES 223 (25% from fat); FAT 6.2g (sat 3.7g, mono 1.7g, poly 0.4g); PROTEIN 1.3g; CARB 43.1g; FIBER 2.4g; CHOL 16mg; IRON 0.7mg; SODIUM 61mg; CALC 17mg

Vanilla Pudding

This pudding takes about 10 minutes to make in the microwave so there is no risk of overcooking or scorching in a saucepan. It can be the foundation for every custard dessert you prepare.

- ⅓ cup all-purpose flour (about 1½ ounces)
- ½ cup sugar
- ⅛ teaspoon salt
- 2 cups fat-free milk, divided
- ¼ cup egg substitute
- 1 teaspoon vanilla extract

1. Lightly spoon flour into a dry measuring cup; level with a knife. Combine flour, sugar, and salt in a medium microwave-safe bowl; gradually add 1¾ cups milk, stirring well with a whisk. Microwave at HIGH 4 to 5 minutes or until thick, stirring after every minute.
2. Combine remaining ¼ cup milk and egg substitute in a large bowl. Gently stir one-fourth milk mixture into egg substitute mixture; add to remaining hot milk mixture. Microwave at HIGH 1 minute; stir well. Stir in vanilla. Pour into a bowl; cover surface of pudding with plastic wrap. Chill. Yield: 5 servings (serving size: ½ cup).

CALORIES 151 (1% from fat); FAT 0.2g (sat 0.1g, mono 0.1g, poly 0g); PROTEIN 5.4g; CARB 31.4g; FIBER 0.2g; CHOL 2mg; IRON 0.6mg; SODIUM 128mg; CALC 126mg

Santa Rosa Plum Crumble

Santa Rosa Plum Crumble

Santa Rosa plums are great in this dessert, although any juicy plum will work nicely. Because it's good served either warm or at room temperature, this is a choice make-ahead dessert. After scraping the seeds from the vanilla bean, use it to flavor sugar: Bury the bean in a container of granulated sugar, and store for up to six months.

- 14 plums, each cut into 6 wedges
- ¼ cup granulated sugar
- 3 tablespoons dry red wine
- 1 (4-inch) piece vanilla bean, split lengthwise
- Cooking spray
- ¾ cup all-purpose flour (about 3⅓ ounces)
- 1 cup regular oats
- 6 tablespoons brown sugar
- 1½ teaspoons grated orange rind
- ¼ teaspoon salt
- ⅛ teaspoon ground nutmeg
- 5 tablespoons chilled butter, cut into small pieces

1. Preheat oven to 375°.
2. Combine first 3 ingredients. Scrape seeds from vanilla bean; add seeds to plum mixture. Discard bean. Toss mixture gently to combine. Spoon into a 13 x 9–inch baking dish coated with cooking spray.
3. Lightly spoon flour into a dry measuring cup; level with a knife. Combine flour and next 5 ingredients in a medium bowl; cut in butter with a pastry blender or 2 knives until mixture resembles coarse meal. Sprinkle flour mixture evenly over plum mixture. Bake at 375° for 45 minutes or until plum mixture is bubbly and topping is lightly browned. Serve warm or at room temperature. Yield: 9 servings (serving size: about 1 cup).

CALORIES 284 (26% from fat); FAT 8.2g (sat 4.1g, mono 2.8g, poly 0.7g); PROTEIN 3.8g; CARB 52.5g; FIBER 3.9g; CHOL 17mg; IRON 1.3mg; SODIUM 134mg; CALC 24mg

Bittersweet Chocolate Mousse à l'Orange

Two appliances, the blender and microwave, simplify the preparation of this easy dish. Fresh orange sections are topped with a thick chocolate mousse for a unique presentation. The mild bitterness of orange rind and bittersweet chocolate temper the dessert's sweetness. It can be prepared up to a day ahead.

- ½ cup sugar
- 7 tablespoons unsweetened cocoa
- 2 tablespoons Grand Marnier (orange-flavored liqueur)
- 1 teaspoon grated orange rind
- ½ teaspoon vanilla extract
- Dash of salt
- 2 (12.3-ounce) packages reduced-fat silken tofu, drained
- 3 ounces bittersweet chocolate, chopped
- 3 oranges, peeled and sectioned
- Mint sprigs (optional)

1. Combine first 7 ingredients in a blender or food processor; process until smooth.
2. Place chocolate in a small microwave-safe bowl. Microwave at HIGH 1 minute or until almost melted; stir until smooth. Add chocolate to tofu mixture; process until smooth.
3. Divide orange sections evenly among 6 bowls or parfait glasses, and top each serving with ½ cup mousse. Cover and chill at least 1 hour. Garnish with mint sprigs, if desired. Yield: 6 servings.

CALORIES 241 (27% from fat); FAT 7.1g (sat 3.6g, mono 1g, poly 0.9g); PROTEIN 9.5g; CARB 35.9g; FIBER 4.1g; CHOL 1mg; IRON 2mg; SODIUM 124mg; CALC 79mg

Polenta Pudding with Blueberry Topping

Cooking grains and cereals in the microwave is very simple. There's no clumping, it's quick, and the cleanup couldn't be easier.

- 1 cup fresh or frozen blueberries
- ½ cup sugar, divided
- 2 cups 2% reduced-fat milk
- 6 tablespoons yellow cornmeal
- ¾ teaspoon lemon rind
- ½ teaspoon vanilla extract
- ¼ teaspoon salt

1. Combine blueberries and ¼ cup sugar in a medium microwave-safe bowl. Cover with wax paper; microwave at HIGH 3 minutes or until thoroughly heated and sugar dissolves, stirring after 1½ minutes.
2. Combine ¼ cup sugar, milk, cornmeal, and lemon rind in a 2-quart glass measure; stir with a whisk. Microwave at HIGH 7 minutes or until thick and bubbly, stirring every 2 minutes. Stir in vanilla and salt. Serve with blueberry topping. Yield: 4 servings (serving size: ½ cup pudding and about 3 tablespoons topping).

CALORIES 226 (11% from fat); FAT 2.8g (sat 1.5g, mono 0.8g, poly 0.3g); PROTEIN 5.3g; CARB 45.7g; FIBER 1.7g; CHOL 10mg; IRON 0.7mg; SODIUM 209mg; CALC 153mg

Individual Tiramisu Trifles

These parfaitlike desserts can be assembled the day before serving and need no last-minute garnishes.

- 1 cup cold strong brewed coffee
- 3 tablespoons Marsala wine
- 1 (8-ounce) block ⅓-less-fat cream cheese, softened
- ½ cup (4 ounces) block-style fat-free cream cheese, softened
- ¾ cup sugar
- 30 cake-style ladyfingers (2½ [3-ounce] packages)
- 1 teaspoon unsweetened cocoa

1. Combine coffee and wine; set aside.
2. Place cheeses in a medium bowl; beat with a mixer at medium speed until smooth. Gradually add sugar, beating until well blended.
3. Cut each ladyfinger crosswise into 3 pieces. Arrange 5 ladyfinger pieces in each of 9 wine glasses or small bowls; drizzle each with about 1 tablespoon coffee mixture. Spoon about 1½ tablespoons cheese mixture into each glass. Repeat layers once; sprinkle evenly with cocoa. Cover and chill at least 1 hour. Yield: 9 servings (serving size: 1 trifle).

CALORIES 228 (28% from fat); FAT 7.2g (sat 4.3g, mono 1.9g, poly 0.6g); PROTEIN 6.4g; CARB 34.2g; FIBER 0.3g; CHOL 62mg; IRON 0.7mg; SODIUM 340mg; CALC 71mg

Chocolate-Raspberry Tiramisu

To make this nontraditional, summery tiramisu even fancier, use a mixture of red, golden, and black raspberries. Use a small strainer to sift the cocoa over the tops of each serving.

- ¼ cup powdered sugar
- ¼ cup (2 ounces) mascarpone cheese, softened
- ¼ cup raspberry-flavored liqueur, divided
- 1 (8-ounce) block fat-free cream cheese, softened
- 12 cake-style ladyfingers, split
- 1½ tablespoons unsweetened cocoa
- 2 cups fresh raspberries
- Mint sprigs (optional)

1. Place powdered sugar, mascarpone cheese, 1½ tablespoons liqueur, and cream cheese in a large bowl, and beat with a mixer at high speed until well blended.
2. Brush cut sides of ladyfingers with remaining 2½ tablespoons liqueur. Spread about 1½ tablespoons mascarpone mixture over bottom half of each ladyfinger; cover with tops.
3. Arrange 3 filled ladyfingers spokelike on each of 4 dessert plates. Sprinkle evenly with cocoa. Arrange ½ cup raspberries over each serving. Garnish with mint sprigs, if desired. Yield: 4 servings.

CALORIES 348 (27% from fat); FAT 10.3g (sat 4.8g, mono 3.5g, poly 0.9g); PROTEIN 13.6g; CARB 46g; FIBER 5.2g; CHOL 144mg; IRON 1.8mg; SODIUM 331mg; CALC 209mg

Chocolate-Raspberry Tiramisu

Sweet Potato Trifle

The two main ingredients in this easy dessert, purchased angel food cake and canned sweet potatoes, mean there's no baking required. Prepare and garnish up to a day in advance.

- 1 (16-ounce) angel food cake, cut into 1-inch cubes
- 3/4 cup sugar, divided
- 1/2 cup reduced-fat sour cream
- 1 (8-ounce) block 1/3-less-fat cream cheese, softened
- 1 (5-ounce) can evaporated fat-free milk
- 1/2 teaspoon vanilla extract
- Dash of salt
- 2 (15-ounce) cans cooked peeled sweet potatoes, drained and mashed
- 3 tablespoons flaked sweetened coconut, toasted and divided
- 1 (8-ounce) container frozen fat-free whipped topping, thawed
- 1 tablespoon chopped pecans, toasted

1. Preheat oven to 350°.
2. Arrange cake cubes in a single layer on a jelly-roll pan. Bake at 350° for 15 minutes or until toasted, turning once.
3. Place 1/2 cup sugar, sour cream, and cream cheese in a large bowl; beat with a mixer at medium speed until well combined. Gradually add milk, beating until smooth. Add cake cubes, and fold gently to combine.
4. Place remaining 1/4 cup sugar, vanilla, salt, and sweet potato in a large bowl; beat with a mixer at medium speed until smooth.
5. Spoon half of cake mixture into a trifle dish or 3-quart glass bowl; top with half of sweet potato mixture. Sprinkle 1 tablespoon coconut over sweet potato mixture; top with half of whipped topping. Repeat layers; sprinkle with remaining 1 tablespoon coconut and pecans. Cover and chill at least 1 hour. Yield: 12 servings (serving size: about 2/3 cup).

CALORIES 303 (20% from fat); FAT 6.9g (sat 4g, mono 1.9g, poly 0.5g); PROTEIN 6.2g; CARB 53.5g; FIBER 1.4g; CHOL 19mg; IRON 0.9mg; SODIUM 434mg; CALC 125mg

Peach and Raspberry Pavlova Parfaits

To make crumbs, place the mini meringue cookies in a plastic bag, and gently crush with a rolling pin.

- 1/2 cup (4 ounces) 1/3-less-fat cream cheese, softened
- 1/4 cup sugar, divided
- 1 cup vanilla fat-free yogurt
- 2 cups sliced peeled peaches (about 6 to 7 peaches)
- 1 cup raspberries
- 1 cup vanilla meringue cookie crumbs (such as Miss Meringue Minis; about 12 mini cookies, coarsely crushed)
- 12 vanilla meringue mini cookies

1. Place cream cheese and 3 tablespoons sugar in a medium bowl; beat with a mixer at high speed 2 minutes or until smooth. Add yogurt, beating until well blended.
2. Combine remaining 1 tablespoon sugar, peaches, and raspberries in a large bowl, tossing gently to coat. Let stand 5 minutes, stirring once.
3. Spoon 2 tablespoons cream cheese mixture into each of 6 (8-ounce) glasses; top each with 1/4 cup peach mixture and about 2 1/2 tablespoons cookie crumbs. Repeat layers once with remaining cream cheese mixture and remaining peach mixture; cover and chill. To serve, top each parfait with 2 whole mini cookies. Yield: 6 servings (serving size: 1 parfait).

CALORIES 193 (22% from fat); FAT 4.7g (sat 2.9g, mono 1.3g, poly 0.2g); PROTEIN 5.1g; CARB 34.7g; FIBER 2.5g; CHOL 15mg; IRON 0.3mg; SODIUM 111mg; CALC 94mg

Key Lime Pie Parfaits

Key limes are smaller, rounder, and have a paler flesh than traditional limes. They add a unique sweet-tartness to this dessert.

- ½ cup fresh lime juice
- ¼ cup sugar
- ¼ teaspoon grated lime rind
- 2 large eggs
- 1 (14-ounce) can fat-free sweetened condensed milk
- 1½ cups canned whipped light cream (such as Reddi-wip)
- 1 cup graham cracker crumbs (about 8 cookie sheets)
- Grated lime rind (optional)

1. Combine first 5 ingredients in a large bowl, stirring with a whisk until smooth; pour into top of a double boiler. Cook over simmering water until mixture thickens (about 6 minutes) or until a thermometer registers 160°, stirring constantly. Remove from heat. Place pan in a large ice-filled bowl 20 minutes or until mixture comes to room temperature, stirring occasionally.

2. Spoon 1 tablespoon whipped cream into each of 8 (8-ounce) glasses; top each serving with 1 tablespoon crumbs and 3 tablespoons lime mixture. Repeat layers once, ending with lime mixture. Top each serving with 1 tablespoon whipped cream; sprinkle with lime rind, if desired. Serve immediately. Yield: 8 servings (serving size: 1 parfait).

CALORIES 258 (17% from fat); FAT 5g (sat 2.1g, mono 1.6g, poly 0.7g); PROTEIN 7.1g; CARB 47g; FIBER 0.4g; CHOL 65mg; IRON 0.6mg; SODIUM 149mg; CALC 161mg

Funky Monkey Parfaits

This easy chocolate pudding is layered with the delicious combination of peanut butter and bananas. Prepare the pudding and make the cookie crumbs in advance; slice the bananas just before you assemble the parfaits.

- 6 tablespoons sugar
- ¼ cup Dutch process cocoa
- 2 tablespoons cornstarch
- Dash of salt
- 1½ cups 2% reduced-fat milk
- ½ teaspoon vanilla extract
- 1 cup peanut butter sandwich cookie crumbs (such as Nutter Butter; about 8 cookies, crumbled)
- 3 cups sliced bananas

1. Combine first 4 ingredients in a 2-quart glass measure; stir well. Gradually add milk, stirring with a whisk. Microwave at HIGH 2½ minutes, stirring occasionally. Microwave at MEDIUM-HIGH (70% power) 2½ minutes or until thick, stirring occasionally. Stir in vanilla. Cover surface of mixture with plastic wrap; chill.

2. Spoon 1 tablespoon cookie crumbs into each of 8 (8-ounce) glasses; top each with 3 tablespoons bananas and 1½ tablespoons chocolate mixture. Repeat layers once, ending with chocolate mixture. Serve immediately. Yield: 8 servings (serving size: 1 parfait).

CALORIES 191 (21% from fat); FAT 4.5g (sat 1.4g, mono 1.4g, poly 0.6g); PROTEIN 4g; CARB 37.7g; FIBER 1.9g; CHOL 5mg; IRON 0.9mg; SODIUM 127mg; CALC 53mg

Deconstructed Flan

YOGURT CHEESE:

- 1 (32-ounce) carton vanilla low-fat yogurt

ICE CREAM:

- ¼ cup sugar
- 3 large eggs
- 1 cup whole milk
- 1 cup half-and-half
- 1 vanilla bean, split lengthwise

SAUCE:

- ⅓ cup sugar
- ½ cup boiling water
- 1 vanilla bean, split lengthwise

1. To prepare yogurt cheese, place colander in a 2-quart glass measure or medium bowl. Line colander with 4 layers of cheesecloth, allowing cheesecloth to extend over outside edges. Spoon yogurt into colander. Cover loosely with plastic wrap; refrigerate 12 hours. Spoon yogurt cheese into a bowl; discard liquid. Cover and refrigerate.

2. To prepare ice cream, combine ¼ cup sugar and eggs in a medium bowl, stirring well with a whisk. Combine milk and half-and-half in a heavy saucepan over medium-high heat. Scrape seeds from 1 vanilla bean; add seeds and bean to milk mixture. Heat to 180° or until tiny bubbles form around edge of pan, stirring frequently (do not boil). Gradually add milk mixture to egg mixture, stirring constantly with a whisk. Return milk mixture to pan; cook over medium heat until thick (about 5 minutes), stirring constantly. Remove from heat. Place pan in a large ice-filled bowl until mixture cools to room temperature (about 25 minutes), stirring occasionally. Discard vanilla bean. Pour mixture into freezer can of an ice-cream freezer; freeze according to manufacturer's instructions. Spoon ice cream into a freezer-safe container; cover and freeze 1 hour or until firm.

3. To prepare sauce, place ⅓ cup sugar in a small, heavy saucepan over medium-high heat; cook until sugar dissolves, stirring as needed to dissolve sugar evenly (about 6 minutes). Continue cooking about 1 minute or until golden. Remove from heat; carefully stir in water (caramelized sugar will seize slightly and stick to spoon). Place pan over medium-high heat until caramelized sugar melts. Scrape seeds from 1 vanilla bean, and add seeds and bean to mixture. Cook 2 minutes or until reduced to 6 tablespoons, stirring occasionally. Remove from heat, and let stand 10 minutes. Discard vanilla bean.

4. Place ¼ cup yogurt cheese into each of 6 glasses or bowls; top with 1 tablespoon sauce and ½ cup ice cream. Serve immediately. Yield: 6 servings.

CALORIES 319 (27% from fat); FAT 9.7g (sat 5.5g, mono 3.2g, poly 0.5g); PROTEIN 13.2g; CARB 43.8g; FIBER 0g; CHOL 140mg; IRON 0.5mg; SODIUM 172mg; CALC 366mg

Deconstructed Flan

Honey Crème Brûlée with Raspberries

Honey Crème Brûlée with Raspberries

You can check your local farmers' market to find honey produced in your area; it will add pleasantly complex flavor. If you don't have shallow dishes for the crème brûlée, use 6-ounce ramekins instead.

- 2 cups 2% reduced-fat milk
- ¾ cup nonfat dry milk
- 2 tablespoons sugar
- 2 tablespoons honey
- 5 large egg yolks
- Dash of salt
- 3 tablespoons sugar
- 24 fresh raspberries

1. Preheat oven to 300°.
2. Combine first 4 ingredients in a large saucepan. Heat mixture over medium heat to 180° or until tiny bubbles form around the edge (do not boil), stirring occasionally. Remove from heat.
3. Combine egg yolks and salt in a medium bowl; stir well with a whisk. Gradually add hot milk mixture to egg mixture, stirring constantly with a whisk. Divide milk mixture evenly among 4 shallow (6-ounce) custard dishes. Place dishes in a 13 x 9–inch baking pan; add hot water to pan to a depth of 1 inch. Bake at 300° for 1 hour or until center barely moves when dish is touched. Remove dishes from pan; cool completely on a wire rack. Cover and chill at least 4 hours or overnight.
4. Sift 3 tablespoons sugar evenly over custards. Holding a kitchen blowtorch about 2 inches from top of each custard, heat sugar, moving torch back and forth, until sugar is completely melted and caramelized (about 1 minute). Top evenly with raspberries. Serve immediately. Yield: 4 servings (serving size: 1 crème brûlée and 6 raspberries).

NOTE: If you don't have a kitchen blowtorch, you can make the sugar topping on the stove top. Place ¼ cup sugar and 1 tablespoon water in a small, heavy saucepan. Cook over medium heat 5 to 8 minutes or until golden. (Resist urge to stir, since doing so may cause sugar to crystallize.) Immediately pour sugar mixture evenly over cold custards, spreading to form a thin layer.

CALORIES 275 (26% from fat); FAT 7.9g (sat 3.4g, mono 3.1g, poly 1g); PROTEIN 12.6g; CARB 39.2g; FIBER 0.8g; CHOL 265mg; IRON 0.8mg; SODIUM 185mg; CALC 364mg

Blueberry Granita with Berry Compote

(pictured on page 402)

The more frequently you stir the granita, the slushier it will be. The less you stir, the icier it will be. Both can be made up to a day ahead.

GRANITA:

- 2 quarts fresh blueberries (about 1½ pounds)
- 1½ cups water, divided
- ¾ cup sugar
- 3 tablespoons lemon juice

COMPOTE:

- 2 cups quartered small strawberries, divided
- ½ cup water
- ⅓ cup sugar
- 1 (2-inch) piece lemon rind
- ¾ cup fresh blueberries
- 1 teaspoon lemon juice

1. To prepare granita, place 2 quarts blueberries in a food processor or blender; process until smooth. With food processor still on, slowly pour 1 cup water through food chute; process until well blended. Strain blueberry mixture through a fine sieve into a bowl; discard solids.
2. Combine ½ cup water and ¾ cup sugar in a small saucepan over high heat, stirring until sugar dissolves. Stir sugar mixture and 3 tablespoons juice into blueberry mixture. Pour mixture into a 13 x 9–inch glass baking dish; let cool to room temperature. Freeze 1½ to 2 hours or until ice crystals begin to form. Remove mixture from freezer; stir well with a fork. Return dish to freezer; freeze 2 hours, stirring every 30 minutes or until slushy. Cover and freeze 1 hour.
3. To prepare compote, place 1 cup strawberries in a food processor or blender; process until smooth. Strain strawberry mixture through a fine sieve into a bowl; discard solids.
4. Combine ½ cup water, ⅓ cup sugar, and rind in a medium saucepan over medium-high heat; bring to a boil. Cook 1 minute; remove from heat. Discard rind. Add pureed strawberries, quartered strawberries, ¾ cup blueberries, and 1 teaspoon juice to pan; stir gently to combine. Let cool to room temperature. Cover and chill. Spoon compote into each of 8 bowls; top with granita. Yield: 8 servings (serving size: ⅔ cup granita and about ⅓ cup compote).

CALORIES 174 (3% from fat); FAT 0.5g (sat 0g, mono 0g, poly 0.1g); PROTEIN 0.9g; CARB 44.5g; FIBER 3.5g; CHOL 0mg; IRON 0.3mg; SODIUM 7mg; CALC 12mg

Citrus Tea Sorbet

Citrus Tea Sorbet

Use an unflavored black tea, or substitute your favorite tea. This refreshing sorbet makes a great ending to a spicy meal. If you use loose tea, strain it and discard solids before adding the sugar.

2¼ cups boiling water
4 black tea bags or 4 teaspoons loose black tea
2 cups sugar
4 cups grapefruit juice (about 8 grapefruit)
1 tablespoon grated orange rind
1 cup fresh orange juice (about 2 oranges)

1. Pour boiling water over tea bags in a large saucepan; steep 5 minutes. Remove and discard tea bags. Add sugar to pan; cook over medium heat 5 minutes or until sugar dissolves. Cool completely.
2. Combine tea mixture, grapefruit juice, rind, and orange juice in freezer can of an ice-cream freezer; freeze according to manufacturer's instructions. Spoon sorbet into a freezer-safe container; cover and freeze 1 hour or until firm. Yield: 8 servings (serving size: about ¾ cup).

CALORIES 252 (1% from fat); FAT 0.2g (sat 0.1g, mono 0.1g, poly 0g); PROTEIN 0.8g; CARB 63.8g; FIBER 0.3g; CHOL 0mg; IRON 0.3mg; SODIUM 2mg; CALC 15mg

Nectarine and Raspberry Sorbet

Fresh peaches also work well for this frozen treat. Garnish with nectarine slices, if you wish.

2 cups chopped peeled nectarines (about 1½ pounds)
1⅓ cups raspberries (about 6 ounces)
2½ cups apricot nectar
½ cup honey
1 tablespoon fresh lemon juice

1. Combine chopped nectarines and raspberries in a food processor; process until smooth. Stir in apricot nectar, honey, and lemon juice. Strain mixture through a sieve into a large bowl; discard solids.
2. Pour mixture into freezer can of an ice-cream freezer; freeze according to manufacturer's instructions. Spoon sorbet into a freezer-safe container; cover and freeze 1 hour or until firm. Yield: 5 servings (serving size: 1 cup).

CALORIES 218 (2% from fat); FAT 0.6g (sat 0.1g, mono 0.2g, poly 0.3g); PROTEIN 1.4g; CARB 56.7g; FIBER 3.4g; CHOL 0mg; IRON 0.9mg; SODIUM 5mg; CALC 21mg

Raspberry Melba

Peach melba—the classic dessert of sliced peaches and pureed raspberries—is reversed with pureed peaches and whole raspberries for an unusual but equally pleasing effect.

¼ cup peach nectar
2 tablespoons sugar
2 teaspoons fresh lemon juice
1 pound ripe peaches, peeled and coarsely chopped
2 cups raspberry sorbet
1 cup fresh raspberries

1. Combine first 4 ingredients in a food processor; process until smooth. Let mixture stand at room temperature 5 minutes.
2. Spoon ¼ cup peach puree into each of 4 parfait glasses; top each serving with ¼ cup sorbet and 2 tablespoons raspberries. Repeat layers with remaining puree, sorbet, and raspberries. Yield: 4 servings.

CALORIES 179 (2% from fat); FAT 0.4g (sat 0g, mono 0.1g, poly 0.2g); PROTEIN 2.3g; CARB 45g; FIBER 4.3g; CHOL 0mg; IRON 0.5mg; SODIUM 5mg; CALC 18mg

Sautéed Apples over Ice Cream

Fuji apples hold their texture during cooking and are so naturally sweet that they need very little additional sugar. Galas are a good substitute.

1 tablespoon butter
1½ cups sliced peeled Fuji apple
1 tablespoon sugar
3 tablespoons brandy
¼ teaspoon fresh lemon juice
⅛ teaspoon ground ginger
1 cup vanilla reduced-fat ice cream

1. Melt butter in a small nonstick skillet over medium heat. Add apple; cook 5 minutes or until lightly browned, stirring frequently.
2. Add sugar, brandy, juice, and ginger; cook over medium-low heat 2 minutes or until apple is tender, stirring occasionally. Serve warm over ice cream. Yield: 2 servings (serving size: about ½ cup apples and ½ cup ice cream).

CALORIES 316 (23% from fat); FAT 8.2g (sat 4.7g, mono 1.7g, poly 0.4g); PROTEIN 3.3g; CARB 46.9g; FIBER 3.8g; CHOL 21mg; IRON 0.2mg; SODIUM 104mg; CALC 108mg

Apple Pie à la Mode Parfaits

Crumble packaged oatmeal cookies for a quick streusel. The apple mixture can be made a few hours ahead.

4½ cups chopped peeled cooking apple (such as Braeburn)
½ cup sugar
1 tablespoon fresh lemon juice
1 teaspoon apple-pie spice
1 cup oatmeal cookie crumbs (about 4 ounces, crushed)
3 cups vanilla low-fat ice cream, softened

1. Combine first 4 ingredients in a medium saucepan; bring to a boil. Cover, reduce heat, and simmer 5 minutes. Uncover; simmer 5 minutes or until tender, stirring occasionally. Spoon into a bowl; cover and chill.

2. Spoon 1 tablespoon cookie crumbs into each of 8 (8-ounce) glasses, and top each with ¼ cup apple mixture and 3 tablespoons ice cream. Repeat layers once, ending with ice cream. Serve immediately. Yield: 8 servings.

CALORIES 284 (24% from fat); FAT 7.7g (sat 2.3g, mono 3.7g, poly 0.9g); PROTEIN 4.4g; CARB 51.4g; FIBER 3g; CHOL 9mg; IRON 0.9mg; SODIUM 129mg; CALC 83mg

Peppermint Brownie à la Mode

If you're a big mint lover, substitute mint chocolate chip ice cream.

1 cup all-purpose flour (about 4½ ounces)
½ cup unsweetened cocoa powder
¼ teaspoon baking soda
¼ teaspoon salt
¼ cup warm fat-free milk
2 teaspoons instant coffee
1 teaspoon vanilla extract
1 cup sugar
2 large eggs, lightly beaten
5 tablespoons butter
¼ cup semisweet chocolate chips
Cooking spray
2 teaspoons powdered sugar
4 cups reduced-fat chocolate chip ice cream (such as Healthy Choice), softened
18 hard peppermint candies, coarsely chopped and divided

1. Preheat oven to 350°.

2. Lightly spoon flour into a dry measuring cup; level with a knife. Combine flour, cocoa, baking soda, and salt in a large bowl, stirring with a whisk.

3. Combine milk, coffee, and vanilla in a medium bowl. Add sugar and eggs, stirring with a whisk until well combined. Melt butter and chocolate chips in a microwave-safe bowl at HIGH in 20-second intervals, stirring between each interval, until completely melted. Add chocolate mixture to egg mixture, stirring with a whisk until well combined.

4. Fold egg mixture into flour mixture, stirring just until moist. Spread batter into an 8-inch square baking pan coated with cooking spray. Bake at 350° for 20 minutes or until a wooden pick inserted in center comes out clean. Cool on a wire rack. Sprinkle with powdered sugar; cut into 12 pieces.

5. Place ice cream in a large bowl. Add ½ cup chopped candies to ice cream, stirring with a wooden spoon until well combined. Return to freezer.

6. Place 1 brownie on a plate; top each with ⅓ cup ice cream. Sprinkle each with 1 teaspoon chopped candies. Yield: 12 servings.

CALORIES 294 (30% from fat); FAT 10.2g (sat 6.2g, mono 2.1g, poly 0.4g); PROTEIN 5.2g; CARB 47.9g; FIBER 1.7g; CHOL 61mg; IRON 1.3mg; SODIUM 160mg; CALC 20mg

Peppermint Ice Cream Cake

Cooking spray
¾ cup unsweetened cocoa
¾ cup boiling water
6 tablespoons butter, melted
1 cup packed dark brown sugar
½ cup granulated sugar
¾ cup egg substitute
1½ cups all-purpose flour (about 6¾ ounces)
½ teaspoon baking powder
½ teaspoon baking soda
½ teaspoon salt
2 teaspoons vanilla extract
3 cups low-fat peppermint ice cream (such as Edy's/Dreyer's Slow-Churned Light), softened
3 cups frozen fat-free whipped topping, thawed
⅛ teaspoon peppermint extract
8 hard peppermint candies, crushed

1. Preheat oven to 350°.

2. Coat 2 (8-inch) round cake pans with cooking spray. Line bottom of each pan with wax paper.

3. Combine cocoa, water, and butter, stirring with a whisk until blended. Cool.

Peppermint Ice Cream Cake

4. Combine sugars in a large bowl; stir until well blended. Add egg substitute; beat 2 minutes or until light and creamy. Add cocoa mixture; beat 1 minute.

5. Lightly spoon flour into dry measuring cups; level with a knife. Combine flour, baking powder, baking soda, and salt. Gradually add flour mixture to bowl; beat 1 minute or until blended. Stir in vanilla. Pour batter into prepared pans. Bake at 350° for 28 minutes or until a wooden pick inserted in center comes out clean. Cool in pans 10 minutes on a wire rack. Remove from pans. Wrap in plastic wrap; freeze 2 hours or until slightly frozen.

6. Spread ice cream in an 8-inch round cake pan lined with plastic wrap. Cover and freeze 4 hours or until firm.

7. To assemble cake, place 1 cake layer, bottom side up, on a cake pedestal. Remove ice cream layer from freezer; remove plastic wrap. Place ice cream layer, bottom side up, on top of cake layer. Top with remaining cake layer.

8. Combine whipped topping and peppermint extract; stir until blended. Spread frosting over top and sides of cake. Sprinkle with crushed peppermints. Freeze until ready to serve. Let cake stand at room temperature 10 minutes before slicing. Yield: 16 servings (serving size: 1 slice).

CALORIES 251 (24% from fat); FAT 6.8g (sat 3.3g, mono 2.1g, poly 0.4g); PROTEIN 4.3g; CARB 44.4g; FIBER 1.7g; CHOL 19mg; IRON 1.6mg; SODIUM 207mg; CALC 63mg

Turtle Ice Cream Pie

When you see how easy it is to melt chocolate in the microwave, you'll never go back to doing it on the stove top. Remove just before it's completely smooth or it'll burn. It'll continue to melt as you stir.

CRUST:

- ½ cup all-purpose flour (about 2¼ ounces)
- ¼ cup unsweetened cocoa
- ⅛ teaspoon salt
- ⅓ cup sugar
- 2½ tablespoons fat-free milk
- ½ teaspoon vanilla extract
- 1 large egg
- 2 tablespoons butter
- 2 tablespoons semisweet chocolate minichips
- Cooking spray

FILLING:

- 4 cups vanilla low-fat ice cream, softened
- ⅓ cup fat-free caramel sundae syrup (such as Smucker's)
- ¼ cup chopped pecans, toasted
- 3 tablespoons fat-free caramel sundae syrup

1. Preheat oven to 350°.
2. Lightly spoon flour into a dry measuring cup; level with a knife. Combine flour, cocoa, and salt in a medium bowl, stirring with a whisk; set aside. Combine sugar, milk, vanilla, and egg in a medium bowl, stirring with a whisk until well combined; set aside.
3. Place butter and chocolate chips in a small microwave-safe bowl. Microwave at HIGH 1 minute or until butter and chocolate melt, stirring every 20 seconds. Add chocolate mixture to sugar mixture, stirring with a whisk. Fold in flour mixture. Spread batter into a 9-inch deep-dish pie plate coated with cooking spray. Bake at 350° for 15 minutes or until a wooden pick inserted in center comes out clean. Cool completely on a wire rack.
4. To prepare filling, place softened ice cream in a large bowl; beat with a mixer at medium speed until smooth. Spoon half of ice cream over cooled crust, and place remaining ice cream in refrigerator. Drizzle pie with ⅓ cup caramel. Freeze pie 30 minutes or until firm. Spread remaining ice cream over caramel. Sprinkle evenly with pecans; drizzle with 3 tablespoons caramel. Cover and freeze 4 hours or until firm. Yield: 8 servings (serving size: 1 slice).

CALORIES 308 (29% from fat); FAT 10g (sat 4.3g, mono 3.9g, poly 1.2g); PROTEIN 6.3g; CARB 50.5g; FIBER 1.8g; CHOL 51mg; IRON 1.3mg; SODIUM 181mg; CALC 104mg

Peppermint-Marshmallow Ice Cream Pie

Brushing melted ice cream into the pie plate "glues" the crust into place. Crushed chocolate wafers create the crust, while the whole cookies define the edges of the pie.

- 4 cups vanilla low-fat ice cream, softened and divided
- 20 chocolate wafer cookies (such as Nabisco's Famous Chocolate Wafers), coarsely crushed and divided
- 1¼ cups miniature marshmallows, divided
- 15 hard peppermint candies, crushed
- 8 chocolate wafer cookies
- 5 hard peppermint candies, crushed

1. Place 2 tablespoons ice cream in a small microwave-safe bowl. Microwave at HIGH 20 seconds or until ice cream melts. Spread melted ice cream in bottom of a 9-inch pie plate. Arrange half of crushed wafer cookies in bottom of pie plate.
2. Place remaining softened ice cream, 1 cup marshmallows, and 15 crushed candies in a large bowl; beat with a mixer at medium speed until well combined. Spoon half of mixture evenly into crust, and sprinkle evenly with remaining crushed cookies. Spread remaining ice cream mixture over crushed cookies. Arrange whole cookies around outside edge of pie; sprinkle top of pie with remaining ¼ cup marshmallows and 5 crushed candies. Cover and freeze 4 hours or until firm. Yield: 8 servings (serving size: 1 wedge).

CALORIES 281 (18% from fat); FAT 5.5g (sat 2.8g, mono 1.6g, poly 0.5g); PROTEIN 5.1g; CARB 53g; FIBER 0.9g; CHOL 20mg; IRON 0.8mg; SODIUM 221mg; CALC 77mg

Peppermint-Marshmallow Ice Cream Pie

Cherries Jubilee Ice Cream Pie

Cherries Jubilee Ice Cream Pie

All the flavors of the classic dessert combine in this easy-to-prepare pie. Since the cherries are cooked, frozen ones work just fine, especially when fresh ones are not in season—and they save you the trouble of pitting.

- ⅓ cup water
- ¼ cup sugar
- 1 tablespoon cornstarch
- 2 tablespoons brandy
- 1 (12-ounce) package frozen pitted dark sweet cherries
- 2 tablespoons butter, melted
- 2 tablespoons honey
- 1½ cups graham cracker crumbs (about 9 cookie sheets)
- 4 cups vanilla low-fat ice cream, softened

1. Preheat oven to 375°.
2. Combine first 5 ingredients in a medium saucepan. Bring to a boil; cook 2 minutes or until thick, stirring constantly. Cool completely.
3. Combine butter and honey in a medium bowl. Add graham cracker crumbs, stirring to blend. Press mixture into bottom and up sides of a 9-inch pie plate. Bake at 375° for 8 minutes. Cool completely.
4. Place ½ cup cooled cherry mixture in a food processor; process until smooth. Place remaining cherry mixture in an airtight container; cover and chill.
5. Place softened ice cream in a large bowl; beat with a mixer at medium speed until smooth. Add pureed cherry mixture, and gently fold in to achieve a swirl pattern. Spoon mixture into cooled crust. Cover and freeze 4 hours or until firm. Top wedges with reserved cherry sauce just before serving. Yield: 8 servings (serving size: 1 wedge and 3 tablespoons sauce).

CALORIES 277 (23% from fat); FAT 7g (sat 3.4g, mono 2.4g, poly 0.8g); PROTEIN 5g; CARB 47.3g; FIBER 1.6g; CHOL 24mg; IRON 0.7mg; SODIUM 165mg; CALC 88mg

Mascarpone-Stuffed Apricots

Can't find mascarpone? Substitute crème fraîche for similar rich flavor and creamy texture.

- ⅓ cup (3 ounces) block-style fat-free cream cheese
- 2 tablespoons (1 ounce) mascarpone cheese
- 2 tablespoons honey
- 3½ teaspoons lemon juice, divided
- ⅛ teaspoon ground nutmeg
- 2 tablespoons coarsely chopped walnuts, toasted
- 10 small apricots, halved and pitted
- Chopped fresh mint (optional)

1. Combine cheeses, honey, ½ teaspoon lemon juice, and nutmeg, stirring well. Stir in walnuts. Chill 1 hour.
2. Sprinkle cut sides of apricots evenly with 1 tablespoon lemon juice.
3. Spoon about 1 teaspoon cheese mixture into each apricot half, and chill 1 hour. Garnish with chopped fresh mint, if desired. Yield: 10 servings (serving size: 2 apricot halves).

CALORIES 61 (37% from fat); FAT 2.5g (sat 0.9g, mono 0.3g, poly 0.6g); PROTEIN 2.2g; CARB 8.4g; FIBER 0.8g; CHOL 4mg; IRON 0.3mg; SODIUM 49mg; CALC 26mg

Gruyère and Cherry Compote

This is a great introduction to cheese for dessert. Gruyère is a Swiss cheese that has a rich, sweet, nutty flavor. Domestic Swiss and Emmental also work well in this recipe. Gruyère is not overly sweet; a sparkling wine, champagne, or even a dessert wine would be a nice complement to this course.

- ½ cup sugar
- ½ cup water
- 1 pound sweet cherries, pitted
- ¼ cup fresh lemon juice
- 5 (1-inch-thick) slices Italian bread (about 5 ounces)
- 4 ounces Gruyère cheese, cut into 15 thin slices

1. Combine sugar and ½ cup water in a medium, heavy saucepan over high heat. Bring to a boil; cook 1 minute. Add cherries, and cook 1 minute. Reduce heat to medium-low; cook 20 minutes. Remove cherries from pan with a slotted spoon.
2. Cook cherry liquid until reduced to ¼ cup (about 15 minutes). Remove from heat. Add cherries to pan; stir in lemon juice. Cool.
3. Preheat broiler.
4. Cut each bread slice crosswise into 3 strips. Arrange in a single layer on a baking sheet, and broil 1 minute on each side or until bread is toasted. Cool completely.
5. Cut each cheese slice in half diagonally. Arrange 3 bread strips on each of 5 plates. Top each bread strip with 2 slices cheese and about 1 tablespoon compote. Yield: 5 servings.

CALORIES 324 (26% from fat); FAT 9.3g (sat 4.8g, mono 2.8g, poly 1.1g); PROTEIN 10.6g; CARB 51.7g; FIBER 3g; CHOL 25mg; IRON 1.3mg; SODIUM 258mg; CALC 281mg

Figs with Ricotta, Honey, and Walnuts

Fresh figs need little adornment. But a drizzle of honey, a good-quality ricotta, and some fresh cracked walnuts conspire to make an enjoyable summer dessert.

- 15 fresh figs, trimmed (about 1½ pounds)
- ½ cup whole-milk ricotta cheese
- ⅓ cup honey
- ⅓ cup chopped walnuts

1. Cut each fig into 4 wedges, cutting to, but not through, base of fig. Spread wedges slightly apart; place 3 figs on each of 5 dessert plates. Spoon about 1½ teaspoons cheese into each fig, and spoon about 1 tablespoon honey evenly around each serving of figs. Sprinkle each serving with about 1 tablespoon walnuts. Yield: 5 servings.

CALORIES 273 (27% from fat); FAT 8.3g (sat 2.4g, mono 2g, poly 3.4g); PROTEIN 6g; CARB 49.9g; FIBER 6.1g; CHOL 13mg; IRON 1mg; SODIUM 23mg; CALC 110mg

Baked Figs and Nectarines

This fruit mixture is great over shortcakes.

- 12 medium fresh figs, halved (about 1¼ pounds)
- 3 nectarines, pitted and quartered
- ¼ cup late-harvest riesling or other sweet white wine (such as Gewürztraminer)
- 2 tablespoons honey
- 3 tablespoons sugar
- 3 cups vanilla reduced-fat ice cream

1. Preheat oven to 425°.
2. Arrange fresh figs and nectarines in a single layer in a 13 x 9–inch baking dish. Pour wine over fruit; drizzle with honey. Sprinkle evenly with sugar. Bake at 425° for 25 minutes or until fruit begins to brown. Serve warm with vanilla ice cream. Yield: 6 servings (serving size: about ½ cup fruit mixture and ½ cup vanilla ice cream).

CALORIES 271 (9% from fat); FAT 2.6g (sat 1.1g, mono 0.7g, poly 0.2g); PROTEIN 4.3g; CARB 58.3g; FIBER 5.3g; CHOL 5mg; IRON 0.6mg; SODIUM 47mg; CALC 136mg

Glazed Peaches in Phyllo Baskets

This delightful dessert is stunning enough to serve at a dinner party but simple to prepare as an everyday treat. The pastry baskets can be made a few days ahead and stored in an airtight container at room temperature.

- ½ cup whole-milk ricotta cheese
- 3 tablespoons granulated sugar, divided
- 1 teaspoon vanilla extract
- 3 tablespoons chopped hazelnuts, toasted and ground
- 6 (18 x 14–inch) sheets frozen phyllo dough, thawed
- 1½ tablespoons butter, melted
- Cooking spray
- 3 cups chopped peeled ripe peaches (about 2 pounds)
- ½ cup apple jelly, melted and slightly cooled
- 1 tablespoon powdered sugar

1. Preheat oven to 350°.

2. Place ricotta, 1 tablespoon granulated sugar, and vanilla in a medium bowl, and beat with a mixer at medium speed until well blended. Cover and chill.

3. Combine remaining 2 tablespoons granulated sugar and hazelnuts. Stack 2 phyllo sheets on a large cutting board or work surface (cover remaining sheets to prevent drying); brush with half of butter. Sprinkle phyllo stack with half of hazelnut mixture. Repeat procedure with 2 phyllo sheets, remaining butter, and remaining hazelnut mixture. Top with remaining 2 phyllo sheets. Gently press phyllo layers together. Lightly coat top phyllo sheets with cooking spray. Cut phyllo stacks into 6 (7 x 6–inch) rectangles. Carefully place 1 layered rectangle into each of 6 (8-ounce) ramekins coated with cooking spray. Gently press rectangles into ramekins to form baskets (phyllo will extend about 1 inch over tops of ramekins). Place ramekins on a baking sheet. Bake at 350° for 20 minutes or until lightly browned and crisp. Cool in ramekins on a wire rack. Carefully remove phyllo baskets from ramekins.

4. Just before serving, spread about 1 tablespoon cheese mixture into bottom of each phyllo basket. Combine peaches and melted jelly, tossing to coat. Spoon about ½ cup peach mixture into each phyllo cup. Sprinkle evenly with powdered sugar. Serve immediately. Yield: 6 servings (serving size: 1 filled phyllo basket).

CALORIES 264 (29% from fat); FAT 8.5g (sat 3.5g, mono 3.8g, poly 0.7g); PROTEIN 5g; CARB 42.9g; FIBER 2.4g; CHOL 18mg; IRON 0.8mg; SODIUM 201mg; CALC 93mg

Strawberry Sauce with Caramelized Sugar and Pink Peppercorns

An immersion blender goes directly into the strawberry mixture to smooth the sauce, eliminating the transfer of the warm liquid to a stand-up blender. The caramelized sugar enhances the strawberries' sweetness, while the peppercorns add a surprising zing. Serve this sauce over frozen vanilla yogurt, pound cake, or sliced fresh strawberries. This recipe can be prepared up to four days in advance and refrigerated in an airtight container.

- 2/3 cup sugar
- 1/4 cup water
- 1 pound hulled strawberries, quartered
- 1/2 teaspoon crushed pink peppercorns

1. Combine sugar and water in a large saucepan; bring to a boil. Cook until sugar dissolves; do not stir. Brush down any crystals that form on edges of pan with a wet pastry brush. Cook 2 minutes or until sugar caramelizes and turns pale amber, swirling pan occasionally. Remove pan from heat; let cool 3 minutes. Add strawberries; cover and let stand 10 minutes or until strawberries are tender. Cook over low heat until caramel is liquefied. Stir in peppercorns. Using an immersion blender in pan, puree sauce until smooth. (Sauce will thicken as it cools.) Yield: 1 1/4 cups (serving size: about 1 1/2 tablespoons).

CALORIES 83 (2% from fat); FAT 0.2g (sat 0g; mono 0g; poly 0.1g); PROTEIN 0.4g; CARB 21.1g; FIBER 1.2g; CHOL 0mg; IRON 0.3mg; SODIUM 1mg; CALC 10mg

Poached Pears with Raspberry-Balsamic Sauce

- 2 cups frozen unsweetened raspberries
- 1 tablespoon balsamic vinegar
- 2 teaspoons honey
- 1/8 teaspoon freshly ground black pepper
- 4 peeled firm Bosc pears (about 1 3/4 pounds)
- 1 tablespoon lemon juice

1. Place raspberries in a 3-quart casserole. Cover with lid; microwave at HIGH 2 1/2 minutes or until thoroughly heated. Press raspberries through a fine sieve over a small bowl, reserving liquid; discard solids. Add vinegar, honey, and pepper to reserved raspberry liquid.

2. Rub pears with lemon juice. Place pears in casserole, and drizzle with raspberry sauce. Cover with lid. Microwave at HIGH 8 minutes or until pears are tender, stirring and spooning sauce over pears after 4 minutes. Yield: 4 servings (serving size: 1 pear and 2 tablespoons sauce).

CALORIES 239 (3% from fat); FAT 0.9g (sat 0g, mono 0.2g, poly 0.3g); PROTEIN 1.5g; CARB 61.1g; FIBER 4.4g; CHOL 0mg; IRON 1.3mg; SODIUM 2mg; CALC 38mg

Tropical-Fruit Pizza

- 1 (18-ounce) package refrigerated sugar cookie dough
- Cooking spray
- 1/3 cup sugar
- 1 1/2 teaspoons grated orange rind
- 1 teaspoon coconut extract
- 1 (8-ounce) block fat-free cream cheese, softened
- 1 cup (1-inch) pieces peeled ripe mango
- 1 cup sliced banana (about 1 large)
- 6 (1/2-inch) slices fresh pineapple, cut in half
- 2 kiwifruit, each peeled and cut into 8 slices
- 1/4 cup apricot preserves
- 1 tablespoon Triple Sec (orange-flavored liqueur) or orange juice
- 2 tablespoons flaked sweetened coconut, toasted

1. Preheat oven to 350°.

2. Cut cookie dough into 8 slices; firmly press slices into a 12-inch round pizza pan coated with cooking spray. Bake at 350° for 25 minutes or until lightly browned. Cool completely on a wire rack.

3. Combine sugar, orange rind, extract, and cream cheese in a bowl; beat with a mixer at medium speed until blended. Spread cream cheese mixture over cookie crust, leaving a 1/2-inch margin around edges. Arrange mango, banana, pineapple, and kiwifruit on top of cream cheese mixture. Combine preserves and liqueur in a small microwave-safe bowl, and microwave at HIGH 30 seconds or until melted. Drizzle over fruit pieces; sprinkle with toasted coconut. Chill 1 hour. Yield: 12 servings (serving size: 1 wedge).

CALORIES 283 (24% from fat); FAT 7.4g (sat 2.4g, mono 0.1g, poly 1g); PROTEIN 4.6g; CARB 48.2g; FIBER 1.7g; CHOL 10mg; IRON 1.3mg; SODIUM 203mg; CALC 63mg

Sesame Sweets

In these traditional Indian cookies, both the nut filling and the cookie dough are prepared using a food processor.

FILLING:

¼ cup slivered almonds, toasted
¼ cup packed brown sugar
2 tablespoons sesame seeds, toasted
2½ tablespoons honey
¼ teaspoon ground cardamom
¼ teaspoon ground ginger
⅛ teaspoon ground nutmeg

DOUGH:

2 cups sifted cake flour (about 8 ounces)
3 tablespoons granulated sugar
¼ teaspoon salt
¼ cup chilled butter, cut into small pieces
4 to 5 tablespoons ice water
Cooking spray
2 tablespoons powdered sugar

1. Preheat oven to 325°.

2. To prepare filling, combine first 7 ingredients in a food processor, and pulse 6 times or until combined and almonds are finely chopped. Remove almond mixture from food processor, and set aside. Wipe processor bowl and blade with a paper towel.

3. To prepare dough, lightly spoon flour into dry measuring cups; level with a knife. Combine flour, granulated sugar, and salt in a food processor; pulse 3 times. Add butter; pulse 4 times or just until combined. Add ice water, 1 tablespoon at a time, pulsing just until combined. (Mixture may appear crumbly but will stick together when pressed between fingers.)

4. Shape dough into 24 balls. Place dough 2 inches apart on a baking sheet coated with cooking spray. Press thumb in center of each ball to form an indentation. Fill each indentation with about 1 teaspoon almond mixture. Bake at 325° for 20 minutes or until set. Remove from pan, and cool completely on a wire rack. Sprinkle with powdered sugar. Yield: 2 dozen (serving size: 1 cookie).

CALORIES 81 (33% from fat); FAT 3g (sat 1.1g, mono 1.3g, poly 0.4g); PROTEIN 1.1g; CARB 12.9g; FIBER 0.4g; CHOL 5mg; IRON 0.8mg; SODIUM 40mg; CALC 8mg

Cardamom-Lemon Polenta Cookie

Cardamom-Lemon Polenta Cookie

The dough procedure is simplified by combining the ingredients in several steps, creating a shortbreadlike texture when baked. The cookie complements Blueberry Granita with Berry Compote (recipe on page 389) nicely.

¼ cup blanched almonds, toasted
1⅓ cups all-purpose flour (about 6 ounces)
½ cup yellow cornmeal
½ cup granulated sugar
1 tablespoon grated lemon rind
¾ teaspoon ground cardamom
Dash of salt
3 tablespoons butter
1 tablespoon water
1 large egg
Cooking spray
1 tablespoon powdered sugar

1. Preheat oven to 350°.
2. Place almonds in a food processor, and pulse until finely ground. Lightly spoon flour into dry measuring cups; level with a knife. Add flour and next 5 ingredients to food processor; process until combined. Add butter, water, and egg; pulse 3 or 4 times or just until combined.
3. Lightly press mixture evenly into bottom of a 9-inch round springform pan coated with cooking spray. Sprinkle with powdered sugar. Bake at 350° for 30 minutes or until lightly browned.
4. Remove outer ring of springform pan; cut cookie into 12 wedges while warm. Yield: 12 servings (serving size: 1 wedge).

CALORIES 150 (29% from fat); FAT 4.9g (sat 1.9g, mono 1g, poly 0.2g); PROTEIN 3g; CARB 24.4g; FIBER 1.2g; CHOL 25mg; IRON 0.9mg; SODIUM 18mg; CALC 12mg

Pecan Sandies

It's important for the butter to be soft when you prepare the dough. That way, it will hold together nicely when you shape it.

2 cups all-purpose flour (about 9 ounces)
¼ cup finely chopped pecans
⅛ teaspoon salt
¾ cup granulated sugar
9 tablespoons butter, softened
2 teaspoons vanilla extract
Cooking spray
¼ cup powdered sugar

1. Preheat oven to 350°.
2. Lightly spoon flour into dry measuring cups; level with a knife. Combine flour, pecans, and salt, stirring well with a whisk.
3. Place granulated sugar and butter in a medium bowl; beat with a mixer at medium speed until fluffy (about 2 minutes). Beat in vanilla. Beating at low speed, gradually add flour mixture, and beat just until combined (mixture will be crumbly).
4. Shape dough into 34 (1-inch) balls (about 1 tablespoon each). Place dough balls 2 inches apart on baking sheets coated with cooking spray. Bake at 350° for 20 minutes or until lightly browned.
5. While cookies are still hot, sift powdered sugar evenly over tops. Remove from pan; cool completely on wire racks. Yield: 34 cookies (serving size: 1 cookie).

CALORIES 81 (41% from fat); FAT 3.7g (sat 1.6g, mono 1.6g, poly 0.3g); PROTEIN 0.9g; CARB 11.1g; FIBER 0.3g; CHOL 8mg; IRON 0.4mg; SODIUM 30mg; CALC 3mg

Chewy Chocolate-Coconut Macaroons

These cookies store well in an airtight container for up to two days. To freeze, layer cookies between sheets of parchment or wax paper in an airtight container. Let cookies thaw about 30 minutes before serving.

- 2 ounces unsweetened chocolate, chopped
- ½ cup sifted cake flour (about 2 ounces)
- 2 tablespoons unsweetened cocoa
- ⅛ teaspoon salt
- 2½ cups lightly packed flaked sweetened coconut
- 1 teaspoon vanilla extract
- 1 (14-ounce) can fat-free sweetened condensed milk

1. Preheat oven to 250°.
2. Line a large baking sheet with parchment paper; secure with masking tape.
3. Place unsweetened chocolate in a small microwave-safe bowl. Microwave at HIGH 1 minute or until almost melted. Remove from microwave; stir until chocolate is completely melted.
4. Spoon flour into a dry measuring cup; level with a knife. Combine cake flour, unsweetened cocoa, and salt in a large bowl. Add coconut; toss well. Stir in melted chocolate, vanilla, and sweetened condensed milk (mixture will be stiff). Drop by level tablespoons 2 inches apart onto prepared baking sheet. Bake at 250° for 45 minutes or until edges of cookies are firm and centers of cookies are soft, rotating baking sheet once during baking time. Remove from oven; cool 10 minutes on pan on a wire rack. Remove cookies from parchment paper; cool completely on rack. Store in an airtight container. Yield: 3 dozen (serving size: 1 cookie).

CALORIES 84 (38% from fat); FAT 3.7g (sat 3.3g, mono 0.3g, poly 0g); PROTEIN 1.9g; CARB 11.7g; FIBER 0.9g; CHOL 1mg; IRON 0.2mg; SODIUM 45mg; CALC 33mg

Maple-Walnut Spice Cookies

Store these frosted cookies between layers of parchment paper or wax paper to keep them from sticking together. You can bake and freeze the unfrosted cookies up to a month in advance; bring the cookies to room temperature before frosting them.

COOKIES:

- 1½ cups all-purpose flour (about 6¾ ounces)
- ½ teaspoon baking soda
- ½ teaspoon ground ginger
- ½ teaspoon ground cinnamon
- ¼ teaspoon salt
- ⅛ teaspoon ground nutmeg
- ⅛ teaspoon ground cloves
- ¾ cup packed dark brown sugar
- ¼ cup butter, softened
- 2 tablespoons maple syrup
- 1 large egg

FROSTING:

- 1 cup powdered sugar
- 2 tablespoons maple syrup
- 1 tablespoon fat-free milk
- 2 teaspoons butter, softened

REMAINING INGREDIENT:

- ½ cup finely chopped walnuts, toasted

1. Preheat oven to 350°.
2. To prepare cookies, lightly spoon flour into dry measuring cups; level with a knife. Combine flour and next 6 ingredients in a medium bowl, stirring well with a whisk.
3. Place brown sugar and ¼ cup butter in a large bowl; beat with a mixer at high speed until light and fluffy (about 4 minutes). Add 2 tablespoons maple syrup and egg; beat until well blended. Beating at low speed, gradually add flour mixture; beat just until combined.
4. Spoon cookie batter evenly into 30 mounds (about 1 tablespoon) about 2 inches apart on baking sheets. Bake at 350° for 14 minutes or until lightly browned. Cool on pans 5 minutes. Remove from pans; cool completely on wire racks.
5. To prepare frosting, combine powdered sugar, 2 tablespoons syrup, milk, and 2 teaspoons butter, stirring with a whisk until smooth. Spread frosting evenly over cooled cookies. Working quickly, sprinkle cookies with walnuts. Yield: 2½ dozen (serving size: 1 cookie).

CALORIES 98 (30% from fat); FAT 3.3g (sat 1.1g, mono 1g, poly 1.1g); PROTEIN 1.2g; CARB 16.3g; FIBER 0.3g; CHOL 12mg; IRON 0.5mg; SODIUM 58mg; CALC 12mg

Macadamia and Ginger Cookies

- ½ cup self-rising flour (about 2¼ ounces)
- ½ cup macadamia nuts
- ¼ to ½ cup crystallized ginger
- 2 large egg whites
- ¾ cup sugar
- 1 teaspoon honey
- 1 teaspoon grated orange rind

1. Preheat oven to 300°.
2. Line 2 baking sheets with parchment paper; secure with masking tape.
3. Lightly spoon flour into a dry measuring cup, and level with a knife. Place flour and nuts in a food processor, and pulse 10 times or until mixture resembles coarse meal. Reserve 1 tablespoon flour mixture in food processor; set remaining flour mixture aside. Add ginger to food processor; pulse 8 times or until finely minced. Stir into remaining flour mixture; set aside.
4. Place egg whites in a large bowl; beat with a mixer at high speed 1 minute or until soft peaks form. Beating at high speed, gradually add sugar and honey; beat 4 minutes or until thick and glossy. Gently fold in flour mixture and rind. Drop dough by level tablespoons 2 inches apart onto prepared baking sheets. Bake at 300° for 18 minutes or until set. Remove from baking sheets; cool on a wire rack. Yield: 30 cookies (serving size: 1 cookie).

CALORIES 51 (30% from fat); FAT 1.7g (sat 0.3g, mono 1.3g, poly 0g); PROTEIN 0.6g; CARB 8.7g; FIBER 0.2g; CHOL 0mg; IRON 0.2mg; SODIUM 37mg; CALC 11mg

Maple-Date Bars

Wrap these moist bars individually, or place them in a cookie tin between layers of wax paper or parchment paper.

- 1¾ cups finely chopped pitted dates (about 12 ounces)
- ¾ cup water
- ⅓ cup maple syrup
- 1 teaspoon grated lemon rind
- ⅔ cup sugar
- ½ cup butter, softened
- 1 cup all-purpose flour (about 4½ ounces)
- 1 cup regular oats
- ¼ teaspoon baking soda
- ¼ teaspoon salt
- Cooking spray

1. Combine dates, water, and maple syrup in a heavy saucepan over medium heat. Bring to a boil; cook 12 minutes or until most liquid is absorbed, stirring frequently. (Mixture will look like jam.) Stir in rind; cool completely.
2. Preheat oven to 400°.
3. Beat sugar and butter with a mixer at medium speed until smooth. Lightly spoon flour into a dry measuring cup; level with a knife. Combine flour, oats, baking soda, and salt. Stir flour mixture into sugar mixture (mixture will be crumbly). Press 2 cups flour mixture into bottom of a 13 x 9–inch baking pan coated with cooking spray. Spread date mixture over flour mixture. Sprinkle with remaining flour mixture. Bake at 400° for 20 minutes or until golden brown. Cool completely in pan on a wire rack. Yield: 20 servings (serving size: 1 bar).

CALORIES 162 (28% from fat); FAT 5g (sat 2.3g, mono 2g, poly 0.3g); PROTEIN 1.6g; CARB 29.5g; FIBER 1.8g; CHOL 12mg; IRON 0.7mg; SODIUM 78mg; CALC 14mg

Maple-Date Bars

Orange Fig Bars

DOUGH:

6 tablespoons butter, softened
1/4 cup sugar
1/4 cup honey
1 teaspoon vanilla extract
1 large egg
1 3/4 cups all-purpose flour (about 7 3/4 ounces)
1 teaspoon baking powder
1/4 teaspoon salt

FILLING:

2 cups dried figs (about 12 ounces)
1 tablespoon grated orange rind
1/4 cup boiling water
2 tablespoons sugar
2 tablespoons honey
2 tablespoons fresh orange juice

REMAINING INGREDIENTS:

Cooking spray
1 teaspoon fat-free milk
1 large egg yolk, lightly beaten

1. To prepare dough, beat butter with a mixer at medium speed until smooth. Add 1/4 cup sugar; beat 2 minutes. Add 1/4 cup honey, vanilla, and egg; beat well. Lightly spoon flour into dry measuring cups; level with a knife. Combine flour, baking powder, and salt in a medium bowl. Add flour mixture to egg mixture, stirring just until moist. Divide dough in half, and gently press each half of dough into a piece of heavy-duty plastic wrap. Cover dough with additional plastic wrap; chill 8 hours.
2. Preheat oven to 375°.
3. To prepare filling, place dried figs and orange rind in a food processor; process until minced. Combine 1/4 cup boiling water, 2 tablespoons sugar, and 2 tablespoons honey, stirring until sugar dissolves. Stir in fresh orange juice. With processor on, slowly add orange juice mixture to fig mixture through food chute. Process until well blended, scraping sides of bowl occasionally; set aside.
4. Working with 1 portion of dough at a time (cover remaining dough to keep from drying), roll each portion into a 9-inch square on a heavily floured surface. Fit 1 portion of dough into a 9-inch square baking pan coated with cooking spray. Spread filling evenly over dough in pan. Place remaining square of dough on top of filling. Combine 1 teaspoon milk and egg yolk in a small bowl, stirring with a whisk. Brush milk mixture over top of dough.
5. Bake at 375° for 30 minutes or until top is golden. Cool 30 minutes on a wire rack. Remove from pan; cool completely. Cut into bars. Yield: 20 servings (serving size: 1 bar).

CALORIES 156 (25% from fat); FAT 4.3g (sat 0.9g, mono 1.8g, poly 1.3g); PROTEIN 2.2g; CARB 28.9g; FIBER 3.2g; CHOL 22mg; IRON 1mg; SODIUM 100mg; CALC 45mg

Streusel-Topped Key Lime Squares

If you can't find Key limes, you can use regular Persian limes. The squares will be just a bit sweeter.

1/4 cup butter, softened
1/4 cup granulated sugar
1 teaspoon grated lime rind
1/8 teaspoon salt
1/8 teaspoon lemon extract
1 cup all-purpose flour (about 4 1/2 ounces)
Cooking spray
2/3 cup granulated sugar
3 tablespoons all-purpose flour
3/4 teaspoon baking powder
1/8 teaspoon salt
1/2 cup fresh Key lime juice
3 large eggs
1 tablespoon powdered sugar

1. Preheat oven to 350°.
2. Place first 5 ingredients in a medium bowl; beat with a mixer at medium speed until creamy (about 2 minutes). Lightly spoon 1 cup flour into a dry measuring cup; level with a knife. Gradually add 1 cup flour to butter mixture, beating at low speed until mixture resembles coarse meal. Gently press two-thirds of mixture (about 1 1/3 cups) into bottom of an 8-inch square baking pan coated with cooking spray; set remaining 2/3 cup flour mixture aside. Bake at 350° for 12 minutes or until mixture is just beginning to brown.
3. Combine 2/3 cup granulated sugar, 3 tablespoons flour, baking powder, and 1/8 teaspoon salt in a medium bowl, stirring with a whisk. Add lime juice and eggs, stirring with a whisk until smooth. Pour mixture over crust. Bake at 350° for 12 minutes. Remove pan from oven (do not turn oven off); sprinkle remaining 2/3 cup flour mixture evenly over egg mixture. Bake an additional 8 to 10 minutes or until set. Remove pan from oven; cool in pan on a wire rack. Sprinkle with powdered sugar. Yield: 16 servings (serving size: 1 square).

CALORIES 121 (29% from fat); FAT 3.9g (sat 1.7g, mono 1.5g, poly 0.3g); PROTEIN 2.2g; CARB 19.9g; FIBER 0.3g; CHOL 47mg; IRON 0.6mg; SODIUM 93mg; CALC 21mg

Streusel-Topped Key Lime Squares

NUTRITIONAL ANALYSIS

HOW TO USE IT AND WHY Glance at the end of any *Cooking Light* recipe, and you'll see how committed we are to helping you make the best of today's light cooking. With chefs, registered dietitians, home economists, and a computer system that analyzes every ingredient we use, *Cooking Light* gives you authoritative dietary detail like no other magazine. We go to such lengths so you can see how our recipes fit into your healthful eating plan. If you're trying to lose weight, the calorie and fat figures will probably help most. But if you're keeping a close eye on the sodium, cholesterol, and saturated fat in your diet, we provide those numbers, too. And because many women don't get enough iron or calcium, we can also help there, as well. Finally, there's a fiber analysis for those of us who don't get enough roughage.

Here's a helpful guide to put our nutrition analysis numbers into perspective. Remember, one size doesn't fit all, so take your lifestyle, age, and circumstances into consideration when determining your nutrition needs. For example, pregnant or breast-feeding women need more protein, calories, and calcium. And men older than 50 need 1,200mg of calcium daily, 200mg more than the amount recommended for younger men.

IN OUR NUTRITIONAL ANALYSIS, WE USE THESE ABBREVIATIONS:

sat	saturated fat	**CHOL**	cholesterol
mono	monounsaturated fat	**CALC**	calcium
poly	polyunsaturated fat	**g**	gram
CARB	carbohydrates	**mg**	milligram

Daily Nutrition Guide

	WOMEN AGES 25 TO 50	WOMEN OVER 50	MEN OVER 24
Calories	2,000	2,000 or less	2,700
Protein	50g	50g or less	63g
Fat	65g or less	65g or less	88g or less
Saturated Fat	20g or less	20g or less	27g or less
Carbohydrates	304g	304g	410g
Fiber	25g to 35g	25g to 35g	25g to 35g
Cholesterol	300mg or less	300mg or less	300mg or less
Iron	18mg	8mg	8mg
Sodium	2,300mg or less	1,500mg or less	2,300mg or less
Calcium	1,000mg	1,200mg	1,000mg

The nutritional values used in our calculations either come from The Food Processor, Version 7.5 (ESHA Research), or are provided by food manufacturers.

index